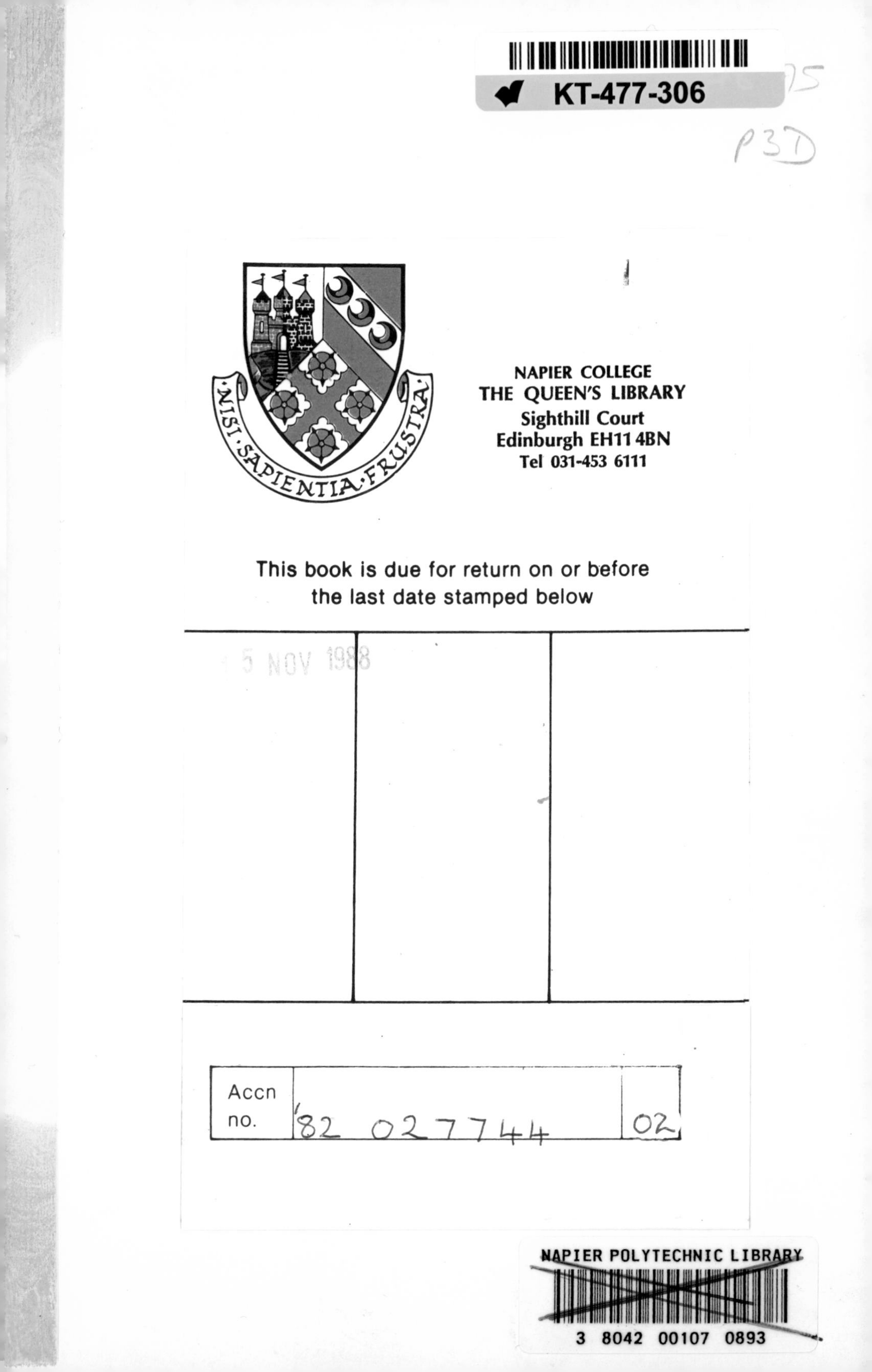

Advances in
Management Education

ADVANCES IN MANAGEMENT EDUCATION

Edited by

John Beck and Charles Cox

Department of Management Sciences
The University of Manchester
Institute of Science and Technology

A Wiley–Interscience Publication

JOHN WILEY & SONS
Chichester · New York · Brisbane · Toronto

British Library Cataloguing in Publication Data:

Advances in Management Education
(Conference), University of Manchester, Institute of Science and Technology, 1979
Advances in management education.
1. Management – Study and teaching – Great Britain – Congresses
I. Beck, John II. Cox, Charles
658'.007'1141 HD30.42.G7 80–40117

ISBN 0 471 27775 4

Set by MHL Typesetting Ltd., Coventry and printed by Page Bros. (Norwich) Ltd., Norwich

Contributors

JOHN BECK	*Lecturer, Department of Management Sciences, UMIST.*
DON BINSTED	*Director, The Centre for the Development of Management Teachers and Trainers, University of Lancaster.*
DAVID BODDY	*Senior Lecturer in Management Studies, University of Glasgow.*
RICHARD BOOT	*Director, Management Learning Project, London Business School.*
PHILIP BOXER	*London Business School.*
TOM BOYDELL	*Principal Lecturer, Department of Management Studies, Sheffield Polytechnic.*
CHRIS BREWSTER	*Manager, Industrial Relations Unit, Kingston Regional Management Centre.*
DAVID CASEY	*Independent Consultant.*
JOHN BURGOYNE	*Research Director, The Centre for the Development of Management Teachers and Trainers, University of Lancaster.*
CARY L. COOPER	*Professor of Management Education Methods, UMIST.*
MARY COX	*Independent Consultant.*
CHARLES COX	*Lecturer, Department of Management Sciences, UMIST.*
IAN CUNNINGHAM	*Principal Lecturer, Anglian Regional Management Centre.*
K.F. JACKSON	*Administrative Staff College, Henley-on-Thames.*

KIM JAMES	*Lecturer in Management, Lanchester Polytechnic.*
PHILIP KESLAKE	*Divisional Training Manager, RHM General Products Ltd.*
RALPH LEWIS	*Senior Management Development Advisor, Cranfield School of Management.*
GEORGE LONG	*Teaching Fellow, The Centre for the Development of Management Teachers and Trainers, University of Lancaster.*
IAN McGIVERING	*Reader in Organization Behaviour, University of Bradford.*
CHARLES MARGERISON	*Professor of Management Development, Cranfield School of Management.*
JOHN MORRIS	*Professor of Management Development, Manchester Business School.*
MIKE PEDLER	*Senior Lecturer, Department of Management Studies, Sheffield Polytechnic.*
PHILIP RADCLIFF	*Management Training Manager, RHM General Products Ltd.*
MICHAEL REYNOLDS	*Senior Teaching Fellow, The Centre for the Development of Management Teachers and Trainers, University of Lancaster.*
MIKE SMITH	*Senior Lecturer, Department of Management Sciences, UMIST.*
ROGER STUART	*Teaching Fellow, The Centre for the Development of Management Teachers and Trainers, University of Lancaster.*
J.H.B. VANT	*Project Manager, Management and Marketing, Petroleum Industry Training Board.*

Contents

Preface ix

Chapter 1 Management Education for the 1980's. 1
John Beck, Charles Cox, and Philip Radcliff

Chapter 2 The Quality of Managerial Life: The Stressors and Satisficers. . . 9
Cary L. Cooper

Chapter 3 Participation in Work and Education. 21
Michael Reynolds

Chapter 4 Inward Bound – A New Direction for Outward Bound: Toward an Holistic Approach to Management Development 41
Philip Keslake and Philip Radcliff

Chapter 5 The Development of Senior Managers for the Future 55
Kim James

Chapter 6 Management Analysis – An Improved Method for Identifying Managers' Training Needs 73
K.F. Jackson and J.H.B. Vant

Chapter 7 Facilitating Re-entry Through Role Analysis. 85
Ian McGivering

Chapter 8 Joint Development Activities: From Practice to 'Theory' 97
John Morris

Chapter 9 Some Issues in the Design of Action Learning Programmes 123
David Boddy

Chapter 10 **Facilitating Behaviour in Work Centred Management Development Programmes** 141
John Burgoyne and Ian Cunningham

Chapter 11 **Is All Management Development Self-Development?** 165
Mike Pedler and Tom Boydell

Chapter 12 **Applications and Uses of Repertory Grids in Management Education** 197
Mike Smith

Chapter 13 **Changing a Manager's Construction of Reality** 215
John Beck

Chapter 14 **Reflective Learning** 231
Richard Boot and Philip Boxer

Chapter 15 **Ten Years of Transactional Analysis** 253
Mary Cox and Charles Cox

Chapter 16 **Management Educators and their Clients** 271
Charles Margerison and Ralph Lewis

Chapter 17 **Evaluation of Management Training: A Focus on Change** 283
Chris Brewster

Chapter 18 **Transfer of Learning – There Are Two Separate Problems**. 303
David Casey

Chapter 19 **Promoting Useful Management Learning: Problems of Translation and Transfer**. 323
Don Binsted, Roger Stuart, and George Long

Chapter 20 **Reflections**. 351
John Beck, Charles Cox, and Philip Radcliff

Index 357

Preface

This book represents the collected papers presented at a conference held at UMIST in Manchester in April 1979 entitled 'Advances in Management Education', which was organized by the Editors. In organizing the conference we were hoping to bring together academics concerned with research and developments in management education in institutes of higher education, with management education practitioners from commerce and industry to enable a dialogue to develop between the parties. Our feeling at the time was that there was much which both parties could learn from one another, practitioners might see scope for applying the ideas generated by the academics, and academics could aware of developments and problems in the industrial and commercial spheres. Problems which could form the basis for future research.

The objectives of the conference were stated as: to identify and appraise current trends in management education, and to identify possible areas of joint research activities between academics and practitioners. In this way it was hoped that the conference might have some practical impact on the way in which management education is conducted in the UK today.

Contributions to the conference, and hence this book, were sought in two ways. We approached people we knew were involved in developing interesting new ideas and asked them to submit a paper about their work. The other approach was to circulate large business organizations, government departments, industrial training boards, colleges of higher education, and consulting organizations with details of the conference, requesting them to submit a paper if they were involved in some developmental activity which would be of interest to others. All contributors were asked to present in their papers outlines of the implications of their work for the management education practitioner, and also some directions for future research which were suggested by their work.

A large number of papers were submitted, including a number from institutes of higher education discussing features of the design of courses or programmes which they were running for managers. There was a sufficient number of these papers to justify a conference on such design issues in its own right, but we decided on 'the process of management learning', as the theme for this conference and not the design of particular programmes.

One disappointing aspect of the contributions submitted was that there were very few which came from practitioners. There are probably a variety of reasons for the reluctance of practitioners to share their ideas and experience, but this does mean that the contribution that they could make to the development of thought and practice in management development is less than it might be. We will be organizing a somewhat similar conference in April 1981 and would welcome discussions with anyone, but practitioners in particular, who would be interested in presenting their ideas at that conference.

We have pointed out that the majority of contributions in this book are by academics, nevertheless we believe that this book will be of value not only to academics in highlighting research and development issues, but also to practitioners in giving new insights and ideas about the design and implementation of their management development programmes.

UMIST, *July 1979*

J.E.B.
C.J.C.

Advances in Management Education
Edited by John Beck and Charles Cox

CHAPTER 1

Management Education for the 1980's

J.E. Beck, C.J. Cox, and P. Radcliff

In this introductory chapter we identify some of the current issues in management and management education, and fit the papers presented in this book into this framework. We do not claim that this book is representative of all the activities which are carried out under the banner of management education. On the contrary, the intention is to identify and appraise new trends and developments in management education. This will be the focus of the second half of this chapter.

But before we do this we need to place management education in a context. A context which illustrates the pressures for change in the way in which managers go about their daily activities. Changes brought about by societal pressures which influence the nature of the manager's role and his responsibilities, as well as changes in the economic, technological and legal order which have a direct impact on the manager's job.

THE CONTEXT OF MANAGEMENT EDUCATION

Social Responsibility

One major theme of the past decade has been concerned with management's social responsibility. Possibly the impetus for this has come more from business academics than industry itself. As early as 1958 Blum was advocating that along with audits of efficiency and profits, civilized western society should have a 'Social Audit of Enterprise'. Drucker (1967) included public responsibility as one of the eight areas in which objectives have to be set for management. But how do we assess whether an organization or its managers are behaving in a socially responsible manner? In many business organizations which are ultimately economic institutions, it will be hard to avoid conflict between some elements of social and business goals. Whether such issues and conflicts are seen as largely within the framework of government legislation is to some extent irrelevant to our concerns. It is difficult to define a clear pattern of the future demands on the manager, but we are entering a world in which business, government, and society as a whole will be in the process of 'renegotiating an invisible contract' whose terms are likely to become increasingly explicit.

A recent survey conducted by Management Centre Europe (Harrison and Humble, 1975) indicated that although policies were not fully formulated, social issues remained a priority concern even in times of economic stringency. Those responsible were either situated at board level or had access to it. Little is mentioned in the survey of involving managers at other levels in this process of renegotiating the contract with wider society and no company reported schemes for developing and educating managers to deal with these issues. In another study Cherrington (1970) suggests that education to deal effectively with social issues is one of the major areas of failing by industry. Are key areas such as race employment problems, workers' rights and preparation for retirement and redundancy being neglected as he suggests?

Our own experience in drawing together these conference papaers would indicate that this is an area of only limited concern for management education. It is significant that we were not offered and did not succeed in commissioning a paper on training in relation to social responsibility. Cooper in Chapter 2 does refer tangentially to such issues, but he is more concerned with responsibility for the quality of the manager's own life rather than wider social issues.

Industrial Democracy

Another factor in recent years has been the increasing pressure on managers as the fundamental relationship between individuals and the organization they work for, has become more open to challenge and alteration. Much management training has been directed towards a new set of values based on democratic ideals. Bennis and Slater (1973) suggest that in new training methods 'status prerogatives and traditional concepts of authority are severely challenged'. Management is therefore being subjected to a new set of values which may conflict with currently accepted role and behaviour patterns. In Chapter 3 Mike Reynolds pursues this dilemma into the design implications for the trainer when preparing managers for organizational democracy.

Another aspect of this development is concerned with the pressures generated by democratic processes on the role and security of the manager. Jenkins (1977) pinpoints one of the major incentives for a move towards industrial democracy. 'In the manufacturing enterprise it can lead to a substantial reduction in the numbers of supervisors, managers, and specialists'. This process of continuing democratization leading towards a possible reduction in managerial positions may well be only one of a variety of new role pressures facing management.

A further dimension is that decisions about work are going to be taken in conditions of greater choice and autonomy and directed, within a more holistic framework of work and non-work life, towards the goals of improving the individual's quality of life. As Higgin (1975) suggests the quality of working life is not divisible.

Management education may need to prepare management to create the opportunities for such changes and managing such periods of transition. This means educating management to be creative, to be capable of coping with the anxieties of change (both in themselves and in others) and the management skills of leading change and monitoring situations for new opportunities and choices. In Chapter 4 Keslake and Radcliff describe a particular approach adopted by a company to prepare their managers for such challenges and speculate on a more holistic approach to management learning.

Discontinuity and Turbulence

We have discussed the importance of the direction of particular changes in society on the managerial role, but an environment characterized by high rates of change and discontinuity will have a marked effect on management and organizations of the future. Change has often been regarded as automatic and always leading to a new stable order. No longer can we think in terms of progressing to a new stable order or returning to an old one, organizations will have to come to terms with turbulence and change. This then is the reality for management, not to cope with or avoid change nor to plan for future stability, but to accept change as a key element in shaping their world and their actions. 'The sheer rate of change will have an impact on our sensibilities and ideas, our institutions, our politics, and values. Most of these to date developed on the assumption that stability was more characteristic of the world than change' (Von Foerster, 1965). Managers must then be educated in a reality shaped by change and not in a myth of social and technological stability. In Chapter 5 Kim James discusses how one company investigated the training of Senior Managers and how best to develop their careers to meet the demands of a complex and uncertain future.

Organizational Adaptability

It has long been assumed that organizations need predictability in their environments otherwise they would be unable to function effectively. The question now becomes how much environmental uncertainty organizations can cope with and still function effectively. Bennis (1966) suggests that the answer lies in changing the way in which we view man and organizational values. Organizations must move into a more fluid state, with a more active response towards change in the environment, and a higher valency towards self-appraisal and renewal.

The implications are clear, managers will have to take uncertainty into their own world. We know very little about how to bring about such changes in managerial attitudes. Some writers have advocated that the only way to speed up this rate of internal change is not by bureaucratic restructuring, but by organizations becoming 'learning systems' in which 'the entire organization must transform itself from a rigid hierarchical mode into a learning mode. When uncertainty increases and new conditions obtain, the collective intelligence of the organization must be mobilized to develop a novel response' (Boettinger, 1971). The concept of a learning system is an underlying theme of many of the papers, e.g. Morris, Chapter 8, Burgoyne and Cunningham, Chapter 10, Pedler and Boydell, Chapter 11.

The Changing Managerial Role

These changes in organizational life involve not only new skills and behaviour, but far more fundamental changes in attitudes, values and authority/power relations. The demands are for managers to take on new roles with wider accountability to society. Management cannot play victim to circumstances, but should realistically manage the future. A basic assumption must be that the management of change will be carried out by managers rather than change specialists. It is they who will be responsible for assessing the situation, making the decisions, and implementing the improvements. Consequently the managerial role is going to require greater capacity in solving problems and acting as agents of change. Pym (1966) refers to a network of new relationship characteristics within which managerial activity will have to be carried out. Basil and Cook (1974) indicate a number of dimensions on which the managerial role is in a state of transition. They offer little in the way of certainty and generally indicate directions and permutations within which there will be a variety of appropriate managerial behaviours. The purpose of management education must be to help the individual manager develop his capacities to solve problems, and enable the necessary changes to be made. Jackson and Vant (Chapter 6) place strong emphasis on problem-solving categories as a new method for identifying managerial training needs. McGivering in Chapter 7 indicates the necessity to enable managers to identify behaviour changes within the context of a clear analysis and understanding of their role and the set of associated perceptions.

ISSUES AND THEMES IN MANAGEMENT EDUCATION

So far we have explored the context in which management education will have to function in the future. What then are the main lines of advancement in the education and training of the individual manager? The remaining chapters can be fitted within five major themes.

1. Experience, Action and Self-Development

Learning by reflection on managerial experience has been discussed from the days of Follet and Taylor through to modern concerns with sensitivity training and self-awareness. Experiential learning is not now exclusively linked to T-groups, but undoubtedly the bulk of such activity has been associated with the T-group, and its derivatives. If experiential learning is to become more fully utilized, greater understanding of, and control of, the processes is essential – 'we wish to do far more than observe our experience, we wish to make it yield up for us its riches' (Follet, 1924). The need is for the development of theories which attempt to explain the processes whereby we learn from our experience and how they can be incorporated in the training and educational setting – 'Experience must yield meaning to lead to knowing' (Harrison, 1968).

For a long time Revans has put an emphasis on the manager learning from direct experience in what he terms Action Learning. One of his major conditions is that 'one has something to lose by making a mistake, as well as something to gain from finding a workable solution. Exercises that involve no emotional threat teach only how to work on exercises that involve no emotional threat' (Revans, 1973). The debate about the nature and value of experiential learning continues in the absence of a theory base, by which we can understand the learning processes involved and also in the absence of any studies of cost and effectiveness. We need some useful theory and scientific investigation if only to establish the needs and appropriateness of the method in particular situations. This is essentially the theme of John Morris' argument in Chapter 8. David Boddy in Chapter 9 contributes some general comments on necessary conditions for effective Action Learning programmes, whereas Burgoyne and Cunningham (Chapter10) place the emphasis of their paper on the development of set adviser skills. Management Self-Development in a wider context is reviewed by Pedler and Boydell in Chapter 11.

2. Role Relations

Attempts to define managerial activities in terms of task requirements has proved inadequate in dealing with the problems of role ambiguity and role conflicts which managers must face. The management educator's goal must be to help management understand the implications, demands, and opportunities of their role situations. Harrison has advocated an approach which allows managers in a team to negotiate and openly establish their role relationships. He reminds us of the need to consider issues of power, competitiveness, and coercion as well as personal styles and values in developing managers. Reed (1974) has emphasized this way of working with management as a means of diagnozing learning needs and establishing education and training programmes. As McGivering (Chapter 7) indicates this may be particularly critical in facilitating the process of learning transfer.

3. Development of Theoretical Models

In order to be effective, management educators require a theoretical base from which to understand the process of growth and development of the individual manager. Many of the theories which management educators use have their origins in developmental or clinical psychology. This is not surprising since these are both areas concerned with change and growth; Pedler and Boydell refer to this in Chapter 11.

There seems to us, however, to have been two major developments in this context in the last few years. One is the use of Personal Construct Theory and Repertory Grid Techniques as a method of exploring an individual's constructs and as a way of helping him develop a new view of the world. Mike Smith in Chapter 12 discusses a variety of applications of Repertory Grid Technique and John Beck in Chapter 13 outlines the use of Personal Construct Theory in understanding the management education process. Boot and Boxer in Chapter 14 on Reflective Learning also use Repertory Grid as the basis of their method.

The other main theoretical system to have an influence on management training particularly on interpersonal skills and perceptions is Transactional Analysis. This is reviewed by Cox and Cox in Chapter 15.

A further reference to Morris (Chapter 8) is also relevant here, as he discusses in depth the types of models found useful by managers in structuring and ordering their experience of the managerial world. If this is taken in conjunction with the paper by Margerison and Lewis (Chapter 16), who point to the differences in thinking between managers and academics, we may have an explanation of why the models so much liked and valued by managers are so often scorned by academics.

4. Evaluation of Training

With the emphasis that has been placed on management self-development and changing managers' models of reality to cope with more uncertain factors, the evaluation of training becomes an even more intractable problem than in the past. The self-developing manager, by definition, is responsible for identifying his own learning goals and is the principal arbiter of whether he has achieved them. It is surely, also, a paradox to identify precise and quantifiable training objectives for programmes designed to prepare managers to cope with uncertain imprecise and unquantifiable futures? However one practical solution to this problem is proposed by Brewster (Chapter 17) with the concept of context re-evaluation as a means of identifying the organizational impact of management training programmes.

One general direction for management education which is mentioned in a number of papers is the development of metaskills which a manager needs in order to cope with a rapidly changing world. The development of these 'learning to learn' skills involves the manager becoming aware of his own learning and development processes and managing his own learning experience, so that all experience becomes a learning experience. Setting these general process goals for the development of managers creates even more problems for the evaluation of training, than were incurred by the strategies of systematic training in the past. Yet our inability to evaluate the achievement of these goals does not in any way reduce their importance or significance. Having said that, perhaps we have to be more precise in defining behaviourally what we mean by these learning to learn skills, in order to design programmes to achieve them.

5. Transfer of Training

It has become traditional to consider 'learning' and 'transfer' as two separate issues. 'Learning theorists have contributed to the apparent schism between learning and transfer by focusing attention on one or other of these two aspects of the training session to the exclusion of the other. More and more writers are beginning to question the reality of this schism'. (McGehee and Thayer, 1961). Written from a background of Action Learning David Casey in Chapter 18 goes further and suggests that the whole problem of transfer is actually created by trainers who have separated the learning situation from normal work.

It is probably true, however, that there are many cases where, for one reason or another, training must be carried out as a special event. It is with this in mind that Binstead, Stuart, and Long discuss the 'transfer problem' from a more traditional viewpoint in Chapter 19.

THE ORGANIZATION AS A LEARNING SYSTEM

We have primarily considered learning for management as interventions at the individual level. The discussion has focused on the individual (either with or without help) confronting his own problem areas. Such a process makes demands on the organizational environment to facilitate development and growth. Learning can only be effective if it achieves a match with the culture of the organization with which it is engaged. There is no one right way to develop managers, any approach is contingent on the style of the organization (Handy, 1974). It is insufficient to look at management education purely in terms of the provision of courses and resources either internal or external to the organization. The development of a manager is something to which many different inputs contribute during his working life. It is this very complexity of the factors involved in this process which makes management education such a difficult area to evaluate. If we are to establish fully effective 'learning systems' then we are confronting our organizations and their management with a new concept of learning and education. Increasingly managers will be responsible for designing, carrying out, and evaluating their own personal change programmes. The old mode of the learner dependent on the educator for the provision of content and structure no longer meets the required objectives. 'The needs least satisfactorily satisfied for the moment appear to lie *primarily* in the area of coping with the complexities of the present situation, in such a way as to learn how to cope in the future.' (Mant, 1969). It requires individuals and organizations to deal with continuous education as a phenomenon in the reality of working life. The question is how far are management and management educators prepared to consider the full implications of the future possibilities in management education.

In this introductory chapter we have attempted to fit the contributions to this book into the context of management education. In doing so we have picked the major themes expressed in the papers, as we see them. There are inevitably other themes and links between papers of which the reader will become aware.

REFERENCES

Basil, D. and Cook, C. (1974). *The Management of Change*, McGraw-Hill, New York.

Bennis, W.G. (1966). *Changing Organisations*, McGraw-Hill, New York.

Bennis, W.G. and Slater, P.E. (1973). Organisational democracy: towards work by the consent of the employed, in F. Best (ed.) *The Future of Work*, Prentice-Hall, Englewood Cliffs, N.J.

Blum, F.H. (1958). Social audit of the enterprise. *Harvard Business Review*, March–April.

Boettinger (1971). *Impact of Rapid Change*, BIM Occasional Paper OPNG.

Cherrington, P. (1970). *Wider Business Objectives in Management Education*, Industrial Education and Research Foundation Occasional Paper 1.

Drucker, P.F. (1967). *The Practice of Management*, Mercury Books.

Follet, M.P. (1924). *Creative Experience*, Longman, London.

Handy, C.B. (1974). Pitfalls of management development, *Personnel Management*.

Harrison, H. (1968). Quoted in Insights and Outlooks, *Journal of Applied Behavioural Science*, **4**.

Harrison, R. (1972). When conflicts trigger team spirit, *European Business*, Spring.

Harrison, F. and Humble, J. (1975). Social responsibility in British companies, *Industrial Participation*, Summer.

Higgin, G. (1975). Scarcity, abundance and depletion, Inaugural Lecture Loughborough University of Technology.

Jenkins, D. (1977). The democratic factory, *Management Today*, April.

McGehee, W. and Thayer, P.W. (1961). *Training in Business and Industry*, John Wiley, New York.

Mant, A. (1969). *The Experienced Manager – a major resource*, BIM.

Pym, D. (1966). Effective management performance in organisational change, *Journal of Management Studies*, **3**.

Reed, B.W. (1974). Organisational role analysis, in Cooper C.L. (ed.) *Experiential Methods of Management Education*, ATM, London.

Revans, R.W. (1973). The response of the manager to change, *Management Education and Development*, **4**.

Von Foerster *et al.* (1965). *Purposive Systems*, Proceedings of First Annual Symposium of the American Society of Cybernetics, Spartan Books.

Advances in Management Education
Edited by John Beck and Charles Cox

CHAPTER 2

The Quality of Managerial Life: The Stressors and Satisficers

Cary L. Cooper

Working in organizations not only provides a large section of the population with life-sustaining income and job satisfaction, but also exerts its own pressures and stresses on them, which can ultimately have negative consequences both for achieving the goals of organizations and meeting the needs of the individuals working within them. Before we examine the various sources of managerial pressure and stress at work, it might be useful to define these two central concepts. 'Pressure' is an external or internal force acting on an individual to perform in a particular way or achieve a particular end result. This can be a source of some discomfort and some anxiety, but it can be at the same time exciting, challenging, and growth-producing. 'Stress', on the other hand, has only negative outcomes for the individual concerned because (1) the individual feels that he or she will not (in the long term) be able to cope and therefore (2) will find it necessary to deal with it in a defensive and maladaptive way. Pressure is a tolerable, manageable condition, includes some positive attributes, and is characterized by activity and productive coping; stress is a regressive and counter-productive condition, can produce extreme and usually undifferentiated anxiety, and is characterized by defensive coping.

Why is understanding the nature and sources of managerial stress important? Why should we be concerned about it? Primarily because a manager's mental and physical health may be adversely affected by these stresses. French and Caplan (1973) suggest that job-related stress and pathologies 'manifest themselves in forms ranging anywhere from passive apathy, job dissatisfaction, and depression to violent acts directed against the organization'. These and other stress-related effects (e.g. tension, poor adjustment) also feed into the family becoming sources of disturbance there, and thus pervading the whole quality of life. The manager can find himself the victim of an unending stress feedback loop. 'Individuals even suffer extreme physiological symptoms from stress at work such as disabling ulcers or heart attacks, which force them to retire prematurely from active organizational life before they have had an opportunity to actualize fully their potential' (Brummet, Pyle, and

Flamholtz, 1968). The mental and physical health effects of job stress are not only a disruptive influence on the manager but also a 'real' cost to the organization, on whom many individuals depend; a cost which is rarely if ever considered either in human or financial terms by organizations, but one which it incurs in its day-to-day operations.

A recognition of the possible sources of managerial stress and well-being, therefore, may help us to arrive at suggestions of ways of minimizing its negative consequences. In this paper we hope to provide a comprehensive account of the sources of work stress on executives.

One of the main problems currently facing research workers in the field of stress is that there is no integrated framework or conceptual map of the area. Much of the early stress research came from two sources. First, from work carried out in 'crisis' situations such as stress in battle situations during wars, the stress effects of major illness or breavement, etc., which focused heavily on the assessment of physical and mental symptoms exhibited in these unique circumstances. Second, from the 'company doctor' literature, which was geared essentially to the needs of industry and based on intuition rather than substantiated fact. These studies were usually descriptive reports by individual industrial medical officers on, for example, the relationship of poor physical conditions at work and worker apathy or stress, or of work overload and nervous complaints by workers and managers, etc. In the last 10–15 years, however, there has been a determined effort by social scientists to consider more systematically the sources of organizational stress. The framework offered in this paper is basically an attempt to integrate the findings of this new wave of research. Much of this work will be in the field of managerial stress. However, from an examination of the 'shop floor' studies it would appear that most, if not all, of the factors to be discussed here are applicable to the labour force as a whole.

MANAGERIAL PRESSURES AND STRESSORS

An examination of the literature and my own research (Cooper and Marshall, 1978; Marshall and Cooper, 1979) reveals a formidable list of interacting factors which might be sources of managerial stress. Figure 1 is an attempt to represent this diagrammatically; below they will be dealt with in a natural progression from individual-centred to total environment-centred.

Intrinsic to the Job

Factors *intrinsic to the job* were a first and vital focus of study for early researchers in the field, and in 'workers' (as opposed to management) studies are still the main preoccupation. Stress can be caused by too much or too little work, time pressures and deadlines, having to make too many decisions, fatigue from the physical strains of the work environment (e.g. too much noise), excessive travel, long hours, having to cope with changes at work and the expenses (monetary and career)

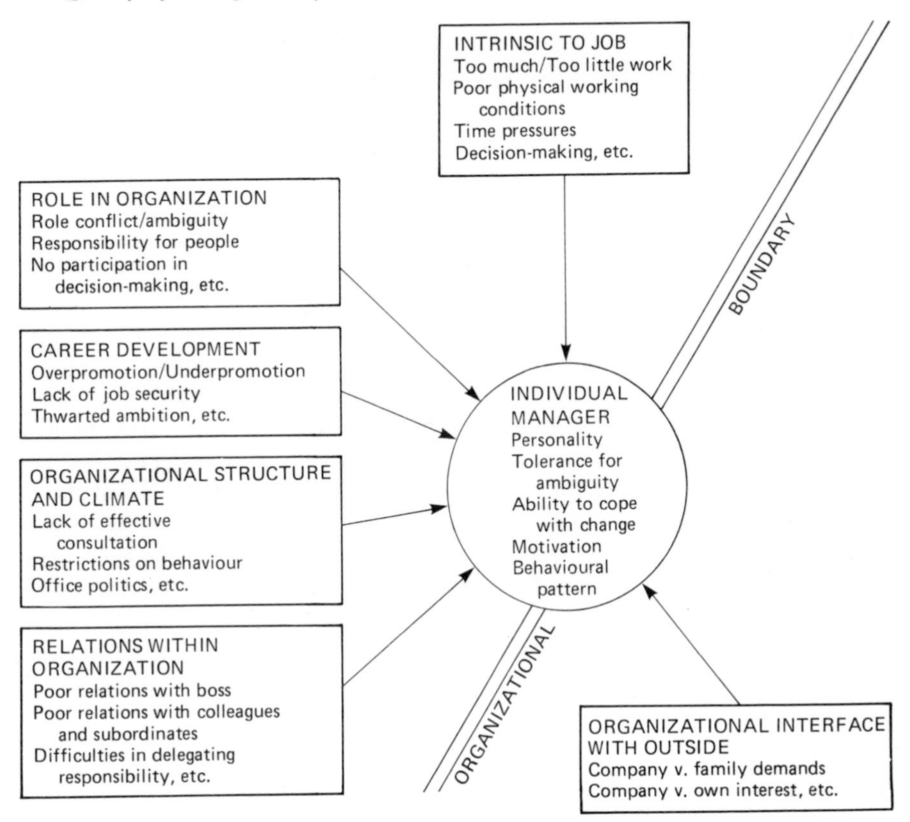

Figure 1. Sources of the Quality of Managerial Life

of making mistakes. It can be seen that every job description includes factors which for some individuals at some times will be sources of pressure. Continual conceptual refinements in this area are being made as more research is carried out. French and Caplan (1973) made an important distinction in terms of work overload between *qualitative* and *quantitative*. In one of their studies, for example, they found that whilst increases in the quality of work overload lowered the self-esteem of university professors, it was only increases in quantity which had the same effects on university administrators.

Manager in the Job

Factors intrinsic to the job are intimately related to the characteristic of the person or *manager in the job* – these include not only the personality and motivational characteristics individuals take with them to work, which may predispose them to stress or to withstand stress, but also situational-related factors such as being ill-equipped to deal with problems, having to come to terms with declining abilities, having to move out of one's area of expertise and lacking insight into one's own motivations and sources of satisfaction and stress. The work of Kahn *et al.* (1964) in this area is of special interest as it represents one of the most rigorous, and at the same time comprehensive, approaches to personality measurement. They examined a sample of managers on a series of personality variables; extroversion *vs.* introversion, flexibility *vs.* rigidity, inner- *vs.* outer-directedness, open- *vs.* closed-mindedness, achievement/status *vs.* security-oriented – and related these to job stress. The following gives an indication of some of their results: (1) outer-directed people were more adaptable and more highly reality-oriented than inner-directed; (2) 'rigids' and 'flexibles' perceived different types of situations as stressful, the former being more susceptible to rush jobs from above and dependence on other people, whilst the latter were more open to influence from other people, and thus easily became overloaded; (3) achievement seekers showed significantly more independence and job involvement than did security-seekers. Individual differences play a vital part in the complex interaction of employee with the job . . . his environment – they largely determine career choice and development, they form the basis of the individual's perception of his situation and, when pressure and stress is perceived, help to dictate the coping style adopted. Kahn *et al.* found, for example, that introverts tend to react to interpersonal tensions by withdrawing from the stress-producing relationships, thus aggravating the original situation by making genuine communication, interaction and problem-solving more difficult.

Role in the Organization

Job intrinsic factors are largely explained by the function the employee performs – whether he is an accountant, market researcher, salesman or production manager – and will be common to a function across companies. Variations in company organization will, however, lead to intercompany differences in the third set of stress variables, those resulting from an individual's *role in the organization.* Factors such as role ambiguity and conflict, responsibility for people or things, too little responsibility, no participation in decision-making, lack of managerial support and explanation or orders, having to reach successively increasing standards of performance and being located at organizational boundaries fall into this category. Kahn and his colleagues at the University of Michigan were the leading workers in this area, and it is due to their work that the concepts of role ambiguity and role conflict have such a wide currency in this field. Using the sociological notion of 'role set' and 'expectation' – that those people who interact with an individual 'send' him their expectations as to how he should behave – the Michigan researchers distinguished certain ways in which role conflict can occur. The most important of these are (1) situations in which one or several members of a 'role set' put pressure on an individual to act in a particular way, and (2) situations in which the individual receives conflicting messages from different 'role sending' groups. To give an example – the buyer in a company will be expected by the research and development division to purchase high quality components in order to produce to their design specifications; the company accountant, on the other hand, will advise him to keep costs to a minimum – seldom will the buyer be able to satisfy both of these requirements. Conflict occurs when the alternatives are reasonably well defined and understood (but incompatible); in some cases, however, the individual is uncertain as to what is expected of him, what his responsibilities are, and what authority he can exercise to achieve them. It is this type of circumstance which is labelled role ambiguity.

A more recent contribution to the area of role-related stress was made in a paper by French and Caplan (1973). They report that whilst there was a high positive correlation between responsibility for people and the measures of stress used in their study, no such relation was found with responsibility for things. Before the full implications of this finding can be explored, further research is needed to discover how it can be generalized. It does, however, highlight a point which has been noted repeatedly by research workers in the field of management stress, that, on the whole, dealing with people is far more stressful than dealing with things.

When interviewed it is those pressures intrinsic to the job and due to role in organization which managers consider to be the most legitimate sources of stress vis-à-vis their jobs. Typically they are referred to as 'what I'm paid for', 'why I'm here', and even when they cause severe disruption, the implication is that they cannot be legitimately avoided. In many companies, in fact, there are institutional ways in which these problems can be handled – for example, deadlines are set unrealistically early to allow a margin of error, decisions are made by groups so that no one individual has to take full responsibility, the employee is allowed to neglect certain tasks (e.g. filing) if he is busy, work can be reallocated within a department if one member is seen to be doing more than his fair share. Like the old age pensioner with supplementary benefits, however, the manager may not always perceive himself as free to use these fail-safe mechanisms.

It is often much easier to do a job alone than to co-operate with other people. Any employee can be seen as the focus of a network of organizational relationships which may be extensive (e.g. a work study officer), or more restricted (e.g. production engineer), depending on his function and level in the company. Minzberg (1973) in a study of how chief executives of a company actually spend their time found that in a large organization a mere 22% of time was spent in desk work sessions, the rest being taken up by telephone calls (6%), scheduled meetings (59%), unscheduled meetings (10%) and other activities (3%). In small organizations basic desk work played a larger part (52%), but nearly 40% was still devoted to face-to-face contacts of one kind or another.

Relations within the Organization

Relations within the organization have been recognized by many researchers as a potential source of stress. All workers at some time will have felt the strains of 'poor relations'; personality conflicts with supervisors, subordinates, or other members of the work team, not being able to call on others for help to solve problems or difficulties in delegating responsibility. These pressures are not so amicably regarded by managers – they are often seen as 'trivial', 'petty', time-consuming and an impediment to doing the job well. It is, however, this category which is likely to be a growing source of stress as (1) there are more clamourings at every level for participation and consultation, and (2) higher management become more 'switched on' to human relations training and expect this area of functioning to come increasingly under the individual's control.

Career Development

In our ambitious, differentials-conscious society, *career development* is a major preoccupation, frustration, and cause of stress. It is currently argued that the days of the achievement-oriented manager, the stereotypic 'whiz-kid executive' are over, and that many of our economic difficulties are caused by a lack of commitment. This appears to be true for only a small section of management, who fall into two classes – the disillusioned young (a minority at present), and those in middle age, who face diminishing promotion and life prospects – perhaps in the past the latter particularly were less open about their cynicism. Some of the more significant sources of stress associated with career development are overpromotion, lack of job security, fear of redundancy or retirement, fear of obsolescence, having to face frustrated ambitions, loss of status, and feeling trapped. As was seen with factors that are 'job-intrinsic', the employee has a strong fear of being under-used. This is severely aggravated by the rapid development of both technology and management techniques. As old ways become devalued, waves of freshly trained recruits come in to upset the age-ordered hierarchy, which puts an added strain on the older manager, especially in an organization or industry which is more receptive to novelty and change. Even those who lead developments in their own area of specialization find it hard to keep abreast of those in 'background' disciplines.

Managers are expected to be men of action, yet they have a limited ability to influence their own career development – for many, also, the rules as to how this can be done are ambiguous, a frequent dilemma is whether it is better to do one's job and rely on results, or to be seen by 'important people' to be doing those aspects of one's job which *they* consider to be important. Sofer (1970) suggested that many executives report that 'luck' plays an important role in their career development – belief in 'being in the right place at the right time' and 'having a face that fits' bear testimony to this.

It is interesting to note that for many managers salary increase is only a partial substitute for promotion; at management levels, pay and working conditions are glaringly absent from the list of pressures reported by researchers. The exact role of pay as a satisficer at shop floor level is much debated, but has been reported as a variable in a number of studies (Daniel, 1972).

Organizational Climate and Structure

There is a ubiquitous set of pressures which face all of us in our day-to-day lives – those related to individual freedom, conformity to authority, etc. 'No Parking' signs, 'Please fill in this form', and the conscientious objector all have their organizational parallels, which can lead to the seventh set of pressures, those we have called pressures due to *organizational climate and structure.* The literature highlights restrictions on behaviour such as budgets and form filling, lack of effective consultation and communication, uncertainty as to what is happening next, no sense of belonging/loss of identity, the tensions of office politics, etc. The larger the organization the more likely it is that these will operate, and the less likely that any one individual will be in a position to influence them. In modern technological society, it is practically impossible to survive without co-operation and compromise, or more specifically, organizational membership – this, however, directly threatens the individual's freedom, autonomy and sense of identity.

Work: Home Interface

Research to date has tended to concentrate on the individual in his organizational setting, ignoring the intrusions of the job into life outside work, and also any feedback in the opposite direction. In the final set of sources of stress, *work:home interface*, only three factors are found with any significant frequency – those of an individual in an organizational boundary position (i.e. where work relations are mainly with persons outside the company), those created by conflicts of individuals' attitudes with those of the company, and the conflict of the company with family demands. Several factors help to explain the rather limited research focus on interface issues:

1. it is easier to study the closed confines of the organization than the individual's total life situation;
2. many researchers are interested in improving the employee's work performance, for them the organization is a natural focus of study;
3. many people have very little life outside their work, particularly at executive levels, where their outside interests are usually structured around job demands.

The manager's life outside working hours is now receiving more attention, partly because of a more humanistic outlook on the part of organizations and researchers in the field, and also because certain of society's problems (delinquent children, drunken wives) are being laid at the breadwinner's door. A recent report by the BIM *The Management Threshold*, Beattie *et al.* (1974), for example, highlights the difficult situation of the young executive who, in order to build up his career, must devote a great deal of time and energy to his job just when his young housebound wife, with small children, is also making pressing demands. The report suggests that the executive fights to maintain the distance between his wife and the organization, so that she will not be in a position to evaluate the choices he has to make; paradoxically he does so at a time when he is most in need of sympathy and understanding. American researchers (e.g. Packard, 1972, in *A Nation of Strangers*, and Pahl and Pahl, 1971, in *Managers and their Wives*) are beginning to examine the disruptions caused not only to home life, but also to the community, by the typical managerial life style, particularly the high level of geographical mobility.

From an examination of the seven main sources of stress one is able to see several overriding theories in the literature. First, for example, managerial stress is repeatedly seen to be the result of *uncertain situations* – poorly defined jobs, role conflict, responsibility without authority, fears about career development or job security, etc. And second, that stress results from conflicting demands at work; the manager does not only take responsibility for his subordinates' actions, he answers for those to his superiors; he not only agrees to a two-week business trip abroad, he goes home to tell his wife he will be away for that time. A way of avoiding these pressures is to segregate sharply the two separate worlds – the manager can seldom do this, as he is continually required to act in the one according to decisions made and norms upheld in the other.

The list of sources of work stress reflects, broadly speaking, the research carried out so far. There are however a number of factors and issues that have not been adequately examined in the research to date that also deserves our attention.

1. So far very little more than lip service has been paid to the fact that the job is only one part of any manager's total life situation, and a part to which he can be either deeply or superficially committed. What part work does play in an individual's overall life pattern at any particular time will have great bearing on how he perceives situations, both at work and at home, and the degree of work stress. It is probable, for example, that at a career-centred time (e.g. when promotion is likely) the manager will find work pressures more damaging than at a family-centred time (e.g. the birth of a baby), when work performance is relatively more likely to deteriorate if there are problems at home.
2. The manager's overall situation is important too, in providing some insight into the ways in which pressure and stress have cumulative or compensating effects, both at one point in time and also over time.
3. Implicit in literature is a fundamental distinction between acute and chronic as applied to pressure and stress. Some pressures (e.g. relocation) are of relatively sudden onset and duration, these can be classed as acute; others

will be constantly present (e.g. a poor relationship with one's superior) and therefore chronic. This distinction is somewhat clouded by the fact that acute pressures (e.g. a wave of unemployment notices in a company) can lead to chronic stress (i.e. the constant fear of being unemployed).

COPING WITH MANAGERIAL STRESS

This paper has concentrated almost entirely on the *sources* of managerial stress, with little attention to techniques of coping with them. This has been done deliberately, because it is only possible effectively to prevent or deal with work stress if one can accurately identify it in a particular work situation. The strategy adopted to cope with work stress will depend upon which of the job or organizational stressor(s) described in this paper is or are operating in the specific work environment. For example, if occupational ill-health stems primarily from poor physical working conditions, then we might want to consider work redesign or ergonomic solutions to the problem. If, on the other hand, work problems originate from conflicting or ambiguous roles, then we might want to utilize techniques such as 'role negotiation', 'role playing', etc. If managers at work are dissatisfied with their rate of career advancement, and this leads to job frustration and stress manifestations, it would not be of any help to them to try relaxation techniques or transcendental meditation; it would be far more useful, for example, to be doing some career planning or to train senior management in methods of career development or job evaluation.

Different job and organizational stressors require different solutions, and only when companies are willing to accept their responsibility and contemplate carrying out specific organizational 'stress audits' will we begin to deal effectively with managerial stress.

Let us briefly explore some of these here. If we examine the factors which are *intrinsic to the job* and the individual there are several possible stress-preventive steps one might consider. Some of the stress research suggests, for example, that certain types of individuals are more susceptible to stress than others. If an organization deems the costs of stress too high it has available the possibility of introducing new criteria for selection and placement. It might consider the possibility of trying to select people who are better able to cope with role ambiguity and conflict, with increased responsibility for people, with work overload, etc., when these are known to be relevant to a particular job situation. An organization's ability to optimize the fit between individual and job by their selection procedures will of course depend on extensive validation work on potential selection tests. This is something that will require a great deal of further work but is currently under review by a number of the larger industrial organizations.

Another way of coping with some of the stress associated with the relationship between the individual and the job is by training. Training programmes and techniques are available or could be designed which might help the individual perform his or her job more effectively and with less stress, or to cope with work overload, or to improve his or her relations with others; that is training people to increase their tolerance and coping abilities. Techniques such as transcendental meditation, role-playing, time management training, personal growth groups, team building activities (as both a source of feedback on the person–job fit and a source of support) and many others are currently available for use in stress prevention and reduction programmes.

'Role in the organization' is a very important source of stress. Role conflict and ambiguity can be dealt with by procedures designed to clarify the duties (role expectations of others) and performance (role behaviour) of each individual in an organization. This could be accomplished by encouraging mutual consultation between individual and supervisor for purposes of redefining the job. A systematic procedure of job clarification should help to achieve a somewhat less ambiguous network of interrelated work roles.

It has been suggested (Kahn *et al.*, 1964) that individuals who experience role conflict should be able to confront those making excessive demands on them and 'renegotiate' their relationships. The organization could help by building in feedback channels of communication which make this possible.

Another important factor associated with the individual's role in the organization is that of *participation.* Based on our research and a number of other research projects (for example, French and Caplan, 1973) we know that stress can result from low participation or lack of autonomy, which leads to job dissatisfaction. The suggestion here is that greater participation in the decision-making process may enhance an individual's own self-esteem and feelings of control and thereby reduce job dissatisfaction and threat. French and Caplan (1973) outline five necessary conditions of any participation programme based on their research findings: first, to reduce stress by increasing participation one must provide a *supportive* supervisor and cohesive work group; second, that participation should *not* be *illusory,* that is that it should not be used as a manipulative tool; third, that the decisions on which participation is based should *not* be *trivial* to the people concerned; fourth, that the decisions should be *relevant*; finally, the decisions should be seen to be a *legitimate* part of their work. These qualifiers are a very useful guide in designing decision-sharing mechanisms, particularly in view of recent moves by the government for greater involvement and wider representation in industry.

If we examine the career development factors we can see that some of these (e.g. overpromotion and underpromotion) depend on an accurate assessment by the organization of the individual's potential and performance at work. Social skill training techniques like sensitivity training (Cooper, 1979), team role laboratories (Reddin, 1970) etc., may help to provide those concerned with promotion and management development with the necessary sensitivity to the individual's achievements, potential, and other relevant factors in making decisions about promotion. Another important issue that falls within the career development category is job insecurity and fear of redundancy. Many organizations handle this issue very badly indeed. This not only creates a climate of distrust and encourages job dissatisfaction but also is personally damaging to the individual concerned. It seems that this is an unnecessary destructive cyclical process, which might be improved by greater openness and honesty on the part of the organization about issues of job tenure and redundancy.

Ineffective communications and lack of trust lead us into another main source of stress – 'poor relations within organizations'. If we are to minimize the potential stress effects of 'being in organizations', with all the behavioural restrictions that implies, and of poor relations between boss and subordinate, and between colleagues, organizations will have to consider change or development programmes that will encourage trust-building activities. Organizational trust-building is characterized by (1) the development of a supportive organizational climate and norms, (2) the building of shared norms on the basis of perceived similarities in attitudes and experiences of people working in organizations, and (3) the development of 'we-ness', a shared identity among workers that implies substantial common direction by all (Golembiewski and McConkie, 1975). More and more work is being carried out in the area of organizational change and development to create the conditions of trust and well-being within the workplace (Cooper, 1976), which should help to improve relations between boss and subordinate and between work colleagues, and help to make the constraints associated with living in an organization less stressful. As Bennis and Slater (1968) suggest in their book on the 'temporary society', industrial life is so fast-moving and changeable that organizations have to adapt by being more flexible and by unfreezing their structures so that individuals are not locked into jobs that might put excessive stress on them. Burns and Stalker (1961) made this point in their book *The Management of Innovation* when they suggested that changing times demand more 'organic' as opposed to 'mechanistic' organizations.

At the moment managers are facing considerable stress at work which is a result of the subtle outgrowth of all the factors discussed in this chapter. Today more organizations are recognizing that it is their responsibility to consider these and to help create the conditions for the psychological well-being of their staff. Kornhauser aptly summarised the condition that organizations should be concerned about today:

> Mental health is not so much a freedom from specific frustrations as it is an overall balanced relationship to the world which permits a person to maintain realistic, positive belief in himself and his purposeful activities. In so far as his entire job and life situation facilitate and support such feelings of adequacy, inner security and meaningfulness of his existence, it can be presumed that his mental health will tend to be good. What is important in a negative way is not any single characteristic of his situation but everything that deprives the person of purpose and zest, that leaves him with negative feelings about himself, with anxieties, tensions, a sense of lostness, emptiness and futility.

REFERENCES

Beattie, R.T. *et al.* (1974). *The Management Threshold,* BIM, London.

Bennis, W.G. and Slater, P.E. (1968). *The Temporary Society,* Harper and Row, New York.

Brummet, R.L., Pyle, W.C. and Flamholtz, E.G. (1968). 'Accounting for human resources', *Michigan Business Review,* **20** (2), 20–5.

Burns, T. and Stalker, G.M. (1961). *The Management of Innovation,* The Tavistock, London.

Cooper, C.L. (1976). *Developing Social Skills in Managers,* Macmillan, London.

Cooper, C.L. (1979). *Learning from Others in Groups*, Associated Business Press, London.

Cooper, C.L. and Marshall, J. (1978). *Understanding Executive Stress,* Macmillan, London.

Daniel, W.W. (1972). 'What interests a worker?', *New Society,* 23 March.

French, J.R.P. and Caplan, R.D. (1973). 'Organizational stress and individual strain', in A.J. Marrow (ed.), *The Failure of Success*, AMACOM, New York. 30–66.

Golembiewski, B.T. and McConkie, M. (1975). 'The centrality of interpersonal trust', in C.L. Cooper (ed.), *Theories of Group Processes*, John Wiley, New York.

Kahn, R.L., Wolfe, D.M. Quinn, R.P., Snoek, J.D. and Rosenthal, R.A. (1964). *Organizational Stress,* John Wiley, New York.

Kornhauser, A. (1965). *Mental Health of the Industrial Worker,* John Wiley, New York.

Marshall, J. and Cooper, C.L. (1979). *Executives Under Pressure,* Macmillan, London.

Minzberg, H. (1973). *The Nature of Managerial Work,* Harper and Row, New York.

Packard, V. (1975). *A Nation of Strangers,* McKay, New York.

Pahl, J.M. and Pahl, R.E. (1971). *Managers and Their Wives,* Allen Lane, London.

Reddin, W. (1970). *Managerial Effectiveness,* McGraw-Hill, New York.

Sofer, C. (1970). *Men in Mid-Career,* Cambridge University Press, Cambridge.

Advances in Management Education
Edited by John Beck and Charles Cox

CHAPTER 3

Participation in Work and Education

Michael Reynolds

There is a contradiction in Management Education which is not being adequately confronted. As the attempt is made to change organizations or some part of them to more democratic structures, so the ability of education and training to facilitate that change seems to be losing ground. There is no single reason for this, yet it seems to be chiefly because our collective skill in the design of educational or training experiences has outstripped our understanding of some of the fundamental processes involved. In particular, we seem to have overlooked the function which education serves in preparing people for membership of work organizations.

Awareness of 'process', as it has come to be known (Schein, 1969), is one of the major contributions which the Human Relations and Group Dynamics Schools have made to our understanding of social interaction and social systems. Much of our recent work is based on the belief that the development of effective social relationships depends upon the ability to identify the processes involved and to understand them. Whatever the setting, work or non-work, we ignore these processes to our ultimate cost. Unfortunately, the range of process we examine is limited, and so therefore, is our understanding of the events of which they are a part.

In summary therefore, the points I should like to argue in this paper are these:

1. Education and training exercises a powerful influence in shaping the beliefs, values, and expectations on which our subsequent behaviour as members of organizations is based. The principles which underlie our relationships with others and our beliefs about the kind of social structures within which those relationships occur, are transmitted and reinforced by the educational settings to which we are exposed.
2. This process of transmission is not simply through the content or the curriculum of educational programmes, let alone of specific courses or sessions. It is at least as much communicated to the student or trainee through the processes involved. The methods used, the trainer–student

relationship and the decision-making structures are all based on principles, social and political. The methods applied transmit these principles even when they contradict the points of the content which it is intended they should convey.

3. It is possible to define those structures and processes, at work or in the classroom, which enable people to learn about taking part and taking responsibility, and those structures and processes which encourage passive acquiescence.
4. For whatever reason and with whatever confusion as to the precise meaning of democracy as practised, there are people in organizations who wish to see authority-structures become less hierarchical. At the same time, our capability – or willingness – to provide the form of educational experience which would enable that change to happen has been eroded. Educational method is slipping back into its more traditional role of confirming and strengthening peoples' acceptance of both hierarchical structures and their own, largely subjugated role within them.

In developing these arguments I shall look at questions like these:

- What in practice can democracy involve, both at work and in educational settings?
- What are the effects of various educational methods on our expectations of, or preferences for the kind of structures and relationships we experience at work?
- To what extent do we, in training and education, understand the effects that structure and control have in shaping peoples' values and beliefs about organizations?
- Are we always aware of how much direction and control we use? Equally, do we have the theoretical grounding necessary to understand why less structured methods create the problems they do?
- Why is it that Management Education seems to have slowed down in its effort to develop its capacity to bring about democracy at work?

For a number of years my interest has been in the development of teaching methods in an attempt to encourage people to participate in the workplace. Those with similar experience would, I think, agree that it is an area fraught with design problems, where even apparent success seems difficult to sustain when students or trainees return from courses to their work and their on-going relationships.

Recently, it seemed to me while on a training programme, that the opposite was the case. The preparation that the course was offering did not appear to match up to the opportunities for participation which were being presented to the course members in their work. So I should like to describe this experience first, and then attempt to define the criteria for an educational culture most likely to support participative forms of organization.

AN ILLUSTRATION – A PROGRAMME FOR THE DEVELOPMENT OF CONSULTANCY SKILLS

Background

This programme was designed for the members of an engineering department which provided a service to a large manufacturing company. The company had a history of being active for a number of years in its use of 'Behavioural Science' methods of development. As a result of this work, an ethos had been developed of collaboration and conflict-resolution in problem-solving, decision-making and Management–Union negotiations. A number of projects designed to improve working relationships and the quality of work life had involved management and unions. So much was this work seen to have changed the culture of the department that it was believed that there was more scope for OD consultants' work than could be maintained by the numbers of consultants available (internal or external).

In view of this, it was decided to sponsor a training programme to develop the methods and skills of process consultancy amongst the members of the department, and at all levels. Until then, people in the consultants' role were a specialist resource to planning, decision-making and problem-solving meetings, or to special events. It now seemed more appropriate that their time should be spent in training the members of the department in the understanding and skills of interpersonal and group process. It was hoped that as a consequence participants would become more effective as members of work groups and be able to provide a consultant resource to their own and other sections of the department. A team of two external consultants, a training officer, and a line manager was delegated the responsibility of designing a programme to meet this need. There have now been over ten programmes, with 16 participants on each and around ten participants have become members of the staff group for subsequent courses. There have been a number of changes in the programme but the description which follows is fairly representative.

The Programme

The programme begins with a five-day residential event and is followed by 6–8 one day sessions spread over the next six weeks. The 16 participants on each programme are managers, supervisors, and shop stewards from the various sections of the department. It is designed and run by a staff team of four people including at least one external training consultant and one new staff member invited from the participants of a previous programme. The aims are:

to understand the nature and problems of the consultant–client relationship.
to understand the various models of organizational intervention.
to develop consulting skills.
to identify those concepts and skills which will be the basis of further development.

This description of the aims is taken from the proposal submitted by the original design team. As the design has evolved, there has been a shift of emphasis from developing consulting skills to the development of the kind of awareness and skills normally associated with Process Consultancy as the basis of effective group membership.

The course consists of various sized groups predominately using the experiential method of the input–exercise–discussion and application type. The topics are:

- *The Helping Relationship* – A blend of the Rogerian client-centred approach applied to work problems, whether personal or organizational, on a one-to-one basis. A good deal of time is given to demonstration and practice of the techniques involved.
- *Group Behaviour* – Exercises to illustrate the various social processes of decision-making, such as communication, leadership, conflict and collaboration, competition and support.
- *Intergroup Behaviour* – Problems of representation and taking authority on behalf of others, structures for communication and negotiation, exploring assumptions and perceptions of other groups. The dilemmas of roles and relationships.
- *Personality Theory* – Some basic (social psychology) concepts to help understand differences in individual behaviour using peoples' experience and impressions of themselves and each other in the context of the week.
- *Organizational Problem-Solving* – An opportunity to apply the content of the week to current back-at-work problems brought by visiting works personnel to the final day of the event.

Principles

Any training programme, whatever its aims and content, is based on implicit principles which will be transmitted to the participants by way of the procedures and processes within which the course content is embedded. From the inception of a course, choices are made by the staff and by management, thoughtfully or otherwise, which manifest principles of social relations mirrored in and originating from the workplace. So for example, the participant role is defined, initially by the design team, at the stages of both design and implementation. The relationship between staff and participants is demonstrated not only in the classroom but in the process of choosing and deciding throughout the entire life of the programme.

At this stage, and before summarizing some of the problems experienced with the programme, it would be appropriate to describe the most salient principles upon which the staff team based their design, wittingly or otherwise.

1. The ethos within which (and from which) the programme had been conceived was one of *'participative management'* as understood strictly within the

profession of management and as opposed, for instance, to the meaning which a political theorist might give to the term.

2. The liberal value-system pervading the course was therefore one of exploring more *collaborative* and *humanistic* ways of conducting social relationships. This was manifest in the emphasis on developing the helping relationship and in the implicit value system for colleague and superior–subordinate relationships which was a characteristic of this type of development work.
3. The conceptual emphasis was on identifying *interpersonal, group and intergroup process* and to focus on ways of becoming aware of and able to deal with those dynamics which determined the quality of work or work relationships.
4. The method was mainly *experiential* (Kolb *et al.*, 1971). The assumption being that learning would be derived from reflection on and analysis of events in which participants either took part or were observers, or – hopefully and eventually – were able to be both observant and involved.
5. It is important to emphasize that the staff took complete responsibility for directing the event. Although all sessions were based on involvement and active participation and the staff's role in discussions often fairly non-directive, *what took place, when and by what means, was largely if not entirely the prerogative of the staff group.*

   In the same way the tasks used as illustrative exercises were tightly structured. The only (and significant) exception to this was an intergroup exercise which took up the whole of the third day on some of the courses. In this the group membership, roles, procedures, and tasks were chosen or designed by participants.
6. The disciplines from which the content and method were drawn were mainly *social or humanistic psychology.* There was little analysis of events in terms of those societal institutions of which they were born and which they reflected.
7. Finally, but perhaps as important as any other principle described so far, it had always been intended that in most of the staff groups there would be a participant from an earlier programme. At least nine people become staff members of subsequent events and three of them at some stage were invited to be the staff team leader.

Problems

Both within and outside the department there was a strong body of opinion that this programme had made a significant contribution to the work of the department and especially to the quality of working relationships. Senior Management continue to give financial and organizational support to the venture and by most accounts, interest in the programme is unusually high. The exercise has been seen by trainers, senior management, and participants as one of the more successful in their experience. The problems were these:

1. There was confusion between 'consulting' and 'consultative management'. Why were people being turned into consultants? Was it the same as being consultative and in either case were the implications for decision-making?
2. It seemed inescapable that the more experienced the staff group became the tighter the structure of the event. Accordingly the rarer were those unpredictable episodes which many trainers recognize contain much of the energy which brings a learning community to life.
3. We have much to learn before we will have solved the difficulty of harnessing the rich material which springs from less structured, less controlled learning settings. It sometimes seemed that the same process which generated material for enlightenment left course participants floundering, confused and frustrated.
4. The follow-up events of a day each (or less usually half a day each), were incorporated for the following reasons: firstly, because of the limitations of any isolated training experience, it takes longer than five days to sustain any significant learning or skill. Secondly, and crucial to the argument of this paper, the ultimate aim of the programme was that people would become more active, participative members of their department and work groups. As training for this it was always hoped that in the follow-up events, the responsibility for co-ordination, choice of topic and, as much as possible, design, would be shared between staff and participants.

Sometimes this worked well. Indeed some course groups designed and ran follow-up sessions without involving the staff group in any way at all. But for the most part it resulted in disappointment. The participants became dispirited, felt let down, and the follow-up sessions faded away. In spite of what the design team thought they would accomplish in the five-day event, more often than not, the offer of a share in responsibility was rejected. Yet it was fundamental to the aims of the programme that peoples' development would lead them to feel more comfortable if not more eager to take an active role rather than to acquiesce, in matters of the department which affected them.

The problems encountered in the consultancy skills programme provided a starting point from which to examine the relationship between participation in the workplace and the culture of educational or training events designed to support it. The steps in exploring the nature of that relationship will be as follows:

1. *Democracy and Participation*: There are difficulties of defining participation. Different degrees of participation are practised and there are quite different rationales for introducing it. Organizational development, however, provides a link between work assumptions and educational method.
2. *Education as Socialization*: Education is one means by which peoples' values and beliefs about organizations are shaped and through which their expectation of roles and relationships at work are developed.

3. *Socialization through process*: Development of organizational assumptions is not simply through the explicit content of education. The decisions and procedures involved in planning and design as well as the transactions during the event itself make up its social and political culture. This is a neglected source of influence on peoples' subsequent behaviour.
4. *Liberating culture in education*: A discussion of what the features of a programme would be for its culture to be consistent with, and supportive of a participative organization.
5. *Participative designs and their neglect*: Models for education do exist which meet most criteria for a more enabling culture. Why are they not used more?

Finally, the points of this argument are applied in an analysis of the consultancy skills programme. Some criteria were met by the programme but some were not.

DEMOCRACY AND PARTICIPATION

The notion of democracy and ideas about democratic structures of organizations are central to this discussion. But there is often a vagueness about what democratic methods mean in practice which makes any discussion of their value or of the appropriateness of various educational methodologies difficult. To put it more strongly, without being conceptually tidier, we may think we are engaging in democratic procedures when we are not.

Ultimately, the definitions of democracy and participation which have meaning are those implicit in practice. The question therefore is not 'what is democracy?' but rather 'what in practice are we doing when we adopt what we believe to be a democratic approach to management or education?'. If we say we wish to humanize the workplace, what structures and practices need to be changed and for what alternative? Are our reasons political, humanistic, or pragmatic? There is a need for more clarity and more honesty about the ideology implicit in what is practised. Participation must involve a change in the structures of authority.

Participation in Work

Participation is generally accepted as a necessary condition for democracy, though there are differing ideas as to how much 'taking part' is desirable or feasible. The ultimate practice of participation would be one which would assume political equality. Each member of the organization would have an equal opportunity to influence any decision. This model is to be found in some collectives.

The most common form of participation is one which is localized within a given level of the organization. Workers on the shop floor may take part in decisions about the tasks which they perform, in the same way as management may collaborate in planning or deciding policy at its level. But this form of participation need not involve much change in the authority structure overall in that it is limited to immediate tasks. Also common to our experience is that decisions may be made after consultation with subordinates. This again is a partial form of participation in that giving or withholding the opportunity for subordinates to influence the final decision is the manager's prerogative, as is the extent to which he allows their ideas to influence him.

Often of course, 'participation' is not to participate at all. It is an exercise in diplomatic communication. A task is performed more willingly, if its rationale has been explained and discussed or when problems in working relationships have been ironed out. However plausible this is as an exercise in 'human relations' it is only a variation in the operation of a hierarchical structure. It is not democratic because it is not, in essence, participative. The nature of the decisions has not been affected by those whose duty it is to carry them out, however willingly they do so.

Of course, partial or local participation is necessary if a more significant involvement is ever to be achieved. Indeed as Pateman points out, the ability of people to take part in the community and its decision-making processes will depend on similar opportunities being available at work.

> Most individuals spend a great deal of their lifetime at work and the business of the workplace provides an education in the management of collective affairs that it is difficult to parallel elsewhere.
>
> (Pateman 1970, p. 43)

Participation in Education

The link between democracy at work and in educational method has been made most explicit in the field of Organizational Development. Its founding fathers, Argyris, McGregor, and Bennis were adamant that pyramidal structures were dehumanizing and that by their nature they promoted and sustained a climate of coercion, subjugation, secrecy and competitiveness. Bennis (1969) writes of

> A new concept of *organizational values,* based on humanistic–democratic ideas, which replaces the depersonalized, mechanistic value system of bureaucracy. (p. 22)

The rationale for this movement was both humanistic and pragmatic. OD people saw a match between the needs for organizations to produce more and the better human conditions which would result from the structures likely to ensure that productivity. But the significance of the practice of OD has been that the approach to training was itself designed to be more participative and more student-centred than conventional methods (Schein and Bennis, 1965). The need was recognized for people to *understand and revise their values and beliefs as preparation for sharing in democratic work structures* (Reynolds, 1979). The consultancy skills programme was of this mould.

EDUCATION AS SOCIALIZATION

Education is one of the agencies by which peoples' assumptions about organizations are shaped. In building on our experience of the family, education indicates the principles on which social relationships are to be based. This experience also serves as a preparation for entry into political structures of various kinds and in various roles. There is thus a rapport between the various arenas in which socialization takes place. The values inherent in apprentice schools or colleges of higher education reflect, more or less, values first introduced in childhood and are usually in accord with the principles upon which organization of the workplace is based. It is certain that there is no such thing as neutrality in education.

As trainers or teachers, how well do we understand the way in which organizational assumptions are transmitted? What experience do we have of those educational structures which prepare people for 'taking part' as opposed to those which reinforce their compliance?

I believe that an answer to these questions must take account of two points. First, that if we are exclusively preoccupied with the explicit content of education, we ignore the socializing influence of process and, by default, allow it to work against any aims which we espouse of developing participation and democracy. The decisions which we make in designing courses and curricula and the roles we define for staff and participants are a means by which peoples' social and political consciousness is developed. Second, that although there is the expertise in management education to identify this process, our designs are often less enabling than we have the ability to make them. Further, the educational culture provided may fall short of the opportunity for participation with which some people are being presented at work.

SOCIALIZATION THROUGH PROCESS

The concept on which this section in particular is based is the distinction between content and process. 'Content' refers to the subject material of a course or programme and which is explicitly conveyed to students through reading, discussion or through instruction, whether that is by lecture or by illustrative exercises of the 'simulation' type. 'Process' refers to those decisions, structures, and transactions within which the content is borne and communicated and the principles which they imply. So to understand the working of socialization, we must think of the entire sequence of events involved in the planning of a programme. This embraces the design of its sessions, the authority-structures which are adopted, and the sequence of choices and decisions made throughout its history. In some subjects, content and process are distinct, as in the teaching of a science or language. But in courses concerned with social relations, including management, they overlap. So in a session dealing with the concept of 'leadership', belief and theories about the role and practice of leader and follower will be communicated by the tutor as content. But equally they will be conveyed by the tutor's behaviour in the classroom and the basis and extent of the authority assumed in the relationship between tutor and participants.

In studies of socialization, the emphasis is usually on the explicit component or less often, on the norms, rules, and values on which the educational organization is based and which determine the social behaviour of its members. But the process involved in education not only affects how much of the content is picked up but constitutes a source of learning in its own right. For example, a teacher who adopts a punitive or controlling stance towards his pupils may inhibit his pupils' learning in his subject. But through his approach will also be transmitted the principles on which his behaviour and mode of teaching is based. Specific relationships between authority and control, power and role, punishment and learning represent the teacher's interpretation of his culture and are conveyed to his students whether he intends that to happen or not.

In a similar way but with a different outcome, a science course based on solving problems in student groups may do more than enhance the learning of scientific principles through the enjoyment which that method generates. Beliefs about the value of collective effort, about the value of self-management, and about taking responsibility are also transmitted, and the social consciousness shaped by this process is available for engaging with other social settings.

So with Management Education, involvement in class or in class design will help generate commitment and enthusiasm for the subject content. But more importantly it provides an opportunity to experience and understand the principles and problems of shared responsibility and of work based on collective effort and decision-making. In this way our inner experience is developed and made available for our involvement in other social settings.

It is fundamental that all social activities, and the rules and procedures they contain, are based on social and political principles of some kind. The same must be true for the structures and procedures of an educational programme which emerge or are invoked in the process of policy, decision-making, and classroom method. The principles on which they are based will be transmitted to course members whether or not that is the intention. How else do we learn about social relationships and the problems of power and control except from our prior experience of these parallel settings? Even the decision whether to have specific or integrated course content affects the nature of the authority relationships between staff and students by determining whether the emphasis will be on learning how to learn or simply on the acquisition of knowledge. In highly specialized courses the authority is more likely to be directive and unquestioned. In integrated courses the teacher–student relationship is more collaborative, as are the student–student relationships (Bernstein, 1975).

Policies which determine specificity of subject matter also affect how subdivided the staff group will become through the separation of their disciplines.

In this way principles of authority, individualism, and competition are conveyed indirectly from the form which the curriculum takes. So for example in management education, do training, industrial relations, and line personnel collaborate in deciding training policy and course design or alternatively do they keep their activities separate? Either way a message is communicated to course members as to the value in practice which is placed within their organization on collaboration as opposed to hierarchy and division.

LIBERATING CULTURE IN EDUCATION

If the context of an educational programme is some degree of democracy in work and if we acknowledge that the processes of such a programme are as much a source of organizational assumptions as its content, then it follows that its fabric should be composed of the principles upon which participative democracy is based.

But even more, for the programme to develop peoples' ability to take part, the opportunity to take an active role in their own learning may not be enough. It would also be necessary to provide the means of understanding how their experience to date may have inhibited their ability and willingness to take part. The design of learning events should be such as to help people understand the genesis of constraint inherent in previous work and educational settings they have encountered and the ways that this is manifest in their present behaviour. In other words, *the educational culture has not only to be participative but 'liberating' as well.* Otherwise the opportunity to participate may only serve to reinforce peoples' lack of confidence in accepting responsibility and increase their sense of failure.

The problem is that as so much training has been such as to encourage subservience, whether in school or at work, that the initial response to a more participative culture will be one of reticence and 'muteness' (Freire, 1972). To have spent many years of receiving information and knowledge and receiving and carrying out instructions is poor training for 'taking part' at all, let alone for becoming involved in the transformation of work structures. The principles which underlie these experiences dominate the way we interpret our role in organizations and make for a considerable gradient up which the educationalist must work. I wonder if, in practice, we do not underestimate this.

Specifically then, and within the context of management education, what would be the salient features of a liberating culture?

(i) Participative Democracy as the Structure of Authority

It is possible, though not commonly practised, to involve the members of a course in decisions at the stages of design and during the course itself. They can take part in providing material about the problems and interests on which the design can subsequently be based and in deciding how that information should influence the design. Course members are more often involved in providing data than in deciding on how it should be used. Similarly during a course, feedback from participants is sought by the staff, but who takes part in deciding what changes should be made as a result? Choices about the selection of participants, location, timetable, and content can also be made jointly by staff and membership. The course need not be wholly predetermined, emergent models leave some of the time to be planned during the event itself.

The goal of participation is not to create merely the feeling of involvement, nor should it be interest or excitement for its own sake. The social and organizational basis of the event should be community as a whole, with a staff–participant boundary permeable to ideas and to influence, with room for individual work within a collective process of learning and deciding. Clearly, on these criteria an 'experiential' event is not necessarily participative. Material for study is generated from past or present experience yet few, if any decisions need to be open to the students' influence.

(ii) Authority based on Knowledge

In an educational event this is a necessary condition for participation. Often we employ, perhaps unwittingly, purely professional authority based on status and on role. It is necessary therefore to identify in which choices it is appropriate to defer to the staff and which it is not. There are usually decisions to be taken which are not academic in nature and where political equality would be realistic. In group dynamics training for example, there is an implication, if not a stated aim, that students take responsibility for their own learning. But if the concepts on which design or interpretation are based are not open to question, this opportunity is limited. The model of authority conveyed is patently hierarchical. By the same token, the way in which the staff exercise their authority should be open to question and influence from participants.

(iii) Process as Material for Study and Historical Reflection

The processes involved in the 'classroom' provide material from which to learn. This is fundamental to some experiential designs but not all. In using structured exercises the dynamics illustrated by the exercise itself are intended as study material but the structure and organization of the session is not. More broadly, the events open to observation and reflection could include those choices made by design or default within the entire programme. As well as there being more from which to learn, this would additionally provide the basis from which structure, procedure, and relationships could be modified. It would also enable the staff and participants to explore any misunderstandings or concerns which arise because of the 'deliberate irony' which is an essence of participative methods (Torbert, 1978).

(iv) Dialogue

Appropriate to the values of participative democracy is the notion in teaching, of dialogue rather than simply of communication. In the same way that a decision may be based on the collective contribution of a work group, so ideas and interpretation of experience can be based on the exchange of views of reality between teacher and students. It is inappropriate, within this model, to assume that the concepts with which the teacher begins his encounter with the students will remain unchanged. But this is only a possibility if the mode is one of dialogue.

> Only dialogue, which requires critical thinking, is also capable of generating critical thinking. Without dialogue there is no communication, and without communication there can be no true education. Education which is able to resolve the contradiction between teacher and student takes place in a situation in which both address their act of cognition to the object by which they are mediated.
>
> (Freire, 1972, p. 65)

Practically, dialogue will encompass the rationale for design, and those problems which the staff have previously encountered and which have influenced the rationale on which their practice is based. Private discussions during the course are a contradiction of dialogue and of any notion of a liberating culture. They deny students the learning which such discussions might contain. In turn, the discussions are denied the benefit of participants' ideas and analysis. Ironically, it is as if experience in teaching limits dialogue. When the rationale is clear and the content precise, there is less need for the process of public question and explanation through which the rationale might be developed and modified.

(v) Objective Detachment

To be fully aware of the social processes of which one is also involved and to understand their nature and origin, requires a degree of mental and emotional detachment. The level of objectivity necessary is difficult to achieve when the learner is both participant and observer.

Take for example a relationship within a course between two people of different organizational status, one which has become characterized as deferential. Given objective detachment, both can examine whether this deference is based on a perception of competence or knowledge, or whether it is because of attitudes about educational or class background. They are able to identify the values upon which their relationship has been developed and, if they wish, modify or discard them.

Objective detachment is necessary in this case precisely because what is to be examined is the manifestation of values which have been internalized. The learning material is otherwise inseparable from those who wish to understand it. If however this relationship is fraught, it may be unrealistic to expect the two people involved to be able, or indeed willing to distance themselves from the event. Some resolution here and now is necessary in order to achieve objectivity later. Only then would it be possible to explore the origins and meanings of the transaction in terms of prior experience. Raising awareness of the nature of the present and raising consciousness of the past as manifest in the present requires both these stages.

(vi) Generic not Specific in Subject Matter

Specialization, or invoking strict rules about what is to be included or excluded from a course session in terms of the boundaries between disciplines (psychology or social history), or between the types of material (emotional or cognitive), or the placing in time of experience to be examined (historical or current, within the course or outside it), transmits assumptions about structure and control which simulate the values of hierarchy.

More immediately it limits the material for examination and the concepts from which understanding may be developed. Indeed it has been a particular handicap that so much experience-based work has been rooted in psychology when this results in the origin of social problems being located within individuals rather than in the structures within which they live and work. At worst this offers unrealistic notions of personal transformation and protects social systems from change of any significance.

Inclusion or exclusion of disciplines or of types of material should be allowed to emerge from the process of dialogue and be based on those interests, concerns, and ideas which have meaning for everyone involved, staff and participants.

5. PARTICIPATIVE DESIGNS AND THEIR NEGLECT

The nearest to these criteria that has been reached in management education is in learning communities, sensitivity training groups, and the student–centred designs which were developed from them, (Rogers, 1969). In these models not only are ideas exchanged, but decisions and choices are both made and collectively examined. Furthermore, their participative structure and basis of authority enable the community to develop and test out its own approaches to collective effort, decision-making, and social interaction. It is fundamental to these designs that there is an opportunity to experience and learn from the responsibilities, rewards, and discomforts of working within a democracy. Participants are able to identify and develop the skills and understanding which make it possible.

Yet in industrial organizations the use of methods like these seem to have declined (Reynolds, 1979). If the movement towards more democratic authority-structures is sincere, what prevents the more appropriate educational methods available being used in its support?

Firstly, not everyone wishes to see an alternative to hierarchy. It is what we have grown used to. Besides which, any teaching method which increases awareness of the social and political environment is likely to encourage expression of discontent. As those in hierarchical authority put their power at risk by engaging in participative management, so teachers and trainers may believe that there is some risk to their acceptability by using participant-centred approaches.

Secondly, however useful as a method of illustration, structured experience-based exercises do not provide a model for democratic organization. But one reason for more student-centred designs becoming more difficult to find is that we have become so skilled in designing games and exercises for classroom use. Less costly in time and often in temper, these methods have come to occupy the place in training which less structured events might have done.

Organization Development is identified with the theory and practice of change but seems to have become preoccupied with mechanistic, value-free prescriptions. Yet if it is the structures of organizations which dehumanize, then it is the structures which need to be changed. If the methods of OD are harnessed unquestioningly to the pursuit of productivity and commercial competition and offer no challenge to the pyramidal structure and practice of an organization, they place its members at risk of further domestication.

Sadly, and concurrently with this development, there seems to be considerable envy of the OD practitioner's role and status by training and education personnel who, in reality, are probably freer to influence change from their present roles.

A fourth for the neglect of participative methods of education is the influence of consumerism which shows itself in the relentless quest for efficiency. At worst, all education is reduced to the acquisition of skills and prescribed units of knowledge rather than of the understanding which permeates our way of looking at things. (Peters, 1973, p. 19).

Lastly, the narrow conceptual basis of Organization and Management Development has retarded understanding of educational methods; of their benefits and problems. In particular, the socio-political spectrum is often thinly covered. Our analysis of events is conceptually monocular and therefore incomplete. The field has seen too much preoccupation with personality theory and theories of interpersonal dynamics. It has lacked the conceptual breadth necessary in order to engage constructively with the problems encountered in earliest attempts at participative education. Perhaps that is why some abandoned its methods altogether.

THE CONSULTANCY SKILLS COURSE AS A LIBERATING CULTURE

It was the course in consultancy skills (CS) which crystallized for me some of the essence and dilemmas of designing educational programmes for enabling people to 'take part'. What analysis can be made of the CS course using these criteria?

For the seven preceding years the Department had been finding ways to involve people at all levels in decision-making and problem-solving. The decision-making body from which the idea of the CS programme came reflected this move to democracy and openness across professional boundaries. This 'Resource Group' was made up of trainers, personnel officers, outside consultants, line managers, and latterly, (through their involvement in CS courses) shop stewards and supervisors. The immediate organizational structure therefore had already undergone a significant shift away from a hierarchical form.

The aim of the CS programme was to enable people to take part in participative exercises and help resource them as OD consultants might. The course received considerable support from all parties involved. The main outcome was seen to be that it raised peoples' confidence and as Pateman (1970) points out, confidence is a precursor of participation.

The problem was that difficulty in 'taking part' proved a considerable hurdle even before the programme was completed. Which of the criteria of liberating cultures had been achieved and from which had our design fallen short?

Criteria met by the Programme

(i) Its participants were mixed in function and level and the staff group too, deviated from the usual educated middle class background. However, in only one of the courses were both sexes represented (Worsley, 1970, p. 182).

(ii) A more radical break from hierarchical or professional values was the central purpose of the course in training people at all levels to provide the kind of resource usually associated with the OD consultants. A feature of the helping relationship is that it enables people to cut across the prevailing culture of hierarchy based on status and experience. It also conveys humanist values of interpersonal relationships.

(iii) Although there was little opportunity for direct participation in decision-making or design, there was a strong emphasis throughout the programme on objective observation, reflection, and analysis. The material used for study was both past experience as well as here-and-now behaviour. Within the limits of the illustrative exercises used there was a good deal of involvement.

(iv) Perhaps most significantly, the staff were committed to a policy of training participants to run the programme by becoming members of the staff group. This gave a number of people an opportunity to share fully in the dialogue within the staff group. Through this means, a number of participants came to have a significant involvement in the programme.

Criteria not met by the Programme

(i) The structure within each session was high. There was little room for change and participant influence on the design was not invited. This somewhat 'packaged' approach generated much interest and enthusiasm but the control of the event was almost entirely the staff's.

(ii) Because of the structured and directed nature of the event, the processes available for observation, reflection, and analysis were limited to those generated by the prescribed exercises. The processes contained in the interstices of the programme were rarely open to discussion or to influence by participants.

(iii) In fact, the opportunity for dialogue about purpose, rationale, and progress was generally low, in spite of the precedent which had been set in previous – less structured – problem-solving events. In these sessions staff and participants had often openly reviewed the progress and problems of a course.

(iv) As a learning community, the consultancy skills course gained little from what can often provide a rich source of understanding of social processes.

It is worth repeating that the course provoked considerable interest. Yet too much reliance on psychology and social psychology may have reinforced fatalism and an attitude of resigned subjugation. The lack of any broader institutional basis for analysing events limited awareness by deflecting attention away from those social structures which inhibit peoples' ability to take part.

The Problem of the 'Follow-up' Events

Returning to the problem of the follow-up, there had been insufficient opportunity on the programme to experience the opportunities and problems of participation and the paradox of sovereignty which is an essence of democratic authority-structures (Magee, 1973, p. 82). This limited the material which could have been analysed in institutional terms, even had the opprtunity for dialogue been greater. Without being conscious of the effects of hierarchy, the further step of willingly and effectually taking part was even more difficult.

Naturally, without this consciousness-raising experience, supervisors especially will express reluctance to take a more active role, having internalized the dominant value system of their culture; but to interpret this as 'dependency' or having 'a fear of ambiguity' or of 'lacking in initiative' is only to relabel what is happening. It still fails to explain it. Explanation must be in structural as well as individual terms. Otherwise, it becomes an unwitting rationalization for preserving the existing state of things. Attempts to change the individual's psychology provide the illusion of action but do nothing to affect the structure which shape that psychology.

In the follow-up sessions, the opportunity to participate had simply been presented too abruptly. We had not correctly judged the limitations of the initial week-long event in overcoming the immense weight of influence on peoples' expectations by means of their prior socializing experience.

Why was this so hard to see? One reason must be that we as trainers also carry in our heads the principles of hierarchy which we have been taught so thoroughly.

This influences our approach and our design even when our own aim is to enable others to become less dominated by that influence.

CONCLUSION

Throughout this paper I have assumed that the goal of democratization is committed involvement not pseudo-participation. For this goal to be realized most of us need, from education, support in undoing the effects of years of socialization into the principles and values of hierarchical systems. In spite of our understanding of this process, education and training still foster more subordination and acquiescence that creativity and enlightenment.

I have drawn the distinction between educational structures which liberate and those which continue the process of subjugation. Ironically, Management Education has been prominent in the development of liberating structures and a good deal of experience and wisdom has grown around these advances. Unfortunately the signs are that Management Education is no longer as active in exploring the methods which prepare us for taking part in participative organization.

The key to liberating educational structures is to understand the means by which varying the degree of staff control can allow participants to practice taking part. But teachers and trainers often seem to demonstrate more fear and prejudice about participative structures than understanding of their processes, opportunities, and problems, or by mishandling them, generate alarm and scepticism in their students.

As I have argued, one of our greater assets is the emphasis we place on process as well as content. We have been hampered in our analysis of this by monocular vision. Critical aspects of process, including the way principles of organization are transmitted through education, have either escaped our attention or not affected our practice. As a profession we know that people should be enabled to think for themselves but we persist in maintaining the structures which make it less likely to happen.

Given these contradictions of what we do, with what we could be doing, the notion of conspiracy or collusion between senior management and teachers could be forgiven. Yet I do not believe that to be the main reason why our educational devices are less participative than they might be. What is lacking is persistence in developing and understanding methods already begun and problems so far encountered. And what could enrich this effort would be exposure to ideas in theory and practice of people in arenas quite different from our own.

REFERENCES

Bennis, W.G. (1969). *Organizational Development: Its Nature, Origins, and Prospects*, Addison–Wesley, Reading, Massachusetts.

Bernstein, B. (1975). *Class, Codes and Control, Vol. 3.*, Routledge and Kegan Paul, London.

Freire, P. (1972). *Pedagogy of the Oppressed,* Penguin, Middlesex.
Kolb, D.A., Rubin, I.M., and McIntyre, J. (1971). *Organizational Psychology,* Prentice-Hall, Englewood Cliffs, N.J.
Magee, B. (1973). *Popper,* Collins, Glasgow.
Pateman, C. (1970). *Participation and Democratic Theory,* Cambridge University Press, Cambridge.
Peters, R.S. (1973). *The Philosophy of Education,* Oxford University Press, Oxford.
Reynolds, P.M. (1979). Experiential Learning: a declining force for change, *Manag. Educ. and Devel.*, Vol. 10. pt 2.
Rogers, C. (1969). *Freedom to Learn,* Merrill, Columbus, Ohio.
Schein, E.H. (1969). *Process Consultation*, Addison-Wesley, Reading, Massachusetts.
Schein, E.H., and Bennis, W.G. (1965). *Personal and Organisational Change through Group Methods,* John Wiley, New York.
Torbert, W.R. (1978). Education towards shared purpose, self direction and quality work. *J. Higher Ed.* 44, 2, 109.
Worsley, P. (1970). *Introduction to Sociology,* Penguin, Middlesex.

Advances in Management Education
Edited by John Beck and Charles Cox

CHAPTER 4

Inward Bound – A New Direction for Outward Bound: Toward an Holistic Approach to Management Development

P.S. Keslake and P.J. Radcliff

Within the last five years there has emerged as a central concern amongst managers the recurring problem of determining the type of behaviour or leadership style necessary to promote effective work groups. Old models of behaviour were no longer appropriate to either the purely business and technical needs or the social and interpersonal elements of the manager's job.

Within RHM it became clear that there was widespread support at senior levels to achieve a more open style of management. Throughout the management structure, responsibility was being delegated down and a policy based on the work group was established for disseminating information more widely throughout all levels of the RHM Group. It was obvious that there was a need to prepare managers personally to face such a challenge. However, unlike many of the respected, and oft quoted, transatlantic organizational change programmes, we, in the food manufacturing industries, were not facing the challenges of rapid growth, high technology and highly qualified professional personnel. In fact the environment was one where power was moving progressively from the manufacturer to the food retailer, and the mission was one of organizing the available resources of people and technology to ensure survival.

RHM held a range of stable products requiring less in terms of innovation and more in terms of supportive marketing strategies, to slow down their decline. Within the context of tight margins, a relatively paternal management team, with traditional views towards its work force, was facing the pressures to achieve a more open style of management. Our task then was to develop a strategy for developing management which could play its wider part in this required organizational change.

In writing this paper we are indebted to a small group of colleagues with whom we shared and developed ideas. These include Peter Sheehan of the River Dart Residential Centre, Chris Creswick of the Food Drink and Tobacco ITB and our fellow management trainers in RHM.

A major part of this strategy was to create a programme of some kind which would help managers to face the difficulties of taking effective action in the work setting. Specifically this required developing their skills in leading and working within small groups. We saw this as integrating learning about the skills of planning and acting on information, with those of communication and sensitivity to events and feelings both in oneself and others. Furthermore the programme had to help develop capacities and awareness in the manager which were needed to create conditions in the workplace conducive to such a change in style.

Consequently we see the line manager not only as a major client in terms of his needs for new skills and understanding, but also as a vital resource in achieving other aspects of the changes required in developing the organization.

Obviously only tentative steps could be made through a training programme, but nonetheless the problem was to attempt to resolve demands of such a long-term policy decision within the constraints of available training technology, financial resources, and prevailing managerial attitudes towards learning and development.

BACKGROUND AND DEVELOPMENT

Training programmes in the area of man-management have proliferated under the diverse banners of practitioners emphasizing the advantages of their respective approaches and, as a group, we had experienced a wide variety of them. Many of these programmes reflected the primary cultures from which they originated; the feelings and self understanding emphasis of the US 'T' group movement, the task and technical orientation of the military-based leadership programmes (some of which include physical development), and the self-development and learning programmes reflecting the interests of UK business educators.

This confusing array of programmes confronted us with an incredible number of different forms, norms, and values. Leadership seemed more trained than understood. In all this, the temptation to reach for a packaged answer existed and the anxiety that we might only be re-inventing the wheel haunted the trainers throughout the early days.

We maintained our belief, however, that we were looking for a tailor-made event which would attempt to integrate certain processes and methods of learning with a model of analysing and changing managerial behaviour.

THE FRAMEWORK OF DESIGN

The fact that we had experienced and shared a variety of learning methods and their differing philosophical bases inevitably proved fortunate, but needed managing.

We set about our task by sharing our beliefs and values about leadership and learning. Our initial discussions produced a series of basic notions about both leadership and learning which provided the framework for the eventual programme design. In addition, as an inevitable result of the development of the programme, we have sought to move to a more complete understanding of the training programme in terms of its processes and its wider implications. Much of this has occurred in a random and irregular manner rather than as a logical progression.

With this in mind, we have left the principles and speculations about learning and leadership until later in the paper as it is difficult to determine which of these formed the base for the first event and which have developed and been internalized over the years.

We did start from a number of shared views about the nature of the programme we required, and these served as the basic components from which the programme has evolved.

The Design Components.

1. We identified a number of situations in which a manager is likely to find himself in terms of communication links, size of groups, length of task and resource constraints. Some fairly typical examples are the manager as a centre of communication, the manager as delegator, as part of an hierarchical small group, the leader taking over responsibility of a new group and facing a range of demands in terms of group participation in the decision-making process. Each of these situations is now transformed into a number of specific exercises on the programme.
2. Managers perform and learn in organizational environments where their actions are executed against a series of demands and expected results. Such pressures and implications provide very real parameters to any business task. We therefore attempted to build in the reality of stress and the consequences resulting from ineffective strategies and behaviour. On this programme participants experience both the anxiety and very often the consequence of poor individual or group performance. It is not a question of delegates coping or surviving the course via careful strategies of limited involvement or withdrawal. The tasks demand full involvement, comparable to that required in the business environment. The programme is designed to 'distract' participants away from *manipulative coping* strategies (e.g. where they reproduce the behaviours they feel are required of them by the trainers). The pressures and challenge of the tasks here bring about real behaviours and, therefore, learning comes from realistic experience.
3. Each task is designed in terms of a cycle of managerial activity. In differing degrees each task requires planning, organizing resources of material and people, effective execution, and review against objectives. The aim is not to involve a high degree of technical learning (although some basic skills are provided at the outset to all participants) but to provide situations where managerial skills can be practised and improved.
4. Managers learn directly from their experience of taking action and reflecting on its consequences. We had also found from our own exposure to experiential

learning programmes that they provide an opportunity for personal growth and development. It thus seemed desirable, to facilitate not only incremental learning about behavioural styles, but also wherever possible to create a climate encouraging self-insight at depth together with opportunity for skill practice. Review sessions, therefore, were designed both to focus on task performance and to include more open group and personal reviews of feelings and values, the latter becoming increasingly important with the use in the programme of such activities as climbing, caving, and canoeing with the demands these made on individuals in terms of emotions and stress.

It is in this area that we still are undecided as to the basic reasons why such activity is so effective in contributing to the learning and development of managers and it is here that we feel more research is needed.

5. The trainer does not teach in the traditional sense. Rather he provides through his behaviour, care, and skills, an atmosphere conducive to personal growth and change. Above all, he must encourage the participants to take personal responsibility for their own learning. The role of the trainer, as we see it, is that:

   - The trainer can help create new learning by providing activity for the groups relating to the problems facing the group and its individual members at any moment in time.
   - The trainer can also help individuals communicate with each other at a more authentic level.
   - Finally the trainer can help group members to expose and critically analyse stereotypic roles and values, thus providing an opportunity for change.

6. From personal experience, we had a growing awareness of the relationaship between learning, understanding, and health. In few of the managerial/leadership programmes experienced by us had the dynamics created by the physical needs of the learner been catered for in the design and we decided to build into the framework of our course the opportunity for balanced development in physical, emotional, and intellectual experience.

   We believe that this area is rich in its potential for research and a growing amount of evidence is being produced about this critical relationship between physical, intellectual, and emotional elements in personal development. As far as we know, however, no work has been done on this in areas of applied adult learning, such as in developing managerial capacities.

As a result of these basic components, we began to design a programme which would include physical, intellectual, and emotional elements. The individual manager would be given the opportunity to take a holistic view of himself as a resource and to develop all his capacities. A variety of vehicles make up the programme and reflect the influence of a whole array of sources.

Each manager organizes his own learning by specifying his own objectives, selecting his own learning opportunities and taking responsibility for maintaining and reviewing his own progress.

THE PROGRAMME STRUCTURE

The nature of the programme is cyclical both in terms of the processes of learning involved and in terms of the way it views managerial behaviour. The processes of learning involve using data both from the delegate's own work environment and also data generated by the learning experiences in the programme (see Figure 1). The delegates both individually and as a group actively participate in reviewing their progress on the programme and in explicitly planning their group targets and learning goals throughout the week. Although they concern themselves with a strategy for re-entry at the end of the programme, they also write a daily diary to identify links between course learning and the back home situation. Our aim is to maintain the intensity of the delegate's experience of the learning programme whilst not building a major barrier to transfer to his work environment.

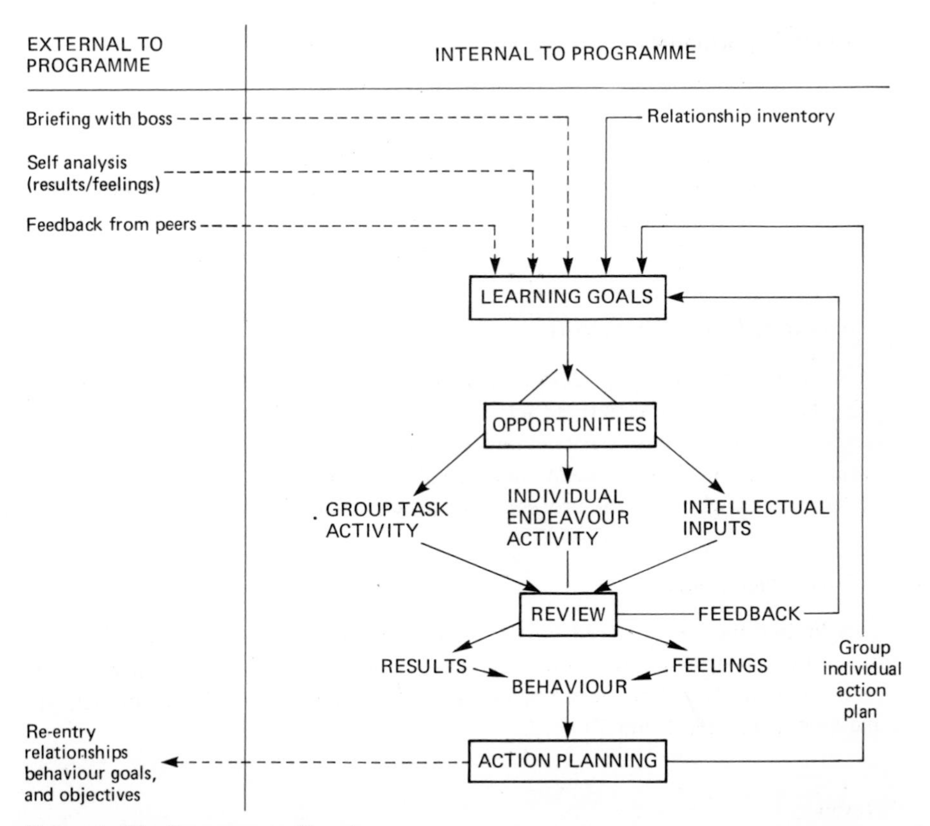

Figure 1. The Programme Structure

Learning Goals

As the course aims to tackle the fundamental problems of the individual managers, each delegate is required to complete a questionnaire, together with his immediate boss before the programme. In doing this, discussion focuses on an assessment of the delegate's current style in dealing with people and outlines areas for change in terms of explicit behaviours, which act as agreed learning goals. Naturally, most delegates come to the programme with their own subjective assessment of their performance and relationships with others at work. We feel it is critical to enter into this personal map of reality which each manager carries with him, as this map is often the basis for his work behaviour. The initial session of the programme (based on the Relationship Inventory) is thus spent analysing the work relationships each delegate perceives as critical to his performance and sharing these perceptions and feelings with fellow group members. This establishes some level of understanding with other members of his learning group, but also helps each individual delegate to add his own personal learning goals for the week to those already agreed.

Learning Opportunities

1. Group Task Activity

For the whole of the course, delegates work in small teams on a series of tasks. These are designed to reflect those factors of individual and group relations which are present in potential problem situations back at work. The tasks are physical in nature and require the complete process of planning, execution, and review.

2. Individual Endeavour Activity

Running parallel to the development of task, group and personal skills, each delegate selects from one of three activities, canoeing, climbing, or caving, to provide further opportunities for personal understanding and growth. This activity does not occur in isolation, but represents individual development which can be utilized by the group, as a whole, in the processes of its own development.

3. Intellectual Inputs

A limited number of intellectual inputs are provided, their selection being determined by appropriateness to the progress of each group. These are explicit in terms of the learning offered by the programme and each trainer uses the input for clarifying and helping meet individual's needs.

Review

Nearly half of the time on the course is spent on review and personal reflection.

This can be artificially split in a variety of ways, but in reality, it is difficult to differentiate between the different focal points. However, the two major areas are:

1. Task Review

Each group is able to assess its performance in terms of task performance and in its capacity to create, develop, and maintain a small work organization under demanding conditions. Plans for improvement are developed and followed.

2. Group/Personal Review

Group processes are reviewed together with the relationship between an individual's behaviour and that of his colleagues. Group process reviews merge into personal reviews and individuals are encouraged to use a diary to focus on significant events. Different interventions are available to the trainer. In the early part of the week these are used to encourage sharing and feedback of individual perceptions. As the week progresses, the delegates take responsibility for the reviews, which become less structured and the expression of feelings becomes more acceptable as a norm.

Action Planning

The programme is designed for each participant to take responsibility for achieving progress and for establishing his own action plan. This involves him in constantly monitoring his own learning goals against the feedback received during the programme and in planning his own performance improvement. Additionally, each delegate notes in his diary, on a daily basis, any links between learning on the course and specific problems at work (such as those identified in the Relationship Inventory).

At the end of the programme each delegate has to make a conscious effort to establish his own strategy for re-entry. This forms the basis for immediate discussion with his boss on his return to work and enables further coaching and monitoring to be carried out within the line management's responsibility.

Examples of Task and Individual Endeavour Activities

1. Exercise Leat Beam

This, an early task in the course, involves the group getting its individual members and a heavy barrel of water over a strip of water with limited equipment. It encourages rapid decision-making and firm direction in use of resources.

2. Exercise Defuse

A manager plans to retrieve a heavy cyclinder from a tree platform 40 feet high, with a small team and some equipment. After completion of the plan he swops groups and becomes the new leader of a group which has been carrying out the same task. His task here is to complete the exercise effectively with the new group and its existing plan. The opportunities to explore the dynamics of entering a group and working on an established plan are significant and it is possible to experiment with a variety of different approaches.

3. Exercise Gilson

This is a full day's exercise divided into a number of parts where the team works in independent pairs as well as a full group for different parts of the total exercise.

A communication system has to be established as at times the participants are separated by many miles, completing activities, which finally will be brought together at the end of the exercise. The task involves combining high equality planning and communication with quick decision-making and independent judgement during the exercise.

4. Individual Endeavour

Climbing, caving, and canoeing are used as activities and although high standards are often achieved, this is not the main purpose. Team work is emphasized with participants sharing responsibility for safety and for carrying out the activity. Primarily delegates gain an insight into their working and that of their partner. Initial selection is a critical factor, as participants can only participate in one of these activities and a group must be represented by at least two team members in each.

PRINCIPLES AND SPECULATIONS

The programme has always represented a learning experience for us and still does, as we both develop the programme and also experiment with new uses such as team building. Consequently this paper is very much a report of progress to date, enabling us to clarify some elements whilst also speculating on its futher implications.

Rather than attempt a precise theory for developing managerial ability, we prefer to outline a series of principles, some on which the programme was originally based and some which have arisen out of the programme as it has developed. In addition we put forward some speculations about the processes involved. We feel that many of these represent fertile ground for further research.

1. Leadership

The modern manager is often confused. He is not quite sure how to behave and there are many times when he is torn between exerting strong leadership or permissive leadership behaviour. With this in mind, the programme represents an opportunity to integrate different behaviours. The design is based on the following principles:

Principles

(i) Effective management requires a selection of flexible behaviours appropriate to the situation and the desired results.

(ii) Leadership depends on coping with uncertainty in oneself and in others.

(iii) Leadership requires the capacities of authentic expression, openness and assertiveness.

(iv) A manager needs to understand and be sensitive to his/her own and others' feelings, particularly in areas of stress and conflict.

(v) Leadership involves full utilization of resources, both personal and material, in successful achievement of the desired objectives.

(vi) Leadership requires dealing with colleagues' fantasies and stereotypic roles.

(vii) Management and leadership does not amount to a series of techniques but is a holistic concept made up of an individual's values, assumptions, and choice of life style.

(viii) A large part of a manager's world is internal, particularly in the areas of leadership and authority. His role is inevitably that constructed by his own interpretation of a series of values, norms and aspirations for himself and others.

2. Learning

The concept of a workshop in which individuals working in small groups develop new insights into themselves is not new. There are, however, a number of fundamental principles built into the design of this programme which, when put together in a single event, make it unique.

Principles

(i) *Challenge, Stress, and Immediate Feedback*. Real learning must involve individuals facing the consequences of their own actions. Learning becomes clear and powerful when participants are faced with real challenges where the direct consequences of their behaviour cannot be ignored or rationalized. Feedback should be in terms of the results of their actions as well as group analysis. The tasks must contain realistic challenges and opportunities in the area of taking risks where stress is an important factor in the situation.

(ii) Learning is facilitated by having real and identifiable learning goals to which participants and their bosses are committed. By this we mean that goals should be stated in explicit terms, monitorable, measurable, and identifiable, particularly in terms of their appropriateness to the situations and problems faced. The explicitness of working towards specific learning goals facilitates dialogue with peers and bosses on return to work. This is particularly critical on a programme, such as this, where the learning achieved is often difficult to express verbally to others and to transfer effectively. The thread of specified learning goals moving through briefing, course experience, and de-briefing helps greatly to increase learning identification and transfer.

(iii) *The Right to Freedom and Choice*. Learning in the group is based on providing freedom for the participant so that he can make informed choices about his own behaviour and learning. The manager must accept the responsibility and pressure of making decisions for himself. The trainer respects the integrity of the learner by having no checklist (either explicit or implicit) of 'appropriate behaviour' and the emphasis is very much on the individual integrating his learning goals, within his own model of management behaviour, with those of other group members.

(iv) *The Process of Unfreezing, Change, and Refreezing.* The exercises and the climate of the event are designed to encourage realistic behaviours. Although a member of a temporary group, each member utilizes his normal array of behaviours in establishing his identity and role with others, while forming an effective work team. Opportunity is provided, therefore, for group members to question the effectiveness of this behaviour and its effects upon them. As a participant receives feedback, it is possible for him to experiment with new behaviours. He then has the option to internalize these new behaviours as part of his own personal criteria of effectiveness and acceptability. The design of any event must therefore provide sufficient time and opportunity for tension to be experienced, behavioural options to be tested and new behaviours internalized. We also feel an event should facilitate the manager considering how best to apply his learning back at work and provide mechanisms for encouraging dialogue between boss and delegate on these specific learning areas.

(v) *Phases in Learning Refinement*. Learning does not rest solely with the individual participating in the experience, but in the consciousness this experience raises in terms of his needs, behaviour and the situation he is in and its relevance to the real world in which he sees himself living.

All activity on the programme is directed towards the satisfaction of learning goals established in the individual manager's model of reality. Learning begins in the programme with gross observations, crude measurements and speculative hypotheses (why don't you . . . ?). Only as each delegate begins to specify and share his model of reality with other members of the group can advanced analysis and interpretation occur. At the later stages both delegates and trainers can help the learning by exploring the reality of others and their behaviour, less from the restrictions of their own viewpoint and more from understanding the other person's perceived world.

(vi) *Learning as a Complete Person*. Learning takes place when each individual can utilize, in a balanced way, all the facilities at his or her disposal. Any learning event, we believe, should take into account the need for a balance of physical, emotional and intellectual experience in order to achieve maximum understanding and personal development. The aim is to increase awareness via a focus on the total person in a balanced and integrated learning design.

To achieve this the programme must be able to bring together the qualities of a variety of approaches. We have attempted to describe this in simple terms in Figure 2 by reference to what be regarded as two poles of the continuum of management learning design.

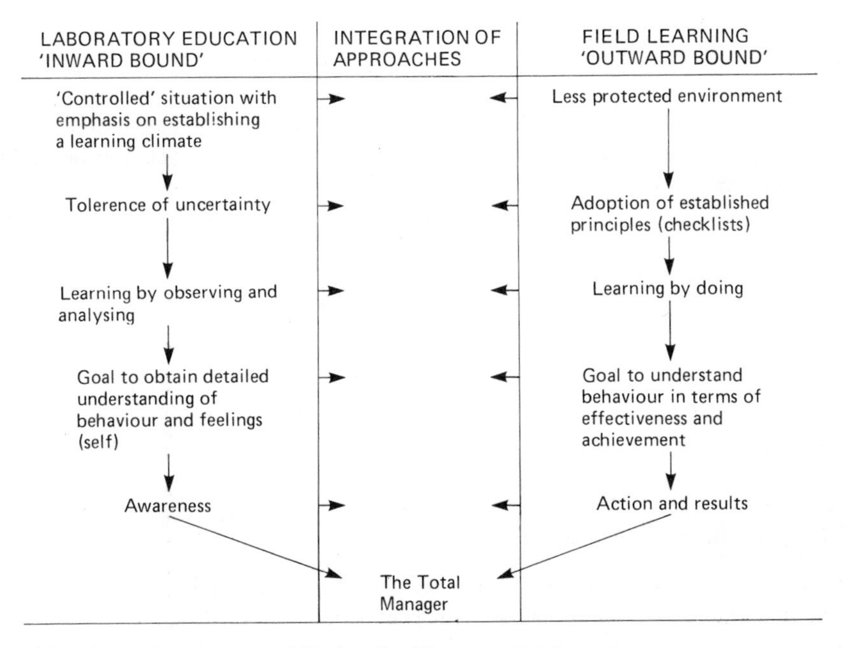

Figure 2. A Continuum of Design for Management Learning

3. Management and Learning – Speculations

As indicated earlier we set ourselves the goal of attempting a design which would integrate the methods of learning with the processes of management. We now tentatively move towards a few speculations about the essential task of management educators, integrating our views on management with our views on learning. This is an area which still contains considerable uncertainty and doubt for us as trainers. In this section we will identify some of those, at this stage, random elements.

(i) *Understanding the Games and Rituals in Leadership Performance*. We started (above) with a general amalgam of values, views, and elements of leadership, which we found more illuminating in terms of understanding what a manager means by leadership than the more conventional breakdown of leadership functions. Further, we have found that by placing people in situations which they can engage with their leadership fantasies and images, they can begin the process of selecting those aspects which are most appropriate to their everyday work needs, and thereby actually develop a more realistic approach to leading a group. They can test reality against unusual demands, often removing many of the fears which they have about their own personal competence. At the end of it, production managers go back and manage their lines against criteria of efficiency rather than against some leadership image – because, in most instances, they have had the chance to check out their previously unvoiced fantasies during the programme.

(ii) *Balanced Managerial Activity*. Increasingly, concern is being expressed about the total health of an organization, team or individual. Much has been written about the growing levels of stress with which people have to cope. Few managers have the opportunity to reflect on that stress, as they are usually too involved in either generating it or having stress induced into their own system. We feel it is becoming more important for managers to take responsibility for managing their own health in its broadest sense. The programme contributes in two ways to getting this process started.

Firstly, every delegate develops through the programme a greater awareness of the needs of the three regimes of physical, intellectual, and emotional activity and the importance to his own effectiveness and development of maintaining a balance of the resources at his disposal. Secondly, whilst the programme operates with a high degree of pressure on both the work groups and the individuals, delegates do develop the capacity to manage themselves better both psychologically and technically. The opportunity to develop new behaviours and check out the way they come over to others seems to lead to a clearer sense of their own boundaries and identity in working as part of a team.

(iii) *The Two Elements in Making Managerial Experience Work*. Often it has been cited that the key to good management is experience. Probably one of the major contributions that can be made by a programme to a manager's development can be to facilitate his learning from his own experience. We believe that this programme has helped identify two major elements involved in changing managerial behaviour.

1. *'Inward Bound'* – involving the processes of reflection and introspection. This is particularly important in understanding past behaviours and habit patterns and the restrictions they impose on an individual's own performance. In the programme the delegate confronts these blockages in a supportive environment, which enables him to understand the anxiety and fears which often prevent effective decsion-making. It also places him in the role of decision-maker about the direction and pace of his own learning.

2. *'Outward Bound'* – involving the process of exploring alternative behaviours and active problem-solving. By making the delegate responsible for monitor-

ing his own learning goals, the programme encourages him to manage the process of changing his current and future behaviours. At all times achievement of results is a critical issue to both the individual and the group, any experimenting with behaviour has to be tested against the reality of performance. Each delegate must undertake the process of learning review and assert himself in both managing the tasks and his own learning goals. Effort is made to suggest, request, and practise alternative ways of expression.

We think that to achieve full managerial learning, a programme must combine reflection and exploration; opportunity to identify the source of concern with the chance to plan new behaviours – i.e. to be both Inward Bound and Outward Bound. Every individual manager will require differing proportions of both to meet his particular needs and this balance may well change throughout the programme, as a result of feedback and self-learning – the delegate chooses his own emphasis.

CONCLUSION

This paper represents our reflections and speculations arising out of our own experience as both delegates and trainers on these programmes. Initially we both considered training of this nature in a highly sceptical manner, particularly in terms of its applicability to the modern industrial scene. The experience has convinced us that whilst it is dangerous to buy a 'package' of leadership training – it is equally ill-advised to ignore others on immediate impression without careful consideration. The fertilization of our own culture, of a more sensitivity training approach, with that of the more 'Outward Bound' approach has proved valuable in moving towards a learning programme which, in its processes, approximates to effective managerial behaviour.

For us, both of the training cultures have an important part to play. The 'Outward Bound' culture, by its strong emphasis and concern for action skills, pressured decision-making and dealing pragmatically with task and organizational constraints. The 'Inward Bound' culture, by its attempts to confront an industrial world which has tried to ignore feelings and self-awareness, and encourage participants to reflect more deeply on individual motivations and processes. Neither represents, on its own, a full operational model to facilitate managerial learning.

Our efforts have been to attempt some synthesis, where at the end of the day, managers attending the programme will not be solely more skilled in the use of a leadership checklist or in eliciting feelings in themselves and others, but will, in fact, be able to manage better and learn from their own total managerial experience. The programme aims to ensure that all elements of the programme, be they managing task activities or learning from the opportunities provided, follow the same cycle outlined in Figure 3.

Consequently we have tried to ensure that the way in which people learn on the programme reflects the way in which they manage. As a result, managers can then

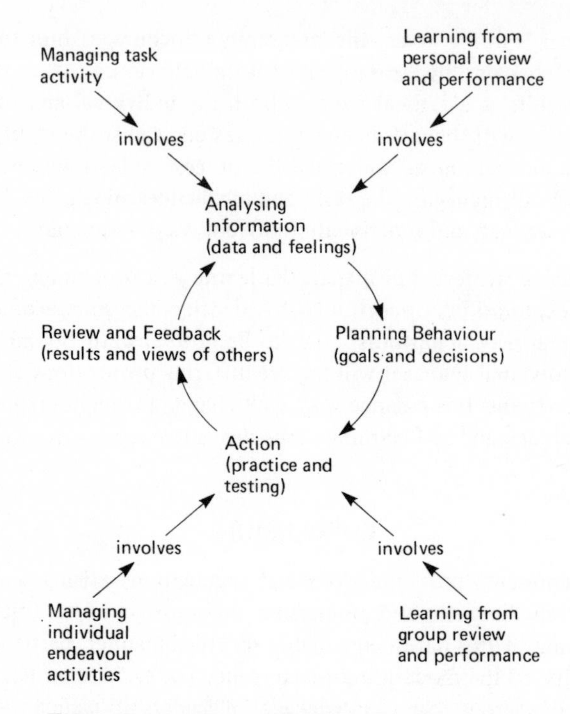

Figure 3. Management Learning Cycle

apply the same approach to learning from experience they use on the programme when they return to work. The group atmosphere and pressures may differ in the back home situation and the character of the tasks may differ, but the learning skills required and the menegerial elements should be relatively common. This, we hope, enables the manager to learn more actively from his own work experience back on the job.

The programme has in itself added to our array of activities in support of a policy to move to a more open and communicative style of management. Much still needs to be researched, particularly in terms of how the learning via insight actually occurs during the programme and the capacities required of the trainer to facilitate it. We also believe that this type of training programme may have more likelihood of success in some organizational cultures than in others. We hope, however, that this paper has helped shed some light on a growing, but little conceptualized or analysed area of management training.

Advances in Management Education
Edited by John Beck and Charles Cox

CHAPTER 5

The Development of Senior Managers for the Future

Kim James

INTRODUCTION

The accelerating rate of change in the social, economic and political environments of business activity has meant that planning for the future occupies an increasing proportion of management's time. An important aspect of this planning is for management itself, preparing people for jobs which may have quite different facets from present senior positions. To solve problems which are without precedent managers will need wide ranging skills, but particularly they will need to have learned to learn. Mason (1974) has described such 'learning managers' as active, innovative, and creative forces in their environment, able to explore unchartered directions and achieve optimal realizations of their own and their clients' potentials in all situations. This paper considers the problem of how people can be helped to develop these abilities, against the background of a study carried out for a large multinational company, Dunlop Ltd.

Organized into fairly autonomous product divisions, the company's problem was to find ways in which the Central Personnel Division could generate ideas which would encourage management development throughout the group.

Though identifying four areas in which a contribution might be made (training, career development, appraisal, and motivation) career development and learning on the job created the most interest. The research problem became clear: how can work experience be structured so that people can be encouraged to become 'learning managers'? Can knowledge of the way people learn from experience be used to improve the practice of career development?

A MODEL OF EXPERIENTIAL LEARNING

A model which has received much attention in recent years from people concerned with learning and training is Kolb's (1971, 1975) experiential learning model. This model develops two themes: that of a 'cycle' of learning abilities, and that of personal development of learning abilities. In the cycle of learning, Kolb describes how learning is facilitated by a cyclical process of here-and-now experience, followed by reflections and observations on that experience, the formulation of abstract concepts and generalizations, and lastly, by the testing of the implications of these concepts in new situations. The effective learner thus requires four abilities (concrete experience, relective observation, abstract conceptualization, and active experimentation) though may choose which set of abilities he will bring to bear on any situation. In practice, argues Kolb, most people develop learning styles that emphasize some learning abilities over others. His own research suggested, for example, that marketing managers tended to emphasize active experimentation and concrete experience, engineers abstract conceptualization and active experimentation, personnel managers concrete experience and reflective observation, and researchers reflective observation and abstract conceptualization. These differences may be because the

Table 1. Kolb's Descriptions of Learning Abilities and Complex Environments

COMPLEX ENVIRONMENTS

Affectively Complex Environment	Perceptually Complex Environment	Symbolically Complex Environment	Behaviourally Complex Environment
Focus on here-and-now experience. Legitimation of feelings and emotions. Situations allow ambiguity. High degree of personalization.	Opportunities to view subject matter from different perspectives. Time to reflect and roles which allow reflection. Complexity and multiplicity of observational framework.	Emphasis on recall of concepts. Thinking or acting formed by rules of logic and inference. Situation structured to maximize certainty. Authorities respected as caretakers of knowledge.	Responsibility for setting own goals. Opportunities for real risk-taking. Environmental responses contingent upon self-initiated action.

LEARNING ABILITIES

Concrete Experience	Reflective Observation	Abstract Conceptualization	Active Experimentation
Receptive Feeling Accepting Intuitive Present oriented Experience	Tentative Watching Observing Reflecting Observation Reserved	Analytical Thinking Logical Evaluative Conceptualization Rational	Practical Doing Active Pragmatic Experimentation Responsible

In each vertical column a Complex Environment is coupled with its corresponding learning ability.

working environments stimulate different learning styles, or because people choose to work in an environment compatible with their style. Kolb argues that by exposing people to non-familiar environments new learning styles may be developed, and it follows from this that the practice of job rotation may be carried out in a way which will maximize the benefit to the managers concerned. Kolb identifies four complex environments, each of which stimulate the development of one of the four learning abilities. His learning ability and complex environment descriptions are given in Table 1.

Kolb's second theme suggests three developmental stages: acquisition, specialization, and integration. Acquisition, which occurs during childhood and adolescence, is the stage in which are developed the few basic learning abilities of the learning cycle. In the stage of specialization the young adult develops some of these abilities at the expense of others. The person acts on the world and the world acts on him without either being fundamentally changed by the other. The third stage, integration, can occur as a gradual process or as the result of a life crisis, though, Kolb remarks, some never move into this stage. The individual experiences a shift in the frame of reference with which he structures his life, the nature of this shift depending on the individual's dominant learning style. Reflection may be complemented by action to bring a new awareness of opportunities to influence rather than be influenced. Action may be complemented by reflection to bring a new awareness of the implications of actions. The person becomes more aware of the self and experiences choice in new ways of being. The four modes become integrated.

Although becoming an integrated learner may be the result of an unplanned experience, stimulating the growth of the four learning abilities might enhance the probability of this development and provide the manager with the learning skills he would need to be effective in the future. But are Kolb's ideas sufficiently well developed to be used as the basis for a management development scheme?

RESEARCH DESIGN

An approach to investigating the Kolb model which seemed appropriate was to ask managers what learning abilities and environments they felt they had experienced. This would provide an opportunity to test the applicability on a British population.

Kolb's own inventory to test people's choice of learning styles (choice of abilities) consists of sets of four words which describe ways of learning. The respondent is asked to rank the four words in each set in order of accuracy in characterizing the way he learns. Totals of rank scores for each of the four learning abilities over the sets of words can therefore be obtained.

However, this inventory was considered to be inadequate for several reasons. Firstly it is a forced choice questionnaire; secondly, phrases in the instructions such as 'best characterize your learning styles' may have little meaning for many managers who do not normally think about the process of learning; thirdly, some of the words employed are ambiguous in terms of representing a particular learning ability (for example, 'evaluative' given as a description of abstract conceptualization, might also be thought of as reflective observation); and fourthly, the standardized population is American.

Kolb also developed a typology of the learning environments, inferred from a study of students completing a course at MIT. The typology was not framed in questionnaire form and the language would require adjustment for application to a British population.

In order to design a questionnaire to examine Kolb's model it was necessary to draw up short descriptions of learning abilities and their corresponding complex environments. The items describing each ability had to be framed independently of the corresponding item describing the environment. This was because according to Kolb, an association would be expected between the two. It was therefore important not to risk the tautology which would have occurred had abilities been worded in terms of the environment or vice versa.

Table 2. Characterizations of Learning Abilities

Abilities	Characterized by the ability to:
Concrete Experience	Understand and influence my own feelings Understand and influence others
Reflective Observation	Choose among competitive alternatives Judge dispassionately the merits of a case
Abstract Conceptualization	Think through problems in a logical way Apply general principles to particular cases
Active Experimentation	Act confidently Take risks when necessary

The four abilities were characterized by the phrases shown in Table 2. Concrete experience was seen to be concerned with here-and-now interactions and it was felt that in order to cope effectively people need to be aware of their own feelings and those of others, and as a result be able to influence interactions. Reflective observation was seen as the ability to view things from different perspectives and see alternatives. Abstract conceptualization was felt to be concerned with ways of thinking and applying concepts and principles to problems. Active experimentation was considered to be concerned with getting things done and testing hypotheses practically, risk-taking. It was felt that these phrases would have more meaning to managers who would answer the questionnaire than the Kolb inventory.

Similarly phrases characterizing the four learning environments were chosen in such a way as to be quite separate from the abilities; for example, the term 'people changed their demands unpredictably' could be true whether or not someone had the 'ability to understand and influence other people'. These phrases are shown in Table 3.

Table 3. Characteristics of Complex Environments

Affectively Complex	Perceptually Complex	Symbolically Complex	Behaviourally Complex
People were liable to change their demands unpredictably. People needed to be advised, instructed or otherwise assisted. It was impossible to get more than a few moments alone. Agreement had to be reached among people of widely differing interests.	There was no clear precedent for judgement. Changing or conflicting evidence kept coming in. Recommendations from a variety of viewpoints circulated concurrently. It was hard to tell whether something would develop into a problem or not.	Copious dossiers were kept about on-going problems. Some problems required adherence to specific procedures for their resolution. Different specialists used their own jargon when called in for advice. If things were not working properly the person responsible was expected to find out what was wrong and correct it.	Crises occurred which required immediate attention. The unexpected happened in spite of all preparation. The consequences of decisions followed swiftly. The results of activity were unpredictable.

A number of other items were included in the questionnaire. Among these are some related to managers' career histories which were felt by managers interviewed in a pilot stage to be of importance. These items were about working abroad, positions of responsibility, promotions, training received, unnerving and domestic experiences.

It was necessary to include in the questionnaire some way of revealing the links between experience and learning ability. It was considered that time of learning was an important factor and therefore the final questionnaire format used five-year time periods as the link-pin. Three sections each listed the career history, environment, and learning ability items. The data was coded in terms of period into career rather than actual years.

THE RESULTS: KOLB'S EXPERIENTIAL LEARNING MODEL

The Kolb model suggests that the data should reveal a number of associations. The two items characterizing each ability should be more strongly associated with each other than with any other learning ability items. Similarly, the four items characterizing each complex environment should be more strongly associated with each other than with any other environment item. Finally, we should expect an association between each learning ability and its corresponding complex environment.

The data was analyzed using periods into career rather than actual years. That is, the first period was taken to be the first five years after full-time education, whenever that occurred, instead of the first chronological period, pre-1953. This was because the managers contacted were of various ages (approximate range 30–65) and this study is interested not in what people learned on particular dates but what they learned in particular periods during their careers.

For each time period contingency coefficients were calculated for all the possible pairs of items representing complex environments and a McQuitty cluster analysis was performed to see whether these items clustered as expected. A similar procedure was carried out for the learning ability items.

Period 4 is used as an illustration of this procedure, for two reasons. Because fewer conditions were encountered in the first few time periods, low discriminations

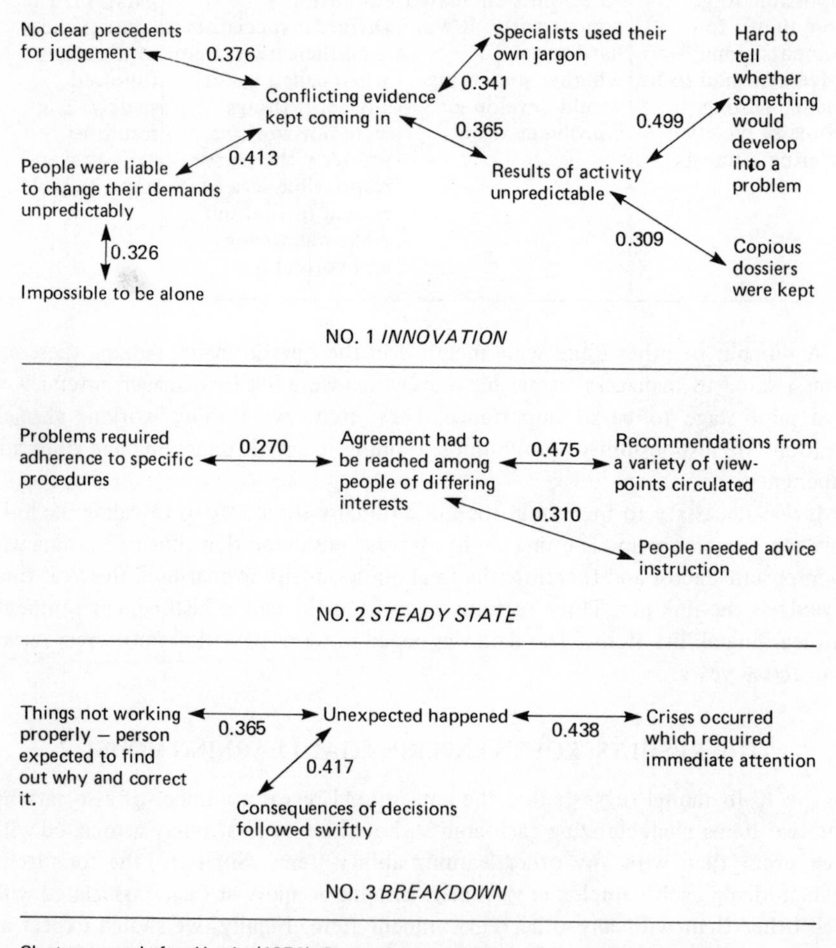

Figure 1. McQuitty Cluster Analysis for the Time Period 4 Environment Items

among items might lend spurious support to the hypotheses by producing high contingency coefficients where there is joint absence rather than joint presence of endorsements. The second reason is that some attrition in periods five and six might have reduced the representativeness of the sample. Figure 1 shows the McQuitty cluster analysis for the environment items.

The first cluster appears to be a combination of perceptual and symbolic complexity; the middle cluster an affective complexity cluster, and the lower cluster a behavioural complexity cluster. There has, however, been a slight shift of items. The remaining time periods were inspected. The clusters change somewhat over periods. Three groups of items were most frequently found to cluster together:

(a) 'crises occurred frequently'
'the unexpected happened in spite of all preparation'
'the consequence of decisions followed swiftly'

(b) 'it was hard to tell if something would develop into a problem or not'
'conflicting evidence kept coming in'
'there were no clear precedents for judgement'

(c) 'agreement had to be reached among people of widely differing interests'
'recommendations from a variety of viewpoints circulated concurrently'.

These may relate to Kolb's environments (behaviourally, perceptually, and affectively complex), or, seem closely allied to Handy's (1976) breakdown, innovation and steady state conditions. These might constitute developmental conditions and suggest experiences appropriate to management careers.

The symbolically complex items did not cluster at all and shifted around the other three clusters over time periods.

Thus the three clusters found by the McQuitty analysis suggest possible environments with which to further the analysis of the data.

However, it might be spurious to force the data into three clusters, because an examination of all the contingency coefficients reveals that some low associations were found within expected complex environments and some high associations were found outside them. This suggested that the environment items interact with each other, and it was therefore decided to aggregate the environmental complexity items to form a single scale.

When the same procedure was carried out for the learning ability items it was again found that although it might be possible to fit the data into clusters, the associations between all the learning ability items were found to be high. Therefore, for further analysis of the data the learning ability items were also aggregated to form a single scale of learning ability. Figure 2 shows a McQuitty cluster analysis of the learning ability items in period 4.

Since neither the environments, nor learning abilities, were shown to separate into four discrete factors, the expected discrete relationships between the learning and the environments could not be observed.

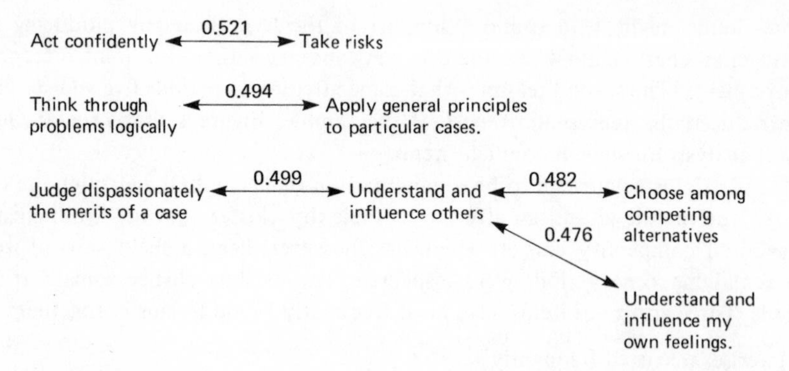

Figure 2. McQuitty Clusters of the Period 4 Learning Ability Items

However, since composite scores were constructed for environmental complexity and for learning ability, it might be expected that the total environmental complexity score in a period would be correlated with the total learning score in the same period. These two new measures were found to be associated.

It appears that in important respects the data does not support the Kolb model. This may be for several reasons:

(a) the measures used are different from the measures Kolb used, and the items did not represent the model effectively;
(b) the population used has different characteristics from the populations Kolb used, e.g., they were all integrated learners, anyway;
(c) additional variables are needed to explain how people gain ability in learning.

Kolb measures learning style by subjective report using a forced choice questionnaire. He suggests dimensions on which environments differ in complexity but does not give any evidence on how people perceive their environments. In this study, people gave their own perceptions of both environment and learning abilities and the questionnaire did not set forced alternative choices but allowed them to endorse all the items that they perceived important to them. It appears that, under these circumstances, people perceive the environments as being complex in many ways at any one time, and perceive their learning skills as being interrelated. The measures constitute a different test of Kolb's model from the one he used, and the results indicate that his categories may not be separate for people and may have been separable in his research as a result of his methods.

Independent judges did not always put each item into the category it was supposed to represent. This was often because they felt items to be strongly related. For example, 'judge the merits of a case' and 'think through problems logically' were put together by one judge because he felt it was impossible to do the former without the latter, so it is not clear whether items were poor items, or whether the four categories are indistinguishable. However, care had been exercised in the design stage to try to ensure that the items did relate to Kolb's concepts.

The populations used in the Kolb study may have different characteristics (Kolb did have a large number of practising managers but there may be cultural differences between USA and UK managers). However it was Dunlop managers in particular with whom it was important to develop a model of learning. It may be asked whether the interrelation of the learning ability items is due to all the members of this population already being integrated learners! Firstly, this is unlikely, for Kolb this stage is not a *necessary* development from the second stage of specialization. Secondly, this questionnaire would not measure this even if this were the case. Merely having these abilities does not ensure that a person is 'integrated'. Kolb implies that this is to do with the way people relate to the world and their awareness of the relationship between these different modes. This questionnaire cannot measure that.

The time scale involved here is also important. Kolb gives no indication how long a period of time the learning cycle covers. In a five-year period, might people make many iterations of it?

The most important reason for the Kolb model not being supported by the data, probably lies in the third category, the importance of additional variables. Kolb's model is akin to a stimulus response model of learning: given a particular stimulus, a learning style develops. He does not pay much attention to how people interpret that stimulus. He does indicate that in the stage of specialization people acquire a particular style of learning as a result of their own inclinations and past experience. However, he does not indicate the mechanism by which they acquire a style or move into the integrated stage. For example, he gives no indication of how much exposure to different environments one needs to acquire another learning style, whether one needs to move through more than one learning cycle, whether people are more receptive to new learning at some periods than others.

The data indicates that people perceive the different learning abilities as interrelated and that they can acquire all of them – this does not mean that they are integrated learners in the sense of self-actualizers, self-starters etc., necessarily. The data indicates that a simple stimulus–response model is insufficient to explain how people learn over a long period of time. The data also shows that in some periods people experience more change in their learning abilities than in others. There must therefore be other variables which are important.

How people *appraise* experiences may play an important part in determining what they learn from them, as further analysis of the questionnaire data reveals.

FURTHER ANALYSIS

In order to examine the data further, three categories of manager were identified: those whose careers had progressed through several different management functions, younger managers, and managers who had begun to gain learning ability predominantly in a particular phase (early, mid or late) of their careers.

For each of these categories the aggregated learning ability scores were divided into low, middle, and high ranges. The aggregated environmental complexity scores were divided into four ranges.

1. Multifunctional Managers

Twenty managers of thirty years or more experience who had indicated that they had changed occupation or function five or six times during their career (by ticking an item 'I moved to a different occupation or function' in the career history section of the questionnaire) were compared with managers of similar experience who had indicated that they had only changed occupation once or not at all. (Change of function is here defined by the managers' own perception of their careers, not defined by the Company).

The two groups were found to have different patterns of learning scores. In every time period the 'multifunctional' group contained a higher percentage of managers with scores in the middle and high ranges, and a lower percentage of managers with scores in the low range. This group appears to perceive themselves as having developed their learning ability throughout their careers much more than the group who have changed functions once or not at all. This is unlikely to be due solely to the number of changes in function since differences exist between the two groups even in periods one and two when the number of changes of function is necessarily small for both of them. These differences in learning ability could be because the managers in the 'multifunctional' group are in some way inherently different from the comparison group (for example, more intelligent, hard-working, or some other dimension not measured) and therefore were invited to change function more frequently. Alternatively, people who have experienced many changes in function may feel that they *must* have learned a lot from a varied experience.

A similar pattern emerged when scores of environmental complexity were examined. In each time period a higher proportion of multifunctional managers scored in the higher ranges, and a lower proportion in the lower ranges when compared with managers with few changes. This is as expected, given the association between learning ability and environmental complexity already demonstrated.

An examination of other career history items in the questionnaire (such as geographical moves, responsibilities, training, meeting people who influenced their career) showed that those with multifunctional careers have a higher frequency of endorsing these items than the comparison group, particularly in the first three time periods.

This could be interpreted as meaning that these managers were recognized as having high learning ability and were given early responsibility and more varied experiences. Alternatively they might have developed a higher learning ability as the result of these experiences.

However, neither explanation seems totally plausible since it is unlikely that career development policies would have identified the higher abilities so accurately, and a comparison of the multifunctional group with the total sample (in which career histories are similar) revealed that the multifunctional group still retain a favourable differential in the scores of learning ability. It cannot therefore be the career experiences, in themselves, which are important. It is more likely that the reason this group have higher learning scores is related to the way that they think of their careers. It is not sufficient just to have a particular experience in order to develop learning ability, it is necessary to construe that experience as valuable progress. The belief that their management skills were valued, and that they were likely to progress to higher management jobs, may have given them the confidence to try out new behaviours (act confidently, take risks) and to place trust in their own judgement. Perhaps perceiving that other people had confidence in them, they had confidence in themselves, to feel that they were originators of action and not merely responding to the actions of others. Those who progress rapidly and perceive other people as taking an active interest in their careers are in a better position to perform managerial tasks themselves, and if succeeding, attribute their success to their own ability.

2. Younger Managers

A group of twenty-nine managers with fifteen years or less experience was compared with managers with twenty or more years experience. For the three time periods which could be compared for the two groups the younger managers scored higher on both learning ability and environmental complexity. A comparison of career histories showed that in the first two comparable periods the younger managers had experienced more career items than had the older managers, and indeed their career profiles were similar to those of the multifunctional managers. However, the differences in learning abilities between the younger and older managers is unlikely to have been due to the more varied career experiences; in the third period the career experiences are similar but the learning ability scores favour the younger managers.

Again, the career history items heavily endorsed by the younger managers supports the suggestion that those who are influenced by other people favourably to their career development, and are given early responsibility, come to construe their experiences differently from those who do not receive this attention. The person who is not carefully groomed and encouraged may take longer to acquire belief in his own abilities.

An interesting point from the data is that in the third period the career history items for the younger and older managers have similar endorsement patterns, and yet the differential in scores of learning ability actually widens. It may be that once managers have acquired the self perception of ability they go on developing their learning ability even if the initial attention is not sustained at a level above that for other managers in this company.

3. Early, Mid-career, and Late Learners

This suggestion is supported by an examination of the data in terms of the period when learning ability is first endorsed and subsequent time periods. The results suggest that, at whichever period managers start to score on learning ability, they are likely to continue to do so in subsequent periods (Figure 3). A large proportion of the group who had scores in the high range in periods one or two had similar scores in all later time periods. Managers who first score in the high range in periods three or four also score highly in periods five and six. Career profiles were broadly similar for the groups and this supports the idea that once self-confidence is acquired people can go on developing their learning ability, independently of what is happening to them in terms of external indicators of career experience.

The environmental complexity scores for the 'early', 'mid', and 'late' developers were also compared. It was found that the scores for environmental complexity increased over time for all groups of managers. Thus the previously observed association between learning ability and environmental complexity may be due in part to the general upward trends in both over time. Yet both trends might have quite separate causes. It has been argued that the pace of change is accelerating and it might therefore be expected that the scores for environmental complexity will rise with the passing of actual years (as distinct from career time periods). Learning ability, however, is more likely to be a characteristic of the individual. The former is indicated by the observation that for managers with varying years of career experience the environmental complexity scores for actual years were broadly similar.

TOWARDS A REVISED MODEL OF LEARNING

Although increasing complexity of the environment and increasing learning ability go together, it was suggested that complexity, as such, might be a less important factor than whether or not managers got early responsibility and encouragement in their career (being given training, or meeting someone who influenced their career). Early responsibility and encouragement would lead people to perceive that they had 'started a career', whereas early job changes which involved few additional demands could be seen as 'just another move'. The concept of *the need to gain realistic confidence in one's ability* was invoked as a mediating variable between experience and learning. Early responsibility and encouragement can be seen as recognition for one's ability.

This concept can only be inferred from the data collected. There is no actual measure of it. Other research, however, can be cited which supports the idea. Bandura (1977) discussed the concept of self-efficacy. A self-efficacy expectation is the conviction that one can successfully execute the behaviour required to produce the desired outcomes. Bandura's conclusions are in accord with the suggestion made here that people need to perceive that they have a career and to have their ability

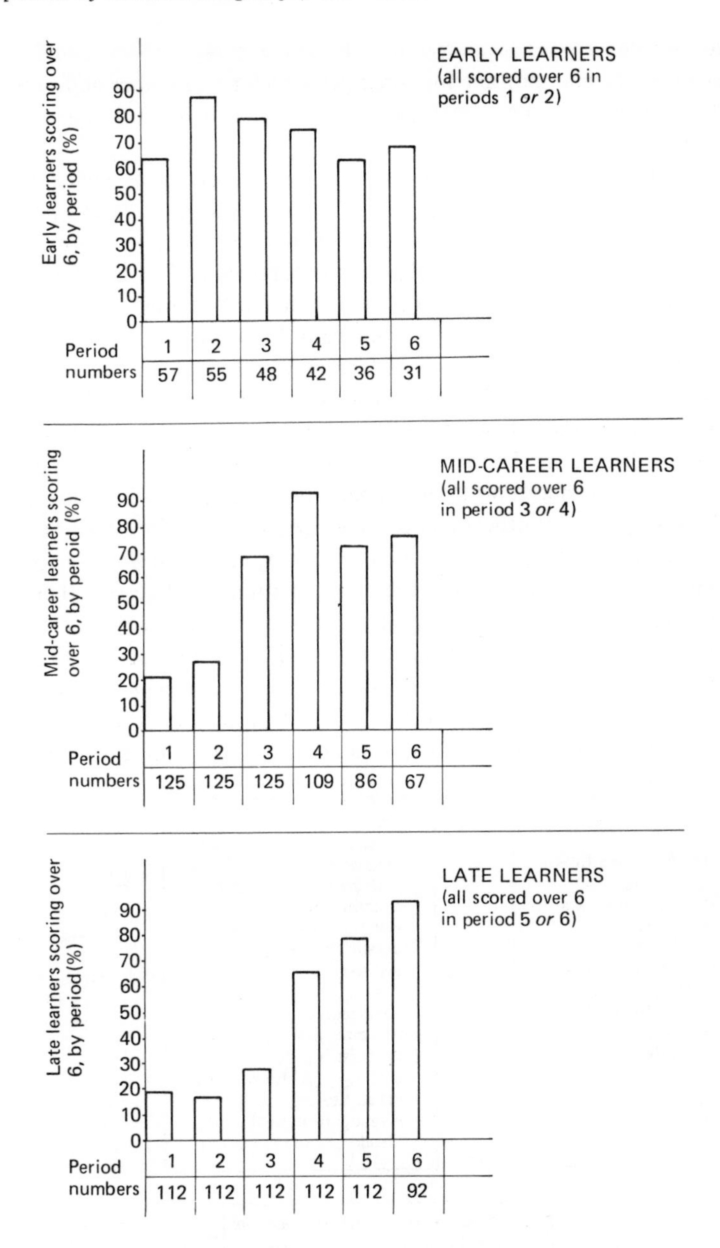

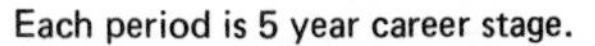
Each period is 5 year career stage.

Figure 3. Proportions of early, mid, and late learners scoring in the high range on learning ability at each period into their career

recognized by being given responsibility. Berlew and Hall (1966) also found that early responsibility is important for subsequent high performance and success. The responsibility given must be congruent with a person's own level of aspiration and personal standards.

Some things enhance a person's self-efficacy expectations and some things weaken them. Enhanced self-efficacy expectations result in a person persisting in new coping behaviour, when a new and demanding task is to be tackled: if success at this new task occurs, then self-efficacy is strengthened. This could therefore be viewed as a 'virtuous' circle – once you have entered a 'virtuous' circle your learning ability may continue to develop. This is shown in Figure 4.

In the same way as 'virtuous' circles of learning and enhancement of self-efficacy expectations can be postulated, so can 'vicious' ones. In 'vicious' circles self-efficacy expectations are weakened so there is less persistence in tackling new things, subsequently. 'Vicious' circles may be entered when a person receives condemnatory feedback from others about his performance which indicates to him that he has not gained any ability, or that others do not recognize abilities he does have. Self-efficacy will also be weakened if the area in which he feels he has failed was one to which he was committed, and also if he thinks the condemnation was deserved, that is, failure was due to lack of personal capability rather than to uncontrollable circumstances.

Not all learning will result in changes in self-efficacy expectations. For example, if a success/failure is attributed to luck or external circumstances rather than personal ability, if a new job is not perceived as difficult to learn, if success is in an area to which a person feels no commitment, or is not seen as relevant to overall progress,

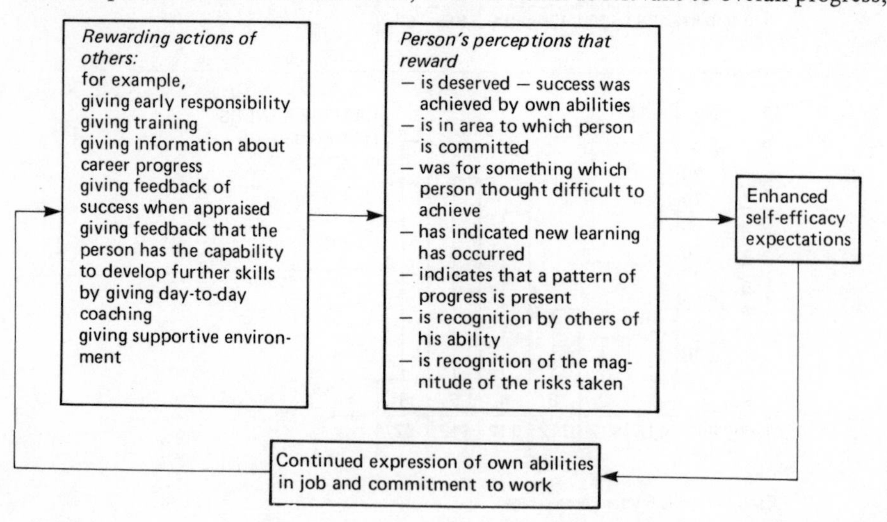

Figure 4. A 'Virtuous Circle' for Learning which strengthens Self-efficacy Expectations

then success or failure will not affect self-efficacy expectations, even when some new learning has occurred.

Rewarding actions (see Figure 3) are things which are within the control of the Company and which can affect the person's perceptions of his ability and thus his self-efficacy expectations.

Recommendations to the Company are therefore based on the kinds of things the Company can do in this area in order to promote 'virtuous' learning cycles and avoid precipitating people into 'vicious' ones.

IMPLICATIONS FOR CAREER DEVELOPMENT

The revised model of learning does not generate an easy list of experiences to which managers may be exposed in the course of career development. It does not merely suggest, for example, that people should experience complexity of the environment. Indeed, the suggestion that it is a person's realistic self-confidence which is important appears to place the onus for development on the individual. However, there may be ways in which managers can foster self-efficacy in their staff.

1. Training Off-the-Job

The way in which training away from the job is presented can have implications for self-efficacy expectations. The purposes of the training should be made clear and the suggestion avoided that training might be a punishment for not having done well enough in the past. It should be seen as part of the person's development and progress and confirmation to him that others perceive him as having ability worth developing.

2. Coaching and Training On-the-Job

Managers will need to be given increasing responsibility, feedback on their successes and guidance on improving their weaknesses in such a way that they are precipitated into virtuous rather than vicious circles. The development of people on the job through being coached by their managers, means that *all* managers with subordinates need to have the necessary skills for coaching. Managers need to know what kind of activities can be used as coaching tools and how to counsel and support their staff. Relatively few managers are given instruction in this area and this therefore represents an important training need. Many managers may not even recognize coaching as being one of the activities for which they are responsible; and this responsibility needs to be emphasized, perhaps by including it as a factor in the appraisal of a manager's performance.

3. Appraisals

The way an appraisal is carried out may have strong implications for self-efficacy expectations. Many managers are expected to carry out appraisals but may not do them well, and again, this is an area in which more training is required. The appraisal is an occasion when a manager can give subordinates constructive advice and criticism of past performance, display his confidence in his subordinates ability, and in setting targets for the future, indicate expectations held of the subordinate.

For appraisals to be effective in improving performance and to enhance rather than weaken self-efficacy expectation there needs to be an emphasis on performance-related behaviour rather than on qualities or abstract grades of excellence.

The appraisal must be seen to be fair (rewards deserved) and the traits assessed within a manager's capability to change (dependent on his own abilities) if it is to have a positive effect on self-efficacy.

4. Career Development

The results of this research suggest that people need to perceive that they have a career rather than a series of unrelated jobs. This implies that career development schemes, however well intentioned, are not likely to achieve their full effect unless the efforts to help them are made apparent to the managers concerned.

Twigger (1978) noted that career development facilities are usually available for 'high-fliers' but 'average' people are left to struggle on alone, and yet most managers indicated that they needed to perceive some overall planning of their career and to have some career counselling. Some career counselling may be useful for all managers but in particular for those who feel that their career is at a standstill. They may not be going to senior posts but some lateral moves might provide new stimulus and confidence. Career counselling may enable people to have some feedback on their overall career progress. Career progress may be construed not only as movement up the traditional management hierarchy but also in terms of the development of a person's managerial abilities. Lateral moves need not be construed as the 'end of a career'.

To introduce the idea that lateral moves can be helpful would need careful counselling. Guerrier and MacMillan (1978) suggest that moving young managers to a small company/division can be an enriching move. They may gain new skills and expertise in an environment which gives them an overview of the business. Middle managers can gain from such a move on a part-time basis and older managers can make sideways moves from large to smaller organizations, thus freeing responsible posts for up and coming managers. They suggest that companies may need to develop such organizations in order to cope with career development in low growth periods. Child (1978) in a study of Dunlop Limited showed that in low growth periods direct production workers decrease in numbers. There is no corresponding drop in managerial numbers. Thus there may develop a 'promotion blockage' for managers in mid-career when more senior personnel no longer move into newly created jobs as they might in a time of expansion. Lateral moves may help to alleviate this problem.

Although the analysis used an aggregate score of environmental complexity, three clusters were found which were labelled 'steady state', 'breakdown', and 'innovative' environments. It is possible that 'multifunctional' experience gives managers exposure to all of these and that these may be readily accessible environments which could be used in career development to develop self-efficacy expectations.

CONCLUSIONS

There is nothing particularly innovatory in many of these proposals for career development. The important issue is the effect that other people can have on a person's self-efficacy expectations, precipitating him into either a virtuous or vicious circle. It is therefore not merely that these activities should be carried out, but that this should be done in such a way as to enhance rather than diminish self-efficacy. In this way a company may develop 'learning managers' capable of meeting novel, complex problems in the future.

REFERENCES

Bandura A. (1977). Self-efficacy: toward a unifying theory of behavioural change, *Psychological Review,* **84**, 2, 191–215.

Berlew D.E. and Hall D.T. (1966). The socialization of managers: effects of expectations on performance, *Admin, Sc Quarterly*, **II**, 2, 207–223.

Child J. (1978). The non-productive component within the productive sector: a problem of management control, in M. Fores and I. Glover, (eds), *Manufacturing and Management,* HMSO, London.

Guerrier Y. and MacMillan K. (1978). Developing managers in low-growth organizations, *Personnel Management,* **10**, 12, 34–38.

Handy C. (1976). *Understanding Organisations*, Penguin.

Kolb D.A. (1971). *On Management and the Learning Process,* Sloan School of Management Working Paper, MIT.

Kolb D.A. and Fry R. (1975). Toward an applied theory of experiential learning, in C.L. Cooper, (ed.), *Theories of Group Processes,* John Wiley, London.

McQuitty L.L. (1967). A mutual development of some typological theories and pattern analytical methods, *Educational and Psychological Measurement*, **27**, 21–46.

Mason R.O. (1974). Towards the learning manager, in R.L. Achoff (ed.), *Systems and Management Annual,* Petrocelli Books, New York.

Twigger A.J. (1978). The managerial career, *Management Today,* December, 54–59.

Advances in Management Education
Edited by John Beck and Charles Cox

CHAPTER 6

Management Analysis – An Improved Method for Identifying Managers' Training Needs

K.F. Jackson and J.H.B. Vant

At the present time, after more than a decade of unprecedented activity in the field of management training, we are still in a position where managers and management trainers are not equipped with adequate methods for carrying out the essential processes of identifying managers' training needs. One has only to look into the booklets put out by training organizations or to start a discussion on the topic among managers or trainers to obtain evidence on this point. This paper offers a partial solution to the problem of identifying managers' training needs. The related problem of turning needs into recommendations or the 'training response', as it is sometimes called, has to be borne in mind, however, because there is little point in finding out about needs if we are going to be unable to meet them. Although we have found that managers and trainers are also not well equipped with adequate methods for making training recommendations we do not regard this problem with the same degree of urgency as the former, since there are suitable methods in existence, and the deficiency seems mainly to be due to poor dissemination of knowledge about the state of the art.

Below is a quotation from a booklet on the subject of the identification of managers' training needs. It is typical of the way in which many tended to write on this subject a few years ago, and it can be seen that it says that training needs can be identified in certain situations, but it does not really explain how to do it.

> 'It is sound practice to carry out performance and potential reviews regularly, asking questions following these general lines:
>
> Is the Manager achieving his goals?
> Is he ready to take on greater responsibility?
> What are his own ideas for the future?

This reviewing leads to an identification of two kinds of training needs:

(i) Training needs for the present job:

(a) What are the skills and knowledge that need to be developed to do his job better?
(b) What help can the reviewer himself give, within the company by guiding, arranging new experience, and organizing internal courses?
(c) What outside experience is necessary such as attending courses or by secondment?

(ii) Training needs for future responsibilities:

(a) If the manager is capable of taking on greater responsibility, what does he need?
(b) In this connection what help can be given within the company?
(c) In this connection, what external help can be given?'

It must be admitted that it is not easy to devise methods that will take us step-by-step to the identification of training needs. One cause of difficulty is the complexity of the chain of logical relationships which needs to be understood. This chain embraces the demands of the job, the capabilities of the person to be trained to do it, and the way that the person organizes himself. It involves the setting of standards, the making of comparisons, the estimation of short-falls, the making of training recommendations, the setting of training priorities, the choice of training methods and resources, and the design of training programmes. The existence of this complexity seems commonly either to be ignored or to invite the taking of short cuts in the identification process.

Other causes of difficulty are the complexity of jobs and the complexity of human capabilities. Here again the methods that are used are often too over-simplified and are incapable of eliciting enough detailed information for an adequate diagnosis of training needs.

REQUIREMENTS FOR A METHOD OF IDENTIFYING MANAGERS' TRAINING NEEDS

1. *Relevance.* The needs that are identified must be relevant to the manager's job, so that when the needs are met he will be able to get better results.

2. *Analysis.* The method must be analytical in order to get down to detail in examining the practical issues of the job. Generalizations, such as 'how to deal with people', are likely to miss the point.

3. *Continuity of concept.* The ideas and words used in investigating the manager and his job must be much the same as those used in describing his needs and in training him. Information will be lost or distorted if we have to translate from one set of concepts or jargon to another as we follow the process through.

4. *Information.* The method must provide an abundance of fresh ideas about

training from which we can choose the most valuable. We must be able to do without the worn-out clichés of the traditional approach.

5. *No arbitrary standards.* We do not want to get involved in target-setting or to have to depend on academic standards of attainment in order to be able to specify training needs.

6. *A procedure which leads to a solution.* The method must work and produce an answer. It must not leave the analyst depending upon his own wits and insight to solve the problem.

OUR METHOD – THEORY

Our method is an eclectic one, bringing together ideas from the orthodox or traditional approach, from the theory of problem-solving, from the theory of management as control, and from a new point of view which we call 'purposeful management'. The orthodox view is that deficiencies or weaknesses which are recognized should be rectified by training. We find this to be a useful and desirable ingredient in the method. The theory of problem-solving (Jackson, 1975) is relevant because managers are paid to solve problems. Work which is not to do with solving problems is presumably of a relatively routine nature and is more suitable for delegation to subordinates.

Problems are difficult situations which people are trying to deal with. In them there is somewhere, either explicit or implied, at least one objective which someone wishes to achieve. There is always at least one obstacle which stands, or appears to stand, in the way. In his book on 'Thinking', George Humphrey (1951) wrote that 'A problem is a situation which for some reason appreciably holds up an organism in its efforts to reach a goal'.

Experience over many years of teaching managers to solve problems has shown that conscious thinking about both objectives and obstacles is crucially important in finding solutions. Consequently, managers need to be clear in their minds about what their objectives are and what obstacles give rise to their problems by standing in the way. The obstacles that they think about should be logically related to the corresponding objectives, in so far as any given objective should not be attainable whilst the relevant obstacle remains.

A full list of the activities which are or may be required to solve problems, including all the different mental processes involved, would be very large and complex. It is convenient to summarize them in the form of a short list. There is no single definitive list which is agreed by all writers on this subject, but the following has been found to be a very helpful reminder and guide and to have stood up well to prolonged use.

1. Formulation
2. Interpretation
3. Constructing courses of action

4. Decision-making
5. Implementation

The items in this list exist both as stages that may need to occur in the problem-solving process and as mental processes or groups of mental skills.

Formulation is the start of problem-solving. It includes the detection, identification, and definition of problems and the recognition of objectives and obstacles. Interpretation is necessary in order to reach sufficient understanding of what the problem is all about and how the various systems that are affected by it work. Constructing courses of action is the creative stage, where we use our imagination, vision, and resourcefulness to devise solutions. Decision-making is the stage for choosing the preferred course of action and obtaining commitment to it. Implementation is the executive stage, where we use all our managerial skills of gathering resources and authority, making plans and preparations, giving instructions, getting things going, controlling and bringing the work to a successful conclusion, and assessing the results.

Research by one of us (unpublished) on the measurement of problem-solving ability by means of tests has shown a marked tendency for certain attitudes towards problems to show up in behaviour. It appears that people tend to be polarized either towards being 'problem-finders' or 'problem-solvers'. The 'problem-finders' are those who think and talk mostly about difficulties and obstacles. The 'problem-solvers' are those who predominantly emphasize decisions or propose and execute courses of action.

The theory of control as applied to management is a branch of systems theory. A manager is responsible for controlling a system or set of systems. He is given inputs, which are objectives, and he gives appropriate instructions to the system to make it do what he requires of it, in order to get certain results. He can get feedback of results for comparison with objectives and thereby work out new control instructions to give to the system to correct its behaviour. He may also be able to get feedback of information about system behaviour more directly, by visiting the system and seeing the work going on, and acting accordingly. For all of this to work, he must know and understand what he is doing and be able to keep the system and its associated information channels working efficiently and effectively.

Purposeful management is a concept which brings together the problem-solving and control-theory points of view. It is based on the axiomatic principle that a manager ought to work in such a way as to make progress towards his objectives. This simple idea has several important implications for judging the work that managers actually do and for identifying their training needs.

The manager has a purpose, or several purposes, and these may be of his own choosing or they may be imposed upon him by other people. The manager is also active. He does things. Some of the things he does contribute to the fulfilment of his purposes, whereas others do not. The manager has strengths. He does some things very well. He does things that are particularly valuable. He could do some things better if he were to be trained or if certain changes could be made. There are also obstacles to the attainment of some of his objectives, which he should try to overcome.

The approach to which this theory leads is clearly a normative one, but it does not depend upon the setting of arbitrary standards of performance. It contains its own internal axioms which serve as a basis for the logical argument that we have now briefly described.

OUR METHOD OF IDENTIFYING TRAINING NEEDS IN PRACTICE

We have developed a standard routine for identifying training needs based on our theory of purposefulness, as well as on the orthodox approach, and on problem-solving and control principles. We use a structured interview which puts questions to the manager in the following form and sequence.

1. What sort of things do you do in your job? How is your time occupied from hour to hour and from day to day?
2. What are you trying to achieve in your work? What are some of the objectives that you have set yourself, and what objectives have been given to you by other people?
3. What, in your view, are the most valuable things that you do for the company? What are you doing when you are really earning your keep? (This question yields information about 'key areas').
4. What are you particularly good at as a manager?
5. What would you like to be able to do better in your job?
6. What obstacles stand in the way of achieving your objectives?

The interview lasts for 30–120 minutes, according to the extent of the manager's desire to talk, and according to whether the interview takes place in his own office or elsewhere. Interviews conducted away from the manager's own office tend to be rather short and less informative, probably because there are fewer stimuli there to remind the manager of various things that he does and various problems that he needs to tackle at the present time.

We write his answers down as fully as possible, making sure to record something of every remark, regardless of its meaning or importance. We use a record form for this purpose, which carries a set of six columns, as well as space for writing down his responses and further space for our own comments which will arise during subsequent analysis. When the responses have been given we read back the record in abbreviated form, picking out the most relevant answers. We then ask the manager what he thinks of the picture thus painted of the way he works and the way he thinks about himself and his work. Usually he feels generally satisfied with it, but sometimes he can also see inconsistencies and ways in which better coherence and purposefulness could be achieved.

Subsequently, we analyse the answers by means of the six columns. A mark is placed on one or more columns against each remark or statement, in order to classify it in problem-solving terms. Column 1 is associated with the formulation of problems, and the mentioning of objectives and obstacles, and is sub-divided into three sub-columns, accordingly. Column 2 is associated with interpretation. All explanations and descriptions are allocated to it. Column 3 denotes creative ideas and couses of action. Column 4 is for decision-making, including all matters to do with criteria, evaluation of courses of action, choosing and giving commitment to action. Column 5 is for everything of an executive nature, including planning and controlling, gathering resources, getting authority, making progress, evaluating results, and so on. Column 6 is for non-problem-orientated remarks, such as interjections, anecdotes, red-herrings, comments on the interview, etc.

By counting the number of remarks classified in this manner we are able to obtain a measure of the relative amount of attention that the manager pays to the different aspects of problem-solving behaviour. We have obtained a collection of interview records from a considerable number of different managers, and are now in a position to be able to grade individual scores as typical, or unusual, or out of balance in some respect. We use a set of rules which guide us in interpreting these quantified results and enable us to make statements about the manager's attitude towards problem-solving and problems generally, such as to distinguish those who are typically 'problem-finders' from those who are 'problem-solvers'.

The next step in the interpretation of the results is to scrutinize each record in detail and apply another set of rules for making comparisons between purposes, obstacles, strengths and weaknesses, and so on. These can be stated briefly as follows:

1. Take what the manager said he would like to do better at face value, and if it means that he would like to learn something, list this as a training need.
2. Where it is apparent that the manager could be helped to reach his objectives, overcome his obstacles, or solve his problems by training, note this.
3. Where the manager's activities do not match up with his objectives, strengths and weaknesses, key areas and obstacles, note this as something that needs to be corrected.

From this we prepare a statement of the consistencies and inconsistencies, needs for better understanding of purposeful concepts, and summarize the training needs that follow from the facts revealed by the analysis.

RESULTS AND FINDINGS

Problem-solving Scores

In Table 1 are shown the average 'problem-solving' scores for the whole sample of managers who were interviewed in a survey of fifty managers in the petroleum industry. These tell of the terms in which the managers expressed themselves when they answered the questions. It can be seen that Implementation is by far the most common category, which means that the managers spoke mostly about what they do, what their executive actions are. This is satisfactory, since managers are employed to get things done.

Table 1. Problem-solving Scores

Average number of responses per person in Problem-Solving Categories

		Average no. of responses	%
1a	Objectives	15.5	18.9
1b	Problems	3.0	3.7
1c	Obstacles	7.0	8.5
2	Interpretation	26.3	32.0
3	Courses of action	1.0	1.2
4	Decision-making	1.1	1.3
5	Implementation	28.1	34.2
6	Other	0.2	0.2
		82.2	100.0

The next largest category is Interpretation, which shows that managers take care to explain what they are saying to the interviewers, as well as to give a factual answer to each question. It may mean in some cases that managers have a real need to talk to someone who is interested in them and their work.

Then follows Objectives, another aspect of work that managers talk about readily. It is noticeable that many managers responded to question 1, which is specifically about activities, by giving a list of their general aims or objectives. They were unwilling, apparently, to let us know what they did in detail without telling us what it was for. Perhaps some managers think that their activities may be judged to be less worthy than their objectives, but this is a point on which one can only speculate, having no independent evidence with which to check it. The fourth most common category is that of Obstacles. These were asked for specifically in the final question, and they turned up occasionally in answer to other questions. Problems described in general terms were the fifth most common category, and are related to objectives and obstacles.

The surprises among the problem-solving scores came in the category referring to Courses of Action, which includes the creative side of management, and Decision-making, which is regarded by some authorities as the most important and characteristic function of managers. Neither of these were scored highly, and most managers made no mention of matters which could be placed in them. We have therefore decided to regard the managers who mention Courses of Action or Decisions more than once as superior in these areas of concern.

We had equipped ourselves with an extra category in which to catch irrelevances and evasions, but it was rarely necessary to use it. However, we think it should be retained because it will be needed now and then, when behaviour is not as courteous and disciplined as that of those met during our survey.

Training Needs

Having extracted the training needs from the individual records of the interviews, the numbers of items per manager were counted, and the frequency distribution of these was drawn up as shown in Table 2. The qualitative nature of the needs was summarized by collecting the needs together in various classes, using categories which seemed to represent the most common and obvious characteristics and to be reasonably mutually exclusive. The numbers of needs found in each category are shown in Table 3. It should be noted that any one manager may have several different needs in the same category.

The largest category of need is to do with relations with other people. We have

Table 2. Frequencies of different numbers of training needs identified per manager

No. of needs	No. of managers
0	0
1	3
2	5
3	4
4	7
5	8
6	3
7	7
8	3
9	4
10	2
11	1
12	2
13	1
total	50

Table 3. Frequencies of training needs in each category

Communications & other 'people' needs (communications 56, other 48)	104
Self-Management	98
Problem-Solving and purposeful management	55
Methods, techniques, specific problems	20
Money	6
Legislation	1
Computers	2
General	2
	288

sub-divided this into Communications and other 'People' needs, although the boundary between them is not distinct. The most common need here is how to communicate one's objectives to other people and other groups and obtain agreement. This is by far the most common need of all in our findings. Among the other 'People' needs the outstanding one is how to train and improve one's subordinates. Another common one is how to make people happy, to retain morale, to motivate, etc.

The next largest category of needs is Self-Management and within it the most common needs are how to delegate, how to set priorities, how to gain credibility, how to gain confidence, and how to manage time and find time to do various activities. How to control work-load and how to cope with various difficult influences are also common.

The third largest category of needs covers the areas of problem-solving and purposeful management. The most common need here is to learn to devote effort to the overcoming of the obstacles of which one is aware. In general, there appears to be a common lack of appreciation of the nature of problems and how to think and talk about them skilfully.

Next comes a mixed category of highly specific problems on which managers need expert advice. Most of these are one-offs, but some are familiar enough to be recognized as typical operational research problems or to come in the general class where known management techniques can be applied. The remaining identified needs are few in number. Those concerned with finance and accounting numbered six, legislation one, computers two, and a general management course two.

In general, we noticed several common tendencies which merit attention in the planning of training and development for managers. One of these is a lack of skill and knowledge in conceptual thinking, which seems to limit management development and is likely to make it difficult to learn quickly from experience. This is important because of the shortage of experience in the expanding sectors of industry. Another general issue is the obstacle of spending valuable time on paperwork and trivial but apparently unavoidable tasks. This may require reorganization as much as training to put it right.

We have remarked that many managers would not give a straight answer to the question about what they actually do in their jobs. They seemed to be compelled to preface any explanations of that matter with a general introduction about their aims and responsibilities. The more intelligent, mature or successful managers, however, seemed to have more disciplined minds and were able to respond accurately to each question as it was put.

Lastly, there was much evidence that managers welcome a chance to talk constructively and objectively about the way they do their work. We gathered that appraisal interviews do not usually meet this need, being strongly associated in managers' minds with the giving of criticism and the making of decisions about rewards.

DISCUSSION

'Traditional' versus 'Non-Traditional' Needs

In formulating the original proposal for our survey it was expected that we would be reporting on both traditional and non-traditional training needs. The distinction between these classes was based on our view that traditional training needs are influenced by the awareness of existing training courses etc., and that our new methods would elicit training needs for which training facilities do not yet exist. Although we still hold this view, we have found that in practice the position of the border-line between the two classes is a matter of opinion and there is no value in separating them. We have, therefore, dropped the distinction in our work and do not propose to discuss it further. We have explained, above, the three principal ways by which we derived training needs from the raw data.

However, we attach importance to the fact that the method on which we are now reporting is focused on the training needs of the individual, not on generalized company training needs. We also believe that if you have an 'engine' and an 'engine-driver', training should not only be directed towards the needs of the 'engine', but towards the improvement of the effectiveness of the 'driving', the way the driver manages the whole situation.

The most important Needs and their Implications

We find that the most common needs are to do with communicating with other people and with solving problems. Since we hold the view that these are the most important areas of manager's work we are not surprised by this finding.

We are concerned that many managers are not careful to ensure that they concentrate their activities on such crucial matters as are indicated by their objectives and on the overcoming of obstacles of which they are well aware. Our data also provides evidence that a matter of great concern to managers is the management of their time, in order to give attention to the various aspects of their work in due proportion. There is surely a strong causal interaction between these two findings in both directions. They are short of time because they misuse it, and so have little time for strategic thinking. The central problem for the trainers is how to help managers to get out of the trap of being overtaken by events, so that they can get 'on top' of the situation again.

The Effectiveness of the Method

One of the purposes of the survey was to try out our method for identifying managers' training needs. We found it to be highly successful. It is acceptable and effective. In every case, without exception, the manager who was interviewed responded willingly to the questions and gave replies which gave us considerable insight into his work, thought processes, attitudes, knowledge, personality, ability, and other attributes. These data indicated a large number of training needs, as we have shown. In several cases we were able to obtain independent evidence of the value of our interpretations, either from the manager himself or from an associate with whom we had his permission to confer. Sometimes the manager told us of useful insights that were produced directly by the process of answering the questions, and in some cases we were able to offer suggestions about how to make improvements which were received appreciatively.

Training of Interviewers and Counsellors

A course of about three days is needed to put over the skills of interpreting the data in terms of training needs, plus two days of coaching and interview practice. However, there may be many trainers who are unused to the counselling method that is required, or who may lack the credibility for acceptance by senior managers, so there is a requirement for selection as well as training of personnel to use our method.

Refinement of the Method

The only change that we have had to make as a result of the survey is to subdivide a question in our structured interview which dealt with strengths and key areas into two separate questions, to make that particular question easier to respond to and to interpret. From now on, we propose to use the average percentages of responses in the problem-solving categories (see Table 1) as norms against which to compare individual results, and to continue to collect quantitative data for building up a set of norms for different occupational groups, etc.

MEETING THE TRAINING NEEDS

We have shown how training needs can be reasoned from the data yielded by the structured interview and what sorts of need have been identified. The next step is to recommend suitable training or other remedies to bring about the desired changes. It is a fortunate aspect of our theories both of problem-solving and purposeful management that they contain within them many indicators which can tell us how to put things right once we are aware of deficiencies that need to be corrected. Suitable courses on problem-solving already exist. We have prepared course designs for training in purposeful management, and are now taking the opportunity to put these into use whenever the occasion arises. However, we have a great deal of thinking and planning to do if we are to find out how to meet the very wide range of individual training needs that are not common enough to warrant the organizing of formal training courses. It is very clear that the kinds of need which we are at present least equipped to meet are those which are closest to the central arts and skills of management, and which are very seldom directly attacked in traditional courses for managers. Once we have begun to find answers to these questions the next step will be to investigate the problems of introducing this novel and stimulating method of identifying managers' training needs into companies and other employing organizations, and of providing line managers and trainers with the understanding and skills that will be necessary both for the introductory phase and for seeing the method through into practical and regular application.

REFERENCES

Humphrey G. (1951). *Thinking,* Methuen, London.
Jackson K.F. (1975). *The Art of Solving Problems,* Heineman, London.

Advances in Management Education
Edited by John Beck and Charles Cox

CHAPTER 7

Facilitating Re-Entry Through Role Analysis

Ian McGivering

It seems to be common for the objectives of management education and training staff to change over time. When the function is first created, the main, if not the only, objective is to achieve recognition and acceptance in the wider organization. The staff are nervous of the scepticism that greets the establishment of any new function and launch their initial training courses with some apprehension. However, as the programme of courses proceeds without obvious disaster and participants show signs of satisfaction, the tension in the training staff diminishes until eventually, with the experience of several months of successful courses behind them, they relax.

The criterion of success during this first period is the degree of enthusiasm with which participants have reacted to the courses which, for one reason or another, they have been required to attend. The needs of the training staff are met, therefore, when participants return to their roles in the organization and report to their superiors and colleagues that the training course provided a valuable, stimulating, and enjoyable experience. Participants are often required to work on training courses until the early hours so that they return to the organization in a state of near collapse. Nervous trainers seem to consider that this demonstrates the rigour of the courses and the dedication of the training staff. The staff are reassured by phrases like: 'I enjoyed that', 'You certainly made us think hard and work hard'; and draw comfort from the personal rapport that has been established with participants.

More formal attempts at evaluation may take the form of a final session on each course, devoted to a plenary discussion of the course content and methods with criticism invited of each individual session and tutor performance. Provided that good interpersonal relationships were achieved between staff and participants, there is usually nothing to fear from such sessions. Sometimes, after a lapse of time following attendance, participants may be invited to complete a questionnaire exploring similar issues in the belief that a more objective, thoughtful appraisal may be thus obtained. Evaluation, however, is still confined to subjective judgements in which enjoyment is a major factor. This is not seen to be naive whilst the primary objective of the training staff is to secure, through their courses, their own credibility and acceptance to their colleagues in other functions in the organization. Indeed, for some trainers, ambition goes no further and although some development in the training function may take place, it is in the form of more sophisticated training techniques and a wider range of courses offered. The objective remains, explicitly or implicitly, the acceptability of the function and hence of the staff. For other trainers, however, this objective gradually begins to pall.

For such training staff, the approval of participants, superiors, and colleagues is a necessary first step in the establishment of a management training function, and of course, it is not being suggested that there is anything reprehensible in running courses that are enjoyable, but once that step has been achieved and the reputation of the staff is felt by them to be reasonably secure, they begin to cast about in search of longer term objectives which will provide them with a more satisfactory justification for their existence. The writer has attended by invitation more than one meeting of training staffs in which they have spent several hours gloomily trying to fathom the meaning of life. Sooner or later, whether they are conscious of it or not, their own value systems come to exert an increasing influence on their perception of the nature and purpose of management training so that they come to view training as a means of bringing about change in the wider organization of which they are part. This change seems invariably to be in the general direction of more open, participative management behaviour and the content of the training courses in the behavioural area reflects these values. They then start to look for evidence of the success of their training activities, not in congratulations from participants or in the flattering completion of post-course questionnaires, important though these may continue to be, but in observable change in the behaviour of participants when they return to their departmental duties.

Of course, not all training courses are expected to induce behavioural change in the participants. Some courses may be informational in character and are designed to acquaint participants with, for example, higher management policy, the activities of different sections of the organization, the rationale underlying the company's organizational structure, recent relevant legislation, the structure and process of the industrial relations machinery, and so on. Courses of this kind may continue to be evaluated in the traditional way and nobody looks to see changes in the day-to-day behaviour of those attending them. But courses in the behavioural science area – interpersonal skills, managerial style, group discussion leading – are a different matter. These courses are hoped by training staff to result in the development of attitudes and the acquisition of skills which will then be applied by participants in their normal organizational roles. The success of the course is now judged by the extent to which participants do, in fact, behave in accordance with the values espoused in the training department.

Unhappily, such behavioural change seems to occur much less frequently than had been hoped, although participants may continue to express their satisfaction with the courses and claim with apparent sincerity that they have learnt from them much that is valuable. The problem of learning transfer has been recognized for many years and the problem is particularly acute in the case of social, as distinct from motor, skills. Accepting that participants are pleased to have learnt new skills but recognizing that they seem not to practise them on their return to the organization, trainers may form the hypothesis that participants have failed intellectually to perceive the relevance of the skills to their daily activities.

Accordingly, trainers frequently conclude a training course with a session in which participants are required to draw up Action Plans consisting of positive sequential steps which will be taken on their return to their departments following the course. It is hoped that this procedure will focus the attention of participants on the applicability of their acquired knowledge and skills and will secure a greater measure of commitment to their use.

It may reasonably be argued that the preparation of Action Plans is a step in the right direction and yet the results are so often disappointing. Despite what might charitably be assumed to be the best intentions, so many Action Plans remain unfulfilled. The ability to prepare an Action Plan in the first place implies that the participant was able to make a connection between the attitudes, knowledge, and skills fostered by the course on the one hand and his departmental role on the other. Presumably, then, the failure to follow through is due to factors, real or imagined, inherent in the work environment, (see Vandenput, 1973). Key to an understanding of these factors is the concept of role, which would seem to be crucial to an understanding of organizational (and other) behaviour and it is therefore astonishing that it receives so little attention in the substantial literature on organizations. Even the article by Vandenput cited above makes no use of the concept.

The absence of an analytical exploration of the forces structuring his role leads the course participant into the preparation of quite unrealistic Action Plans to which he feels under some pressure to pretend a commitment. His intuitive appreciation of their unrealism is often apparent in the lack of enthusiasm displayed in their preparation. If action planning is to have any meaning, it must be carried out in the full appreciation of the problems likely to be encountered when behavioural change is attempted. There is a need, therefore, to provide participants with a simple, theoretical model for them to use as a means of analysing their departmental roles and, by so doing, to become aware of the constraints which surround that role. Action Plans must include steps to handle the negative pressures likely to be encountered.

THE ROLE ANALYSIS MODEL

At some stage in the course, possibly in the session immediately preceding the action planning, participants may be offered the concepts of Role and Role Set for consideration and discussion. The detailed structure of the model will doubtless reflect the theoretical orientation of the trainer and his perception of the participants' needs but the model described below is sufficiently general to have a wide applicability and yet it is of such detail as to be of apparent specific use. It will, presumably, be explained with the use of anecdotal illustrations from the trainer's own repertoire. It can hardly be claimed that it represents an intellectual breakthrough, yet the model embodies two features not normally encountered in the literature on role: the role set includes the actor himself and two impersonal role senders – the reward system and formal lists of duties and responsibilities or job descriptions. With this exception the Role Analysis model offered here is not unlike the concept of Role Analysis which has been used as a training method by workers at the Grubb Institute (Reed, 1974).

Formal Role

Role is defined as 'the behaviour expected of the incumbent of a given position in a social system' or in more popular language, 'The behaviour expected of a person because of the position he occupies'. The term is also used to refer to the position itself. The person whose behaviour is being considered is called the 'actor'. In an organization of hundreds or thousands of people, it is obvious that expectations about behaviour must be formulated in some detail and communicated so that not only the actor himself is clear as to what is expected of him but all those with whom he comes into work contact. The expectations may be in writing but the bulk will be communicated verbally or are simply understood, being learnt by developing a 'feel' for the organization and by sensitive observation. The expectations concern not only the procedures which must be known and followed but also the more subtle aspects of behaviour governing dress, for example, language, and style of relating with other organizational members. The actor will perceive some freedom of movement for the constraints on his behaviour are not absolute and organizations differ in the extent to which deviation is tolerated. Nevertheless, control systems may be devized to ensure as far as possible that behavioural expectations are met and performance may be measured to provide information about the effectiveness of the actor's efforts. Aspects of performance which are subject to scrutiny by the control system or are measured by some method of quantification are likely to be assumed by the individual as being regarded as particularly important and behaviour may be directed to the satisfaction of those implied expectations to the detriment of others. A manager on one training course described how his organization had recently installed an elaborate system of Management by Objectives with clearly defined, quantified objectives for each individual in the management hierarchy. The first observable effect of this, he reported, was that the foremen had stopped talking to each other! The literature now contains many examples of behavioural distortions arising from the application of performance measures (Ridgeway, 1956, Jasinsky, 1956).

Boss

Supplementing, one may assume, the formal job description and its concomitant procedures are the expectations of the actor's organizational superior, or Boss. These are likely to be formulated and transmitted in more detail than would be found in any list of duties and are a potent influence on the actor's behaviour.

The power of the Boss to influence comes from at least two sources: the authority system and his ability to manipulate the actor's rewards. The system of authority, as expressed in the organizational hierarchy, generates its own expectations about command and obedience. The way in which the Boss himself behaves, his beliefs about people and management, his values and attitudes are all seen to imply expectations of the actor. Reinforcing these implications is his ability to influence the actor's rewards ranging from salary increases, promotion prospects, and job security at one end of the scale, to expressions of approval and support at the other.

The Reward System

What behaviour does the organization reward? Or perhaps more accurately, what behaviour is the organization *believed* to reward? What behaviour produces what organizational reactions? When are reactions punitive and when are they positive? Will deviation from the conventional be noticed and, if so, what will happen? Is experiment or initiative encouraged or discouraged? Rewards in this context refer to more than the obvious salary increments and promotion. They include manifestations of approval or disapproval from those in positions of comparative power in the organization and, hence, the general opinion which is formed of the actor. Through his personal observations and his contact with colleagues the actor will have formed views concerning these issues and will have drawn inferences about the effect on his role.

Colleagues

Colleagues are an important source of expectation and, depending on the purpose for which the model is being presented, it may be useful to expand the discussion of this area to include the relationship of the individual to the work group of which he is a member. Particularly if the course participants are younger managers with shop floor supervisory responsibilities, it may be helpful to them to dwell on the shop floor emphasis on social cohesion, the functional and dysfunctional nature of work group membership, the development and reinforcement of attitudes, and the phenomena of social control.

To some extent these issues will be relevant to the manager in his own relationship with members of his peer group but at supervisory and managerial level, peer group expectations, although important, are probably less powerful than they are at shop floor level. Even so, if the actor believes that colleagues expect certain behaviour of him, he may well hesitate to act in defiance of those expectations for fear that his relationships will be damaged, necessary co-operation may be less forthcoming, and he may be subject to criticism, sarcasm or other displays of disapproval.

Subordinates

Subordinates will have developed expectations of the actor's behaviour based on their experience of him over time and, perhaps, on their perceptions of managerial behaviour in general. These expectations may be reinforced by ideological assumptions derived from the culture of the wider society, including the trade union movement. The violation of expectations by sudden behavioural change can cause unexpected reactions. Argyris, for example, reported anxiety amongst subordinates until the actor resumed his traditional behaviour patterns. (Argyris, 1962).

The Actor

The actor himself is more than a passive recipient of expectations, responding unthinkingly to the script provided by others. He will have his own expectations of the behaviour appropriate to a person in the position he occupies in the organization and these expectations will be determined by his personal values and attitudes, his knowledge and skills, and his goals and needs.

Clearly the values of the individual will colour his approach to his role. Behaviour felt to be in violation of principles which are important to him or which impugn his integrity is likely to be rejected. His own interpretation of the expectations communicated to him will be consonant with what he considers to be morally proper, so that, for example, he will try to relate with others in accordance with his moral precepts of openness and honesty and resist attempts to persuade him to behave more deviously. In other words, in so far as he is free to interpret his role, he will try to do so in ways that harmonize with his value system.

Similarly, although at a less deep level than his values, the actor's attitudes will affect his perception of his role. His behaviour will be influenced by notions about the nature of manager–subordinate relationships, the importance and purpose of adjacent organizational activities like production scheduling, costing, quality control, the validity of the authority system, obligations to colleagues, and so on.

The existing state of his skill and knowledge will also effect the expectations he will have of his behaviour. There seems to be a strong tendency for people to structure their roles so as to use such knowledge and skills as they possess. Few, apparently, wish their skills to waste through lack of use. Similarly, expectations of others which appear to assume the possession of knowledge or skills he does not possess are likely to be resisted as unreasonable.

Personal goals and needs influence the perceptions that the individual has of his role. Not only do they help him to decide among the conflicting pressures which may impinge upon him but they help to give rise to distortions in the role as he seeks to establish and maintain an acceptable balance between his own needs and those of others in the organization. For example, the operative on highly repetitive work may seek some measure of personal satisfaction by varying the prescribed detail in his task in order to break the monotony or to create some elements of personal challenge or judgement. Such variations, of course, may be difficult to achieve in the face of a tight control system or close supervision.

Other

These several sources of expectation constitute the model for virtually any role in the context of a formal organization, but for any given individual, specific provision must be made for noting other influences which may be highly significant for his role but insignificant for others. These have been labelled 'Other' in the diagram and might be deemed by the actor to include, for example, shop steward, customer, trade union branch official.

Organizational Culture

All the above sources of influence on the individual's role may be subsumed under the pervasive heading of the organization's culture, which may be defined as the sum total of the beliefs, attitudes of mind, knowledge, and customs which prevail in the organization, or, as sub-cultures, in different parts of the organization. The culture is itself substantially influenced by many factors, including the culture of the wider society in which the organization is located, the predominant technology, the philosophy of higher management, the extent to which its activities are subject to public scrutiny, its economic position and market circumstances, its history, and so on. Roger Harrison has attempted a typology of organizational cultures. (Harrison, 1972).

Latent Roles

To complete the model, attention must be given to latent roles. The individual occupies many roles in life and the behaviour expected in one may imply behavioural expectations in others. For example, the domestic roles of husband and father (or, of course, wife and mother) may make demands on the individual which affect his capacity to meet the expectations structuring his occupational or focal role (Pahl and Pahl, 1971). To label one role and its attendant role set 'latent' and another 'focal' is not to imply any value judgements about the relative importance of the two roles. Focal refers simply to that role which is currently being analysed and latent to all other roles. The model is shown in diagrammatic form in Figure 1:

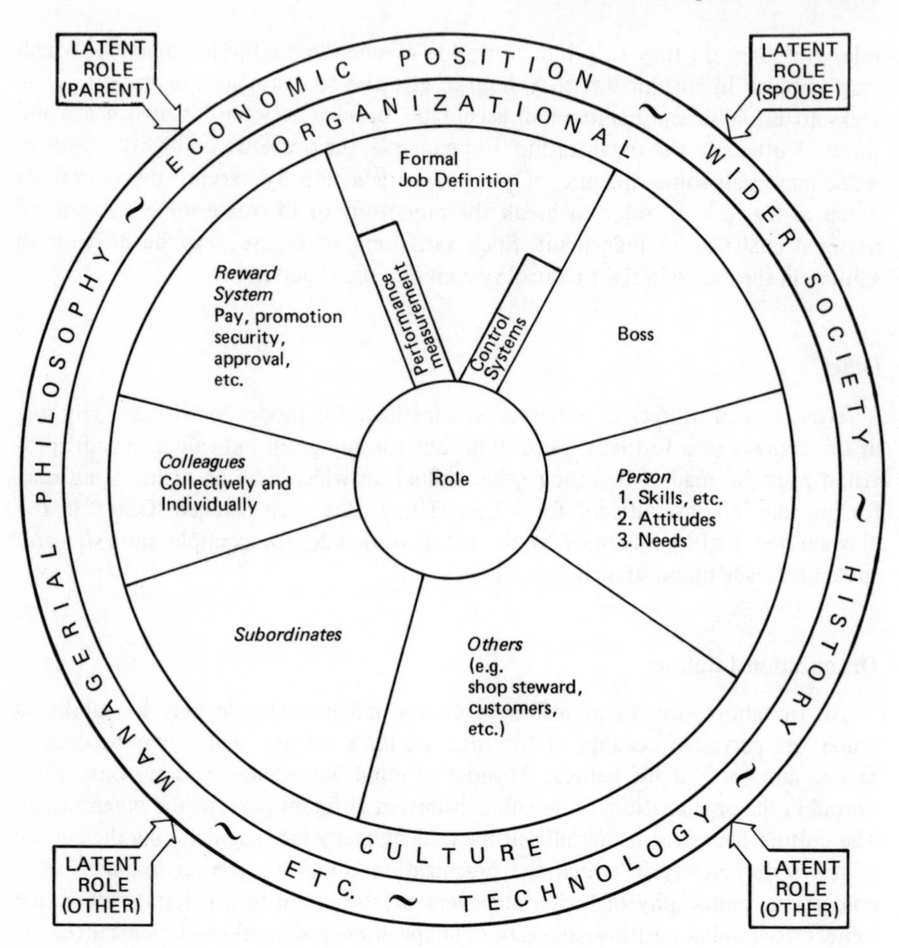

Figure 1. The Role Analysis Model

USE OF THE MODEL TO FACILITATE RE-ENTRY

The view was advanced earlier that action plans drawn up in the euphoria following a training course were inclined to be unrealistic and may be produced by participants because the structure of the course requires them to and not because they have any real intention of carrying them out. The use of the role analysis model is no guarantee whatsoever that behavioural change will take place when the participants resume their normal roles, but such evidence as we have (and it is very scanty evidence indeed) suggests that participants are more likely to attempt some modicum of change even if only tentatively and on an experimental basis. Furthermore, for what it is worth, the presentation of the model as part of the course, indicates to participants that the training staff are aware of the problems facing them on their return, and have realistic expectations concerning the extent to which new concepts and behaviour will be applied.

A suggested procedure for the final session is for participants in pairs or trios matched by organizational affinity – that is to say, if possible from the same department or, at least, with shared knowledge of each other's situation – to review the course content and its impact on them; to decide what, if anything, each would like to apply, and then each in turn, assisted by the others, to analyse his role using the model, identifying and carefully assessing the support or constraints offered by the various role senders, and planning how to tackle each of them. In this way, the realities of their departmental situation are examined and evaluated and the presence of others with some knowledge of the situation helps to ensure that the evaluation is thorough and serious and that any commitment will be that much stronger for having been made in public. The involvement of others in the action plan also provides sympathetic allies who can offer support, even if only at the emotional level, if and when plans are thwarted through unforeseen or inadequately assessed constraints.

This process will not guarantee that appropriate applications of course material will take place, for an examination of constraints may lead to the conclusion that they are too strong to overcome. For example, one young manager, following an in-company course on small group problem-solving and decision-making, appeared to complete his action plans in double quick time. On enquiry, he assured the trainer that he had enjoyed the course very much, that the material had been stimulating and that he had learned a great deal. But application in terms of a more participative managerial style was out of the question. In no circumstances would his boss tolerate the sharing of authority with the shop floor. The other members of his planning trio agreed entirely with him. This reaction is disappointing to a trainer yet it may be argued that it is preferable to the elaborate preparation of bogus action plans and it does demonstrate the greater degree of realism with which participants approach the task. The model legitimizes the examination of constraints and its use is likely to result in more sincere, if more modest, action planning.

OTHER USES OF THE MODEL

Even if not used to facilitate the preparation of action plans, the model seems to have uses as a conceptualization in its own right. It provides a useful antidote to the common tendency to interpret behaviour solely in terms of the personality of the actor. In this way, it encourages the manager to see behaviour, including his own, situationally and, by so doing, to become more aware of the complexity of factors influencing behaviour. This awareness increases the manager's range of options in his attempts to deal with behavioural problems when they arise. Behaviour results from the interaction of an organism with its environment and there is more chance of successfully changing the behaviour if the environment is manipulated rather than the organism. Trying to change people is seldom a sensible strategy.

So-called 'personality clashes' may similarly be reinterpreted in terms of the organizational or situational pressures to which each of the protagonists is responding. Conflict which can be depersonalized in this way permits a more objective analysis of its causes and hence a better chance of resolution or accommodation.

The model also makes it easier to understand the various phenomena of role conflict – those which the manager himself may be experiencing and those to which he may be, perhaps unwittingly, subjecting subordinates or colleagues. The strategems and subterfuges which people adopt in an attempt to cope with role conflict and which frequently prove so irritating to others may then be understood and their causes appropriately attributed (Kahn *et al.* .1964). It may be suggested that it is the rule rather than the exception for the actor to perceive conflicting expectations emanating from role senders:

> The formal organization emphasizes the importance of co-operation amongst managers (the 'management team') but the reward system appears to reward successful competition;
>
> The formal organization's procedures are seen to be time wasteful;
>
> The actor's boss has expectations which clash with the expectations of his subordinates (Roethlisberger, 1945);
>
> The actor has his own perceptions of what the job needs but his boss expects it to be done his way;
>
> The organization expects employees to work overtime and to travel frequently whilst the actor's wife, housebound with an infant family, expects him to be available to take his share of domestic responsibilities and to offer emotional support.

Finally, an inspection of the model shows immediately the limitations of training as a means to bring about behavioural change in organizations. Of the many factors influencing behaviour, only one, the person (attitudes, knowledge, skills) is available to change efforts: the other factors remain untouched. Once this is appreciated, it will not be surprising that behavioural change is difficult to accomplish and many management training officers have been reassured when they have explored the implications of the model. These are trainers who have hoped, through the medium of their courses, to bring about a gradual change in the organization in the general direction of openness and participation. The content and conduct of the training will have reflected this value orientation, and satisfaction will have been felt at the eagerness with which participants embraced the philosophy during their time in the training unit. When, however, the hoped-for transformation of organizational processes failed to occur, there is a tendency for the trainers to assume that their courses were, in some way, inadequate and to question their own professional competence. Reassurance came from the realization that their ambitions were at fault and not their professionalism. Participants may well have derived benefit from courses in ways that are not apparent to observers and the absence of dramatic behavioural change should not be taken as implying that the courses have had no value.

The model indicates, also, the circumstances in which training is an appropriate activity. When the various sources of expectation are more or less consonant but the actor is failing to produce the desired behaviour due to failures of understanding, attitude, skill or knowledge, then training would certainly seem to be suggested. However, if one seeks to change organizational behaviour by changing *roles,* success is unlikely unless attention can be directed to more than one variable. The message is the basic message of Organizational Development – the proper target for such a change effort is the organization's culture.

REFERENCES

Argyris, C. (1962). *Interpersonal Competence and Organisational Effectiveness,* Irwin.

Harrison, R. (1972). How to describe your organisation, *Harvard Business Review,* **50**, No. 3.

Jasinsky, F.J. (1956). Use and misuse of efficiency controls, *Harvard Business Review,* **34**, No. 4.

Kahn, R.L. *et al.* (1964). *Organisational Stress,* John Wiley, New York.

Pahl, J.M. and Pahl, R.E. (1971). *Managers and their Wives,* Allen Lane, The Penguin Press, London.

Reed, B. (1974). Organisational role analysis in C.L. Cooper (ed.), *Experiential Methods in Management Education,* Association of Teachers of Management.

Ridgeway, V.F. (1956). Dysfunctional consequences of performance measurement, *Administrative Science Quarterly,* **1**.

Roethlisberger, F.J. (1945). The foreman master and victim of doubletalk, *Harvard Business Review,* **23**, No. 3.

Vandenput, M.A.E. (1973). The transfer of training: some organisational variables, *Journal of European Training,* **2**, No. 3.

Advances in Management Education
Edited by John Beck and Charles Cox

CHAPTER 8

Joint Development Activities: From Practice to 'Theory'

John Morris

Some years ago, a friend of mine who is a training and development manager with a far-flung company with a household name came to visit me in the School, accompanied by a group of line managers whose faces were stamped indelibly with their experience. Their mission was to discuss a programme for which my colleagues and I might be invited to tender. They had come for lunch, and fortunately the food was excellent. My colleagues, invited to lunch to show the extent of the School's commitment, turned up in encouragingly vast numbers. The ensuing conversation was – at least from the visitors' side – at an impressively high intellectual level (the Company picks only the best graduates, leaving the rest to the Civil Service and the universities). Only one thing was wrong. The visitors had decided what they wanted, and they were clearly mistaken. They were bent on planning a 'Retreat' for their frayed and dented line managers. 'You don't need a Retreat', I thundered, maddened by their wrong-headedness in the face of reasoned argument, 'You need an Advance!' The amenities of civilized discourse were preserved. The lunch ended. My colleagues went back to their other concerns. The visitors left affably, with desultory handshakes. The household name held its 'Retreat' very successfully at another School, on many fruitful occasions, and I was left to Advance with others.

This incident came uncomfortably to mind when I pondered on the title of the conference on which this book is based 'Advances in Management Education'. Now it is my turn to retreat. Joint development activities have been reasonably strong in practice but distinctly weak in theory ever since they started under that name, in 1970. They still lack a recognizable theory, in the traditional sense of a coherent body of testable propositions, empirically grounded. I suspect that this particular defect will not be remedied. But around the activities – mainly in my mind and in a small trickle of papers over the years – can be found a few distinguishable sets of ideas. Let others, then, sound the drums and beat the trumpets for whatever advances they choose to make. For me, these notes are a firm retreat into some hard thinking about these ideas. What are they? How do they relate to joint development activities? Do they relate to one another? What is the nature of their contribution to these activities?

I refer to 'these activities' as if everyone would necessarily have heard about them. Such is the vanity of those who have placed their modest brand-label on a well-known form of educational experience. Many other labels could be used, with only slight differences of substance – project-based learning, learning by doing, and (in many ways the best generic label) action learning. The essential element in all these labels, cherished dearly by those who apply them, is that people take responsibility for learning from their own experience, under conditions which enable them to reflect on what they are doing, have done, and propose to do. If they take responsibility for the questions they raise, the answers they accept, and the actions that they take – in real life – on these answers, then labels are not important. Living questions, deeply felt and thoughtful answers, and responsible actions on those answers: if these vital conditions are met, then we should be too grateful to worry about the descriptive label that is applied to them.

But before the label 'JDA' goes out of the window, perhaps I could say a little about how it came to be used. In 1970–71, Manchester Business School was facing a move from temporary accommodation to a large new building on the University campus. Firm commitments had been made to double the volume of work. The three-month course for experienced managers was well-established and successful. There should be little difficulty in doubling its membership. But was that the best way of meeting the challenge of an increased volume of work? After much discussion, the School staff came to the view that the course should continue as before, and the extra work should be directed to developing a set of new programmes. One such programme – really an umbrella label for a diverse range of in-company activities – came to be given the collective label of Joint Development Activities.

The idea for such activities originated in a part-time, experimental programme that had been jointly set up with a subsidiary company of Rolls-Royce in 1969 and 1970. This had taken one substantial project as a development opportunity for six senior managers who needed supplementary experience to their current jobs if they were to be promoted to other parts of the parent company. The programme was jointly designed and managed by top managers from the subsidiary company and senior staff from the School. The management committee was not the kind of arm's length 'steering committee', commonly found in many projects and new activities; but a deeply interested group of people, forming an executive committee taking part in the meetings, assessing the work of the project team, providing support wherever appropriate, and acquiring funds for the work. (Morris, 1977a).

This programme was judged as very successful, by all parties, and seemed to provide a useful point of reference for new programmes. As those of us at the

School thought about its distinctive qualities, we concluded that these were three: joint management; professional development through guided experience; and an emphasis on activity and initiative on the part of the project team. Put 'joint', 'development', and 'activity' together and you have our chosen label. Over the ten or so years since the School started such activities, we have developed the concept greatly from its origins, without losing the two essential elements of a jointly designed and managed programme between School and sponsor, and the project-method as the major vehicle for learning.

'Project' in this context has always meant an activity – something new – that is both a contribution to the real work of the enterprise, and also a reference point for new thinking, feeling, and activity, from which those taking part can consciously learn. Much effort has gone into splitting work from learning in the world of education and training. The arguments for doing so have been varied and persuasive. Learning, we are told, is associated with a poor quality of performance and output during the process of learning. Let it therefore take place 'off line', so that the faults and fumbles of the tyro can be kept well away from potential clients. In this way, reputations are safeguarded, and costly materials saved. Again, it is suggested that the skills of effective work and those of helping people to learn are quite different. The best craftsman is not necessarily the best teacher. Let the craftsman take charge in the world of work, and the teacher will lead the way in the world of learning.

A little reflection reveals that these arguments apply most strongly in areas in which the materials to be learned are already known to those who are being paid for displaying their knowledge in the world of work. Where the task of learning is to establish a level of skill that is required from those at work, the split between work and learning can be sustained. But when we are presented with questions to which the answers are not yet known, and our work is to find some kind of answer that will be both effective and acceptable, then the task of working on the question and learning from the work are one and the same. And it is to this kind of learning that projects are addressed.

Joint development activities, then, are most definitely not a high-powered way of replacing routine training in established knowledge and skills. They belong to the world of unfamiliar questions and fresh answers. Their 'theory' is for this reason a quite different kind of theory from the theories – or consistent sets of principles – that relate to established fields of knowledge. It is perhaps because the 'theory' of JDA's is of this kind that John Burgoyne and his associates, in their splendidly succinct account of JDAs, place the word, as I have just done, in inverted commas: 'The underlying "theory" of JDA's is linked in with concepts of "resourceful managers" (those who act as agents rather than patients, are self-developed and self-developing) and development functions within organizations (those concerned with developing new patterns of activity, adapting existing ones, revising or coping with those that become non-viable.)' (Burgoyne, Boydell, and Pedler, 1978, p. 40).

A 'theory' of resourcefulness and development is not likely itself to be lacking in freshness and capacity for reflection and renewal. Indeed, the internal dialectic within such a 'theory' is more likely to give one a sense of diversity and even divergence than of bland coherence and unity. In these notes, I want to present and briefly discuss a number of conceptual frameworks, which have been constant associates of joint development activities. I shall dignify these frameworks by the title of 'models', though they are nothing like 'models' in engineering or in mathematics. They are loosely linked sets of ideas, rather than well-engineered components or quantitatively-related propositions. I cannot claim that these models have been shared fully with those taking part in JDAs. Indeed, if any one lesson has been learned from my work with highly intelligent managers and 'self-managing professionals' (a term I shall develop later), it is that they only use models in the technical aspects of their work. They keep models at arm's length when they are actually managing, and the more engrossing the task, the more reluctant they are to dim their vision of the realities of the current situation, in all its freshness, by straining it through a model. (I overstate, but the point is worth making).

The models have been helpful to me in sorting out my own thinking, especially when I am writing for academic colleagues. They are tenuous links with the 'disciplines relevant to business', so beloved of business-school curriculum planners. I am convinced that model-building and managerial realities are necessarily in a state of continuing tension, and the fact that I am spending nearly the whole of these notes in presenting a set of models places us in dire danger. As a prophylactic against infection, perhaps I could preface my discussion of sundry models with a statement prepared for an SSRC conference in 1977. (Morris, 1977b).

'Very little direct use was made of social-science research in joint development activities. . . . The provisional conclusion is reached that much social science research aims to be general, rigorous, quantitative, logical, replicable, and cumulative; while managers find their practical experience confirmed by project work, to be specific, relevant, qualitative, historical, dramatic, and serial. Social science in its conventional form hungers after data-based algorithms; managers use multi-level heuristics based on the critical events of their personal experience.' The notes went on to examine some of the approaches which seemed to make most sense to the managers taking part in an extended JDA in a medium-sized manufacturing company.

'Consideration of the approaches . . . reveals that they have the following characteristics:

- they are narrative, or 'historical' in form – they represent events in sequence, with some attempts at showing sources of influence
- they focus on the nature of people's work, and changes in the organization of the company
- they attempt to form practical notions of the nature of the relevant business environment, and some of the likely future influences on their company and its products

- they are interested in company policy, and the reasons for its taking a particular form
- they are interested in the values, assumptions, and priorities of the participants in the JDA, and the relevance of these to company operations
- they have a strong sense of company 'personalities' and their distinctive influence on company decisions and operations
- they have a highly developed sense of contingency and complexity in company affairs, and are especially aware of the difficulty of interpreting the business environment
- they are eager to use the project work to exercise some personal and group influence on the conduct of company affairs. But they recognize the 'political' problems of exercizing such influence effectively.

In short, the orientation of the work is strongly company-centred, purposive, and personal. It is also strongly realistic: fitting into no one "school" of social science thinking, except perhaps the pragmatic/ecletic.'

(Morris, 1977(b), pp. 4–5).

It is with this kind of experience in mind, and it has been typical of experience in joint development activities, that I seek to review some of the models that seem of particular interest.

SOME MODELS RELATED TO JOINT DEVELOPMENT ACTIVITIES

I have chosen six models that have provided useful orientations to the distinctive kinds of work and learning fostered in joint development activities. I have picked six, out of a much larger number, because a limited number of models of rather different kinds serves the purpose of sharpening the issues of theory and practice that seem most relevant. More than six models would have led to incoherence, and fewer than six would have given a misleading impression of a possible 'fit' between activities and models that might suggest a 'master model' in view. This would have been the precise opposite of my intention, which is to suggest that the possible outcome of 'learning by doing' is to gain a growing sense of one's self as a whole part of a universe of experience, relating to other whole parts – each whole part a person who is a unique sampling of universal experience. Such a vision of life certainly leaves one with a sense of unity – of personal integrity (which enables us to say 'I' or recognize another as an 'I'). But it most certainly does not suggest that a formal, explicit representation – a 'model' – can do more than help us to focus on a particular issue chosen for attention and action at a particular time.

The First Model: Three Contrasting Stages, and a Need to Bring them Together

Figure 1 shows the model in a relatively recent form (Morris, 1975). I developed it step-by-step from a set of earlier ideas, all of which focused on the managerial

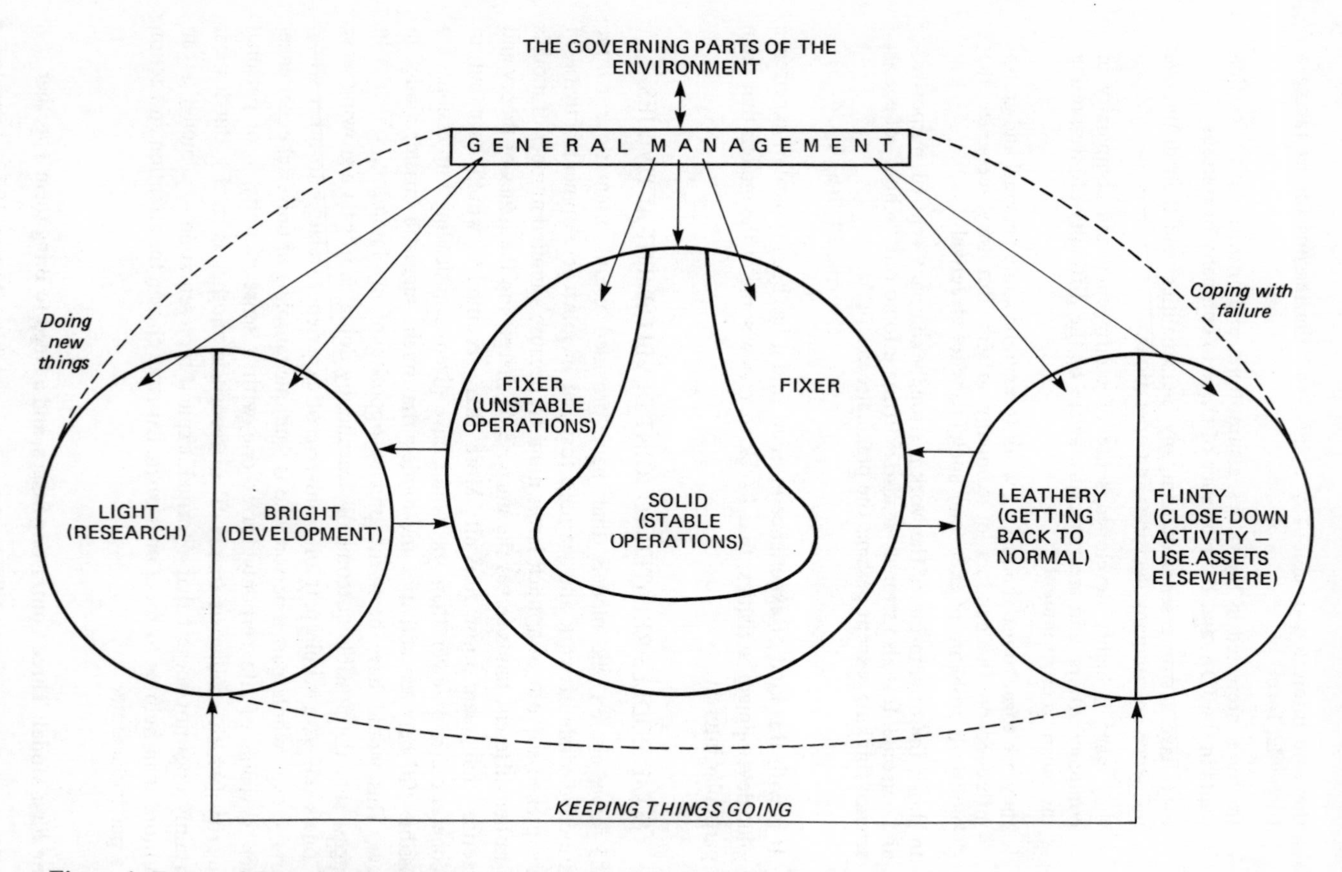

Figure 1. Types of Organizational Activities and related Types of Management

differences between 'keeping things going' to a familiar pattern and managing discontinuities. The two main forms of discontinuity that I found interesting were (and are) 'opportunities' and 'problems'; which I translated into 'doing new things' and 'coping with breakdown and failure'.

The model shown in Figure 1 is suspiciously neat and tidy. 'Keeping things going' sits quietly in the middle, with opportunities and problems looking as if some hidden hand is ready to balance them, one on either side. And to take orderliness even further, I popped two contrasting stereotypes into each of the three types of activity: light, bright, leathery, flinty, solid, and fixer. I have chosen the 1975 version, rather than some more complex later modifications, to bring out an important aspect of the models as I have used them. They have been dramatic devices – means of condensing some key ideas into a readily communicable pattern, so that experienced practitioners can quickly see the 'logic' and relate the model as a set of practical ideas to their own distinctive experience. Obviously, if experienced managers had looked blank when shown the model, and had quickly changed the topic of conversation, the model would have disappeared from view. But it served as a useful communication link, and enabled managers to discuss the ways in which their own enterprises handled the three forms of activity, and – most important – how the activities are brought together. In the model I have usually called the integrative function by the homely label 'pulling things together'; but with more cognitively-oriented managers I have turned this into 'putting things together'. As we move into the participative mode of senior management, both phrases are often replaced by 'bringing people and things together'.

Many managers comment on the implications of placing 'doing new things' and 'coping with failure' on opposite sides of the 'steady-state' activity of keeping things going. Many of their enterprises make such a contrast, but managers with experience of discontinuity observe that success and failure, opportunities and problems are often closely intertwined. The more risky and uncertain the new venture, the more likely it is that the solid ground of 'keeping things going' will be missing or far-distant, and events will be hard to identify with any great confidence as successes or failures. When such points are made, the model has served its purpose, and can be modified to match the appropriate shape of the managers' experience, and the implications of making the change can also be examined.

I have recently given more emphasis than before to the evaluative aspects of the activities depicted in the model, and have dramatized these in turn as 'Good News', 'Bad News', and 'No News'. Those who spend their days engaged in skilled and effortful activities can be disturbed to find that their orderly and productive activities are taken for granted by senior management as 'No News' – the non-exception that Management-by-Exception does not have to do anything about. The trouble-shooting manager finds that his mixed feelings are justified: he is trying to turn bad news into good news, or perhaps less ambitiously into no news. But the cost of his 'good news' can be bad news for many others.

Managers working with the model quickly note that it can be readily shifted from one scale of enterprise to another. The level of analysis can move within a particular enterprise from an individual job to a work team to a profit centre to the whole enterprise. This adaptability is a feature of 'general systems models', and will be found in all the other models discussed in these notes. It has been most explicitly recognized in the work of Stafford Beer, but before discussing this, I would like to bring in a further model which neatly supplements the first (Harrison, 1972).

The Second Model: Harrison's Four Ideologies

A simple but penetrating model that has been widely used in organizational consultancy is Roger Harrison's study of four 'ideologies' commonly found in organizations. Harrison delineates these ideologies and their related 'orientations' very richly and persuasively, and a brief outline scarcely does them justice. But, using his own words as far as possible, they are (i) *power orientation* – such an organization 'attempts to dominate its environment and vanquish all opposition'. Within the organization, 'the law of the jungle often seems to prevail among executives as they struggle for personal advantage against their peers'. Sometimes, one finds a milder form of the power orientation, in the form of paternalism, but 'when the benevolent authority is crossed or challenged . . . the iron fist is very likely to appear again'. (ii) *role orientation* – 'in contrast to the wilful autocracy of the power-orientated organization, there is a preoccupation with legality, legitimacy, and responsibility'. The role orientation often appears in reaction to the power orientation. Legally-controlled or monopolistic organizations often display a role orientation. (iii) *task orientation* – 'achievement of a superordinate goal is the highest value'. Organizations characterized by this ideology often struggle to survive and flourish in complex environments, but use knowledge and skill as their chosen instruments of effectiveness rather than power. Small, market-oriented enterprises often have a high task orientation. In larger enterprises, there are often specially-designed 'task forces' or 'project teams' to deal rapidly and effectively with specific tasks. (iv) *person orientation* – 'unlike the other three types, the person-oriented organization exists primarily to serve the needs of its members'. Such organizations often have a very short life; since they have no rationale when they cease to meet the requirements of their members. Despite problems of structure and coherence, 'there seem to be increasing pressures from the members of modern industrial organizations to move towards person orientation'.

Charles Handy, in his well-known study of organizational theory and practice (Handy, 1976) has an interesting attempt to relate Harrison's ideologies and orientations (which Handy prefers to call 'cultures') to the first model that I have discussed. In this attempt, 'doing new things' is seen as a task culture; 'keeping things going' a role culture; and 'coping with breakdown and failure' is seen as a power culture. The overall integrative function, performed by top management, is also seen as a power culture.

My own impression is that the top-management 'culture' is a shifting combination of all four orientations – powers, role, task, and person. The top team often deals with the problems of achieving an effective mix by crystallizing the distinctive qualities of each culture into some powerful individual. The team then has the task of balancing the diverse and even contradictory qualities of these individuals – each a one-person 'pure culture'. The person at the top is usually the most complex and diverse person in the team. One could hardly call this continual 'balancing act' a person culture. Perhaps a better label for it would be a 'personality orientation' or even a 'personage orientation'. One could then see the claims to distinctive qualities of personality slowly growing as one moves from the bottom to the top of an organization. At the bottom the 'non-persons', then the specialized task-persons, power-persons, and role-persons. Finally, full-fledged personalities (names displayed on their office doors, and other insignia of Having Arrived). And, topping it all, the Personage Himself (or even Herself, if current trends are to continue).

A further variant of the Harrison model is a pairing of cultures into readily recognizable combinations. First, the power-and-role organization, which has people doing the programmed work at the lower levels, displaying all the qualities of a role cultures, and at the senior management level, the 'manual over-ride' of powerful people. Second, the task-and-person organization is in strong contrast to the power-and-role organization. It is the distinctive style of the small, project-based enterprise which has yet suffered no major setbacks, and does its 'trouble-shooting' with a task approach rather than a power approach.

I find that my strong inclination is towards the task-and-person type of organization. The pattern of joint development activities that I have described, with its temporary projects and close association between self-managing professionals, has therefore been very congenial. But by the same token the combined culture of the task-and-person enterprise has seemed very strange to both the power-people and the role-people in long-established organizations of the type that abound in the British economy.

At a recent seminar run for the senior management of the Leyland Components Group, I was greatly interested when Colin Selby, their OD Manager, in a radically simplified presentation of managerial style, brought together Harrison's four cultures and the four quadrants (not corners) of the Blake Managerial Grid – 'low task and people' then became the role culture, and was designated as stagnant bureaucracy; 'high task and people' became task culture; 'high task/low concern for people' became power culture; and low task/high concern for people' was seen as person culture. I found this a neat and thought-provoking first approximation.

What do these two models – which we may think of as the four organizational modes and the four organizational cultures – have to offer our work in joint development activities? In my view, they have a lot to offer. They are simple yet comprehensive. They firmly place these activities in the development segment of enterprises, and, on the whole, in the task culture, though I would now amplify both these comments and argue that I increasingly see JDAs as helping resourceful managers to see how development *relates* to the overall concerns of the enterprise, rather than merely occupying a detachable specialized segment called 'corporate planning' or 'R-and-D' or 'OD' – all of which can be axed by the power culture when the market turns down, and the going gets rough. It is characteristic of the fragmented, mechanistic thinking of our times that we could place 'development' in a specialized box of its own, and expect it to permeate the culture and activities of the whole enterprise of which it is an integral part. Alas, the mistake is not merely conceptual: it has been expensively built-in to the most sophisticated enterprise, with a fearful loss of effectiveness as a result.

As to the Harrison model, my comment is that JDAs are affected by all four cultures, though a firm hold of the task is absolutely vital. As stated, the hybrid culture of task-and-person seems to come closest; with a strong awareness, however, that implementation of what has been achieved in the project work has to work through both 'power' and 'role'. The continuing emphasis on all four roles suggests that the JDA work is close in spirit to the level of challenge presented to top managers. Although ostensibly one is concerned with only part of the task of the enterprise, in order to be effective, one has to encounter all of the others. It was this thought that provoked me in the paper already mentioned (Morris, 1975) to delineate two contrasting stereotypes of managerial styles in each of the three differentiated parts of an organization, with the 'light' and the 'bright' doing new things, the 'solid' and the 'fixers' keeping things doing, and the 'leathery' and the 'flinty' coping with breakdown and failure. I then suggested that JDAs are an excellent way of using practical opportunities in the enterprise to develop resourceful managers who would be 'bright, leathery fixers'! Needless to say, it did not take a great deal of reflection on the implications of this combination of crudities to encourage me to refine the model. The only characteristic to survive is 'bright'.

A Third Model: the Viable System

The 'viable system' approach that seems most relevant to JDAs is that of Stafford Beer. Stafford has been visiting professor at the School since 1970. In 1971 he produced a fascinating report on how the School might be organized in order to achieve its chosen tasks. I played a fairly central part on the working parties that met in the School from the Autumn of 1970 to the following summer, and this activity coincided with the early work of JDAs. Stafford's report suggested a set of action-research activities, with small project teams working on complex real-world issues. They would use their work as a living link between practitioners and research workers. As I think about the profoundly creative work of Stafford Beer, I am struck by its close affinity with that of Reg Revans, although they have worked along independent lines. Both of them have taken activities that are usually mundane, even dull, and made them sparkle. Stafford is often stereotyped as a technocrat, deep in a mysterious computer-based branch of applied science called cybernetics. By a similar process of stereotyping, Reg is often seen as over-committed to Action, at the expense of sensible Planning and Programming. Such stereotypes miss the point of their work completely: they are both intensely practical people, with an equal commitment to helping people improve their effectiveness and to adding to the fund of useful knowledge, intelligently arranged.

I shall come to Reg Revan's work in action learning a little later. At this point it may be useful to give an outline of Stafford's thinking on 'viable systems'. A viable system is quite simply one that can be recognized by an observer as a system, which survives over time in its environment. It does this by adapting itself in detail to those parts of the environment which it needs for its requirements, and linking these parts into a reasonably balanced whole. Not only is it engaged with its present environment, it is also picking up messages about likely changes in vital parts of that environment. It uses this information to plan ways of responding effectively to those changes. If one separates out the distinguishable functions, argues Stafford, they come to five. No less and certainly no more than five. How can he be this confident? Because his analysis shows that these five functions together create the necessary and sufficient conditions of viability. What is more, they can be readily discerned as the essential operating-characteristics of actual systems. The parts of the system that are specialized to meet system requirements are together called 'System 1': they are the basic operating units of the system. 'System 2' co-ordinates these in such a way that they do not trip over one another, and compete destructively with one another. 'System 3' adds to this form of co-ordination an ability to make rapid adaptations to the parts in the interests of overall survival. These three systems are rather well recognized in common-sense thinking about systems such as animals, and systems such as enterprises, or armies, or nations. Stafford adds to these three layers of the viable system another two. 'System 4' is a set of relationships with the internal and external environment, picking up messages about likely change, and preparing possible ways of coping with these. Since 'System 3' is concerned with current urgent needs, and 'System 4' with possible contingencies, they work on different assumptions and with different time-scales. So an overall adaptive system, balancing the needs of the two systems, must exist. This is 'System 5' – the top-management, as it were, of the whole system (Beer, 1970, 1972).

Our conscious thinking about systems, in the modern world, tends to be intensely practical. We feel that we should start with the 'facts'. We expect these to differ greatly from one type of system to another, depending on size, complexity, and purposes. There seems something unacceptably arbitrary about five levels – no more and no less, each with a designated function, if a system is to be viable. Stafford would argue – and very persuasively does so in the studies cited – that the specific *contents* of each of the five systems will vary greatly depending on the nature of the system of which they are parts. Furthermore, the relationships between these systems will also vary. In some cases, they will share common resources, though they will be functionally distinguished. They may be clearly recognized as what they are: or they may work effectively, as a by-product of their main task. In short, differences abound. It is only the five basic functions that remain consistent: because these are logical and practical necessities for the survival of the system in a complex and changing environment.

When we applied this model to the Manchester Business School, Stafford noted that for a fairly small School, a large and complex work-load of programmes was being sustained. There was little in the way of an effective System 2, although it was the proud boast of many senior staff members that they were valued resources on each programme in the School. Furthermore, System 4 was not recognized as a collective need on the part of the School, only as a personal interest on the part of long-sighted individuals and small groups. System 5 existed reasonably clearly, but did not perform its necessary task of balancing Systems 3 and 4, both of which were distinctly fuzzy. A key proposal of the report was that 'System 1' should focus on action-research project groups, working on significant organizational issues.

I will not go into the details of the year-long response to Stafford's report: in the form of five part-time working parties studying the report in detail. I will merely note that I saw the JDAs – as individual 'activities' and as a loosely-related 'programme' – as very close in spirit to Stafford's envisaged action-research teams. A major difference was that the staff members working with the project groups were not primarily committed to the research mode: they were more interested in teaching, and learning-consultancy. It has been argued (Revans, 1980) that research, teaching, consultancy, and counselling have the same underlying structure, when they are stripped of their normal protective covering and seen in their essence. I can follow this argument a long way. But an important difference is that the research approach works painstakingly with a body of published information, sets up formal propositions, and seeks to test them in detailed records and comparisons. Our JDA work did not follow this pattern. The activities took off, instead, from a particular state of affairs within each enterprise, set out what seemed agreed to be an improved state of affairs, and made detailed proposals on how to move from one to the other. The reports, which in the research model are the focus of the activity, were only one aspect of a complicated set of activities and relationships.

I remember a blinding glimpse of the obvious when I was talking with some colleagues in the School about the research implications of the JDA reports. As I thought about them, it became glaringly apparent that these reoprts were intensely political documents, intended to present arguments that would persuade senior people in one's own entreprise of the truth of a set of propositions and the value of particular recommendations. These were documents committed to advocacy, within a culture that assumed certain things to be self-evident, and others to be agreed to be desirable. Research papers also assume a culture, but it is the culture of the particular branch of the research discipline, basing its arguments on evidence gathered by certain agreed procedures, and within a framework of assumptions and achievements indicative of 'the state of the art'. If one stood back a step or two, and looked at the JDA reports and the research papers under such headings as 'statement of an issue', 'statement of starting point of the investigation', 'use of accepted techniques of investigation', 'statement of findings', and 'analysis of implications of findings' – one would find close similarities between the two kinds of materials.

The differences were in the nature of the intended audience, the particularity of the investigation, and the sense of the 'object of the exercise'.

The differences are obvious when we look at the basic form of a joint development activity: it is focused on a specific issue rather than a general class of issue: on the use of any means for getting a grip on the issue, rather than on agreed techniques established within the research discipline. The joint development activities were intended to provide opportunities for experienced managers to learn with and from one another, rather than to make a cumulative contribution to a discipline. With these differences, it may be the similarities that are surprising. And indeed, I must ask myself whether the similarities have grown naturally out of the work of JDAs, or have been the result of the well-meaning contributions of the School staff, in the consulting role. I must confess to feeling occasionally acutely uncomfortable when one has seen an ill-digested gobbet of 'research' within the easy flow of a report aimed at senior managers. One senses that the gobbet is thrown in to appease the academics: and the resultant sense of strong difference makes one almost despair.

These comments are the result of thinking about differences between JDA reports and conventional research papers. They were inspired by reflection on whether the JDAs have grown from Stafford's ideas of project work as 'action-research' or from a different tradition. I conclude that the projects are not at any point really envisaged as research projects, but as business development projects, with all the differences of audience, time-scale, and methods that this distinction implies.

One of the important implications of the Beer approach is that a 'systems theory' can be applied wherever one has identified a system. One can trace systems at different levels of generality – with viable systems containing viable systems, and in turn being contained by viable systems even more comprehensive than themselves. As one thinks about the implications of systems 'nesting' within systems, it becomes clear that the most flexible and potentially productive 'viable system' of all is the resourceful person. Stafford deliberately models his five-level viable system model on the nervous system of the individual human being, for just this reason. If one asks what form of work a resourceful person would be likely to choose, it would be a creative, unique activity in which there would be full opportunity for all one's energies and talents to find useful employment; in short, some form of self-managed project. One certainly could not claim that the projects thrown up by successive management groups on JDAs met these demanding criteria, unfortunately, but they all had something to offer.

Fourth Model: Design, Negotiation, and Trust

It was no accident that the enterprises associated with the early JDAs were those which had long-established relationships with the School, and were able to work with us on a basis of trust. Without such trust, the JDAs would not have got very far. The precedents for such activities were few – Reg Revan's work in Belgium being little known at the time. The School had begun to use projects in its educational work, but most of these were located in the School, in close proximity to other educational methods that were familiar and reassuring, such as cases, syndicate discussion, exercises, and business games. Most of the School projects were short, and firmly under the direction of senior members of staff. The JDA projects were all drawn from the real life of the client enterprise, and not part of a well-designed training programme, but the core of the activity itself.

The fourth model is sensitive to such issues. Briefly, it consists of three concepts which can be inter-related in a reasonably coherent framework for the analysis of basic approaches in training and education programmes. 'Design' refers to all those approaches in which the learning to be achieved is clearly related to a clearly defined set of activities, for which one can discern a 'programme'. If a School staff member is asked to 'design' a course, he will assume that the design should include such matters as the aims and objectives of the course, the intended participants, the duration, and so on.

What does 'design' mean in this context? It means setting out explicitly the boundaries of the activity in space and time: that is, providing the programme. Since people often think of a 'design' as a visual display of something in space, perhaps 'programme' is a better term. But 'design' catches very well the notion of a purposive choice of this element or that, and a consequent 'shape' to the activity that can not only be precisely stated, but somehow justified. A 'design' in this sense certainly presupposes one or more 'designers'. And these designers have, by implication, set up their design to achieve a particular purpose, using particular resources.

At the other end of the scale from a carefully set-out 'design', we trust that a *relationship* will somehow find whatever resources are needed to meet a need as it arises. The sense in which 'trust' is being used here is of an implicit, human relationship which takes things as they arise, in contrast with a controlled use of resources to meet a purpose through the medium of a design. The use of design establishes something 'out there' in the world – the design. With trust, there is only strong feeling as the binding element. It is jointly 'in here' rather than aesthetically or technically 'out there'.

I use the two terms in juxtaposition because I am aware that the early JDAs were able to offer little in the way of a justifiable design: they were the outcome of a set of relationships based on trust. In between design and trust, one finds – very appropriately (because its very nature is to mediate) – the concept of 'negotiation'. If we establish a relationship of trust with others, we can then work alongside them at whatever turns up, without having to transform our relationship into a clear-cut design or programme that serves as a guarantee of how things are going to turn out. If we are not sure of someone, we can bind them to a design. In between the two extreme conditions, we can negotiate with them as to what is to happen. I have noticed in my work in management development that if one is close to the state of mutual trust, negotiation is broad-brush and genial, leaving the details of what has been negotiated to be worked out as circumstances make it appropriate. But if one is at the design end of the spectrum, the negotiation tends to be formal and detailed, leading to written statements in legal form.

Thus, one could speak of trust-based negotiation, which aspires after the condition of a gentleman's agreement, and design-based negotiation, which always seeks formal commitment on details. (It seems no accident that 'designing' and 'calculating' are applied to people that we do not feel we can trust!)

I hit upon this three-concept model when I was considering some of the problems of staffing our project-based in-company activities. My first thought was that some colleagues pride themselves on professing rigorous, often quantifiable disciplines that must be taught in a certain cumulative sequence. The emphasis is on the word 'taught'. Not for these colleagues the idea of working alongside an experienced practitioner to help him comprehend the latent structure of his existing judgements and experiences. They would be inclined to consider the practitioner as being at least as ill-informed as their most inexperienced students, straight from school or a first-degree. (Or perhaps even more so, since the practitioner might feel that his experience was of some value!) This approach to learning through systematic teaching I saw as the 'design' approach, and it seemed to lend itself well to those disciplines of a strong physical and scientific bent. I came to the conclusion: 'If you have to deal with things and physical processes, you can *design* them!'

In striking contrast with the insistence on linear paths of teaching and learning were those colleagues, like myself, who felt that they were the happy, but occasionally rather defensive, exponents of arts that people had acquired in many ways – the arts of making effective judgements under tight constraints of time, the art of getting on in a variety of relationships with their fellow human beings, and – not least – the art of understanding what could be achieved in complex and changing circumstances – the 'art of the possible'. All these arts have been learned, few have been systematically taught. Having been learned, they can often be further improved. And there is clearly an art in fostering artistic skills. Practitioners of this secondary art are called guides, philosophers, friends, mentors, rather than instructors or teachers. The sense that one had of one's range of knowledge and skills was of a widely ramified and incomplete network, or loose set of networks, rather than of a systematic body of knowledge with a clearly defined anatomy.

'Design', in the usual educational sense of a curriculum and a well-defined syllabus seemed inappropriate when one started with such 'subjects'. So mutual trust seemed to be the place to start. What, then, of the place of 'negotiation'? Well, fortunate is the manager who can find a way of working with others in which trust alone is the relevant characteristic. Organizations – as differentiated systems – often put people on opposite sides of a fine line, without anyone intending to do so. Organizations start with decisions to draw a distinction between one skill and another, one form of resource and another, and these distinctions become firmly established and even become ways of life – careers and professions. The manager inherits much of this specialization – and it breeds mistrust among those who are on the same side of the fine line – are brothers and sisters of the same cloth, the same set of skills and interests. The manager who cannot work on a basis of brotherly or sisterly trust will often have to negotiate. One hopes that the negotiation will always respect the importance of trust, and not take the form of force, fraud, and fear.

In subject-teaching terms, we often limit our thinking about negotiation to the two well-established forms of industrial relations and commercial negotiation. Apart from the lamentable tendency to keep these well apart, since they work through different institutions and one is seen as being on the cost side and the other on the revenue side, there is a much greater pervasiveness to negotiation than in these two fields. The flourishing theme of 'role negotiation' bears witness to this, and there is also widespread popular interest in political negotiations of every kind. Slowly, we are coming to see that the common factor in all negotiations is that of reaching agreement under difficult circumstances: again, we are helped by the origins of the word 'negotiate', which means 'not easy'!

The model helps us to understand the difficulties encountered by many managers in dealing with joint development activities. They are used to thinking about all forms of education and training as straightforward matters of design, conducted by appropriate specialists. This way of thinking has the advantage of making the complex processes of individual learning sound reassuringly like commercial products. By extension, the people being brought into the courses of learning (typically thought of as courses of 'instruction') are themselves products to be processed, as many of the metaphors about training suggest. Not surprisingly, training-specialists have played into this habit of thinking, and have chosen approaches that confirm the notion that they are indeed experts in design, taking all worries about learning away from the harassed line manager, and placing them in a well-insulated protected situation – the training centre. The only way left, in the terms of the model, for thinking about joint development activities is of an act of faith that is too strong to be really businesslike.

I would now want to *combine* elements of negotiation, design, and trust into effective forms of management development activity. Trust in the competence of the joint development staff consultant can be fostered by engaging in short, well-designed workshops in which a management group can work together at understanding what is really happening. Experience of working as a member of a management committee plays a large part in enabling experienced managers to see that learning is not always a simple contrast between uncontrolled, 'on the job' learning and the trainer-controlled well-defined learning of the typical training course. In the middle ground there are powerful forms of experience in which novelty plays such a large part that constant awareness of what is going on is not merely a luxury, but a basic necessity. This combination of work and learning can only be 'managed' if it is continuously monitored, by a management group.

A combination of design, negotiation, and trust along these lines can serve to foster trust, and negotiation is then concerned with working intelligently to share responsibility for learning between participants, sponsors, and staff consultants. The fruits of such endeavours are in mutual trust in the possibilities of learning from one's work opportunities and problems.

Fifth Model: Kolb and Styles of Learning

As I set down these notes, at a higher and more critical level of awareness than is common to my work on joint developments, I am surprised by the lack of an explicit model of learning among my sources of influence. The four models discussed so far are (i) a model of modes of organized activity; (ii) of organizational 'cultures'; (iii) of viable systems in complex environments; and (iv) of positive ways of relating to people and things in order to express diverse interests. The word 'learning' has popped up again and again, but as though it were itself problem-free. In a sense, this describes my normal way of thinking about 'learning', which seems such a normal everyday activity that I find it difficult to enclose it in a model. In contrast, the other models refer to modes of organized activity, in which I want to locate my own preferred activity in constructive relationship with another activity. Thus, the contrasts between 'doing new things' and 'keeping things going' which I have found continuously helpful in those numerous enterprises which appear to be single-mindedly committed to 'keeping things going' over and over and over again. On the same grounds, I have found it helpful to contrast opportunities with problems, though I recognize that each has its valued place in human affairs. It just so happens that one cannot have such unalloyed delight in working on a problem (because there is always the question of why it was allowed to develop in the first place) as one has in finding and taking up an opportunity.

This point seems germane to a model that I have only begun to use fairly recently – David Kolb's four-phase learning cycle, succinctly described in a volume devoted to 'Theories of Group Processes' (Cooper, 1975). It starts with a strongly felt experience. Such an experience provides an opportunity to gain some understanding of it by reflective observation, checking one's own feelings with those of others.

This may be followed by an attempt to relate this experience with some general principles – the 'theorize' about it. Having theorized, one may wish to test out one's enhanced understanding by fresh experience. This can be engaged in consciously – as an experiment in experience. At this point, the fresh experience can lead to further reflection and observation and the cycle begins again. But this is not a closed circle of repeated experience, so much as an expanding spiral of enlarged experience at a level of heightened awareness.

These four phases, covering active experiment and reflective observation, theory and experience can be seen as elements in all continuing processes of learning. Sadly, Kolb's investigations show that many people do not feel free to cycle continuously through all four phases, but shuttle between pairs of learning phases. These become established, customary ways of learning. For example, the 'accommodative' style of learning works between the experiment and the experience; while the strongly contrasting 'assimilative' style works between reflective observation and theorizing. Two more styles are 'converging', which combines theorizing and experiment, and 'diverging', which combines concrete experience with reflective observation.

If one stays with these limited styles, it is clear that joint development activities, unlike sensitivity-training, which uses a diverger style, are more focused on an 'accommodative' style. This is one reason why a theory has been so slow in coming along! But if we look closely at Kolb's model one can see that, despite all this talk about styles, it still shows clear signs of its origins as a learning theory derived from responses to sensitivity-training. In its 'full-fledged' form, taking all four phases into account, it starts with a strongly emotional experience, and moves up to a conceptual model from this point. But if one starts with a different kind of learning activity – the phases of the model subtly change. Instead of theory and experience being at opposed poles, separated by reflection and experiment, one finds a continuous process of planning, programming, monitoring, and reviewing novel action. Awareness and action are closely intertwined. 'Theory' in the sense of a set of formal propositions, which may take years to test formally, is of course seen for the frigid thing it is – a long-drawn-out travesty of clear thinking. The phase of 'activity' is not a strongly emotional experience, of the kind that happens in sensitivity-training, in which trainers pull the rug from under people by refusing to meet their conventional social expectations, and thereby precipitate a rash of reflective observations. The activities are those of agents, not patients, and are related to achieving an interesting task – an opportunity – rather than recovering from unpleasant feelings.

The labels given to the phases in the Kolb model are at a high level of abstraction and so these differences are not clearly reflected in the Kolb labels – which are 'concrete experience', 'reflective observation', 'abstract conceptualization', and 'active experimentation'. The labels I would propose are 'project planning', 'active achievement', 'reviewing progress/setbacks', and 'interpreting activities'.

Re-interpreted in this way, the phases can move together in a continuous spiral of learning. But as I look back on my experiences of joint development activities, I am aware that they have emphasized the project planning and active achievement phases relatively more than the interpretation (theorizing) and reflective (reviewing) phases. I think that this has been in part a conscious reaction on the part of the School staff and the sponsors against the limitations of the University-based management programme in generalized analysis and formal modelling of situations.

An uncomfortable aspect of sitting down to think through the lack of theorizing in these development activities has been the element of over-compensation. No one sees more clearly the limitations of the analytic/reflective approach than a career academic like myself. And when, after years of noting the gross mismatch between formal analysis and the distinctive skills needed for project work one is given the chance of working with project teams as a consultant, then one finds many promising babies being hurled out ruthlessly with the dirty bathwater.

All of these experiences of over-reaction are themselves grist to the learning-model. Unfortunately, they remind one of the strength of the forces blocking free movement from one phase to another.

Sixth Model: More than a Model, More a Way of Life

My section-heading, referring to action learning, is an affectionate reminder of the collection of pieces on action learning at GEC. It is called 'More than Management Development' (Casey and Pearce, 1977). I have always recognized that action learning, especially in the form made famous by Reg Revans, is a powerful way of putting models through their paces, not so much through formal testing as by having to show their usefulness to practitioners as they struggle with painful and intractable problems of high importance to them (Revans, 1980).

Joint development activities have often stopped at the diagnostic phase of project work, leaving the business of implementation to the existing operational resources of the enterprise. This is not very satisfactory, though the project teams are themselves members of the enterprise in which the project work takes place, and have a strong sense of organizational politics. While JDAs are undoubtedly in the spirit of action learning, they still have a long way to go before they raise the level of awareness of the whole enterprise of which they are a part. Because, when all has been said and done about the different models and their implications for JDAs, the main task is always to stand firm against the two enemies of conscious and responsible action – Repetition and Randomness. Repetition lulls us into a sense of false security, believing that the more things change the more they remain the same – there is nothing new under the sun. Out of repeated activities – such as personal habits or collective custom – we build an illusory world, deceived by its air of familiarity. Sooner or later (and nowadays sooner rather than later) the solid crust crumbles, leaving us helpless in what seems to be an abyss. Randomness – blind chance – convinces us that the world is meaningless, and that in a meaningless world, any action – or lack of action – is as appropriate as any other. No light is needed when we spin a coin, and do not care which side is uppermost.

As one reflects on this key function of the models – of keeping the level of awareness raised – the question can be asked: Does one model achieve this function better than the others?

Models, Mandalas, and Metaphors

There is a point in the development of some models at which they seem to become fully articulate, and fit a given reality so closely that they provide the means of generating it. Such models have then become virtually interchangeable with that reality. There is no longer any mystery remaining: the reality has become completely open to understanding, completely comprehensible and controllable. Examples of such relationships between a model and its reality are a blueprint and the machine that it delineates; a formula and the process that it controls; a technique and the product that it produces; a prototype and the flow of goods that it foreshadows.

For many practical people, such achievements are an indication that the model 'works'. A model that does not seem to have the degree of elaboration that suggests its point-to-point correspondence with a particular reality is then seen to be lacking in conviction, is 'airy-fairy', thin, or (the ultimate term of abuse) 'academic'. Yet there is a dilemma here. The successful model – once it has been achieved – naturally is put to work in routinely keeping things going, and becomes 'No News'. It is taken for granted. This line of reasoning suggests that the kind of model that best serves the raising of awareness is that which presents a continuing tension with the reality to which it relates. Clearly, a 'routine reality' – the kind of reality that is readily controlled by technique or formula – is ill-served by such a model. But a flow of real life – rich with diversity and fresh with individuality – is best appreciated by a model in the sense discussed here. Such a model will never claim to reproduce or control its appropriate reality. It focuses the attention of a person, or a set of persons, upon some aspect of reality, and serves to reveal it to the appreciative or active eye.

The kind of models that we have been discussing are closer to what Schumacher (1977), in his thought-provoking last book, calls a 'guide to the perplexed'. Schumacher talks of philosophical maps, and in a related sense, I would wish to speak of models for focusing attention, preparatory to appropriate action. Not habitual or customary *responses* to familiar beliefs as to what a situation might be, or might require. Far from it: fresh seeing, fresh feeling, and a fresh answer to the unique question that has been perceived.

It seems no accident that the models that are close to such fresh, personally significant questions and answers are not detailed, factually-based 'maps' in the form of blueprints. They are rather more like the strip maps provided for drivers urgently wishing to reach a destination than the richly detailed maps provided for the leisurely holiday-maker wishing to savour the countryside, or the bed-ridden patient who wants a substitute for the reality of which he is currently deprived.

Some models do not even set out to provide a dramatic indication of how to move in the right direction (the Blake grid, for example). They provide a framework for contemplation, in the light of intuitively perceived situations. As I see it, the models that have been discussed here are mandalas for clear thinking, deep feeling, and right action.

The relation of mandala to model is that between the essential structure of experience – the invariants in our lives – and the adaptation of this structure to circumstances. The most effective models, of the kind discussed in these notes, stay firmly in the middle ground between detailed mapping of a specific situation (though they are powerful guides in such a process) and an invariant so deeply rooted that one cannot easily see how it can be generalized to greater durability. A model can be incrementally developed until it matches one unique circumstance (the kind of 'working model' familiar to lovers of Heath Robinson or Emmett). But a mandala can only be complicated in a symbolic sense, if it is not to lose its capacity for focusing our attention on the essential values in our situation. I speak assertively here, but hasten to add that it is the assertiveness of inexperience. The relationships between models, mandalas, and metaphors have only come clearly to my attention in the process of writing these notes, and I am still fumbling.

By a process of spiralling, and moving from complexity to essential simplicity, I come to metaphors. In 1973 John Burgoyne and I went through the movement from models to metaphors in the other direction (Morris and Burgoyne, 1973). We started with the metaphors that practising managers and management development specialists commonly use when talking about both management and the development of management. We found that six metaphors were constantly appearing, in writings about these topics and in casual conversation. These were (a) building (laying the foundations for a career in management: the top manager is the keystone in the organizational arch); (b) engineering (interfaces, modules, components, structures); (c) agriculture (seedcorn, preparing the ground, cutting out deadwood); (d) zoology (getting the right kind of animal; proper breeding; managers born and not made; organizational jungle); (e) medicine (diagnosis, therapy, prognosis, company doctor); and (f) military (strategy, tactics, logistics, mission, task force, victory, defeat, campaign, line, staff). We also noted, but did not discuss, metaphors derived from family and community.

When the metaphors are grouped in the above order, one can discern an underlying pattern. The metaphors at the beginning of the list assume a fixed order – a structure. Managers are weight-carriers, durable and indispensable elements in a fixed structure. Such elements do not easily change their shape. But as one goes through the list, the elements become more flexible, self-aware, and recognizably human. The essential break-point is between engineering and agriculture: between the living and the purely material. We noted that those *using* the metaphors tacitly keep themselves outside them, especially when they are using them actively, rather than as a source of criticism ('they treat us like cogs in a machine in this place'). The active use of the metaphors enables managers and management development specialists to assume a fully human status in a world of building blocks, engineering components, plants, and animals. Even the medical metaphor has the person using the metaphor as a presumed fully-qualified medical specialist (a Consultant at the very least) and those to whom the metaphor applies, a set of patients suffering from various forms of disorder from which they must be cured. The key contrast, in other words, is between stable human resources and resourceful human beings.

I now feel happier in ending with metaphors than beginning with them. If one begins with metaphors and moves on to a model, however simple, one is asserting the superior adequacy of the model. And for the purposes of systematic research, this may well be so. Research workers are seldom happy with the homely simplicity of a metaphor, a simplicity which is purely apparent; a simplicity which can open up to a complexity that encompasses the universe (God as loving father of his own creation, with the human species as part of his family). Since the metaphor never states the rules of its application, or of its unfolding from simplicity to complexity, the research worker – wedded to explicitness and single meanings – cannot help but demur from its use.

And yet, when we turn to managers, who as research workers we may seek to understand, we find a confident and powerful use of metaphor as a way of preparing for action, as guide to action, and as justification for action (if you don't like the heat, get out of the kitchen! You can't make an omelette without breaking eggs!). The more senior the manager, the more pungent and apt the use of metaphors. This inclination is notoriously the despair of the well-trained staff specialist, who produces well-documented grounds for deferring action, only to be ridden over rough-shod by the Old Man, trumpeting his refusal to succumb to paralysis-by-analysis.

But even the Old Man recognizes that metaphor is not entirely a substitute for maps, plans, and programmes. It is the relationship between the two worlds that he works hard to keep before him, and that has been my concern. Of course, I am dramatizing the contrast between top manager and staff specialist; but the distinction between key metaphors and specialist techniques remains. In my view, it is one of the major communication barriers between practising managers and research workers. A glance at the works of those terrible popularisers who are read with enjoyment and profit by busy managers – Drucker, Townsend, Parkinson, William Davis, Bob Heller – shows their predilection for the striking incident, the leading personality, the exemplary case, the revelation of a pattern beneath the welter of events. The point is not that they are simple rather than complex: but that they are dramatic, and human, placing events on a scale that can be understood *and related to*.

RECENT DEVELOPMENTS IN JOINT DEVELOPMENT ACTIVITIES

Before attempting to make some concluding comments on the links between 'theory' and practice in joint development activities, it might be useful to comment briefly on recent developments in the activities themselves. These have taken three forms. First, the establishment of a four-month full-time programme for starting a business – The New Enterprise programme. Sixteen managers wishing to take the plunge, but eager to have a four-month period for detailed planning of their business ideas, engage in a one-month crash programme in the key factors making for success and failure in new enterprise. In this phase, they get to know one another and their business aspirations well. In the remaining three months, members of the programme work on their new enterprise as their development project, and are encouraged to start trading as soon as this seems feasible. There is no pressure on members to take this decision, if their plan does not mature, but if a business decision is made to begin trading, members of the programme and the supporting staff do whatever they can to foster the development of business.

The shift from in-company projects, focused on opportunities, to projected new enterprise is entirely compatible with the original purpose of joint development activities. Work and learning are even more intimately interwoven, and the problem of in-company projects – that they have often needed to hand over the responsibility for implementation of the recommendations to the existing mainstream functions – is resolved by the very nature of the project members as prime movers in their own business enterprises.

New enterprise and small business have become major talking points in the last few years. Big companies, realizing that their continued economic effectiveness will not be associated with increased employment opportunities, are wishing to serve as 'good neighbours' (Pocock, 1977). All political parties too seem to be making common cause on the need for grass-roots business activity, though not surprisingly, each party wants new enterprise in its own image – common ownership and co-operatives on one side, and thrusting entrepreneurship on the other.

These changes of viewpoint on the role of small business and new enterprise vis-à-vis big companies and government agencies have offered innumerable opportunities for project work, of which the New Enterprise Programme at the School is only one example. In the last few years, many other programmes have emerged at University schools, regional management centres, and the training centres of commercial consultants. We have established a New Enterprise Group in the School, which is extending its work from the nationally-based four-month programme just outlined. A continuing part-time programme has recently been initiated, in association with the Development Board of Rural Wales. The Board has conducted marketing surveys and envisages excellent opportunities for both existing companies, especially those able to meet the steadily growing tourist demands, and new companies.

The second development has been in the extension of corporate finance programmes; all of which grew from programmes with one sponsor, Barclays Bank International. The School now has an affiliated activity in the International Centre for Banking and Finance, working with major banks from many countries, with special reference to the corporate banking interests of the Middle East and African oil countries. All of these programmes are a combination of intensive work in chosen topics, and project work in close association with the bankers' parent institutions.

The third development has been of joint development activities for several companies working together. The first of these, for the Hotel and Catering Industry Training Board, is scheduled to start next September, and will take up to twenty experienced managers from companies in scope to the Board. They will combine two sets of activities; (i) project work in action learning sets and (ii) development work in five one-week modules, related to issues arising on different levels of managerial work.

All of these developments retain the key features of JDAs: work on real-time projects of importance to the sponsoring companies; joint management by sponsors and the School; and support work in the form of consultancy services rather than formal teaching. My hope is that these wider forms of activity will enable the School to stay with the work throughout all its phases, and not only in the early project phases of analysis, diagnosis, and detailed recommendations. The signs are that this is already happening.

CONCLUDING COMMENTS

The two themes that we held fast to at the beginning of JDAs, amid the welter of day-to-day contingencies, were 'resourceful managers' and 'development projects focused on organizational opportunities'. These themes now seem to me to have rather broader application. The 'resourceful managers' have become not only managers but owner-enterprisers. Some of them are not primarily managers, but highly-skilled professional people whose management skills are primarily devoted to managing their own quite complex network of relationships with clients and associates.

Perhaps a word on these 'self-managing professionals' is in order at this point. I believe that with growing disaffection with large-scale organization – anathematized as 'bureaucracy' and 'Big Brother' – and the concomitant growth of sub-contracting, franchising, consultancy groups, agencies, and other fluid forms of work association, self-managing professionals are becoming a major force in economic activity. They tend to treat organizations as vehicles and impersonal sets of resources rather than as higher levels of intelligence or authority. They move from one organization to another with great alacrity, and often feel happiest when they are part of a set of associates.

I feel sure that the organizational bias of conventional 'management development' – with its familiar set of answers to the top-management question 'what should we do with/to/for *our* managers?' – will be totally inadequate to the needs of the self-managing professionals. Their interests focus on work and learning rather than employment and training: and the management that they call for – as self-managing people – is of the nature of *support* rather than *control*.

Not only have joint development activities broadened in the kinds of people to whom I think they should be appealing, but also, as I have indicated, in the form and extent of the development projects. Is there a parallel to the notion of 'self-managing professionals' and 'resourceful owners' on the project side of the activities? I think so. The change is not so much in the label, because 'project' can expand prodigiously to cover any amount of human initiative and daring. It is in the nature of the projects that the change has occurred. No longer do we limit projects to the 'doing new things' sector of an existing enterprise, guided by a top manager from that enterprise. It is increasingly clear that projects can be seen as any form of activity that is new, renewed, or renewable. Freshness is all. A project is the natural habitat of a self-managing, resourceful human being, of whatever age, sex, ethnic or social status. It is a purposive, initiated event – neither random nor repetitious. Between chance and necessity, we find our true being. Not an original thought, perhaps, but certainly one to live with, and to grow with.

REFERENCES

Beer, S. (1970). *The Organisation of Manchester Business School for the Seventies,* (The Beer Report), Manchester Business School.

Beer, S. (1972). *Brain of the Firm,* Allen Lane, The Penguin Press, London.

Burgoyne, J.B., Boydell, T., and Pedler M. (1978). *Self Development,* Association of Teachers of Management, London.

Casey, D. and Pearce, D. (eds). (1977). *More than Management Development,* Gower Press, London.

Cooper, C.L. (ed.). (1975). *Theories of Group Processes,* John Wiley, London.

Handy, C. (1976). *Understanding Organisations,* Penguin Books, London.

Harrison, R. (1972). Understanding your organisation's character, *Harvard Business Review,* May–June, 119–128.

Morris, J.F. (1975). Developing resourceful managers in B. Taylor and G.L. Lippitt (eds), *Management Development and Training Handbook,* 109–125. McGraw-Hill, London.

Morris, J.F. (1977a). Tacking down the middle: ten years of organisational development by a British business school, in C.L. Cooper (ed.), *Organisational Development in the UK and USA,* Macmillan, London.

Morris, J.F. (1977b). *The Use of Social Science Research,* Unpublished conference paper.

Morris, J.F. and Burgoyne, J.B. (1973). *Developing Resourceful Managers,* Institute of Personnel Management, London.

Pocock, C.C. (1977). More jobs: a small cure for a big problem, Ashridge Lecture, London.

Revans, R.W. (1980). *Action Learning,* Blond and Briggs, London.

Schumacher, E.F. (1977). *A Guide for the Perplexed,* Cape, London.

Advances in Management Education
Edited by John Beck and Charles Cox

CHAPTER 9

Some Issues in the Design of Action Learning Programmes

David Boddy

INTRODUCTION

This paper considers the design of action learning programmes for managers. A variety of programmes of this sort have been conducted, and interest in this general approach to management education continues to spread. A central principle of action learning is that action is followed by reflection or review, in order to see what can be learned from the experience. This paper represents one such reflective phase, and is focused on some specific issues in the design of action learning programmes.

The immediately practical purpose is that such a discussion may help those concerned with running or taking part in such programmes. If the potential of this approach is to be widely realized, it will do so when it is used as part of an organization's *internal* development work, rather than in relatively expensive *external* forms. This implies that many more people will become involved in the design and operation of such programmes. Although they will learn most about action learning by doing it, there are some pointers from earlier programmes which may help their own learning process.

The paper begins with a brief account of the theoretical bases of action learning. Each of the main elements in an action learning programme is then discussed, highlighting the variety of forms in which the general approach has been expressed. This is followed by an examination of some dilemmas inherent in action learning, and a concluding section suggests how these might be handled, in a way consistent with the basic ideas of the process.

1. THE BACKGROUND TO ACTION LEARNING

A business environment increasingly characterized by change and uncertainty has fundamental implications for those concerned with management education. In particular, it raises the question of how to help managers at all levels to learn to deal with change – not only to respond to change initiated by others but how they themselves can bring it about. It is unlikely that satisfactory education for change, for dealing with 'what will be', can be achieved by methods designed to educate managers to deal with 'what is'. Pedler (1974) has emphasized that 'To help people to cope with new situations and new problems which have not yet arisen, objectives cannot be set in the usual way. What we can do is to try and prepare the individuals themselves for the difficulties involved.'

Although it is by no means clear how this preparation can best be carried out, one starting point is to consider the kind of learning most likely to be useful. What is it that will help people develop the skills of proactivity, of asking new questions, of creativity and so on, which are most likely to help them work successfully in a changing environment? Professor Revans distinguishes between two kinds of learning, P and Q. P refers to the acquisition of existing, programmed knowledge, while Q refers to the acquisition of the ability to ask fresh questions – of learning how to cope with new problems and new situations. Both types of learning are necessary for managers – they need to keep up to date in the technical aspects of their work, and also to develop the skill to cope with the ambiguities and uncertainties of innovation and policy-making. Conventional institutions and courses have developed to transmit established knowledge – but the problem remains of how to develop the ability to pose useful questions in conditions of change.

The specific model of the learning process which Revans (1971) put forward was a particular application of the classic Western model of scientific enquiry. Faced with a problem, the manager uses his existing stock of understanding in general and of the situation in particular to decide a strategy and to decide how he will go about implementing it. He then goes into an action phase, when he tries to put his ideas into practice. This is followed by a stage of reflection in which the results expected are compared with what has occurred. This comparison, between what was expected to happen with what actually happened, often leads to some critical insight into earlier assumptions about, for example, market growth or the reaction of subordinates. This, probably different, understanding can then be used by the manager as the next problem is faced, and so on through an unending cycle of

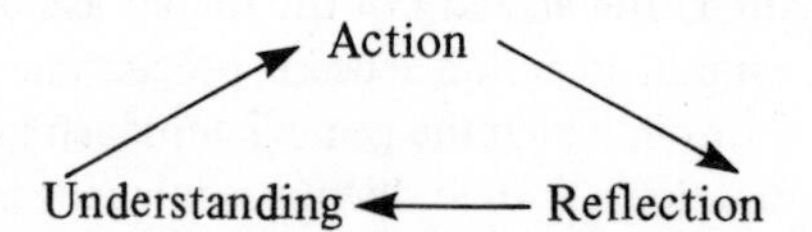

A final point is that great stress is placed on learning as a social process. That is, the insights a manager gains from working on a significant problem are likely to be enhanced if he undertakes the learning experience in the company of several others who are doing likewise. Not only can such groups provide new ideas or approaches to each other's problems, but the group meetings themselves can become vehicles for significant learning.

In some degree, a manager will be going through this cycle in the course of his everyday work, though clearly managers vary in the experiences they have and in what they learn from them. The problem seems to be that of how to confront the manager with new situations which require a more intense activity at each stage of the cycle. In particular, that he is *obliged* to ask new questions, or look at things in a different way in order to make progress on the analysis of the problem; that he goes beyond the comparative safety of diagnosis, and into the riskier stage of action; and that there is a deliberate review of the results of action against what was expected.

The way of doing this suggested by Revans (1966, 1971) and which is central to action learning, is to give the manager a real project to work on, either in his own or in another organization. Managers, being essentially practical people, are more likely, he implied, to undertake and to benefit from this learning process if it is geared to a current organizational situation, in all its realistic complexity. He also viewed learning as a form of social process – 'managers learn best with and from each other.' Therefore although each manager is responsible for his own project, he meets regularly with others who are engaged on similar exercises, to give and seek assistance.

Stated like this, it will be immediately clear that many quite common practices in organizations embody some or all of the ideas of action learning. For example, planned job rotation could be very similar to the provision of a project; setting up a project team to work on a particular assignment could be used for learning as well as for task purposes; while a well-conducted appraisal system can be a basis for learning from the actions of the previous period.

All of these clearly have much to contribute to management development: but the discussion in this paper is concerned with what might be called 'explicit' action learning programmes in the sense that someone (either in a company or a training institution) deliberately sets about putting together projects, participants, set meetings, and so on.

Early examples of such explicit action learning programmes were those developed by Revans himself, notably the Hospital Internal Communications project (Wieland, 1971) and the Belgian Inter-University project (Revans, 1971). More recently there have been some well-documented programmes within GEC (Mansell, 1975; Casey and Pierce, 1977; Foy, 1977), as well as those offered by the Irish Management Institute/Trinity College Dublin, the Institution of Works Management, the Anglian Regional Management Centre, ALP International, and so on. In addition to these 'public' programmes there are also several in-company, and hence little publicized, activities which are explicit action learning programmes.

Each of these programmes is explicitly based on the ideas of action learning: yet closer examination reveals that each one is unique in its design. Clearly the basic concepts have been put into operation in a variety of different ways, suggesting that, as with organizations themselves, there is no universally appropriate way of designing an action learning programme. The strength of this is the adaptability of the approach to meeting the needs of particular managers and organizations – diverse managers do not have to be processed through a standard package.

The challenge, however, is that not all forms of action learning programme will be universally appropriate – action learning is not an easy option, or 'a change from going on a course'. Conscious attention to the complex processes which an action learning programme can generate is necessary if this approach is to be used successfully. What then, are the choices available in the design of action learning programmes, and what considerations ought to influence these choices? We shall examine these issues in the following sections, dealing in turn with the related themes of the project, the participants, the group meetings, and certain structural arrangements in the programme. Issues arising from the relation of these to each other are discussed in the final section.

2. THE PROJECT

The project is a central and distinctive element in action learning. Its use reflects a basic theoretical assumption that the experienced manager will learn best when he is testing his existing ideas against a real managerial situation, and reorganizing his ideas in the light of this experience. How much a participant learns from an action learning programme is therefore assumed to depend heavily (though not solely) on the opportunities for learning which can be generated by the project. What are the key features of a project which need to be taken into account in deciding its suitability?

A project can be seen as a combination of a task to be done, and the setting in which it is to be done. Both the task and the setting may be familiar or unfamiliar to a particular participant, as shown in Table 1. For example, Box 3 would be represented by, say, a marketing manager doing a production project elsewhere in his own company; Box 4 would be a marketing manager doing a production project in another company, and so on.

Although the original action learning programmes were based on Type 4 projects, work since then has taken place in all four boxes. An example of the 'classic' type 4 project with which the author has been connected was carried out by someone who had been a regional sales director for a division of a brewery. He was released from this to work for six months on an action learning programme, and he undertook a project in another company. The 'client' company was in the electronics business, and the project brief was to 'improve the management information system' – a field in which he had no previous experience. The problem was that several similar contracts ran in parallel, and acute difficulty was being experienced in ensuring that costs, particularly for materials were, (a) allocated correctly to the various contracts, and (b) that this was done in sufficient time for management to exercise some control. His project was therefore to investigate the present situation, to make realistic and acceptable proposals, and to arrange for these to be put into effect. Clearly this project was of Type 4, as neither the task nor the setting were familiar to the participant.

Type 3 projects would be represented by those recently undertaken in an action

Table 1.

		Task	
		Familiar	Unfamiliar
Setting	Familiar	1	3
	Unfamiliar	2	4

learning programme within a company manufacturing semi-conductors. This programme was designed for 20 first-line supervisors from all areas of the factory, including finance, personnel, and various production areas. They were divided into four groups on the basis of a variety of skills, work experience, etc.; and each group was then given a project which was in an unfamiliar area for that particular group of participants. So although the setting was familiar (i.e. their own company), the problem they were asked to tackle was not – and therefore Type 3.

A well-established example of a Type 1 model is the Irish Management Institute/ Trinity College Dublin Management Practice Programme. This is intended for chief and senior executives, and the projects here are closely related to the normal jobs of those taking part. They were not, however, concerned with day-to-day routine or with managing recurrent crises: they were concerned with bringing about major new developments in systems or areas of business. Such projects involved work which would have been done anyway, but which was given extra impetus by the participants' involvement in an action learning programme.

Clearly, then, projects of at least Types 1, 3, and 4 are feasible within an action learning programme. In no sense are they limited to the 'classic' Type 4, and it may well be that, numerically, many more projects of Types 1 and 3 are now being carried out than Type 4.

A further structural dimension of the projects which must be clarified is that projects are undertaken by participants on either a full-time or a part-time basis. Although some programmes require full-time participation, many with which the author is familiar are part-time, or occasionally a mixture of the two. In one recent group, two participants had been released from their job to work full-time on the projects for about six months, while a further two were part-time. The latter were able to spend about a day a week on their projects, continuing to do their normal work for the rest of the time. The in-company supervisory course mentioned above and the IMI/TCD programmes are both part-time. Thus in terms of Table 1, a further dimension could be added to show each of the four types being possible on a full- or part-time basis. Incidentally, an emphasis on part-time projects would probably lead to a consequential emphasis on 'own-company' projects (i.e. Types 1 and 3): with limited time available, there is some evidence that it is wasteful to spend significant amounts on simply finding the way around another company (in a physical, let alone political, sense).

A final 'structural' question in relation to the projects is whether they are carried out by individuals, or by groups. The usual model is for individual project work, although the participant works as a member of a group, as we discuss below. There are a few cases, however, of the members of a group working together on a joint project – the supervisory programme mentioned earlier is an example. This approach may be particularly appropriate where an action learning programme is set up within a single company or plant. In such a situation five or six managers (or multiples thereof) working on a variety of individual projects would have evident disadvantages, and group projects offer a solution.

3. THE ROLES IN AN ACTION LEARNING PROGRAMME

Projects are the main focus of activity in an action learning programme, and the conduct of that activity generates a variety of roles. What specifically are these roles, and what are the relationships between them which need to be managed? The participant undertaking the programme is at the centre of a role set including other participants, his boss and/or his nominator, his colleagues, the person who 'owns' the problem on which he is working (often referred to as the client or the customer), perhaps an adviser or tutor to the group, and those other organizational members upon whose co-operation he or she will depend in carrying out the project. How aware he is of these other roles' occupants, and of their respective expectations of him, can materially affect the outcome of the exercise; and the ways in which a participant manages these relationships can in themselves be a valuable learning experience.

Although the early image of action learning was probably that it was intended mainly for relatively senior managers, this is not necessarily the case. Programmes are now being run for supervisory staff in several companies, and there is no evidence that position in the hierarchy affects a person's ability to cope with action learning, provided of course that projects, formal inputs, etc. are designed with the participants' level and ability in mind.

A common problem relates to the expectations which participants have at the outset of the programme. Since by its nature the participant is joining a relatively open-ended activity both in terms of the project outcome and of his own learning, his expectations can be based on very little prior knowledge. Coping with this ambiguity, particularly in the early stages, may, however, correspond to the uncertainties which prevail the higher up an organization one goes, so that again this may be a source of insight to the participant. Whether a member is prepared to work with this uncertainty will depend mainly on his general commitment to the programme, which in turn will depend as much on structural and environmental factors as on individual characteristics. For example, beyond some point the pressures arising in a manager's continuing job may begin to override his commitment to his action learning project, if he has not been helped to develop a reasonably acceptable set of expectations about the programme.

Unusual demands are also placed on the manager who 'nominates' another for an action learning programme, whether the nominator is an immediate boss or a management development specialist. To send someone on, say, a one-week financial planning course, or on a three-month executive development programme at a reputable business school are accepted, safe, and fairly predictable forms of development. Action learning is characterized much more by its unpredictability – it cannot be known at the start what will have been learned at the end. The nominator (and indeed the participant) may therefore need to be ready to withstand criticism that current work-time is being sacrificed for very uncertain, often intangible, benefits. Moreover, it may sometimes be necessary to ensure that expectations of the nominator are realistic, and appropriate to action learning.

Similarly, whoever contributes a project, has demands placed upon him. He is expected to take a significant, challenging problem with which he is seriously concerned, and hand it over to someone else, perhaps from a different department or company, to work on as a training exercise. Moreover, his own staff are likely to be approached and asked to provide information and help to the learner, with no obvious benefits to themselves.

The adviser to the group has a variety of functions to perform, above all he is concerned with the learning processes of the group. These include the critical function of group formation to ensure that members give assistance to each other, both in relation to the projects and to their learning objectives. He may also need in the early stages to maintain a relationship with nominator and client, to ensure the environment is conducive to learning by the participant. Later his role is likely to concentrate more on helping participants to learn from what they are doing – to keep stressing the reflective phase, in which learning can occur.

None of these roles can be specified in advance, and must therefore be negotiated in the course of the programme itself. Nominators, clients, and participants each approach the programme with a variety of expectations about the programme as a whole and the part each will play in it. There are likely to be discrepancies in these expectations, and these need to be recognized and managed in the course of the programme. The adviser's role in particular may need working out: the participant's expectations may well be that he is there 'to lead' or 'to teach' the group, neither of which would be compatible with action learning.

4. GROUP MEETINGS

All action learning programmes involve the participants in regular joint sessions, variously described as project meetings or set meetings. These derive from a basic idea of action learning, namely that learning in general is most effective when it takes place as a social process, and in particular that managers are most likely to learn in an environment of 'mutual self-help'. A fairly common pattern seems to be that the project groups meet every two weeks, either for a day or a half-day, together with one or more 'advisers' with responsibility for the learning processes taking place.

At least six distinct functions can take place in such meetings, and it is for the group members and those responsible for the programme to work out a suitable balance between these at various stages of the programme. The first function is that the meetings provide an opportunity for members to seek the help of other members in carrying out their project. Such help may be of a fairly straightforward technical variety. For example in one group a member found that his project began to raise questions about the machine loading system in the factory in which he was working. Although he was unfamiliar with the topic, another member of the project group worked for a company with elaborate systems of this sort, and he was able to arrange a briefing. Clearly, the more varied the experience of participants within a group, the more scope there will be for this type of help.

Help from the group may also arise from other members raising questions or suggesting possible approaches to the project which had not occurred to the individual. It is well-known that our search for solutions to a problem tends to be limited to areas relatively close to those we have used before. Raising an issue with others almost inevitably widens the area within which a search for ideas or solutions will occur. This should benefit the immediate project; and the manager's long term development should also reflect the now widened area of experience on which he can draw. This aspect can obviously occur at all stages of the project, but may be particularly important at the earliest stages of the activity when issues of problem-definition arise. A common experience seems to be that the 'client' or customer will offer an apparently straightforward problem as a project, and the action learner begins work, on the basis of his interpretation of the information provided by the client. Other members of the group, with their different perspectives, may make a quite different interpretation – and questions such as 'is that *really* the problem?' 'Why has it been raised now?' 'Is he *really* the client?' have been raised in early group meetings. Such questions usually raise sufficient doubt in the participant's own mind for him to seek clarification from the client, generally resulting in a higher degree of mutual understanding about the project.

As work proceeds, action learning projects require activities like the collection of data by interview or questionnaire, and the presentation of written or oral proposals to the client or other managers. Here again the group meetings can serve as a place at which to try out and practise such presentations, revising them in the light of group reactions. As with the earlier activities, the learning about, say, more effective presentations should carry over to the manager's work after the project.

A second major function which the group meetings serve is as an external source of pressure upon members to keep their individual work moving. Particularly when it is a part-time programme, members will experience many immediate, job-related, calls upon their time, and it is very easy for the project work to be pushed to one side, and any initial momentum lost. However good the intentions, the individual participant will usually bend to accommodate pressures from his colleagues at work, and give priority to their concerns. The group meetings can help here by providing a countervailing source of pressure on the individual to spend time on his project – their time at the next meeting will be wasted if he has not made progress and they will probably make this clear to him. This does not immediately make life any easier for the participant, but it does help to keep up momentum, and presumably learning.

Apart from the discipline regarding time in general, the group may act to prevent a participant edging away from a particular task or problem in the project which he finds threatening or difficult. For example one group sensed that the project of one of their members could not make useful further progress until he had held a further meeting with the customer. The participant was evidently reluctant to do this as he had not yet succeeded in establishing a proper *rapport* with his customer, and had found earlier interviews unsatisfactory. After several instances of delay and avoidance, reflecting the participant's understandable uneasiness at a further meeting, the group finally exerted enough pressure upon him to go immediately to the phone to fix an appointment: and as a result a significant 'log-jam' was broken. The group pushed him into doing something – with which he then realized he was able to cope, despite earlier fears.

A third function, which contains elements of the other two, is that of providing a regular opportunity for members to generally review what they have done since the last meeting, to exchange relevant ideas and information about the projects, and to make detailed plans regarding the work they are now going to do: a review of progress on these plans can then provide a starting point for the next meeting. A variant of these occurs when a common group project is being carried out. Here we have found that an additional function occurs as the work to be done in the next stage is specifically shared out or delegated amongst the group members (a process, incidentally, which can in itself be a source of learning).

Fourthly, group meetings can be the occasion for any 'formal inputs' to be made to the group. Action learning is an inductive process, and this may be a peculiarly difficult one for experienced, successful managers to undertake. As Charles Handy (1973) has argued, this can make it hard for him 'to leap beyond the bounds of his previous experience. Too often he sees situations only as mirrors of something he has done before.' The contrasting experience of the other group members can of course provide one way of breaking the bonds of earlier experience, and formal inputs can provide another. Action learning programmes vary widely in terms of the amount of time devoted to 'formal inputs', some giving little or none, while in others (mainly those based in academic institutions) they form a significant part of the programme. Well-presented, relevant formal inputs do appear to be welcomed by participants, serving the intended purpose of broadening the range of ideas available to them.

Where included, they can relate to the programme both in task and process terms. For example, it may be thought necessary for all participants to at least be able to read a balance sheet, or conduct an interview successfully, or to conduct competently some basic statistical analyses: all of these would relate to the project as a task. Formal inputs may also relate to process issues arising from the way the group itself is managing its work as an action learning programme. This approach could include topics such as the analysis of learning needs, group dynamics, or evaluation. It would be consistent with the main ideas of action learning for such formal inputs to be incorporated only as the group perceives a need: though particularly in the process area these may properly be seen as part of the overall responsibility of the adviser for the learning within the group.

Fifth, the group meetings are expected to be the times when, in terms of the overall action learning model, most of the reflection on what has happened is likely to take place from which insights and learning may be derived. Thus, in cognitive terms, and following from one of our earlier points, consider the case of a member who is working on the basis of his interpretation of the client's problem, when another member, with a different background, poses some awkward questions as to what the project is basically about. If this leads, as it often does, to a re-orientation of effort, this experience can lead to the exploration of several large topics – for example it may help members realize more than before the many-sided nature of management problems; differences in perception based on different backgrounds and careers; issues of divergence in organizational goals, and so on. Similarly experience in the project can lead to wider discussion and reflection on issues like information systems, decision-making, or influence.

At the affective level, groups may have been exposed to situations where emotions and feelings were being more readily expressed, partly because of the stress generated within the programme. They will be able to reflect upon their own reactions and feelings towards the risks and opportunities within the programme, and thus have a greater understanding of themselves as individuals – particularly of how they react to risk and stress. In turn, a participant may be more sensitive to the attitudes and feelings of others with whom he has to work in future.

In terms of skill, the group meetings provided opportunities to reflect on the skills the individuals have used in doing their project work, and in conducting themselves as a group. For example, when a member has planned and conducted a series of interviews, or has persuaded someone to implement a change in procedure, this experience in the programme can also be the subject for reflection in the group meetings. What did members find out about getting people to willingly contribute information, about preparing for a difficult meeting, about working without the formal authority on which they normally rely, and, from their own meetings, about ways of seeking the assistance of others in such a way that they are willing and able to help?

The group's own operations may also be a vehicle for learning a more specific set of skills. Managers as a rule spend a large part of their time working with others in small, task-related groups, and any skills or understanding which can be gained from reflection on the working of the project group itself should assist managers in their usual work. For example, action learning groups discover the value to task performance of quite simple things like working to agreed objectives for a meeting, allocating time to each agenda item, or keeping records, as well as the more subtle issue of listening to others or expressing ideas clearly.

Finally, the group meetings can provide for mutual encouragement and support – they can serve as a kind of psychological prop at critical times. If action learning projects are to succeed as vehicles for learning, they cannot be straightforward exercises. Particularly at the problem-definition and action stages members can experience considerable frustration at the apparently insoluble nature of their projects; and this source of tension may be in addition to other distractions with which part-time members must be coping. The project group meetings should be able to encourage and help a member to admit openly that his project is in a mess, and that he is seeking help from the group. The sense of support, and degree of common ownership of problems can provide the reassurance needed to maintain their commitment to the programme. Given the competitively-oriented organizations from which participants tend to come, the experience of working in such a supportive group can itself be a new experience for members, and something they expect to remember and value long after the programme is finished.

5. STRUCTURAL ARRANGEMENTS FOR THE PROGRAMME

The activities of action learning – participants working on projects and meeting regularly as a group to review progress, to learn, and to make new plans – take place within some structural or institutional framework. Since behaviour, including learning behaviour, is likely to be influenced by the nature of such a framework, it follows that this is something which the designers of an action learning programme can usefully consider. We shall therefore outline some of the alternative structural forms which have been used in various action learning programmes, working from the simple to the more elaborate.

At one extreme we can visualize an almost structureless programme, consisting simply of self-organizing, 'self-help' groups, created and run by the participants themselves. These could be project-based, or simply based on the current issues exercising the managers themselves. This model corresponds closely to Professor Revans' account of his National Association of Colliery Managers in 1952. He was convinced that this particularly independent group would not take kindly to advice from outside experts and that they alone would need to 'work out their own salvation'. He therefore suggested that they should set up a series of meetings in their respective pits, at which they exchanged ideas and generally sought to help each other in coping with the substantial problems of the time. There are doubtless many instances of this kind of activity going on at the present time – but by its very nature it does not get publicized or written about.

The well-known Institute of Works Management Programme (Lawlor, 1976) appears to have a similar absence of structure. There is some structure, however, in the sense that the Institute has established the programme, publicized it, and operates it through a network of local branches. Beyond that, however, the pattern appears to be that the managers concerned meet each week or fortnight, to exchange ideas and problems – rather as the colliery managers did. There are not necessarily distinct projects, and little in the way of formal input – so it follows that little is required in the way of formal structure.

Other programmes, however, are characterized by an increasing complexity of structural arrangements, designed to cope with particular relationships within the action learning process. For example, the GEC programmes (Casey and Pierce, 1977; Boddy, 1979) normally have both an internal and an external adviser attached to the set – the former to cope with 'internal' issues within GEC, as well as contributing to the learning process, while the latter dealt only with learning processes. There was a greater level of formal inputs on such programmes, involving a more structured timetable. Finally, recognition was given to some of the relationships arising in an action learning project by formally designating people as 'nominators' or 'clients' respectively, arranging initial and concluding meetings between the participants and clients as a group, and so on.

In the programmes run by the ALP consortium, specific reference is made to the continuing relationship among the group of companies which take part, by the institution of a steering group. This is composed of members drawn from teaching staff and from the companies taking part, serving to monitor the successive programmes and to manage particularly the relationships between the various parties to the arrangement.

The most elaborate arrangements are probably those where the successful completion of an action learning project leads to the award of a University degree. Two current examples would be IMI/Trinity College Dublin programme, and the more recently founded programme at the Anglian Regional Management Centre. Quite apart from any of the arrangements mentioned earlier which may be adopted, these programmes have necessarily built in a number of structures governing the relationship between the participant and the Institution awarding the degree. This covers such things as formal entrance qualifications, assessment procedures during the course, and assessment of the final project report in accordance with Masters Degree standards.

6. DISCUSSION OF ISSUES

The intention of this paper has been to examine the range of choices which exist within the general action learning model. It should be clear by now that this range is very wide and therefore that the principles of action learning can contribute to the development of any manager, not merely to that of a few 'high fliers'. It is equally the case that action learning is not an easy option – setting a group of managers to work on a few random projects is not in itself a sure way of achieving a satisfactory learning experience. The process does need to be thought through, and managed, by all concerned – particularly by those with a particular responsibility for advizing on management development. In this section, therefore, we examine some of the most important issues which seem to arise in this connection.

(i) The Project

Since the project is seen as the principle vehicle for learning, the first broad issue to consider is 'what makes a good project?' More formally, the issue is whether we can identify those characteristics of an action learning project which are most likely to affect its suitability as a learning vehicle. Any such judgement will necessarily be subjective, but it may nevertheless be useful to identify and discuss some relevant characteristics, particularly as projects may be offered by managers unfamiliar with action learning.

The first characteristic to consider in relation to a proposed project is 'will it involve the participant in *action* – in implementing or bringing about change?' Given the very name of the process this may seem an unnecessary question, but in the author's experience it is all too easy for projects to be used which offer little prospect of action in the original sense of action to bring about some organizational change. For example, a project 'To assess the role of the supervisor' was used in one programme, while in another the brief was 'To examine the various forms of flexi-time available, and make recommendations about their suitability for this factory'. Even in projects which could involve an action phase, the time-scale required for changes to be introduced into an organization may out-run the period available to the participant, with the danger that once again it deteriorates into a set of recommendations.

It is possible, though unsatisfactory, to argue that although the recommendations were not followed by action, the participant was nevertheless involved in a mini-cycle of hypotheses formation, action, and reflection in the course of carrying out his investigation. This is true, as conducting an interview is a form of action from which something useful can be learned: but it is unsatisfactory when compared to the risks and difficulties involved in bringing about change.

It seems important to re-assert the requirement that a project should be such that the participant is clearly expected to initiate some change, to achieve some tangible end-result from his work on the project. The first argument for this view goes back to the theory of learning on which the process is based – the model in which assumptions and beliefs about what will happen are *tested* by putting them into action, and the results of this action compared with what was expected. If the project stops at the diagnostic phase, the opportunities for learning, both about the project itself and one's skills as a manager, are lost.

A second argument has to do with the expectations of the various members of the organization from whom the participant seeks help in the course of his work. The usual experience is that many busy people give substantially of their time, in helping the participant understand the situation, put together data for him, talk over his ideas. Although, of course, there may be resistance to change, it is proposed here that if action learning projects end up as 'just another report' then many contributors to the participant's work will feel let down, and the image of action learning will suffer.

Of course there are difficulties arising from the time-scale of change: if it involves, say, capital expenditure or negotiations with trade unions, the timetable of these activities may simply not match the timetable of the action learner. Two quite respectable, and managerially realistic, solutions are possible. For example, a project was recently carried out which basically said 'define and improve the general stores system'. Since those concerned quickly identified numerous possible improvements, it also became clear to them that they could not possibly aim to implement them all; but it would be quite feasible to select some which could be achieved within the time available. They therefore planned the work so that they would face up to the experience of trying to implement *some* changes in hallowed practice, though others would be left as 'further recommendations'.

Another approach was used when the full implementation of the results of a project depended on their being fitted into a wider modification of the company's computing arrangements – which again, though imminent, lay beyond the learner's time on the project. His solution was to involve a number of key members of the organization as 'allies', in such a way that they became as committed to the change as he was. Together they worked out exactly how the internal people would effect the change after the participant had left, with quite satisfactory results.

Although there may be difficulties in getting to an implementation phase, they can be overcome if 'philosophical' projects are avoided, and if the kind of measures suggested above are used.

Another, related, issue concerning the project is whether it is perceived by the person or group carrying it out as feasible, in terms of their personal skills and/or their authority. A central element in expectancy theories of motivation is that the effort a person puts into a task is significantly affected by their belief in their ability to perform the task. This suggests that if a project is genuinely seen as being too difficult, in view of its technical complexity or the time and other resources available, the commitment of members is likely to suffer. Of course, this perception may change if skilful use is made of the resources available or which can be acquired; but there remains a responsibility for ensuring projects are within the grasp of those taking part, particularly as lower levels of management become involved.

Yet it has also been argued that there is an obligation to ensure that the project extends the person's field of vision – either by exploring more deeply an aspect of his own work, or taking him into unfamiliar areas. In other words that it should take him beyond the relative security of his existing learning and skill, and expose him to the risks and uncertainties of taking action in unfamiliar areas. On the criterion that facing up to risk is an important aspect of development, it is worth asking what is at stake in a project – what are the risks of failure in terms of money, position, reputation, etc.

The issue of risk also brings in the relationship between the project, the participant, and the customer. While it may benefit the participant for him to be working on a project where he is experiencing significant risks, this does raise a dilemma for the customer. For if it is a real problem which he is offering to the participant, he too will be sharing the risk of failure, and he will need to continue to live with the negative consequences, as well as the positive. The same issue arises, in only a slightly different form, when the participant is working on an 'own-job' project. There is clearly no easy answer to the issue of the balance between feasibility and risk, but it can readily be a source of tension, possibly creative tension, throughout.

Just as there may be tension surrounding the level of risk, so there may also be difficulties about the 'significance' of the project. In order to raise the level of risk and stress faced by participants, it is common to emphasize that projects must have the characteristics of being 'real and significant' in the sense that at least some key people in the organization are bothered by the situation, and preferably that there will be a crisis of sorts if something is not done about it. There is little doubt that a project of this sort is desirable – but we may ask how realistic it is to expect many projects to be of this type. What proportion of managers are likely to entrust that kind of problem to someone on an action learning programme, particularly if they are only engaged upon it part-time?

(ii) Roles and Expectations

Our discussion of the project leads us to the area of roles and expectations, since some of the dilemmas posed above arise from possibly inherent conflicts in the expectations of the various parties. This is probably true of any development programme, but can be particularly acute for action learning on account of the particularly intense demands the process makes, and its own comparative novelty: there is still a very small stock of experience of how to cope.

We outlined earlier the various roles which arise, and one source of difficulty lies in the exaggerated expectations that the various parties may have of the process as a whole, and of each other. For example, if the participant has been briefed with some of the background reading, he may reasonably expect the customer to be providing him with a project which is significant and of quite direct interest to the customer. But is the customer's knowledge and expectation about the action learner such as to encourage him to offer a project with these characteristics? What does the nominator expect will be gained by the participant? What does the participant expect, and are either or both of these consistent with the interpretation placed on his role by the customer? (Again, very similar issues arise in the course of own-job projects, with the added complication that the one person may experience the roles of participant and customer!)

People may also experience difficulties in coming to terms with the demands made upon them and the other parties in the course of the work, particularly time. The commonest difficulty at the start of a programme, particularly a part-time one, seems to be that of members persuading their managers or colleagues to leave them sufficient clear time to create some momentum on their project. Particular problems of participants working on night-shifts have arisen on two of the programmes with which the author has been involved. Moreover, other organization members may be called upon to give of their time to the action learner: and they may well begin to query what they will receive in return – a point which relates to the importance of a tangible outcome from the projects, as discussed earlier.

Finally, it may only be as the project progresses that some of its inherent risks become apparent. For example the participant may pursue his enquiries into unexpected areas, arouse expectations, or stir up dormant problems.

Although these several issues may be posed as problems, they are perhaps more usefully seen as characteristics of *successful* action learning programmes. For if a project proceeds smoothly from beginning to end, scarcely stirring up comment or controversy within the organization, what will have been achieved? It probably means the problem was unimportant or the solutions put forward uninteresting – thus denying the participant an opportunity to examine how he coped with organizational conflict. Yet if managers are told that the programme may well result in difficulties and conflicts which will need to be sorted out on the way through, how will this affect their willingness to undertake action learning?

(iii) Managing the Environment of Action Learning

As we become more aware of the kind of issues outlined above, the further question arises of what to do about them? To what extent should such issues or potential difficulties be worked over by those responsible for the organization of the programme before it begins, and to what extent are they best left ambiguous, to be sorted out by participants as part of their learning process? Again there is no obvious answer, though where part-time programmes are involved, with particularly difficult time problems arising, the balance of advantage would probably point to more rather than less preparatory work.

This is really part of the wider issue, of the extent to which we structure or preplan action learning programmes, as our understanding of the process increases. In anticipating a difficulty which participants will face, the temptation will often arise to do something to help them over it: but will doing so contribute to their learning?

Such questions can only be resolved by referring back to the basic ideas behind action learning – seeing its value as a way of helping people to develop their skills at coping with change, uncertainty, and ambiguity. This is not likely to be achieved by so structuring a programme that much of the uncertainty is removed, and it becomes a relatively routine exercise. On the other hand, the threats, intended or otherwise, to a programme of this sort, may be such as to endanger the commitment and learning of the participants if they are left completely to their own devices.

A specific example would be the way in which conflicts are handled. If, as we argued earlier, projects are established which can involve real action and decisions, then a participant who does the job well is bound to meet resistance. People will defend their territory, 'he'll be told he's gone too far', and so on. If the participant is not used to coping with conflict, because he lacks the mental and procedural frameworks for working through these differences coherently, he may back off. The results of an environment in which conflicts are avoided, or played down, would probably be that significant learning opportunities would be lost, and action learning would become as safe as sending someone on a course.

The opposite danger, of course, is that conflicts break out which are badly handled, with consequent loss of face, a build-up of personal animosity, and so on. This could result in an abrupt end to the project, or in a harmless report which could be conveniently forgotten. Again, nothing much would be learned.

So perhaps the answer lies in the idea of 'holding the ring'. In other words, to set up or help participants and companies to set up, some framework or structure which encourages conflicts to be faced and managed competently, but which does not do it for them. The same model would probably apply to the many other environmental pressures which bear upon an action learning programme. The participants learning may be impaired if, say, the adviser yields to the temptation to manage these issues for participants, but equally pressures cannot be allowed to build up which destroy the programme.

The line to explore, then, seems to be how best to create an environment which copes with the more extreme external threats to the programme, but which still leaves scope for participants to develop their own mechanisms for dealing with acceptable levels of conflict, ambiguity, and uncertainty within that framework.

This 'boundary function' may consist of personal interventions by the group adviser or someone in a related role, or it could lie in the creation of some more formal structure, such as a 'steering group'. Several examples of this approach have begun to develop, in which managers of the companies taking part in a programme, and of the institution meet from time to time in the course of the event. This can produce both short- and long-term benefits. The immediate job of such a group is to help create and maintain a favourable learning environment for those on the current programme – to help create a structure within which learning is fostered. In the long-term, however, it should also increase the general level of understanding of action learning amongst a number of leading companies, hopefully developing an increased readiness to face up to the very considerable challenges of taking part in action learning.

CONCLUSIONS

In this paper we have outlined the basic ideas behind the use of action learning in management education, and considered in some detail the various forms programmes based on these ideas have taken. This consideration has led us to raise a number of issues which should have the attention of those, particularly management development advisers within companies, who may be involved in establishing some form of action learning programme. In particular, we have reasserted the view that the projects should involve action, despite the obstacles to this which can readily arise. We have then examined the relation of *action* projects to the expectation of and demands upon, the various parties to a programme, and the conflicts which need to be managed. Finally, we have discussed the idea of 'managing the environment' of an action learning programme, and considered the issues of how best to create a structure most conducive to the learning experience of the participants.

REFERENCES

Boddy, David (1979). 'Some lessons from an action learning programme', *Journal of European Industrial Training,* **3**, No. 1.

Casey, M.D. and Pierce, D.J. (1977). *More Than Management Development,* Gower Press, London.

Foy, Nancy (1977). 'Action learning comes to industry', *Harvard Business Review,* Sept–Oct.

Handy, C. (1973). 'Educational theory in practice – the design and concept of a management programme'.

Lawlor, A. (1976). 'Management clinics', *Journal of Industrial and Commercial Training.*

Mansell, C. (1975). 'How GEC learns action', *Management Today,* May.

Pedler, M. (1974). 'Learning in management education', *Journal of European Training,* **3**, No. 3.

Revans, R.W. (1971). *Developing Effective Managers,* Praeger, New York.

Revans, R.W. (1966). *The Theory of Practice in Management,* Macdonald, London.

Wieland, G.F. and Leigh, H. (eds), (1971). *Changing Hospitals: A Report on the Hospital Internal Communications Project,* Tavistock.

Advances in Management Education
Edited by John Beck and Charles Cox

CHAPTER 10

Facilitating Behaviour in Work Centred Management Development Programmes

John Burgoyne and Ian Cunningham

INTRODUCTION

Many of the current trends in management development, towards self-development, learner centredness, participation, task relatedness, and discovery methods, find their practical expression in what we will be calling 'work centred management development programmes'. 'Action Learning' as promoted by Reg Revans and the Action Learning Trust must by now be the best known of these approaches, but we intend our definition to be broad enough to cover any approach in which the emphasis is on learning from actual experience encountered and generated by the learner in a work setting.

We do not wish here to go back over the varied and complex arguments for this form of learning as against any others, but to focus on the question, given that they are now an established part of the management development scene, of what is involved in making them work.

Here it seems that the crucial point must be to do with how work centred management development is different from plain, ordinary work, as a learning experience, rather than how it is different from any other kind of development programme. For if the work centred learning approach is to say anything other than that managers and organizations should be simply left alone to learn naturally in the course of their work, then there must be some process by which work centred learning programmes allow, support, encourage, cause, or facilitate learning from work experience, which would not otherwise happen. Furthermore, whatever that crucial process is, it must self-evidently have its crucial existence at the point of contact between the participant and the programme, rather than in the metaphysical speculations of the proponents of such programmes.

The authors would like to acknowledge the assistance of Ms Caroline MacLean in the preparation of the section in this paper dealing with 'Leadership in Experiential Groups'.

Thus the crucial question seems to be, what precisely is it that impinges on the participant that is owing to the programme, and how can this be assumed or observed to enhance learning from and for work? In other words, the crucial topic is to do with what happens at the coal face of work centred programmes, for without this essential action all the organization, philosophizing, the steering groups, and co-ordinating bodies, are just so much excess baggage on a journey that is not even going to take place.

In the context of action learning the major part of the coal face activity, both as intended and perceived, is the group meetings of participants, with someone in a 'tutoring/facilitating' role. In the jargon these groups are called 'sets' and the 'tutors', 'set advisers'. Much of the essence of action learning in action must therefore be captured in the way in which set advisers conduct themselves in setting up, and acting within, these set meetings. This then, simply, is our focus of attention here; how do facilitators of work centred learning conduct themselves, how can their behaviour be described, in what ways is it similar to and different from behaviour in the context of other educational approaches, and what can be said, either theoretically or empirically, about how this influences learning?

We have drawn on a number of sources in order to develop our ideas about set adviser behaviour:

(i) our own experience of acting in the 'set adviser' role;
(ii) our observations of others carrying out this role;
(iii) our analysis of published and unpublished reports on sets, action learning, etc.;
(iv) discussions with people who have acted as set advisers.

We have also looked at published research evidence on

(a) what teachers in other settings do;
(b) the qualities associated with effective counsellor behaviour;
(c) the role of trainers/facilitators in T-groups, encounter groups, etc.

As work centred approaches are so markedly different from traditional teaching settings the research on teacher behaviour and function has not particularly illuminated our thinking, except that the failure of most such research to contribute to our knowledge of what makes an effective teacher has influenced our thinking about the kind of research needed. Attempts to define quite microscopically the precise detail of what teachers do (using instruments such as those devised by Bales, Flanders, and numerous others), have not advanced our understanding of the teaching process as much as was originally hoped. It appears that reductionist research programmes aimed at isolating the minutest details of teacher behaviour can lead us up blind alleys. The totality of a teacher's activity does not seem to be adequately describable by summing all the parts of that teacher's behaviour. (A good example of this is cases where behaviours which appeared to correlate with teaching effectiveness were drilled into trainee teachers, but the result was no significant improvement in the effectiveness of these teachers).

The published material on set adviser activity is quite different. It largely concentrates on describing in fairly global, non-analytical terms who set advisers are or what their role is. This is useful but limited data. In our view some analysis of the set adviser role is needed, and models which provide a basis for improving set adviser effectiveness ought to result from such analysis. This is the task we have set ourselves. However, we have drawn on the descriptive data to help us in this task.

SET ADVISER ROLE, BEHAVIOUR, AND STYLE

(i) Who are they?

Revans (1974) suggests that a set should be 'under the tutelage of a senior manager, a professor, an experienced research worker or a qualified behavioural scientist'. (p. 4). Casey and Pearce (1977) stated that in choosing set advisers for the GEC action learning programme:

> 'they needed to be people of stature and ability'.
> 'they should have had experience of working with small groups'.
> 'they would have a grasp of industry and the broader commercial and political scene'. (p. 23).

The broadness of these statements is fairly typical of the published literature. This is not to criticise the authors quoted, but rather to suggest that these generalized comments are only a starting point for considering who makes an effective set adviser. Casey and Pearce's comments give some idea of the kind of person a set adviser might be, but they do not indicate what he would do in order to carry out the job effectively. In selecting and developing 'set advisers' it is clearly necessary to consider what an effective set adviser does. For example, there are probably many people who fit the criteria mentioned above, but who would be quite ineffective as set advisers. Therefore, we need a clearer, more precise definition of the qualities required. Later we shall review the research on trainers of T-groups/encounter groups etc., as this does give us some useful insights.

(ii) Philosophy and Principles

The basic principles of action learning are spelled out by Revans (1971) and others and clearly set advisers need to espouse such basic ideas as the value of learning from live experience. However, it does appear that different set advisers operate from different philosophical bases. Burgoyne and Stuart (1977) discuss more fully the range of learning theories used by teachers and trainers. Here it will be appropriate just to refer to two such theoretical frameworks.

Those with an orientation towards experiential/humanistic views of learning seem attracted to work centred approaches. As such approaches do not use traditional curriculum based teaching methods, the set adviser role is appealing to those who are committed to learner centred, humanistic modes of learning.

However, pragmatists are also attracted to action learning. They tend to take an 'if it works, I'm prepared to consider using it' mode of evaluating management development methods. Thus they are less likely to be concerned with deeper views about the nature of human beings (at least not explicitly so) or indeed about the nature of learning. Rather they are interested in whether it does indeed develop competent managers.

Our contention is that the particular orientation to people and to learning of the set adviser is likely to influence his behaviour in a set. Hence, although we have tried to develop models specifically around the question of what set advisers do, we are conscious that a fuller understanding of the philosophical assumptions made by set advisers will shed more light on the factors influencing their effectiveness. This matter is the subject of some of the research we are currently undertaking.

PARTICULAR VIEWS OF THE SET ADVISER ROLE

Revans (1971) makes the following statement regarding the Belgium programme:

> 'The staff of these five university centres had several roles some not traditional for management teachers. Their main responsibility was to help with the design and development of the projects in which the fellows were engaged. In so helping, they themselves were called upon to supply practical advice on sampling, programming, statistical analysis, and questionnaire design, and to introduce fellows to other experts on the university staff able to discuss the many general questions – economic, cultural, technological – that the fellows occasionally confronted. Each member of staff was expected to act in the *traditional role* of personal tutor to the four or five participants at his centre, especially in advising them on any supplementary reading that they found necessary. Each was also responsible for developing the catechisms of cognitive subjects and for engendering an opening balance of operational skills among the participants. Each played an active part in visiting the participants at their supporting enterprises, and in the weekly seminars at which the progress of the participants was examined. Each also acted as a contact between the fellows and any academic research at their own universities, of which the field projects of the fellows provided practical application. The university staff also kept in touch with nominated persons at the supporting enterprises, and discussed from time to time with them, and among themselves, the main implications for management science and other scholarly pursuits, of what was discovered, suggested, or disproved. Perhaps the strongest among the staff were those who saw their role not as teachers but as providers of an opportunity to learn; not as sources of knowledge or information, but as collaborators in the framing of questions and in the sharing of doubts'.

Only in the last sentence does Revans start to approach a model of the set adviser role. Casey (1976) has taken this thinking further, and has postulated four basic tasks for the set adviser, namely '1. To facilitate giving; 2. To facilitate receiving; 3. To clarify the various processes of action learning; 4. To help others take over tasks 1, 2, and 3'. This takes the analysis a stage further but it still leaves the role unclear. Casey goes on to express his opinion of the skills and knowledge required of a set adviser (and, interestingly, the ones not required).

THE DEVELOPMENT OF A MODEL

We want here to build up a model of set adviser functioning. We see that it is important that any model should cover both what goes on inside the person (intrapersonal) and what goes on between people within the set (interpersonal). Interestingly, Lippit (1977) has suggested that group facilitators (in the T-group/encounter group context) need 'trifocal perception', i.e. an awareness of

(a) what is going on inside a person
(b) what is going on between people
(c) what is going on in terms of group phenomena

Our own thinking matches this quite closely.

A MODEL

Firstly, the core of the set activity is the real problem, or task or project that each member brings with him to the set. We will refer to this simply as 'task'. One option open to the adviser is simply to 'tell' the participant solutions to his problem. This can be called 'traditional expert consultant' behaviour, as in Figure 1.

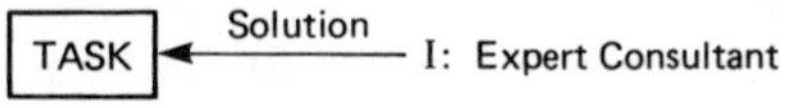

TASK ← Solution — I: Expert Consultant

Figure 1

The participant, with greater or lesser help from the adviser and other participants, works on the task, using some kind of problem-solving, or task process. One option the adviser has is to 'tell' the participants *problem-solving procedures* with which the participant can work out his own specific task solutions. This can be called 'traditional expert teacher' behaviour. See Figure 2.

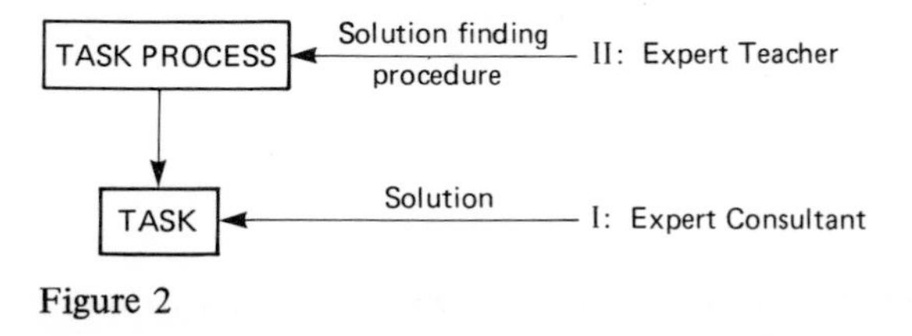

Figure 2

The participant's 'task' or problem is almost certainly grounded in a human context in his work situation, and the set itself, in which he works on the task and the task process, is itself in a human context in the form of the set small group. An option open to the adviser is therefore to make 'interpersonal process' interventions intended to help the participants deal with interpersonal processes that may get in the way of working on the task in either the set or the work situations.

There are many styles and approaches available to the adviser in making 'interpersonal process interventions'. We will simply distinguish 'surface' interventions to do with things immediately affecting task activity, like the utilization of group skills, clarifying mutual expectations, bringing out unannounced needs and hidden agendas, from 'depth' interventions based on more profound interpretations of the psycho-dynamics of the situations concerning, for example, individual or collective repression of guilt, fight or flight from certain issues or people, individual and group rationalization, transference, projection. Figure 3 shows the options:

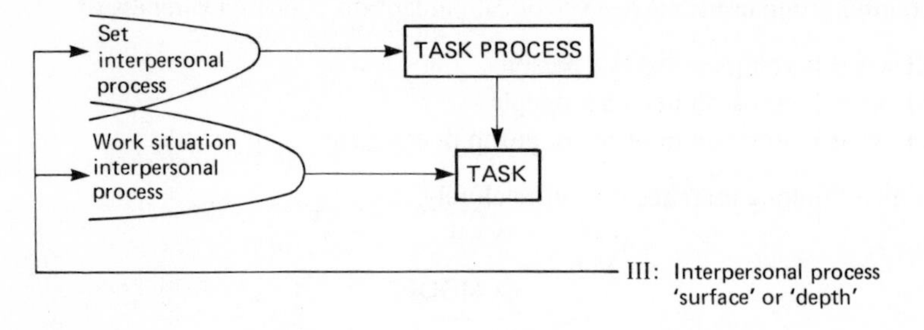

Figure 3

As an alternative to 'telling', 'giving' or 'managing' the task and interpersonal processes for the participant, the adviser can attempt to structure and manage a learning process or situation in which the participants can discover for themselves ways of dealing with both the task and interpersonal aspects of their situations. Thus the adviser could structure an agenda for the set in which they invent, try out, and evaluate some task-solving processes for themselves, or review their own group working, propose new conventions and norms, and try them out (see Figure 4).

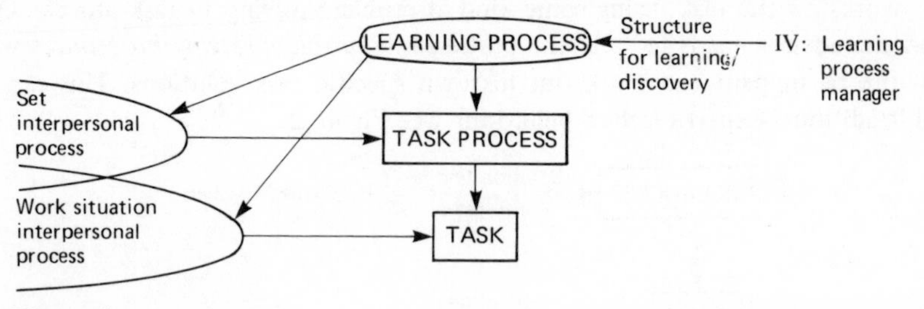

Figure 4

Yet another option open to the adviser, either with or without having shown the effects of structuring activity for learning/discovery process by type IV behaviour, is to encourage the set and/or its members to manage the learning process for themselves. This would amount to the adviser trying to manage a 'learning to learn' process by encouraging the group to try out different learning/discovery procedures for themselves (see Figure 5).

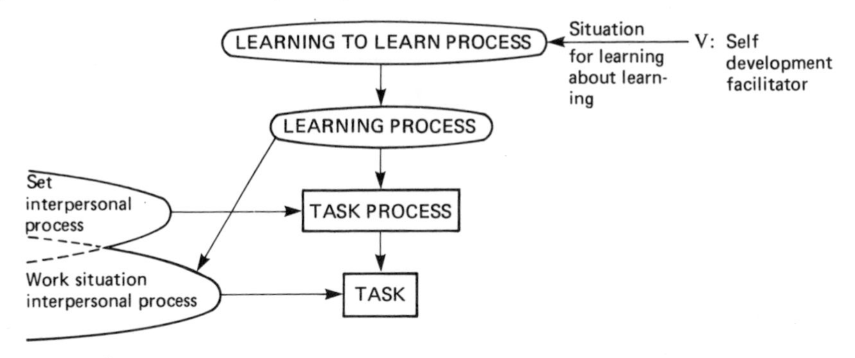

Figure 5

This is, unfortunately, not the whole story. Just as interpersonal process dynamics can help or hinder work on the task and the task process, so it can help or hinder both the *learning process* and the *learning to learn process.* Thus the adviser may wish to use 'type III' behaviour in close conjunction with Types IV and V behaviours to enable learning, or learning to learn, processes to occur. He may also wish to manage the learning process, (type IV behaviour) at a certain stage in the proceedings, to develop in the set the capacity to manage their own interpersonal dynamics. Figures 6 represents this modification of the situation.

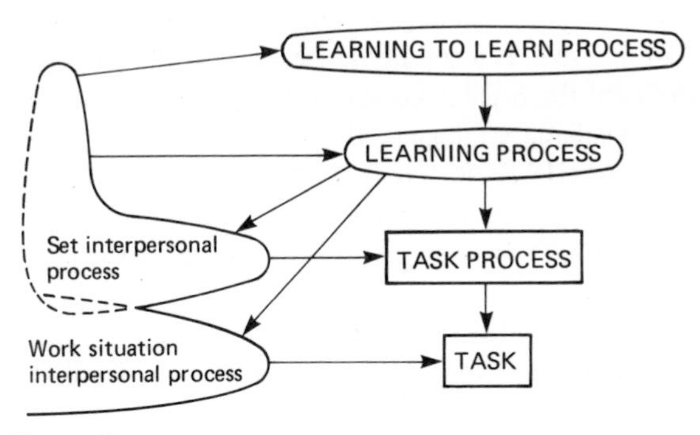

Figure 6

Finally, it has been a universally accepted observation from the set running experience that 'initiation' has been a particularly difficult and time-consuming activity. Initiation consists of all the activities necessary to gain the acceptance, commitment, and consent from all the interested parties to enable participants to join the sets, and see the programme through. Initiation is therefore a complex activity of communicating the nature of the programme, getting various mutual expectations right, and developing explicit and implicit contracts about what will happen. In a sense this is an extension of process consultation in the work situation, but it seems to be important enough to count as an activity in its own right. See Figure 7 for the complete picture with all the possible forms of intervention shown.

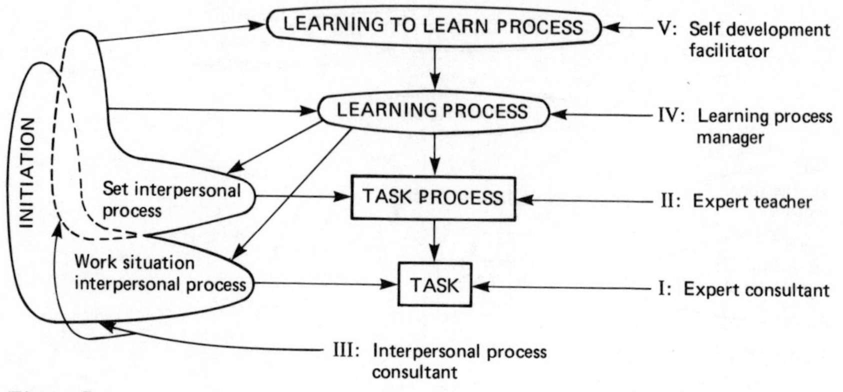

Figure 7

Our aim in developing this framework is to offer a way of interpreting and discussing what goes on in sets, with particular reference to the behaviour of the set adviser, in the hope that this can be a useful formative contribution to the development of work centred programmes.

EVALUATING THE MODEL

The model does seem to accommodate a number of views about set adviser work e.g. Garratt (1977) on his role as a set adviser in GEC said: 'I rarely said anything on the technical aspects of the project, concentrating on the participants' behaviour (III) and their problem-solving strategies (IV), acting more as a learning catalyst (V), umpire (III) and tutor (II)' (p. 82). N.B. the brackets include our interpretation of where Garratt's ideas fit into the model (see Figure 7).

The Casey and Pearce (1977) book suggests the following for the set adviser role:

1. Personal development – tutor/friend (II, IV, V).
2. Negotiator both within and outside the organization to facilitate the progress of the project (III).
3. Technical adviser, either personally or by pointing out others who know (II).
4. Process consultant (III).
5. Learning catalyst (V).
6. Problem-solving adviser (IV, II).
7. Political adviser (II).

Again these ideas can be accommodated in our model.

Revans (1976) suggests that 'the primary task of the management professor should be to acquaint his students with an insight into their own learning processes' (IV, V) (p. 8). Once again, it seems to fit the model.

EXTENDING THE MODEL

We want now to make some addition to the basic model. Firstly as we see it set adviser behaviour is not a constant throughout the life of the set (see e.g. Lundgren and Knight, 1978). This dynamic, changing quality needs to be built into an analysis of set adviser work. One factor that occurs to us is that as the set progresses it may be necessary to make less process interventions (type III behaviours) and more interventions concerned with the individual's learning. If the set starts to work effectively as a unit, and interpersonal issues become resolved, the set adviser has less need to tackle such problems. On the other hand, as participants start to open up more, it is likely that factors concerning their personal learning will become more important. Hence it is possible to suggest that a situation such as that shown in Figure 8 may frequently occur.

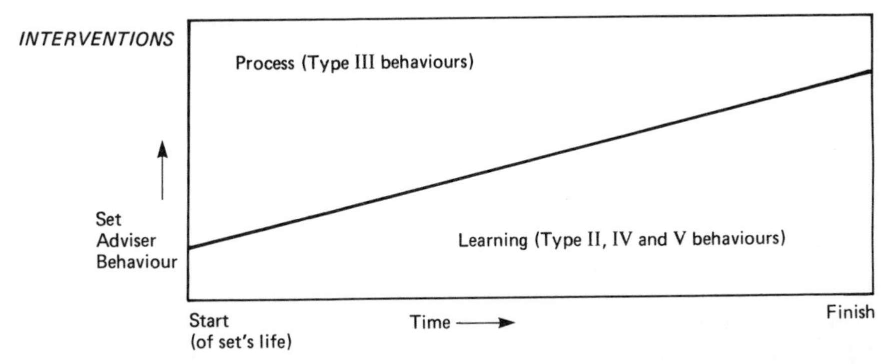

Figure 8

A second point we would like to make about the model is to try to relate the crucial type II, IV, and V behaviours to some view of what the learner is gaining from the process and how he is changing. Figure 9 shows diagrammatically how the situation appears to us. Thus this hierarchical arrangement indicates a spectrum of 'ease of changing' for the manager (with personality change being the most difficult).

In considering this hierarchy, it might be important to consider to what extent some would see type V behaviours as being more in the realm of 'therapy' than 'education'. We find the distinction between these terms difficult. Certainly as the two activities are currently practised, most therapists are concerned almost solely with personality change and most educators are concerned mainly with skill and knowledge development. However that may not be the ideal situation. What the distinction does throw up, though, is some thoughts on the qualities required of a set adviser. If indeed at the learning to learn level we are in the area of personality change, then it may be important to look at the evidence on the facilitation of

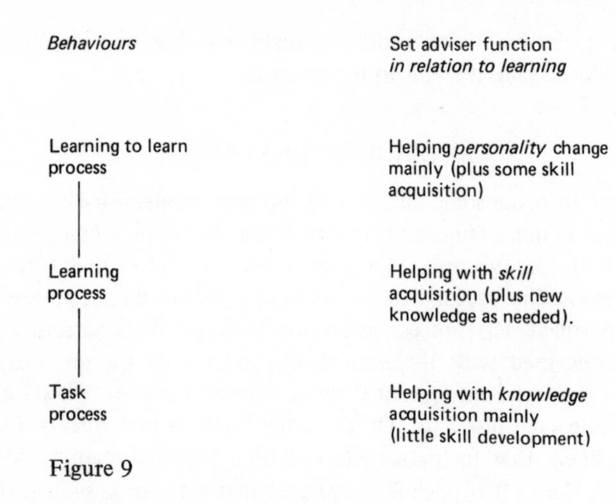

Figure 9

personality change to see if this helps us to understand what a set adviser might do at this level.

We would like to review here some aspects of the current state of knowledge of leadership in experiential groups (mainly personal growth groups or T-groups). Such groups are not, of course, exactly like sets. However, it is an area which has been researched, and as personality change is an important factor in such groups, it appears to be important to see if it is possible to draw on existing knowledge in this area.

LEADERSHIP IN EXPERIENTIAL GROUPS

In most experiential groups, there is a formal, designated leader who is usually referred to as a trainer or facilitator. His role in the group differs from that of the participants in that while the leadership position may be assumed by any member of the group temporarily, the trainer has overall responsibility. The research evidence indicates that the trainer's style and behaviour has an impact on the group's outcome (see Figure 11). Indeed, Cooper and Bowles (1977) from their study of T-groups conclude that 'trainer personality and style of intervention in particular seem the most potent potential risk aspects in experiential learning groups'.

In this section, we shall look at the leader's personality (input variable), the leader's behaviour and style (process variable), and finally draw together existing research evidence to present a picture of effective group leadership.

Personality

Much of the research on the personality of the facilitator comes out of the counselling and psychotherapy world. Based on his professional experience, Rogers (1957) stated that the process of therapy is highly dependent upon the kind of person the therapist is. Indeed, he considered that the therapist's personal qualities are more important than any techniques or skills he may have mastered. He defined the necessary personal qualities as empathic understanding, unconditional positive regard, and congruence. Roger's formulation stimulated much research into the personal characteristics of the therapist. Some of the most important research was carried out by Truax and Carkhuff, who in their review of the research (1967), redefined the necessary characteristics as accurate empathy, non-possessive warmth, and authenticity or genuineness.

Tyler (1969) in her work on the practice of counselling also concludes that it is the personal characteristics of the counsellor which are of major importance. She states:

> At the very heart of the counselling process is a *meeting* of counsellor and client. Whether they meet for fifteen or fifty minutes, whether they talk about symptoms, explore feelings or discuss facts and schedules, whether the client confronts the counsellor alone or as a member of a group – whatever influence counselling has is related most closely to the nature of the relationship that grows out of this encounter.
>
> The reason it has been difficult to analyse what good counsellors *do* in this situation, so that others can be trained to do likewise, is that the essential components are attitudes rather than skills. By his actions, words, gestures, and facial expressions, the counsellor must communicate *acceptance, understanding,* and *sincerity*. (p. 33).

Figure 10 summarizes the characteristics of the competent counsellor as presented by Rogers (1957), Truax and Carkhuff (1967), and Tyler (1969). Although these studies on personal characteristics are concerned with the counsellor or therapist, a later work by Rogers (1967) shows that the same characteristics are pertinent to the group leader (facilitator). Therefore, to expand on the personal qualities themselves, we shall use the terms given by Rogers.

	ROGERS (1957)	TRUAX AND CARKHUFF (1967)	TYLER (1969)
	Necessary and sufficient conditions of therapeutic personality change.	Central therapeutic ingredients.	Essential qualities of the effective counsellor.
1	Empathic understanding	Accurate empathy	Understanding
2	Unconditional positive regard	Non possessive warmth	Acceptance
3	Congruence	Genuineness of authenticity	Sincerity

(From Gilmore, 1973)

Figure 10

Empathic Understanding

The Oxford English Dictionary defines empathy as 'the power of projecting one's personality into (and so fully comprehending) the object of contemplation'. Thus, in the interpersonal encounter, the facilitator needs the ability to 'get into the skin' of the other person(s) in order to understand the problems of that person, yet without taking ownership of those problems. In addition, he needs to be able to communicate that he has understood.

Unconditional Positive Regard

By this, Rogers means that the facilitator must experience an acceptance of the members of the group and show a warm caring for them – 'a caring which is not possessive, which demands no personal gratification' (p. 263, 1967). This acceptance must be total and unconditional.

Congruence

If the facilitator is to create a trusting, open climate then he must be perceived as being congruent. In other words, his behaviour must be in accordance with his feelings. The participants in a group must know 'where they stand' with the facilitator and can only do this if he is a congruent person. This is a view which appears to be confirmed by Sadler's work (1968) on leadership in industry. He found that employees were most satisfied when their boss acted consistently in terms of his leadership style.

Personality would seem to be one of the fundamental factors in determining whether a trainer is successful or otherwise. Certainly, according to the data obtained by Pfeiffer and Jones (1974) from their 'Opinionaire on Assumptions about Human Relations Training', 57% of 238 experienced group leaders think that 'the effectiveness of the trainer is more a function of his personality than it is a function of his academic preparation' (Q50) whilst only 18% disagreed with this statement.

In the experiential group, the leader's position differs from that of the participants in that, among other factors, he has more power. French and Raven (1968) define five bases of social power: legitimate power, reward power, coercive power, expert power, and referent power. In some situations, the trainer may have legitimate, reward or coercive power (for example, in a college situation) but if he does not, his power is dependent on his expertise and on reference i.e. his interpersonal attractiveness, which is a personality factor.

Surprisingly, in few studies have there been attempts to test the personality of group trainers. An exception to this is Cooper and Bowles (1977) who compared the trainers in their study with the normative population data of the Cattell 16PF and found that they differed from the norm on eight of the twelve scales and in a consistently positive direction. 'Experiential group trainers and facilitators are more tender-minded, more experimenting, more self-sufficient, more assertive, less suspicious, less apprehensive, less controlled, and less tense than the general population' (p. 25).

While the validity of the 16PF has been seriously questioned in recent years (see, for example, Peck and Whitlow, 1975), the results of Cooper and Bowles' study are not surprising, in that the trainers in their study were experienced and well respected.

Behaviour

At the process level, it is important to look at what a trainer does and what functions he performs. In doing this, we shall refer to the works of Bolman (1976), Heron (1977), and Lieberman, Yalom, and Miles (1973).

Bolman (1976), in his survey of existing research on group leader effectiveness, suggests that there are six 'educational functions' which a leader can perform in an experiential group:

1. *Providing Feedback:* a leader may facilitate learning through providing members with feedback about the consequence of their behaviour.
2. *Questioning:* the leader might facilitate learning by asking questions which stimulate participants to think or behave in new ways.
3. *Modelling:* the leader might produce learning through providing a behaviour-model which participants can imitate or identify with.
4. *Support:* the leader may facilitate learning through providing psychological support, thereby creating a climate which is safe enough to support defence lowering and risk-taking.
5. *Conceptualization:* the leader might facilitate learning by providing conceptual frameworks.
6. *Structuring:* the leader might facilitate learning by structuring either the environment or the participants' behaviour (e.g. through the use of structured exercises) (p. 38).

Heron (1977) has been influenced by the findings of Bolman and has built on this to provide a model of group facilitation styles which are available to the trainer to use. He considers that there are six dimensions of the leadership function. Within each dimension there is a wide spectrum of specific behaviours which a group leader can choose to adopt. Thus:

Group Facilitation Styles

1. Directive ———————————— Non-directive
2. Interpretative ———————————— Non-interpretative
3. Confronting ———————————— Non-confronting
4. Cathartic ———————————— Non-cathartic
5. Structuring ———————————— Non-structuring
6. Disclosing ———————————— Non-disclosing

1. Directive/Non-directive

Heron suggests that the spectrum runs from autocratic (directive) behaviour to a 'do nothing' mode (non-directive). In between he argues that there are options such as proposing action and then consulting the group (relatively directive) or consulting the group and then proposing action (somewhat less directive).

2. Interpretative/Non-interpretative

Highly interpretative interventions would be for instance theoretically based psychodynamic interpretation (i.e. interpretations of intrapersonal behaviours using theoretical notions). Being non-interpretative would include reflecting peoples' comments without putting any interpretation on them. Again there is a range of possible behaviour, which Heron discusses quite fully in his paper.

3. Confronting/Non-confronting

A high confrontation style would be for instance verbal attacks on group members; low confrontation includes keeping silent even in situations of high tension or deliberately backing off from problems.

4. Cathartic/Non-cathartic

This kind of intervention is common in encounter groups but less likely in other contexts. Encouraging catharsis would include promoting the discharge of emotions, making explicit the acceptability of cathartic release, etc. Discouraging catharsis (at the other end of the spectrum) would include interrupting someone when it appeared that they might show emotion (e.g. by crying).

5. Structuring/Non-structuring

One way of highly structuring is to use rigid ground rules in a group or to use a highly structured exercise, whereas the encouragement of an open, non-structured group clearly belongs at the other end of the spectrum.

6. Disclosing/Non-disclosing

Highly disclosing behaviour includes the group leader being open about his own personal circumstances and his reactions in the group. Being non-disclosing clearly implies a highly closed style, e.g. refusing to express views about something even when asked.

It is interesting to use this model to look at a facilitator in a particular approach. For example, Tavistock T-group trainers have a particular style of operating. Using Heron's model, one could describe it as low structuring (save for setting ground rules) low directing, high interpreting (use of sociodynamic interventions), low cathartic, low disclosure, and medium confronting (questioning). While the Tavistock trainers have a distinct identifiable style, this is not true for many other orientations, (e.g. Transactional Analysis leaders use the same conceptual framework, but this does not determine their style of leadership).

The third work we wish to refer to here, is that of Lieberman, Yalom, and Miles (1973). This study has received much criticism (see, for example, Schutz, 1974) and its reliability in some aspects must be questioned (e.g. with regard to reports on casualties). However, it is useful to look at here, as the researchers investigated group leader behaviour quite comprehensively. They isolated 27 variables describing leader behaviour, these were then intercorrelated, the result of which suggested that fewer variables were needed to describe leader behaviour. When the 27 variables were factor analysed four clusters emerged which led the researchers to believe that much of what trainers do can be subsumed under four basic functions: emotional stimulation, caring, meaning attribution, and executive behaviour.

Emotional Stimulation

The emotional stimulation dimension relates to behaviours designed to release emotion. The critical leader behaviour here is the use of intrusive modelling. As the authors note: 'Emotional stimulation appears to be centred in the person of the leader; the very presence of the leader is a salient feature of the group experience' (p. 149).

Caring

The caring dimension encompasses those behaviours which are designed to support members of the group. Those leaders who scored highly on this dimension were perceived as 'love-oriented' by participants but this dimension was not related to members' feelings about the leader.

Meaning Attribution

Meaning attribution behaviours are designed to help members understand experiences they undergo. Specific behaviours include conceptualizing, explaining, interpreting, and clarifying.

Executive Function

Executive function represents behaviour which is directed primarily towards managing the group, and behaviour which makes use of structured exercises as a vehicle for goal achievement. Specific behaviours include setting rules, limits, norms; setting goals, managing time, stopping (limit setting); and inviting, eliciting, questioning, suggesting procedures (command response).

The authors note that these four dimensions are basic in that all the leaders exhibited some of the behaviours they encompass. They found that apart from the four dimensions noted, there was a fifth variable, which accounted for a small percentage of variance, which they term the leaders' interpersonal attractiveness.

Of the sixteen group leaders observed in the study, ten separate theoretical orientations were represented. (They used 3 T-group leaders, 2 Transactional Analysts, 2 Synanon leaders, 2 Gestalt leaders, 2 Psychodrama leaders, 1 Rogerian leader, 1 Psychoanalytic leader, 1 Eclectic marathon leader, 1 Verbal encounter leader and 1 Sensory awareness leader).

They found that the theoretical orientation of the leader was a poor predictor of how he would behave. For example, on the care dimension, one Transactional Analyst gained the second highest score while the other rated thirteenth. These differences can be seen among other orientations. Lieberman (1972) concludes:

> Whatever the labels of the diverse encounter leaders, the findings are indisputable that conventional categories of leader orientation are poor predictors of leader behaviour (p. 156).

This is a finding repeated by Bolman.

It would seem then that there are distinct functions which a group leader performs but that there are individual differences in style among trainers even when of the same theoretical orientation.

Clearly, there are similarities between the three studies looked at here. Figure 11 attempts to show the relation between them.

LEADER BEHAVIOURS/FUNCTIONS

LIEBERMAN, YALOM, AND MILES (1973)	BOLMAN (1976)	HERON (1977)
Emotional stimulation	Modelling; providing feedback	Confronting; cathartic; disclosing self
Caring	Support	Disclosing; catalytic structuring
Use of meaning attribution	Conceptualization	Interpreting
Executive function	Structuring; questioning	Structuring; directing

Figure 11

Emotional Stimulation

As stated previously, the emotional stimulation dimension relates to behaviours designed to release emotion. These include the leader 'revealing feelings, challenging, confrontation, revelation of personal attitudes, beliefs . . . the emphasis on the release of emotions by demonstration' (p. 235). This clearly fits the function

Bolman terms 'modelling'. In addition, a leader can stimulate emotion by providing feedback. Bolman notes that leader feedback is related to self-disclosure. Therefore, the categories of behaviour Heron terms confronting, cathartic, and self-disclosing are incorporated into the emotional stimulation dimension.

Caring

Bolman notes that the function he describes as support is dependent on the leader's communication of 'caring'. The specific behaviours from Heron's model which are included here are expression of care, touching, validation (disclosing dimension), and catalytic structuring (bringing in, supporting). The caring dimension seems also to be related to the personal characteristics isolated by Rogers and indeed this is recognized by Bolman.

Use of Meaning Attribution

Lieberman *et al.*, state 'Meaning attribution involves cognitizing behaviour-providing concepts for how to understand, explaining, clarifying, interpreting, and providing frameworks for how to change' (p. 238). Given this, the relation between their category and the category Bolman calls 'conceptualization' is plain. The behaviours from Heron's model pertinent to this category are those along the interpretative dimension.

Executive Function

Executive function behaviours centre round two activities: limit-setting and command response. Limit setting behaviours from Heron's model include proposing or imposing ground rules (structuring dimension), and behaviours along the directive dimension. The second activity, command response, is related to Bolman's categories of structuring (the leader's use of structured exercises) and questioning. This in turn is related to some of the behaviours in Heron's structuring dimension, use of structured exercises, devising structured exercises, etc.).

The Effective Group Leader

There seems to be a fairly clear picture emerging of what makes an effective group facilitator. Bolman concludes that he will possess the following characteristics:

1. The leader is able to empathize with the participants, and communicates a consistent respect and caring for them.
2. The leader is sufficiently congruent and genuine that the participants experience him as trustable.
3. The leader is willing to be open, to confront, and to provide feedback but

does not do it in a way which is punishing or which results in his completely dominating the group's activities.

4. The leader possesses a theory with which he is personally comfortable and which enables him to help participants develop more effective cognitive maps (p. 49).

As can be seen, items one and two are dependent on the personality of the leader and can be related to those qualities isolated by Rogers. Item three is also partly dependent on personality but it also rests on the leader's interpersonal competence. Item four, and, to a large extent, item three are concerned with the leader's ability to perform his task efficiently (i.e. to help people to learn and change).

That the leader must be both people-orientated and task-orientated is consistent with the findings of Lieberman *et al.* Taking their four basic functions, they found that the effective group leader's style would combine moderate stimulation, high caring, use of meaning attribution, and moderate expression of executive functions. Conversely, the ineffective leader would be either very high or low on stimulation, low in caring, do very little meaning attribution, and display too little or too much executive function.

The Cooper and Bowles' (1977) study related trainer style to risk. They found that the trainer style most likely to produce positive outcome with the least risk was one where the trainer was highly supportive, used structured exercises and was, in himself, relaxed. The trainer style which seems to produce most *short-term* risk was where the trainer was 'assertive, aggressive, uninhibited and spontaneous, impulsive and lively, sensitive and open', although they showed that in the long-term this style may produce learning.

In conclusion, there seems to be agreement that the effective trainer is highly supportive and this is probably more a function of personality than a 'learned' style. There also seems to be approval of some use of structured material. Finally, it would seem that the effective leader uses some conceptual framework to help participants gain meaning from their experiences.

Sets v. Other 'Learning' Groups

The above analysis related only to leaders in personal growth groups, T-groups, etc. Clearly in a number of respects the set is different from these. For instance, many set advisers seem to emphasize that they are not in a leadership role (see Casey and Pearce, 1977). Also they would tend not to favour moving a set closer to a 'personal growth' group. (Garratt (1977), for instance, emphasises his dislike of T-groups and related activities): this will especially apply to those set advisers who do not espouse the humanistic/experiential school of learning, (but it might also include those with humanistic orientations who see that sets are inappropriate for such work).

Harrison (1970) has suggested an approach to choosing the depth of organizational intervention, which might also be appropriate for the set adviser in choosing how deeply he 'intervenes' at the interpersonal and intrapersonal levels. He makes two propositions regarding the choice of level of intervention:

1. the consultant should 'intervene at a level no deeper than that required to produce solutions to the problems at hand' (p. 181);
2. the consultant should 'intervene at a level no deeper than that at which the energy and resources of the client can be committed to problem-solving and change' (p. 181).

He defines depth of intervention in the following terms, 'By depth we mean how deep, value laden, emotionally charged, and central to the individual's sense of self are the issues and processes about which a consultant attempts directly to obtain information and which he seeks to influence' (p. 181). This definition relates to the previous analysis regarding our model of set functioning. It may be convenient to show the model visually in an inverted form to emphasize the issue of *depth* of intervention (see Figure 12).

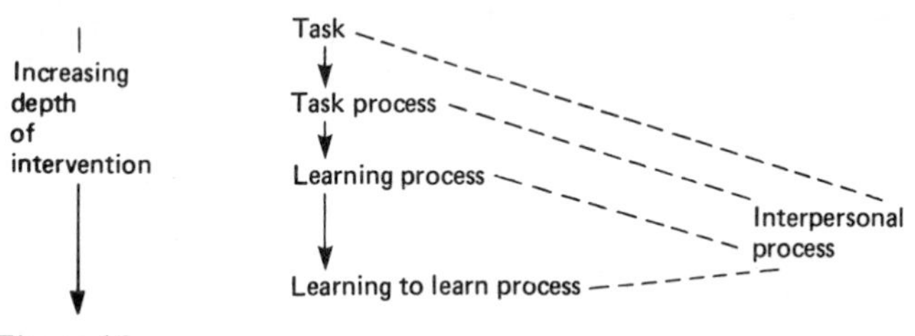

Figure 12

We have deliberately shown 'interpersonal process' at a relatively deep level. Harrison himself gives an example of increasing depth shown in Figure 13. (N.B. this is related to organizational consulting). At the top, surface interventions involve

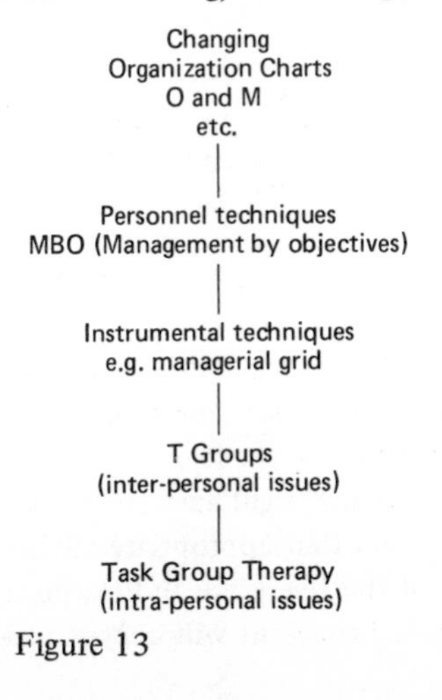

Figure 13

say, shuffling jobs in an organization chart. It is based on public information and requires relatively little knowledge of individual people in the organization. At the other end, therapeutic interventions deal with deeply held, often sensitive, personal values and attitudes. The two situations (a set and an organization) are not exactly analogous, but it is possible to consider Harrison's two basic propositions on their merits.

It is now perhaps convenient to return to the comparison between sets and T-groups/personal growth groups. We would argue that with our current state of knowledge, we should make use of empirical evidence from this source. Sets do concern themselves with interpersonal and intrapersonal processes, though probably at nothing like the intensity of a T-group or encounter group. If, as Harrison suggests the consultant (set adviser) should take the clients' (set members) view of the problems he faces, then it may be that for some set members level V is never tackled (because they do not wish to work on their general learning competence, only on developing the skills to tackle their project). In our experience, however, most set members do want to consider how they are as people; they want to know how they come over to others and how they can develop their personality, e.g. by becoming more self-confident, more pro-active. Hence it might be convenient to broaden our type V behaviours to include a wide range of intrapersonal factors (see Figure 14).

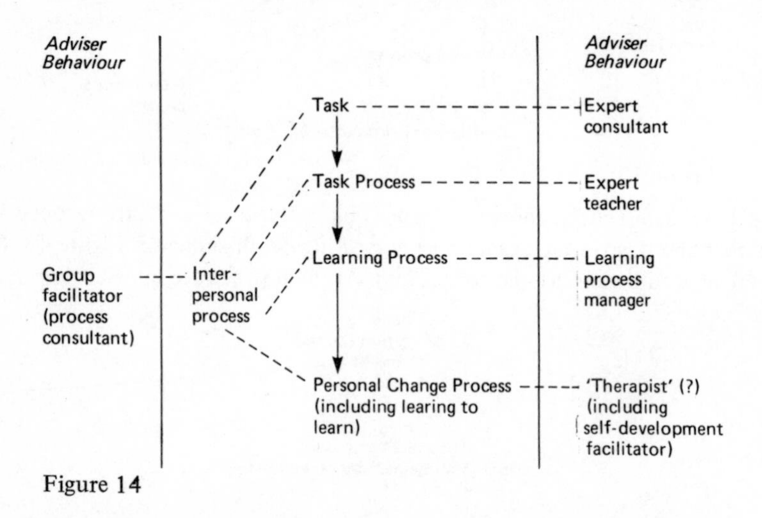

Figure 14

We do not like the term therapist and do not see that a set adviser is involved in 'therapy'. However at that level the set adviser does have to be competent to deal with issues around the personality of the learner.

We do not want to propose any 'right answers' to the question of how an adviser should behave. It seems certain that appropriate adviser behaviour is not a matter of choosing the right one of the five kinds of behaviour and sticking to it. It seems more likely that appropriate behaviour will consist of a dynamic pattern of these behaviours – like a tune made up of notes where the sequencing and timing of the notes contribute to a whole which is greater than the sum of the parts. Furthermore, to stretch this analogy a little further, it seems likely that the appropriate 'tune' will adapt in 'real time' to the participant reaction, rather than be read off a pre-structured script.

However there may be some general rules or heuristics about adviser behaviour that the language of this framework makes it possible to articulate and possibly test. It is very much central to the notion of Action Learning and sets that the adviser avoids behaviours of types I (expert consultant) and II (expert teacher), at least as the 'lynch pin' of the adviser approach. It seems to be an open question as to whether the adviser should ever go in an 'expert teacher' approach as a tactic in a larger strategy that allows him to act as an 'expert resource' for a while. Another option is to bring in outsiders to do this as appropriate. The debate hangs around whether it is better to let the participants learn everything by discovery for themselves, or whether they should be helped over certain problems quickly, to allow them to engage with more complex issues more quickly. Our view is that since Action Learning is a reaction against 'expert teaching' there may be a degree of over-reaction, and there is a case for the use of the expert resource role.

There seems to be implicit agreement that the 'expert consultant' (type I) behaviour has no place at all in the adviser's repertoire. This seems appropriate as the giving of a solution does not imply any but the most trivial level of learning for the receiver.

The general notion of action learning and sets (amongst those professionally concerned) is, in terms of the framework, that the adviser is concerned mainly with III, IV, and V type behaviours. In some discussions the term 'process facilitating' is used in a general way to cover all three, and possibly the distinction between 'interpersonal' and 'learning intrapersonal' process facilitation, may help sort out some ambiguities. It does make it possible to see how advisers' skills might need to be different from, say, an OD consultant's skills, since the latter is concerned primarily with interpersonal process facilitation.

Finally, it may be possible that in the development of a set there is a need to start at II, if only to clarify that this is not the prime focus, move to IV, and only after that to V, with III interventions supporting throughout (but decreasing in quantity if the set is working effectively). It may not be feasible to *start* at level V. (This is, in effect, strongly implied by Harrison's views on the depth of intervention).

CONCLUSION

Our attempts to understand what a teacher might best do in work-centred management development programmes has led us to develop particular models of what goes on in 'sets'. Our testing of these ideas is still in progress. However we feel that management teachers and trainers wishing to work in this area will benefit from having analytical tools which could help them become more effective.

Our feeling is that the evolving theory in these kind of programmes may have use to others who are considering what might be called 'non-curriculum based' modes, (i.e. approaches which do not use courses with predefined topics to cover). It may be, for instance, that tutors supervizing student projects might usefully consider how their style of supervision can maximize potential learning.

REFERENCES

Bolman, L. (1976). Group leader effectiveness, in Cooper C.L. (ed.), *Developing Social Skills in Managers,* Macmillan, London.

Burgoyne, J.G. and Stuart, R. (1977). Implicit learning theories as determinants of the effect of management development programmes, *Personnel Review,* **6**, (2), pp. 5–14.

Casey, D. (1976). The emerging role of set adviser in action learning programmes, *Journal of European Training,* **5**, (3).

Casey, D. and Pearce, D. (1977). *More Than Management Development: Action Learning at G.E.C.*, Gower Press, London.

Cooper, C.L. (1977). Taking the terror out of T-groups, *Personal Management,* January.

Cooper, C.L. and Bowles, D. (1977). *Hurt or Helped?* HMSO, London.

French, J. and Raven, B. (1968). The bases of social power, in Cartwright, D. and Zander, A. (eds), *Group Dynamics,* Harper and Row, New York.

Garratt, R. (1977). Don't call me teacher, in Casey, D. and Pearce, D. (eds), *More Than Management Development: Action Learning at G.E.C.*, Gower Press, London.

Gilmore, S. (1973). *The Counsellor-In-Training,* Prentice-Hall, Englewood Cliffs, N.J.

Harrison, R. (1970). Choosing the depth of organisational intervention, *Journal of Applied Behavioural Science,* **6**, (2), pp. 181–202.

Heron, J. (1977). *Dimensions of Facilitator Style,* British Postgraduate Medical Federation, London.

Lieberman, M. (1972). Behaviour and impact of leaders, in Solomon, L. and Berzon, B. (eds), *New Perspectives on Encounter Groups,* Jossey-Bass, San Francisco.

Lieberman, M., Yalom, I., and Miles, M. (1973). *Encounter Groups: First Facts,* Basic Books, New York.

Lippit, R. (1977). Interview with Anthony J. Reilly, *Group and Organisation Studies,* **2**, (3), September, pp. 266–267.

Lundgren, D.C. and Knight, D.J. (1978). Sequential stages of development in sensitivity training groups, *Journal of Applied Behavioural Science,* **14**, (2), pp. 204–222.

Peck, D. and Whitlow, D. (1975). *Approaches to Personality Theory,* Methuen, London.

Pfeiffer, J.W. and Jones, J.E. (1974). Assumptions about human relations training: an opinionaire, *Structured Experiences for Human Relations Training,* **1**. University Associates Publishers, Inc, San Diego.

Revans, R.W. (1971). *Developing Effective Managers: A New Approach to Business Education,* Longman, London.

Revans, R.W. (1974). *Autonomous Leadership Programmes: Development without Exchange,* A.L.P., London.

Revans, R.W. (1976). Management education: time for a rethink, *Personnel Management,* July, pp. 20–24.

Rogers, C.R. (1957). The necessary and sufficient conditions of therapeutic personality change, *Journal of Consulting Psychology,* **21**, pp. 95–103.

Rogers, C.R. (1967). *On Becoming a Person*, Houghton Mifflin, Boston.

Sadler, R. (1968). Executive leadership, in Pym (ed.), *Industrial Society,* Penguin, London.

Schutz, W. (1974). Not encounter and certainly not facts, in Pfeiffer, J. and Jones, J. (eds), *Annual Handbook for Group Facilitators.*

Truax, C.B. and Carkhuff, R.R. (1967). *Towards Effective Counselling and Psychotherapy: Training and Practice,* Aldine Pub. Co., Chicago.

Tyler, L.E. (1969). *The Work of the Counsellor* (3rd edn), Appleton-Century-Crofts, New York.

Advances in Management Education
Edited by John Beck and Charles Cox

CHAPTER 11

Is All Management Development Self-Development?

Mike Pedler and Tom Boydell

INTRODUCTION

The statement: 'All management development is self-development', was made by a participant at a seminar held for the Inter-ITB Study Group on Self-Development at the Training Services Agency early in 1977. It was delivered in a mildly attacking manner and it has caused us some puzzlement and confusion ever since. Much thinking went into trying to define just what is distinctive about management self-development when compared with current concepts of management development. Nevertheless the puzzle refuses to go away and in some ways all management development *is* self-development.

For some time much of our work concentrated upon the *self* part of self-development. This has been defined in two ways, namely:

- development by self
- development of self (Burgoyne *et al.*, 1978, p. 5; Boydell and Pedler, 1979, p. 4).

The first part of this paper reviews and summarizes this past work. The following section moves the focus on to the *development* rather than the self aspects of self-development.

BY SELF AND OF SELF

The first of these – the 'by self' dimension – is the conception of self-development as a process. The 'of self' dimension conceives self-development as a goal. If these dimensions are taken to be independent and put in a simple matrix, they give rise to four classes of development as in Figure 1. Whilst type A can be characterized as the 'purest' form of self-development, and type D as not at all self-developmental, types C and B are self-developmental in part.

Perhaps because we have been working on self-directed learning programmes for a number of years we have found the 'by self' dimensions easier to elaborate. From

GOALS / PROCESS	OF SELF	NOT OF SELF
Relatively self-responsible	A	B
Relatively non-self-responsible	C	D

Figure 1. A Typology of Self-Development
(From Burgoyne *et al.*, 1978, p. 13)

experience of short courses run on 'autonomy laboratory', 'learning community' or 'Free University' lines; and of our CNAA Post Graduate Diploma in Human Resources Management which we try to operate as a 'learning community', we can posit a clear distinction between conventional management development and management self-development, as shown in Figure 2.

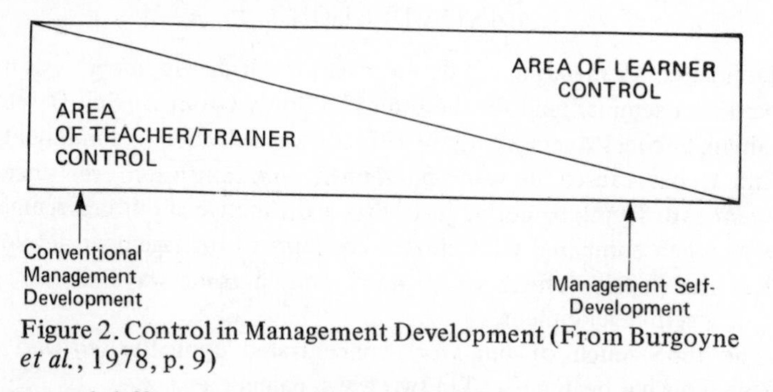

Figure 2. Control in Management Development (From Burgoyne *et al.*, 1978, p. 9)

The essential difference on the 'by self' dimension rests upon the focus of control. Control is critical with regard to several choices, decisions or stages in the learning and development process. Typically these include:

– choosing the *goals* for development
– deciding the *means* to achieve these goals
– deciding *when* and *in what sequence* to tackle the goals
– evaluating the success or otherwise of the development programme.

Elsewhere we have elaborated these choices, decisions, and stages in a matrix which allows for the choice of an overall profile for any learning or development situation (Burgoyne *et al.*, 1978, p. 10), as shown in Figure 3.

On the control/by self dimension, it is clear that much management development is not self-development. Management training and development is a relatively recent field which has inherited much of the systematic training 'philosophy' earlier developed for operator training. With a systematic approach to training and development, an external agent or 'expert' (i.e. someone other than the learner) determines needs, sets goals, plans and implements training programmes, and evaluates them in his terms. This approach to training and development has been widely propogated

DEGREE OF CONTROL / PROCESS STAGE	Teacher/ Trainer Unilateral	Learner Right to Information	Learner Right to Consultation	Negotiated or Shared Control	Teacher/ Trainer Right to Consultation	Teacher/ Trainer Right to Information	Learner Unilateral
Problem/opportunity recognition	TU	LI	LC	SC	TC	TI	LU
Developing commitment	TU	LI	LC	SC	TC	TI	LU
Choosing learning goals	TU	LI	LC	SC	TC	TI	LU
Identifying resources	TU	LI	LC	SC	TC	TI	LU
Planning action	TU	LI	LC	SC	TC	TI	LU
Taking action	TU	LI	LC	SC	TC	TI	LU
Testing learning in application	TU	LI	LC	SC	TC	TI	LU
Evaluation and reviewing	TU	LI	LC	SC	TC	TI	LU

ANY LEARNING/DEVELOPMENT SITUATION CAN BE PROFILED BY CIRCLING ONE OF THE POSTIONS ON EACH ROW

Figure 3. A Control Profile of a Development Situation

by Industry Training Boards and is still the dominant approach used for operator and clerical training. Whilst we are concerned here with management development, it is worth noting in passing that the dominance of this approach for operator training is not unchallenged. Systematic training makes certain assumptions about the person which apply whether that person is manager or operative. However, the de-skilled and circumscribed nature of much operative and clerical work enables the systematic approach to more easily be sustained. We have elsewhere suggested that managerial work is characterized by four inter-related factors which make it less easy to sustain a systematic approach (Burgoyne *et al.*, 1978, pp. 15–16). These factors are:

- the complexity and variability of managerial work;
- the fact that managers exist to deal with unprogrammed as opposed to programmed problems;
- managerial work involves ordering and co-ordinating the work of others; to do this the manager must first be able to create similar order and co-ordination in himself;
- the need for managers to move and work across technical, cultural, and functional boundaries demands an ability to adapt quickly and to have 'learned how to learn'.

These factors create conditions for which we would argue the especial relevance of self-development strategies. Quite often systematic strategies simply do not 'work' in terms of developing managerial competence. Whilst they may seem to 'work' with operative a clerical training, it is worth noting that they may only do so because of the limitations, which in the view of an increasing number of writers, are leading to a widespread rejection of work and employment (Pym, 1979; Sheane, 1978).

Whilst we limit ourselves here to managerial work, the development approach chosen usually reflects a basic split in the concept of the person – his talents, his potential, and his nature.

In preparing an annotated bibliography on management self-development, we reviewed the literature in a number of apparently distinct theoretical perspectives such as psychology, adult education, politics, and general systems theory. It appeared to us that these apparently diverse perspectives led to a common set of guiding principles which assumed a view of either the 'learner as patient' or the 'learner as agent'. Whilst we had noted this dichotomy earlier when examining families of learning theories (Burgoyne *et al.*, 1978, pp. 12–13) the bibliography work showed that 'patient' and 'agent' rested on the philosophical dichotomy of determinism *vs* free will. This dichotomy could be seen at work not only in learning theory but in any field of study which involved human action as a focus. This genealogy of development principles, strategies, and outcomes was presented diagrammatically (Boydell and Pedler, 1979, p. 10), as shown in Figure 4.

Whilst non-self-development principles and strategies do exist widely in management development, we are concerned here with those situations where managers *do* set their own development goals, decide how, when, and where to achieve them, and evaluate success against their own criteria. In the ATM publication and the bibliography a number of these self-development strategies were identified – strategies which involve the learner as self-directing agent. These included:

- action learning;
- self-improvement;
- learning communities/autonomy laboratories;
- experiential groups;
- mind/body approaches;
- learning conversations and focused feedback;
- structured activities.

Obviously there are others, including most of those being presented at this conference. One major criticism of these approaches is that they are nearly all in a sense 'contrived' (Temporal, 1978) involving organization by others and being off-the-job. Much, if not most, management self-development takes place during the course of everyday work and life experience. This point has been made forcefully by Alan Mumford (1978) who favours self-development 'in real situations and not in classrooms or other hypothetical and abstract settings'. The approach of Hawdon

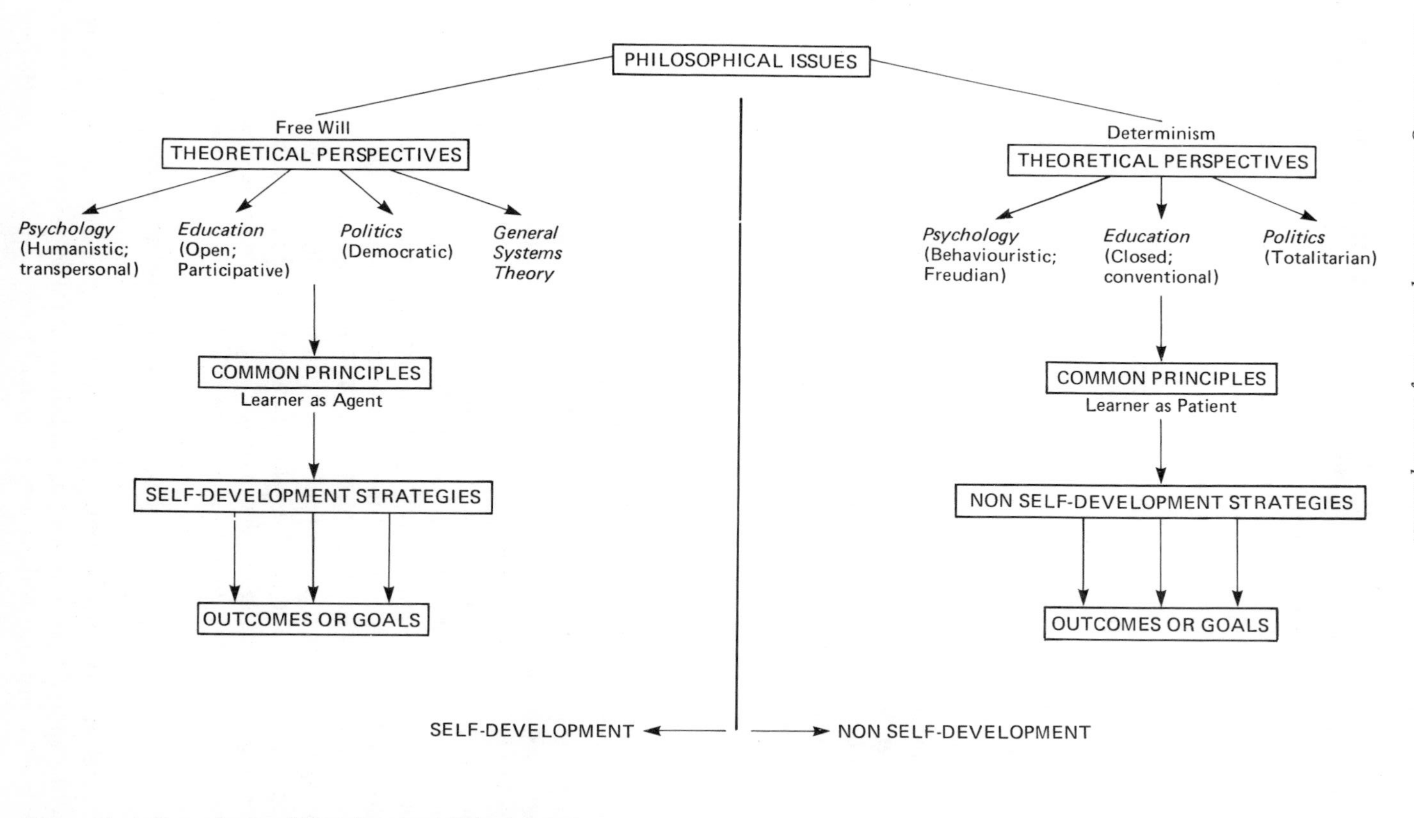

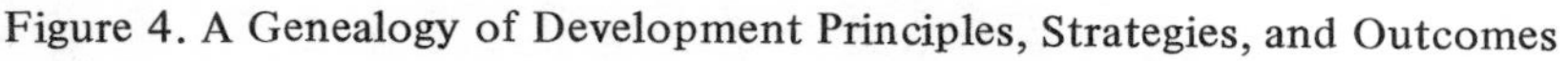

Figure 4. A Genealogy of Development Principles, Strategies, and Outcomes

Hague (1977, 1978) seeks to utilize these 'real time management situations'. We return to this point later.

One puzzle which remains from Figure 4 is that self-development and free-will strategies are seen as 'good' whilst deterministic and non-self-development strategies tend to be classified as 'bad'. However much we may rationalize it, a very definite value position exists. Does this then mean that no place exists for non-development strategies? Clearly not, as in certain situations both in teaching and in managing we find ourselves behaving 'as if' learners were 'patients', i.e. largely determined and limited by genetic and environmental factors. Environmental contingencies may lead to deterministic and non-self-developmental strategies being adopted even where a trainer/teacher is ideologically committed to free-will and self-development. For example:

- *the nature of the learning,* i.e. by domain, e.g. cognitive, psychomotor, affective, interpersonal; or by *level* e.g. memory, understanding, application, autonomy;
- *the learning style and state of readiness of the learner* including his expectations of the teacher/trainer and various blocks to learning;
- *the teaching/training style of the teacher/trainer* including his personal preferences, expectations of the learner, and ideology of teaching/learning;
- *the nature and availability of resources* interpreted widely to include other people, work and life situations, and the learning climate;

are all factors which affect the choice of the development approach to be taken. We might assume that the more a trainer or teacher is committed to a 'by self' strategy of development the more he will involve learners in the free-will/determinism issue, raising it, exploring it, and returning to it as it appears during the learning and development process. We cannot assume that self-development strategies are 'right' for all types of learning, all trainers, and all situations.

Thus far we have concentrated upon the 'by self' dimension. What then of the 'of self' aspect of self-development? We have often used the concept of the 'self-actualized individual' – as found in the writings of Maslow, Rogers, Argyris and others – to illustrate the 'of self' dimension. This puts forward the concept of the person who has realized most of his or her potential, who is 'fully grown' in a developmental sense. The putative value of 'self-actualized individuals' in management rests on the proposition that more 'fully grown' people are generally more competent in what they do and therefore specifically more effective as managers. Obviously this is open to question.

Some of the qualities of the 'self-actualized individual' are set out in Figure 5 (Boydell, 1976, p. 41). The question then arises: are there any aspects of management development which do not give rise to the development of self? At first glance the answer appears to be 'yes' and in the ATM publication we cited the example of a manager working with a 'by self' process on a non- 'of self' goal

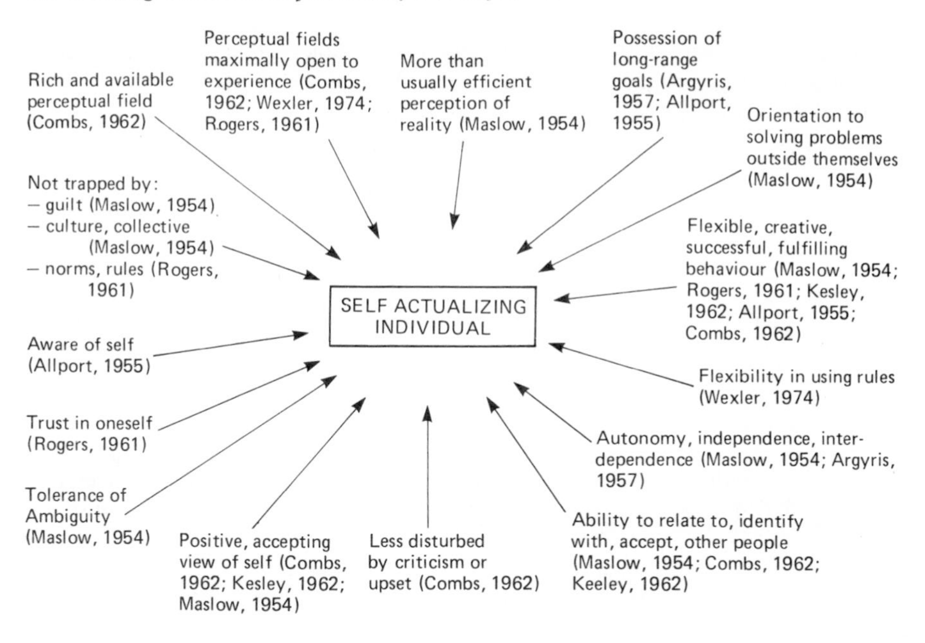

Figure 5. Characteristics of the Self Actualizing Individual

(Burgoyne *et al.*, 1978, p. 13). This manager was working on his own initiative to understand and get better at stock control through a self-designed programme of reading and practical work in his own situation. Understanding and being better at stock control would seem to have little to contribute to the development of self. In fact, and after some more recent efforts with managers looking at events which were developmental for them, this assumption cannot be sustained. If managers (or other people) are asked what events in their lives stand out as critical or especially salient to their development, a most remarkable variety appears. Whilst some of these events have an obvious link to the 'of self' dimension, e.g. being put on the spot by senior managers; absence of boss or death of close relative, there are others that do not, e.g. learning to drive; serving on committees at work; being forced to do a 'boring' job. The reason for this is straightforward: development is a function of the individual interacting with some part of his environment either actually or symbolically – there is no development without a developer. The event which leads to development may appear mundane, but its meaning for the individual concerned is what matters. If he or she finds significance and personal meaning in the event, then that is a self-development experience. It is the finding of meaning which turns the event into a developmental experience of the individual self. Each person then, has to name or define his own self-goals and only the individual can decide what is or has been a self-learning for him. Quite clearly, learning about stock control can be a mundane piece of drill or routine for one person, and for another it can mean a considerable self-achievement, perhaps changing a self-image, adding to self-esteem through changing the views of others about the person, and so on. It is by no means paradoxical to imagine this manager, a few years later, saying 'one of the most significant self-development events in my life was when I finally got to grips with the stock control business'.

In his discussion of 'experiential learning' Chickering (1977) makes this point rather well. His usage of the term 'experiential learning' is synonymous with our use of the term 'development'.

> 'In this chapter the term experiential learning means the learning that occurs when changes in judgements, feelings, knowledge, or skills result for a particular person from living through an event or events. It is not confined, as some usages have it, to such events as encounter groups, field trips, and work experiences. Within our usage experiential learning may result from attending a lecture, but the learning would be that resulting from living through the event with its attendant joy or suffering, and not simply from the content of the lecture, though that is clearly part of the event. Experiential learning may also result from an encounter group or an exam., discussion or demonstration, work or play, travel or sitting on a stump.'

So our earlier position is shown as being simplistic. It now seems that what constitutes an 'of self' development event is individually-specific. We cannot postulate, e.g. that being given an action learning project or being attached for a while to another department will be developmental. Equally we cannot assume that being neglected or left to do a boring job will be non-developmental. To return briefly to our title we can conclude that not all management development, as designed and implemented, leads to development 'of self'. This raises more questions, principally: what do we mean by development in this context?, and secondly: what characterizes the development process in managers?

WHAT IS DEVELOPMENT?

The brief examination of the 'of self' dimension leads to a more detailed examination of what we mean when we talk about 'development'. As we cannot recognize of-self development from external events in that what constitutes such a self-development event is individually-specific, is there a generalized model of the development process which we can recognize? We would like to approach this issue in two ways – first using data collected from managers, then from the viewpoint of 'developmental psychology'.

Some Data on Development of Self

First then, the 'real-data' approach. In fact, so far we have collected only a limited amount of such data, using a quick, informal collection method with approximately 50 managers and management trainers. These managers and trainers were asked to identify five or six key development events in their lives. Each event may have lasted a very short time or been spread over a period of months or years. For each event the participants are asked to describe its characteristics (using adjectives and short phrases) and also to list some of its outcomes and effects. This data was collected not so much for 'research purposes' as for 'here-and-now' use in group sessions. We hope to set up a more formal enquiry in the near future.

In keeping with the way this data was collected, we have avoided a formal analysis in favour of an attempt to give an overall flavour. Thus Figure 6 shows a sample of the listed outcomes of various developmental events. Even a casual glance at Figure 6 raises a number of interesting issues. For example, most of the outcomes are positive, but some are negative. In fact, some events led both to apparently positive and negative outcomes, at the same time.

- Maturity
- Communication
- Shattering of self-image but very productive in my own learning
- Credibility with staff
- More self-questioning
- Concern for my wife
- Realization of how much I can do for myself as a person
- Much clearer idea of directions I want to pursue
- Physical skill
- Improved and worsened personal relationships
- Changed views on meaning of life and death
- Feeling of completeness
- Feeling that fun is legitimate
- Independence
- New sense of personal capabilities
- Greater willingness to stick to a point of view/to look after own interests
- Started to form my own values (previously I was just conditioned)
- Confidence (mentioned frequently)
- Empathy
- Desire for more experiences
- Changed relationship with wife and children
- Perceived the world as less safe
- Don't know yet (still working with it)
- Limits of endurance and tolerance of fear
- More flexible and relaxed approach to relationships
- Less tied to things
- Opened up new modes of consciousness
- Removal of claustrophobia
- Bad feelings and sexual jealousy
- Boredom
- Physical fitness
- Improvement in judgement and perspective of what is good and evil

Figure 6. Some Outcomes of Key Developmental Events

A number of clusters seem to appear – for example, general 'confidence, maturity, independence'. Other tentative groups might include:

- making my own mind up, thinking for myself, own values;
- interpersonal relationships
  - with family
  - with others;
- motivation, direction, purpose in life;
- modes of consciousness, feelings about life and death.

Thus it can be seen that, although a large number of different outcomes are reported, certain themes appear to emerge.

Development, Growth, and Change

We would now like to compare these themes with established models from developmental psychology. A number of these exist, associated with various dimensions of development.

First of all, what is 'development'? Langer (1969a, pp. 3–4) distinguishes between *alteration* and *growth* (after Aristotle) in that the latter is quantitative change, whilst the former is 'a qualitative change by which the system is conserved, but its mode or structure is transformed . . . This type of qualitative change means both continuity and discontinuity in the system'. An example of such a qualitative transformation would be learning to walk, as opposed to crawling. Langer then goes on to note that 'properly speaking both alteration and growth may be considered as the two elements of "development".' Seen this way, development has both a gradual, incremental, improvement aspect and an abrupt, step-jump, transformation aspect: a continuous and a discontinuous aspect.

This view is not shared by everybody, however. Langer (1969b, pp. 22–37) suggests that the various theories of development can be classified into three types – mechanistic/behaviouristic, organismic, and psychoanalytic. The first of these 'assumes that psychological growth is nothing but the increasing quantitative and continuous accumulation of behaviour. There is no qualitative discontinuity – structural or functional – in development' (Langer 1969b, p. 22). The other two schools stress the importance of qualitative change. In psychoanalytic theory, this change is largely around the re-establishment of equilibrium between the conflicting forces of intrapsychic forces. The organismic approach involves changes in the way in which the person perceives and makes sense of the world. Thus, development here refers to qualitative changes in the way I interpret what is going on around and within me. (Baldwin, 1969, Kohlberg, 1969, 1971).

Models of Development

Dale and Payne (1976) suggest that Maslow's hierarchy can be seen as three developmental bands termed (after Alderfer), Existence, Relatedness, and Growth. Progress can be within bands or between them and *within*-band progress is seen as incremental and continuous development, whilst *between*-band development is essentially discontinuous and involves a step-jump. The generalized model of three broad bands of development ties in with a great deal of work done by researchers in other fields.

Each specialist tends to have studied one or two very specific dimensions of development (e.g. Piaget – intellectual; Kohlberg – moral; Loevinger – ego; Maslow – needs/motivation). These dimensions have been studied in rather great detail, usually with considerable supporting empirical data. Some of these primary sources have then made parallels between two or more dimensions of development. Kohlberg (1969, 1971) for example, relates his stages of moral development to five other models of moral development, to four models of ego development, and to Piaget's model of intellectual development. This approach has also been adopted by a number of secondary sources (e.g. Rowan, 1975; Chickering, 1977; Dale and Payne, 1976).

In this paper we will first attempt such a synthesis involving some different dimensions from the sources referred to, and this raises one or two questions about its validity. Both Rowan (1975) and Dale and Payne (1976) use as a base three stages of development – Existence, Relatedness, and Growth. This too will be our base.

In Table 1, then, we present six dimensions of development, seen in parallel with corresponding stages on each. Since this table contains rather a lot of data, it might be as well to attempt a brief overview.

At the level of Existence, the individual is basically fighting for survival. He sees the world as threatening, and is defensive, fearful. He sees things in terms of stark contrasts – of right and wrong, goodies and baddies. His actions, aimed at physical safety, are governed by fear of retaliation and punishment. He is competitive, aggressive, unconcerned for others. Many organizations seem to assume that their employees are at the existence level with authoritarian structures and power ideologies (Harrison, 1972). Perhaps this is a self-fulfilling prophecy or a self-sustaining cycle. After all, in a power-oriented organization, most of us are indeed having to fight for survival. Learning is, naturally enough, seen as a means to survival. Hence the individual has to be content with the minimum knowledge necessary to do his job – although of course, he may well be trying to learn more, in order to have some competitive advantage over someone else to gain promotion. As far as working life is concerned, at any rate, all too many of us are forced to live at existence level.

As we move up to level 2 – Relatedness – the individual, now secure from basic threat, begins to feel a need to belong, to have friends, to achieve recognition from others. He begins to share with others, to trust them – although often this trust is confined to his own group, to 'us', with strong negative feelings towards other departments, outsiders, foreigners. He gradually becomes aware that perhaps the world is not all good/bad, right/wrong, and that some questions are rather complex Nonetheless, in coping with this ambiguity he gradually becomes committed to the rules and norms of his organization or group, with which he now feels a strong identification. Order, rules, 'role culture' (Harrison, 1972) are strongly valued in such organizations. However, at times conflicts, game playing, interpersonal stress, and double binds occur. Learning may be aimed at overcoming these conflicts (e.g. most Organization Development interventions), although there is also a 'luxury good' element in learning which is designed to enhance their feeling of esteem and worth, 'the size of each such package being in accord with the person's probable social prestige' (Fromm, 1978). Thus junior to middle managers with lower middle-class backgrounds attend the DMS at a local college. Upper middle-class managers and/or those with aspirations to higher management, go to a Business School, a Staff College, or even go to Harvard.

Most organizations are attuned either to Existence or Relatedness. Few seem to

Table 1. A Synthesis of Some Development Theories

Level (Alderfer, 1972)	Ethical/Moral Development (Loevinger, 1966 and Kohlberg, 1969)	Ways of Knowing (Various)	Interpersonal Style (Loevinger, 1966, Argyris and Schon, 1975)
Growth[1]	Integrated – reconciling inner conflict[2] Moral principle[3]	Inspiration, intuition[4] Coalescence of knowing and being[5] Prehension – non-duality (i.e. polarity)[6] Growing confidence, acceptance that apparent opposites are not in conflict[7]	Move from tolerating to cherishing individual differences[2]
	Autonomous – coping with inner conflict[2] Social contract legalistic[3]	Imagination[4] Emergence of prehension[6] Beginning to make no-right-answer decision[7]	Recognition of mutual interdependence and others' needs for autonomy[2]
Relatedness[1]	Conscientious – internalization, commitment to, rules and norms of particular group[2] Authority, rule, and social order[3]	Imagination[4] Duality[6] may appear. Realization that perhaps there cannot be a right answer[7] Luxury version of having knowledge – depends on social prestige[8]	Reciprocal but often mutual trust; often extended only to those in narrow in-group[2] Model II – minimally defensive interpersonal relations[9]
	Conformist – adherence to external rules and norms[2] Good boy approval[3]		
Existence[1]	Opportunistic – rules recognized, obeys out of fear of being caught[2] Instrumental egoism[3]	Material knowldge[4] Distinction between knower and known[5] duality[6]	Exploitive, manipulative, varying degree of dependency[2] Model I – defensive, competitive, controlling, fearful, withholding feelings, relative unconcern for others[9]
	Impulse ridden – no recognition of rules; fear of retaliation[2] Obedience and punishment oriented[3]	There must be an answer seen in terms of right/wrong, good/bad, us/them[7] Having knowledge – minimum to do one's job[8]	

Notes related to Table 1

1. Alderfer, C. *Existence, Relatedness, and Growth*, New York. Collier Macmillan, 1972.
2. Loevinger, J. The Meaning and Measurement of Ego Development, *American Psychologist*, Vol. 21, No. 3, March 1966, pp. 195–206.
3. (i) Kohlberg, L. Stage and Sequence: The Cognitive Developmental Approach to Socialization, in Goslin, D.A. (ed.), *Handbook of Socialization Theory and Research*, Chicago, Rand McNally, 1969, pp. 347, 480.

and/or (ii) Kohlberg, L. The Concepts of Developmental Psychology as the Central Guide to Education. Examples from Cognitive, Moral, and Psychological Education, in Reynolds, M.C. (ed.), *Proceedings of the Conference on Psychology and the Process of Schooling in the Next Decade: Alternative Coceptions*, Washington DC: Bureau for Educational Personnel Development, US Office of Education, 1971.

Needs, Motivation (Maslow, 1968) Preoccupation (Loevinger, 1966)	'Potentials' (Wilber, 1975, 1977)	'Dys-ease' after (Wilber 1975)
Self-actualization[10] Identity[2]	Transcending of space–time (Maslow) Mythological awareness (Jung)	Transpersonal anxiety
Esteem (own)[10] Development, Self-fulfilment[2]	Existential freedom Authenticity (Perls) Centredness Being mode (Fromm)[8]	Existential anxiety – fear of death, of the void
Esteem (from others)[10] Achievements[2]	Civilization Culture Social membership Language Law Logic	Double-binds Social alination Conflict War 'Normal neuroses' Games People Play (Berne)
Belongingness[10] Things, appearance, reputation[2]		Acquisitive Society
Safety[10] Advantage, control[2]	Deliberate self-control Civility Verbal communication	Chronic low-grade emergency (Paris) Depression as out-of-touch with one's body (Lowen) Having (Fromm)[8]
Physiological[10] survival Bodily feelings, especially sexual and agressive[2]	Pride, drive to success Righteous indignation Romantic love	Panic anxiety; Guilt; Hatred; Depression as retroflected; Rage; Fear

4. Steiner, R. *The Stages of Higher Knowldge*, New York, Anthroposophic Press, 1967.
5. Deutsch, E. *Adavnta Vendanta, A Philosophical Reconstruction*, Honolulu: East-West Centre Press, 1969.
6. Whitehead, A.N. *Process and Reality*, New York, Macmillan (Free Press), 1969.
7. Perry, W.G. *Forms of Intellectual and Ethical Development in the College Years*, New York, Holt, Rinehart, and Winston, 1970.
8. Fromm, E. *To Have or to Be?* London, Jonathan Cape, 1978; also Sphere Books, 1979.
9. Argyris, C. and Schon, D.A. *Theory in Practice*, San Francisco: Jossey-Bass, 1975.
10. Maslow, A. *Towards a Psychology of Being*, New York, Von Nostrand, 1968.
11. Wilber, K. *The Spectrum of Consciousness*, Wheaton, III. Theosophical Publishing House, 1977.
12. Wilber, K. Psychological Perennis: The Spectrum of Consciousness, *Journal of Transpersonal Psychology*, Vol. 7, No. 2, 1975, pp. 105–132.

be interested in – or prepared to allow – Growth. Perhaps this is not surprising, since it seems that few of us reach the top of this level (the self-actualized individual is a rarity). In any case, since Growth tends to be associated with a decline in materialism (with a parallel rise in spirituality, using the word in a rather broad sense), the nature and purpose both of one's own existence and, presumably, that of one's organization, then such a person is seen as pretty threatening by others. This threat is reinforced by the move away from established norms and rules towards a desire to think for oneself, to struggle with uncertainty and doubt (not relying on the crutch of established practice), together with a refusal to see things in over-simplistic ways, to be pushed into right-answer solutions. 'Such men are dangerous', although a few organizations – often co-operative (not the Co-op) – with an individual ideology (Harrison, 1972) seem to thrive on such danger. A possible example here is Social Ecology Associates, the UK offshoot of the Dutch NPI group of consultants, founded consciously on Anthroposophical principles (Easton, 1975).

Conclusion

Notwithstanding the relative recency of stage theories of development, there seems to be some consensus on what characterizes the higher levels of development compared with the lower ones. For example development tends to mean autonomous rather than conforming behaviour; altruism and respect for others rather than egocentricity; tolerance of ambiguity rather than conceptual simplicity; synthesis and evaluation rather than memorization. What Table 1 shows is that the higher stages of development have much in common with the characteristics of the 'self-actualized individual' described earlier (see Figure 5).

Stage theories add to this concept in two ways. First of all they show the pathways to these characteristics rather than just the rather exalted state of the 'self-actualized individual'. This offers self-developers, and those who would help, some sort of a map, although most theorists are agreed that progression through their hierarchies of stages, whilst sequential, is not a simple matter of course, e.g. of ageing. Progress depends upon the 'specific person–environment interactions influenced by genetic predispositions and limitations.' (Chickering, 1977, p. 66).

The second contribution of stage theories is to illustrate how we may be at different levels of functioning on different dimensions, e.g. 'growth' level intellectually, 'existence' level in terms of 'ego' or 'ethics'. In different 'specific person–environment interactions' we can be at different levels on the same dimension e.g. at the 'growth' level interpersonally with colleagues and 'existence' level with one's spouse! Whilst they provide us with no excuse for our frequently bizarre or 'under-developed' actions, stage theories do help to explain them.

There does seem to be some commonsense and generalized corroboration for the applicabilities of the theories summarized in Table 1 in other relevant writing. Two examples are Argyris (1957, pp. 49–50) who postulates seven basic self-actualization trends in the human personality and Knowles (1970, pp. 24–29) who puts forward fifteen dimensions of the mature individual.

One remaining puzzle is the extent to which 'development' is culturally specific. Most of the researchers involved come from Europe and the USA and it seems that stage theories must rest upon assumptions and values which are to some extent culturally specific. On the other hand, several stage theorists including Piaget, Kohlberg, and Maslow claim universal applicability for their work, often based on weighty empirical verification in a number of societies. Dale and Payne (1976, p. 2) remind us that their model of development is anything but new and has its roots in 2000 years of human history in diverse cultures. This is a point illustrated by Wilber (1975, 1977) who ties his development model into a number of Hindu and Bhuddist traditions.

Having gone some way towards answering the question 'What is development?' the next question concerns the 'how' of development – what does the process look like?

WHAT DOES THE DEVELOPMENT PROCESS LOOK LIKE?

Whilst there is some consensus about what development is, evidence on the process seems less easy to capture. There are a number of questions which can be identified as important in terms of describing this process, some of which are discussed below.

Incremental or Step-jump?

We have already commented on these twin aspects of development and noted Dale and Payne's (1976, p. 3) view that movement *within* broad developmental bands may be incremental, movement *between* bands involves a step-jump. In particular, movement between the second and third bands – relatedness and growth – involves crossing the 'great gap'. The 'great gap' represents the effort required to leave behind comfortable life lived according to societal standards and norms, in order to achieve the autonomous stage where standards are self-set and individuals are self-directed.

This concept of 'leaping the void' or the 'leap of faith' is a familiar one which can be found in many ancient writings and more recently in the existential philosophers. Recently Hampden-Turner (1971, pp. 50–52) has made the 'existential leap' to bridge the gap between self and other; old and new; thesis and antithesis; a central part of his model of psycho-social development. In Don Juan's teachings, Castenada (1970, 1974) can only achieve a 'separate reality' through suspending himself, through literally dissolving the ego and 'embracing the enemy', i.e. the other, that most feared etc. Most of the theorists discussed in the last section point out that movement from one stage to another in their stage theories of development is not a simple matter of course.

We are personally most familiar perhaps with incremental development. After all, our whole educational system is constructed to achieve this and the influential family of behaviourist learning theories strongly supports this view. The thought of

– stimulating	– competitive
– shattering experience	– positive
– different from what expected	– releasing
– traumatic	– emotional
– alien	– unsure
– exciting	– relief
– trust	– horror
– shocking	– wow!
– pain	– aesthetic
– nuisance	– unmanning
– dangerous	– ecstacy
– exciting	– tremendous

Figure 7. Some Described Characteristics of Key Development Events

discontinuous 'leap over the void' is unfamiliar and frightening. By definition the steps cannot be clearly mapped out, there is only one alternative: either to jump or to stay safely but consciously limited on this side. As an illustration, Figure 7 shows some descriptions of development events taken from our data.

Obviously some risks are greater than others – to risk a new form of dress at the office is not of the same magnitude as to risk another lifestyle by emigrating to Tierra del Fuego. Nevertheless both can lead to development of the step-jump type. The simplest conclusion from this discussion seems to be that whilst incremental, safe, development may be possible 'within bands', it is not likely to produce *qualitative* as opposed to *quantitative* development. Thus Revans (1971, p. 113) concludes that the managers on his Belgian programme learned 'relatively suddenly'. To achieve quality the existing order and some risk seems essential, with the inevitable, but hopefully temporary, dislocation and disorder which must accompany these. (This 'temporary' dislocation may last a long time – months or even years – it is 'temporary' in the sense of the general tendency towards equilibrium).

Is Crisis Necessary?

If development is of the step-jump rather than the incremental kind, then the person will almost certainly experience the development period as a 'crisis'. A period in which the skills and competences hard-won over the years are of no avail to him; a period in which a substantial part of his reality has collapsed or disappeared. A manager made redundant, a wife losing her husband, and at a less critical level an authoritarian teacher being answered back, are all examples of potential crises. The 'crisis' occurs when the existing system or competences cannot cope with the new challange – which may come from within or without.

In line with the individually specific nature of self-development events, what is a crisis for me, is often not one for you. Obviously there are some generalizations that can be made here and Thomas Holmes and his associates at the University of Washington have developed a list of life crises ordered by stress level based upon the

Death of Spouse	100
Divorce	73
Jail term	63
Marriage	50
Fired at work	47
Change to different work	36
Outstanding personal achievement	28
Trouble with boss	23
Change of residence	20
Change in eating habits	15
Minor violations of the law	11

From: Holmes and Rahe (1967)

Figure 8. Life Crises and their relative stress Values

results of 5,000 interviews. Figure 8 gives a sample of some of these life crises and their relative rating according to Holmes *et al*., (Death of Spouse = 100).

Any change seems to involve a level of stress and in management development terms there are crises and crises. Stress has a positive function in that it mobilizes us for action, which turns to a negative function when it rises beyond the optimum for any individual at any point in time.

Dale and Payne (1976, p. 9 and Figure 4) present a further model which elaborates the within-band and between-band types of development. The step-jump needed for band development comes from environmental pressure, i.e. development occurs when the individual is pushed beyond the comfortable, where things begin to hurt or get out of control. They point out quite firmly that most management development does not create this type of environmental pressure and therefore does not lead to between-band development:

> Since many educational and training experiences do not generate the sustained element of pressure which pushes the person into the zone of maximum development potential, *we believe they lead to development within a level but rarely to development across levels* (Their emphasis).

Perhaps a better word than 'crisis' which may be overly dramatic, is 'perturbation'. A 'perturbation' is some turbulence that disconfirms our previous view or judgement and which makes us stop and think. Too much perturbation and we will not be able to think. In talking to managers about self-development experiences, we have often asked them whether the development took place as a flash of insight or as a gradual process. What they have frequently said is that whilst the event which led to the development was sudden and of 'crisis' proportions, e.g. death of a loved one; the development process is best described as the *recovery* from that crisis. It has usually been quite a time before they could even acknowledge the new reality and often over a period of years they have kept returning to the experience in order to reflect, puzzle, and eventually assimilate it. On the other hand, what leads to development is often less than 'crisis' – a niggling or worrying about something previously taken for granted.

We may conclude this section by saying that perhaps development attends upon perturbation in that some disconfirmation must occur before the development process is set in action.

How does Perturbation Link with Development? (or not)

We are often perturbed you may say, but this does not always lead to development. Well, perhaps not. Clearly this is only a first step and all sorts of factors will affect whether development 'takes' in a given perturbation. One of these is our own belief in self-development as a concept and as a way of living. Whether this holds for a particular individual may well depend upon personality factors, belief systems, and current environmental factors. Before considering these three elements however, we can postulate something of a generalized perturbation or surprise models of development.

A great many writers point to the need for surprise, perturbation or disconfirmation as the necessary prerequisite for attention and hence learning. Charlesworth (1969), for example, presents a model which has many parallels with that of Kolb *et al.* (1971, pp. 21–29) and Revans' (1971) System beta (see Figure 9). This surprise captures attention and reflection which leads to an advance in the level of thinking about the problem or situation. This development leads in turn to new expectations or 'hypotheses' which, when tested on reality may lead to new surprise and enquiry.

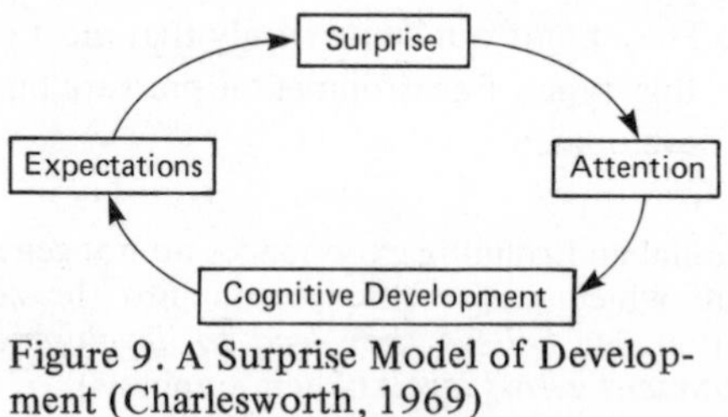

Figure 9. A Surprise Model of Development (Charlesworth, 1969)

Given what was said earlier about requisite stress levels for learning, must 'surprise' always lead to learning? It has often been apparent to us in situations when we and others have been attempting to learn about something, that some people are more able than others to take certain things 'on board' and learn from them whilst others could not. Box 1 gives an example of this.

BOX 1: Negotiating the Surprise level

On a recent in-company programme for production managers, an intergroup 'Planners' and 'Operators' exercise created the usual failures to communicate and cross boundaries. This exercise followed a morning analysing the host organization pin-pointing such problem areas as liaison between sales and production, production planning and production departments, and generally lateral communication throughout the company. In the view of the trainer the exercise had 'worked very well' – the communication gaps discussed earlier were very apparent in the intergroup exercise. Naturally this was no 'surprise' to the trainer, he'd planned and 'seen it all before'. The managers however, had great difficulty in 'seeing it' and strenuous efforts were made to fend the 'surprise' off. There were attempts to deny the reality and therefore the relevance of the exercise; attempts to blame the trainer for 'bad briefing'; and, especially by the 'planners', the attempt to blame it on the 'operators'. The trainer's response was to use humour in reviewing the exercise; to identify himself personally with some of the 'surprises', and to continually point up the universalistic aspects of various actions, i.e. 'all managers, all people, have a tendency to do this'. These responses are designed to reduce the anxiety attendant on the 'surprise' to a level where it can be 'taken-on-board' and receive proper attention. In effect the level of surprise is being negotiated between trainer and group (and perhaps between and within group members).

Although different individuals can clearly 'take-on-board' different levels of surprise, there is a definite group level of acceptance before discussion and reflection is legitimated. Once this has been achieved it obviously does not guarantee that each individual will learn from his/her experience but it does give everyone the opportunity in theory.

Charlesworth's (1969) Surprise Model seems to neglect the possibility that the 'surprise', 'crisis', 'perturbation', or 'shock' may be too strong to allow for it to be 'taken-on-board' and for learning to take place. We can envisage a number of possibilities stemming from perturbation which do not always result in learning. Figure 10 emerged from discussions which we had with Dale Young (Diploma in Human Resources Management, Sheffield City Polytechnic, 1978–79) about learning from 'bad' or 'unpleasant' experiences. Our personal experiences suggest that reflection on such experiences is not automatic or necessarily productive, and that to exorcize the experience, and probably to learn from it, requires strenuous emotional and intellectual efforts and perhaps the help of skilled others. Fink's (1971) 'Shock Model' is clearly relevant here.

Thus in Figure 10, whilst there is the possibility of a developmental outcome, there are also several options which do not lead to learning and growth. Two of these, REPRESSION and OBSESSION, may have serious consequences for future action and are perhaps not resolvable except with skilled help from another. The others, RATIONALIZATION and ATTACKING SOURCE, are common enough defence mechanisms which we use daily. Whereas the two non-developmental outcomes which are concerned with denying the perturbation are basically 'rejecting' strategies, RATIONALIZATION and OBSESSION are 'accepting' strategies where

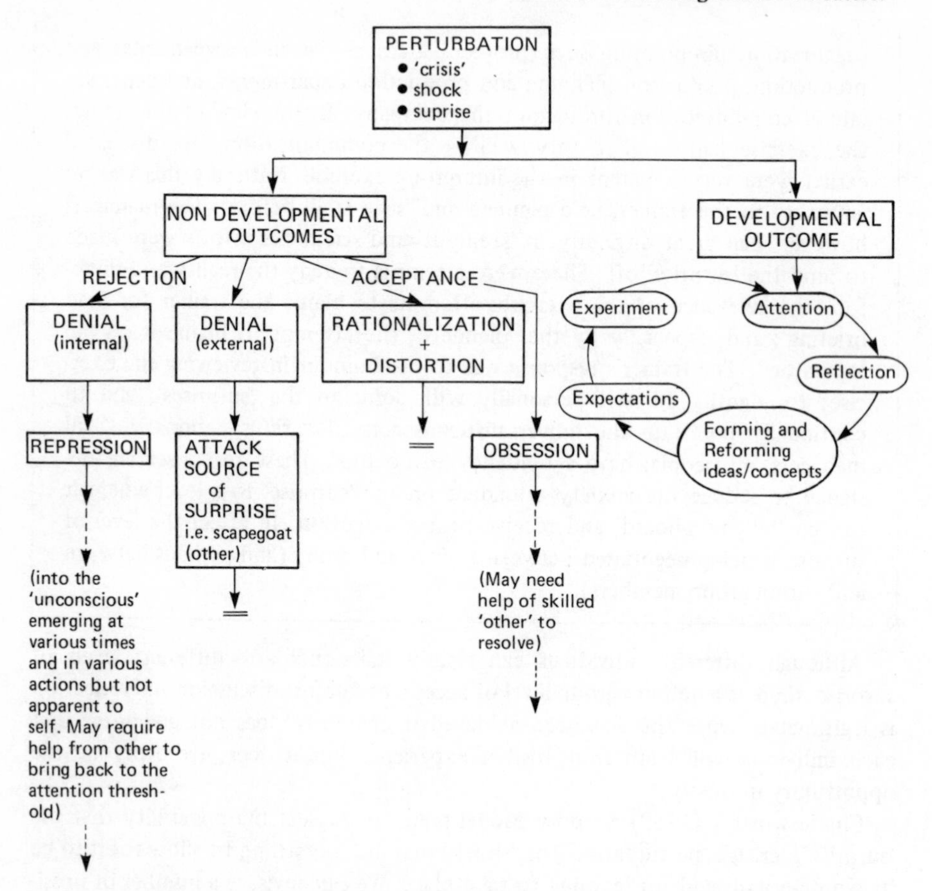

Figure 10. Developmental and Non-Developmental Outcomes from Perturbation

the perturbation has been partly or wholly 'taken-on-board' but where we do not have the resources or capacities for developing it.

The developmental outcome can only be achieved if we possess, or can obtain, the necessary resources and skills to reflect, form ideas, etc. A very painful experience such as a bereavement may take a long time to result in a developmental outcome as in Frankl's (1963) example of the man who only accepted the death of his wife after the therapist had pointed out what agony the woman would have undergone had the man died first. Whilst such experiences may be brought to development with the help of a therapist, our own experience suggests that we can, and do, often do it for ourselves with somewhat less shocking experiences. Nevertheless the more painful the experience the more the process will be a tentative and backwards-and-forwards one – now taking a step towards the painful experience and now away from it – gradually getting closer until we can contemplate it without fear, then touch it, explore it, and learn from it.

In terms of management development, as we have already remarked, the 'learning situations' are often so structured as to eliminate the possibility of perturbation – either for the 'learner' or the 'trainer'. If we are interested in qualitative, step-jump development it seems that the trainers' role is two-fold: (a) to provide opportunities for perturbation; and (b) to help with turning this perturbation opportunity, once taken-on-board, into development. Essentially this has to be self-development on the part of the manager – only he can decide to 'take-it-on-board'.

It might be remarked here that the trainer has indeed a heavy responsibility in a situation where there can be so many non-developmental outcomes and even potential damage. It is certainly true that the trainer's responsibilities are onerous and demanding – not to say daunting – but perhaps the dangers are not so great as they seem. Cooper and Bowles' (1977) research into the effects of T-groups on participants showed a very small proportion 'adversely' affected in the long term (< 2%) compared with those who experienced positive effects. A notable point was that 5% reported adverse effects immediately after training, suggesting that perhaps some adverse emotional reaction is a necessary pre-condition for long-term change in some people. This sort of tentative conclusion would fit well with the discussion above following Figure 10.

What seems to be a much greater danger in reality is that either the trainer prevents the possibility of development through his structuring of the programme and his own needs for order and predictability; or whilst providing perturbation opportunities he lacks the skills to realize the development potential inherent in these. We are only too familiar with our continuing failings in both these respects!

Essentially the trainers' responsibilities are not as daunting as they may seem, because most adults do take responsibility for themselves most of the time. Thus the manager *chooses* whether or not to take a perturbation on board. The trainer should be ready to offer, but not force, perturbation and be ready to help with development, if the offer is taken up.

Having established the link between perturbation and development, what factors influence the likelihood of successful development outcomes apart from the perturbation or surprise level? Three of these are discussed briefly below:

- the question of basic personality orientations
- belief in freedom of choice
- the nature of the environment

What turns Perturbation into Development? (or not)

(a) There are, of course, as many personality theories as there are schools of psychology and it is not our intention here to enter this arena. In pointing to the possibility that certain aspects of personality may be critical in turning perturbation into development we are only noting the frequent offerings of others. For example, Alan Mumford (1978) comments:

Although we have no scientific method of identifying them, it is surely the case that some managers will take more readily than others to the disciplines and processes of self-development.

We questioned a training manager who had set up some self-development groups in his organization as to how he had chosen/invited participants. He was unable to give a specific answer, saying that he chose people he could get on with and who in many cases had already shown signs of being 'self-developers'. He added that his prejudices had been confirmed by a manager who joined one group and had left it after two meetings. The training manager felt uncomfortable with this particular manager and did not 'see him as a self-developer'. Without seeking to identify specific character traits in people which increase the likelihood of their being self-developers, it does seem that a broad conclusion is possible.

Whether or not a person 'sees' the development opportunity in a given situation is based partly on genetic inheritance and early learning. The question of temperament seems to be important. For example, the optimist/pessimist construct is one which has wide currency in general terms and which seems relevant here as the story in Box 2 illustrates.

BOX 2: There Must be a Pony!

There was a psychiatrist who had twin sons aged 10. They were completely different in temperament, one being an incurable optimist, whilst the other was an incurable pessimist. Their father decided that he should try and alter these increasingly fixed patterns and on the night before their 11th birthday he made extensive preparations. He filled one room of the house with presents, everything a boy could want – books, toys, games, sweets, and so on. Outside he filled a large shed with horse manure.

In the morning he greeted his sons and sent the pessimist to the room full of presents and the optimist to the shed. After a while he went to see how they were reacting. The pessimist sat with a worried look in the midst of all his presents, hardly opened. 'What's the matter son?' said the father. 'Father, with all these presents here, there just has to be a catch somewhere' replied the pessimist.

The father sighed and walked in search of the optimist who could hardly be seen for flying shovels of horse manure. He was standing waist deep in the manure, laughing and shovelling with great gusto. 'Son,' said his father, 'what's the matter with you, why are you so happy?' The boy turned, still laughing, and replied, 'Well, dad, with all this horse shit, there must be a pony!'

(b) As well as temperamental factors, the adult is one who has a measure of free choice. Essentially he can choose the development opportunity or not. Frankl (1973, p. 64–65) points out that whilst man can never free himself completely from the ties that bind him, there is always a certain residue of freedom left for his decisions. In the stand he takes towards the conditions that face him he proves his humanness. He gives the example of a conversation with a famous American psychoanalyst in Vienna whom he invited to join him climbing in the mountains. The American refused, having had a life-long aversion to climbing stemming from early trips with his father. Frankl then disclosed that his father had taken him on similar trips and that he also had been annoyed and fatigued by these. Nevertheless he had gone on to become an Alpine Guide.

> To this extent man is not only responsible for what he does but also for what he is, inasmuch as man does not only behave according to what he is, but also becomes what he is according to how he behaves. In the last analysis, man has become what he has made out of himself. Instead of being fully conditioned by any conditions, he is constructing himself.

Now whilst Frankl presents this as a self-evident truth, it is of course, his basic value or belief – perhaps his most basic choice. In everyday life one constantly comes across people with a very different basic set of beliefs, i.e. that man is the product of a deterministic process which largely through heredity and early conditioning has made him what he is today and about which he can do little.

Perhaps the choosing of sides on this fundamental position relates back to personality or temperament, but it seems to us that a crucial factor which contributes to the effectiveness or otherwise of self-development strategies with any given person is whether that person has a belief in his or her own freedom to choose or not. An associated belief is whether the person sees him or herself developing over a whole life time, i.e. always having something new to learn.

A graphic example of this was given to us recently when a friend described a series of seminars for primary school teachers. The seminars dealt with language development in young children and required the teachers to record, analyse, and examine their verbal actions. Many of the teachers in their 30's and 40's found this 'perturbation' too threatening to take-on-board. Many spoke of its irrelevance to their work or that they had no time to work in such a way. One of the notable exceptions was a 60 year-old head mistress – about to retire – yet as full of energy and enquiry as a 20 year-old should be. She saw herself as always having something to learn, as being incomplete.

Box 3 gives a short extract from two managers talking about themselves, the difference in their fundamental beliefs being apparent.

Box 3: Some Personal Beliefs affecting Self-Development

Jim: 'Basically I know who I am. My character and personality were formed early on in life and that's it – I'm stuck with them. My father died of cancer when he was 48 and I expect that I'll go around that time too. That's why I continue to smoke heavily, I've never tried to stop. Smoking is part of me, I need to smoke and although I know it's dangerous, I'm going to enjoy life now. You can't alter fate . . . this T-group nonsense is dangerous I think, it's interfering with certain processes that no-one understands. I prefer to stick to engineering and matters that we do understand. Personal relationships just happen – either you get on or you don't. I do have some good friends and others I don't get on with, these are just personality clashes, you can't do anything about that except avoid the buggers . . .'

Colin: 'I'm continually struck by situations in which I realize I could have done so much better than I did. I think . . . damn! I could have been much more helpful, aggressive, risky, etc. there. I see myself having more to learn about this job now than I did when I started and much of it's to do with helping and persuading other people to do their work.

I don't know what I'll be doing in five years' time . . . in some ways I don't care . . . there's so much happening right now. One of the things I've tried to do with my present job is to make room in it for some of the things I want to do. Of course, there are parts of it which I find boring and onerous, but I've also negotiated a lot of good new things like accompanying the personnel people on their 'milk round' trips and helping with the interviewing'.

Obviously there is more than a basic belief involved here as Colin has found the will and the resources to follow up his inclinations. It is clear, however, that the value, belief, attitude, or inclination underlying this commitment of will and acquiring of resources is crucial.

(c) The third factor which influences the extent to which self-development will 'take' is not to do with particular individuals, their temperament and beliefs, but to do with the environment in which they operate. Environments can be 'enabling' or 'restraining' and there are many potential blocks to self-development strategies in most organizations. Alan Mumford (1978) has described some of these, including the attitudes of boss, colleagues, and subordinates; the organizational reward and value systems and the manager's own previous experience of management development. In our ATM publication we suggested that the culture of the organization was a key variable and that person-centred and task-centred cultures would be more fertile ground for self-development strategies than power- and role-centred ones (Burgoyne *et al*. 1978, p. 16–17).

Are self-development strategies harder to adopt in large formal organizations than in small co-operative ones? Derek Sheane (1978) has suggested a 'federal' structure for ICI and other large organizations which would combine the needed size for production purposes, with the self-managed culture needed to motivate and satisfy people. The major point is that self-development strategies for management development fit better with certain ways of managing and certain designs for organizations.

Nor should the environment be limited to the work organization. Ultimately work organizations reflect the values of the wider society. The model of man prevalent in our society is in many ways a very limited one, which is not supportive of a life-long developmental process. To illustrate the possibilities Figure 11 contrasts a physical with a spiritual development curve.

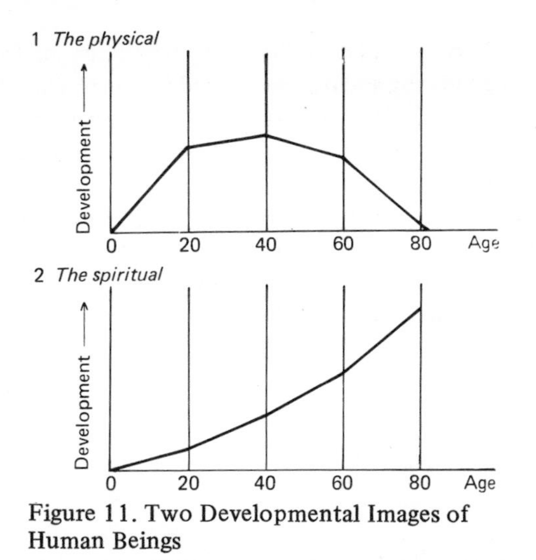

Figure 11. Two Developmental Images of Human Beings

Whilst ever we follow a primarily physical model of human potential, with the inevitable decline in powers and hence value after, say, 40, self-development cannot be but of very limited appeal. It may operate in a materialistic and selfish 'self-improvement' way for the fittest who survive. The primarily spiritual view of human beings sees us not simply as a product of plant-like blueprints, but as potentially unlimited in what we can be and understand. Certainly we all decline physically and many of us decline in spirit too, but this does not have to be so. We can if we will attain these higher levels of consciousness.

In western Europe and North America we are still strongly tied to the physical model of man. Examples of how this is manifest are numerous, but the following are an indication:

- 'Ageism' – the old have little value either in society (put them in special 'homes' etc.) or in work organizations (retire them as early as possible or make them redundant first). In contrast youth is prized, revered and over-nurtured.
- The marketing of sport and sex are exceptional examples of how our over-concern with the physical body is fed back to us through various media and commands a great deal of our attention.
- IQ is just one concept which continues to attract us and which, when graphed over a life-time, follows a 'physical' rather than a 'spiritual' curve. Thus we can easily find the 'right answer' to which children are 'gifted' or not, and structure our educational system accordingly. In using concepts like IQ we operate at the 'existence' level.

There are some signs that Western societal norms are changing to facilitate a more supportive climate – in a swing towards matrist rather than patrist values

(Rattray-Taylor, 1972, p. 47–71); in the rising popularity of Do-it-yourself approaches, first in home building and decoration and now in physical fitness (jogging!) and even divorce; in the increasing realization of the importance of interpersonal skills and the provision for helping develop them, and in a turning of the tide towards more spiritual rather than material values.

Closer to the individual in the organization, by far the best strategy still seems to be the establishment of a 'support group'. A cocoon perhaps, or better a web or network of collaborative 'others' who will help him/her and he/she helps them, to development on self-set goals. Some of the organizations with which we have had contact are working in this way and we hope to intensify this effort in the near future.

Some Implications for Trainers

Development, then, can either be

- qualitative, between stages, involving relatively turbulent processes of disequilibrium followed by restructuring;
- quantitative, incremental, within stages, involving steady growth.

We will refer to these as Types I and II respectively (after Bereiter (1970) and Kohlberg (1970).)

Now what are the principles on which most 'management development' appears to be based? It seems that these principles tend to revolve around notions of careful planning; avoiding unexpected issues; specifying outcomes precisely in advance; avoiding confusion, doubt or uncertainty; 'running a smooth ship'; and so on. After all, Systematic Training is – or tries to be – systematic. Thus, we have management development defined as 'any attempt to improve current or future managerial performance by importing information, conditioning attitudes, or increasing skills' (House, 1967), and 'any attempt to improve managerial effectiveness through a planned and deliberate learning process' (TSA, 1977). These characteristics appear to match the needs of Type III development fairly well. By avoiding the unexpected, the painful, the traumatic, the existing, the emotional, gradual increments in knowledge or skill can be accumulated.

It must be noticed, however, that the features that systematic training seeks to avoid are those very characteristics of reported 'key development events' (as per Table 2). That is, Type I development seems, in the main, to be more significant. This may, of course, merely be due to the fact that one is more likely to *remember* emotional events of this nature. Much 'significant' but incremental development may be forgotten – or, indeed, one may not even be aware of it. That being so, what types of event are we talking about? Our data suggests that about 75% of them are things that happened in the course of everyday work or life experience thus very much reinforcing the view of Temporal (1978) that we need to 'restore the balance' of views on management development processes by 'examining how managers can and do learn through natural, non-contrived experiences'.

Table 2

Non-contrived Events (Approx. 75% of total reported)	Contrived Events (Approx. 25% of total reported)
'Work-based'	
Confrontation by a subordinate	Tabistock Organization Laboratory
Chairing a hostile meeting	Bioenergetics Workshop
Dropping first clanger at work	T-group
Having to give a lecture on a certain topic	Co-counselling Workshop
Feedback from a colleague	DMS
Changing job	Feedback from a teacher
Redundancy	Outward Bound Course
	Open University Degree Course
'Not Work-based'	
Living abroad	
Car crash	
Broken leg	
Sailing - caught in a storm	
Marriage	
Death of parent	
Birth of child	

This is not to say, of course, that contrived experiences cannot be of use in Type I development. As already indicated, our data suggests that approximately 25% of the reported key events were of this nature. Of this 25%, some were what might be called 'relatively unusual contrived events' (e.g. Bioenergetic Workshops), and some were more conventional (e.g. the DMS). However, it is interesting to note that in the case of the latter, the significant development was seen not so much as a result of the content of the course, but due to the learning processes involved (i.e. discussion, confrontation, etc.) (Table 2 shows a small sample of the reported developmental events).

Thus, in the main, it appears that for Type I development, we need:

– ways of helping managers learn from non-contrived experiences (which may include 'learning to learn', contrived events);
– contrived experiences that provide an optimum level of perturbation, disequilibrium.

Table 3 is intended to suggest some such ways.

CONCLUSION

This paper addresses itself to the question 'Is all management development self-development?' and has summarized earlier work on the 'by-self' and 'of-self' aspects of self-development. It has then concentrated on the question 'What is Development?' and attempted to synthesize the ideas of a number of influential theorists who have postulated stage theories of development. In process terms

Table 3

	Learning from non-contrived experience	Learning to learn experiences (i.e. contrived specifically to help with non-contrived learning)	Learning from contrived experiences: Relatively established	Learning from contrived experiences: Events that would be currently considered rather 'way out' by most trainers
Type I Development	Coaching Counselling Co-counselling Certain structured packages Joint-development activities Action-learning Self-development groups Job rotation Committees/task-groups Talking with colleagues Active reading Taking risks Living	Certain structured packages Learning conversations Focused feedback	Possibility of process learnings from 'conventional' courses T-groups Certain structured packages Transactional Analysis Learning Communities Autonomy Laboratories Gestalt Therapy Encounter Groups Self-development groups	Biography Workshops Outward Bound Logotherapy Bioenergetics Alexander Technique Rolfing EST Zen Various Yogas Various Meditations Psychosynthesis Bio-feedback Kundalini Massage Retreats Martial Arts
Type II Development	Presumably Type I experiences can also have Type II outcomes		Most planned, intended outcomes of 'conventional' courses. Programmed Learning	

a distinction between incremental, quantitative and step-jump, qualitative development has been explored. The latter part of the paper has concentrated upon a more detailed examination of what triggers and supports the development process. It seems clear that some perturbation in equilibrium is necessary to start the process and that the extent to which development will 'take' afterwards depends upon several factors including the temperament and beliefs of the individual and the nature of the environment.

Clearly there are gaps and avenues unexplored, some of which will be pursued in our future research. Two particular areas stand out for us here.

1. Detailed explorations with individual managers to find out how key development events come to have meaning within that particular individual's biographical developmental process.
2. The establishment of self-development groups in organizations to increase our understanding of how supportive climates can be provided for individuals pursuing self-development strategies.

Another obvious and continuing area of research is the role of the trainer and we have suggested that the trainer's responsibility is (a) to offer opportunities for perturbation and to help turn this into development once taken up; and (b) to help the individual to develop from perturbations that he will inevitably encounter as part of his normal everyday work and living experiences. In line with our conclusion that what constitutes a self-development event is individually-specific, the thrust of recent researches, including most of those reported at this conference, has not been in designing *events/strategies* for self-development (e.g. T-groups, autonomy labs. etc.) but in methods which are designed *to help managers understand their development processes* (e.g. Repertory Grid applications).

Appendix 1 to this paper is a simple format used for collecting data on self-development experiences together with a suggested forced-grid for self-analysis of these experiences.

REFERENCES

Argyris, C. (1957). *Personality and Organisation,* Harper & Row.

Baldwin, A.L. (1969). 'A cognitive theory of socialization', in *Handbook of Socialization Theory and Research,* Goslin D.A. (ed.), Rand McNally, Chicago, p. 325–345.

Bereiter, C. (1970). 'Educational implications, J. Kohlberg's cognitive-developmental view', *Interchange,* **1**, No. 1, p. 25–32.

Boydell, T.H. (1976). *Experiential Learning,* Manchester Monographs 5, University of Manchester Department of Adult and Higher Education, Manchester, England.

Boydell, T.H. and Pedler, M.J. (1979). *Bibliography: Management Self Development,* MCB Publications, Bradford, England.

Burgoyne, J.G., T.H., and Pedler M.J. (1978). *Self Development,* Association of Teachers of Management, London.

Castenada, C. (1970). *The Teachings of Don Juan,* Penguin, London.

Castenada, C. (1974). *Tales of Power*, Penguin, London.
Charlesworth, W.R. (1969). 'The role of surprise in cognitive development', in Elkind D. and Flavell J.H. (eds)., *Studies in Cognitive Development*, Oxford University Press, New York, p. 257–314.
Chickering A.W. (1977). 'Developmental change as a major outcome' in Keaton M.J. *et al.* (eds), *Experiential Learning: Rationale, Characteristics and Assessment*, Jossey Bass, San Francisco.
Cooper, C.L. and Bowles D. (1977). *Hurt or Helped? A Study of the Personal Impact on Managers of Experiential, Small Group Training Programmes, Training Services Agency*, Training Information Paper No. 10, HMSO, London.
Dale, A. and Payne, R. (1976). *Consulting Interventions using Structured Instruments: A Critique*, Working Paper presented to a seminar on Client–Consultant Relationships, Groningen, Holland.
Easton, S.C. (1975). *Man and World in the Light of Anthroposophy*, Anthroposophic Press, New York.
Fink, S.L. *et al.* (1971). 'Organisational crisis and change', *Journal of Applied Behavioural Science*, **7** (1).
Frankl, V. (1963). *Man's Search for Meaning*, Washington Square Press, New York.
Frankl, V.E. (1973). *Psychotherapy and Existentialism*, Penguin, London.
Fromm, E. (1978). *To Have or To Be?* Jonathan Cape, London.
Hague, H. (1977). 'Getting self-development to happen', *Journal of European Industrial Training*, **1**, (5, 6).
Hague, H. (1978). 'Tools for helping self development', *Journal of European Industrial Training*, **2**, (3, 5).
Hampden-Turner, C. (1971). *Radical Man*, Duckworth, London.
Harrison, R. (1972). 'How to describe your organization', *Harvard Business Review*, Sept–Oct.
Holmes, T.H. and Rahe R.H. (1967). 'The social readjustment rating scale', *Jnl. Psychosomatic Res.*, **11**, 213–218.
House, R.J. (1967). *Management Development: Design, Evaluation, and Implementation*, University of Michigan, Ann Arbor.
Knowles, M. (1970). *The Modern Practice of Adult Education: Andragogy versus Pedogogy*, Association Press, New York.
Kohlberg, L. (1969). 'Stage and sequence: the cognitive developmental approach to socialization', in Goslin D.A. (ed.), *Handbook of Socialization Theory and Research*, Rand McNally, Chicago.
Kohlberg, L. (1970). 'Reply to Bereiter's statement on Kohlberg's cognitive-developmental view', *Interchange*, **1**, (1), 40–48.
Kohlberg, L. (1970). 'The concepts of developmental psychology as the central guide to education' examples from cognitive, moral, and psychological education', in Reynolds, M.C. (ed.), *Proceedings of the Conference on Psychology and the Process of Schooling in the Decade: Alternative Conceptions*, Bureau for Educational Personnel Development, US Office of Education, Washington DC.
Kolb, D., Rubin, I. and McIntyre, J. (1971). *Organisational Psychology: An Experiential Approach*, Prentice-Hall, Englewood Cliffs NJ.
Langer, J. (1969a). *Theories of Development*, Holt, Rinehart, and Winston, New York.
Langer, J. (1969b). 'Disequilibrium as a source of development', in Mussen, P.H., Langer, J. and Covington, M. (eds), *Trends and Issues in Developmental Psychology*, Holt, Rinehart, and Winston, New York, 22–37.

Mumford, A. (1978). 'Self development – flavour of the month?' *Paper written in response to the Inter ITB Study Group on Self Development Meeting,* Gloucester, England.

Pym, D. (1979). 'Work is good, employment is bad'. *Employee Relations* **1**, (1), 16–18.

Rattray-Taylor, G. (1972). *Re-Think,* Penguin, London.

Revans, R.W. (1971). *Developing Effective Managers,* Praeger, New York.

Rowan, J. (1975). 'Exploring the self', *New Behaviour,* 11/9/75 London.

Sheane, D. (1978). 'Organisation development in action', *Journal of European Industrial Training,* **2**, (8), 8.

Temporal, P. (1978). 'Non-contrived management education', *Management Education and Development,* **9**, (2).

Wilber, K. (1975). Psychologia perennis: the spectrum of consciousness, *Journal of Transpersonal Psychology,* **7**, (2), 105–132.

Wilber, K. (1977). *The Spectrum of Consciousness,* Wheaton, Theosophical Publishing House.

Appendix 1 A format for collecting data on key development events:

	KEY DEVELOPMENTAL EVENTS	OUTCOMES	DESCRIPTION (what did it feel like)
1			
2			
3			
4			
5			
6			

Appendix 2 A forced grid for analysing data on key development events:

	KEY DEVELOPMENT EVENTS					
	1	2	3	4	5	6
1 Planned by Self Planned by other						
2. At work Not at work						
3. Pleasant Unpleasant						
4. Sudden Incremental						
5. Alone With others						
6. Life centred job centred						
7. Distant recent						

Advances in Management Education
Edited by John Beck and Charles Cox

CHAPTER 12

Applications and Uses of Repertory Grids in Management Education

Mike Smith

If you attempt to carry out a computer literature search on Repertory Grids you need to be very careful. Slovenly use of key words can easily produce an enormous list of references concerning either poor famished rats crossing electrified grids to obtain food, or poor harassed managers gazing into the entrails of a questionnaire trying to discern a management style that is both considerate and structured. Repertory Grids are neither of these things. It is an enormously powerful and statistical technique which can chart the ideas of individuals. As a technique, it has great potential as a part of the management education process and in evaluating management education.

In this paper, I have two main objectives. *First*, I want to outline four specific applications of Repertory Grids. *Then*, when I have established the potential of Repertory Grids, I want to draw back a little and consider some of the practical difficulties which may arise from their use. However, before either objective is attempted, it may be necessary to lay some groundwork and draw a thumb-nail picture of the Repertory Grid Technique. A more detailed exposition is given by Smith and Stewart (1978).

INTRODUCTION TO REPERTORY GRIDS

The impetus for Repertory Grids arose out of Kelly's (1955) work on the theory of Personal Constructs. In essence, Kelly believed that men behave like scientists exploring their environment. On the basis of our explorations we construct our own individual maps of the worlds about us. We then use our individual cognitive maps to guide our behaviour. It follows that if we know a person's map then we should be in a strong position to predict his behaviour. It also follows that if we can find ways to alter a person's map, either through management training or, say, planned experience, we should be able to alter their subsequent behaviour.

Kelly's map of the maps which we use suggested that our cognitive maps and his cognitive map of our cognitive maps, have two main contents: the *elements* are the *objects* of thought and typically these objects are the other people in the world about us, but they can be inanimate objects or abstract nouns such as justice or democracy; secondly, there are the *constructs* which are the *qualities* which we use to describe the elements – they are the goggles through which we view the objects in our world.

Repertory Grids are merely a way of obtaining an individual's elements and constructs and subjecting them to a statistical analysis so that an objective and quantifiable map can be produced. Although the impetus for the development of Repertory Grids came from Personal Construct Theory, Repertory Grids constitute a statistical method in its own right and there is no obligation to accept Kelly's underpinning theory.

The production of a Repertory Grid is deceptively simple. *First,* the objects of a manager's thoughts are obtained; *second,* the qualities he uses to describe the objects are elicited; *third,* the grid is produced with the elements along the top of a matrix and the constructs are arranged down the side of the matrix. Then using, say, a seven-point scale the manager works along the rows rating each element on each construct.

Providing there are no empty cells in the data matrix which results – in other words, provided that it is sensible to rate every element on every construct – there are a number of powerful and sophisticated statistical techniques which can be used to analyse the underlying structure of the data. Because the analytic techniques are so sophisticated and exhaustive, it is almost always necessary to process the results by computer. A number of pre-written programs are available. The two best known packages are the Grid Analysis Package (GAP) developed by Dr. Patrick Slater, under a grant from the Medical Research Council (Slater, 1972) and the PEGASUS package developed by Dr. L. Thomas and Mildred Shaw. To an extent, both packages are similar in that they use related multivariate techniques. But, as a generalization GAP adopts a principal component approach while Pegasus adopts a cluster analysis approach. The merits of both approaches have been argued in the literature (Rump, 1974; Slater, 1974). All four of the applications described in this paper have used Dr. Slater's GAP package.

Although some of the advantages of Repertory Grids have emerged from this thumb-nail sketch of the technique, many of the advantages and variations are best demonstrated by a number of practical applications.

APPLICATION ONE: VOCATIONAL GUIDANCE

This Vocational Guidance application (Smith, Hartley, and Stewart, 1978) is relevant to Management Education in two ways. *First,* the application with Vocational Guidance demonstrates the classic Repertory Grid Situation where the aim is to obtain the cognitive map of one individual and where both the elements and constructs are elicited. *Second,* the application is relevant because there is a clear parallel between vocational guidance and the counselling, and development, and career planning of managers.

The young man involved, Anthony P. came to our attention because he was unhappy with his University course in history. He had completed the first year of his course and previously he had attended a major public school where he had taken exclusively Arts 'A' levels. He reported that family influence, combined with school pressures had led him to read history at University.

The first stage of producing Anthony's grid was to establish the elements in his occupational choice. In this case, the elements were the various occupations on Anthony's mental map. To help him produce a comprehensive list of jobs, Anthony was provided with some general prompts such as: jobs you have thought of doing; jobs done by members of the family; jobs you would hate; jobs you thought of doing when you were younger. In response to these prompts, Anthony produced the following list of 15 jobs:

historian	businessman	PE Teacher
clerk	postman	climbing instructor
nurse	accountant	barrister
naval officer	policeman	fireman
jet-set executive	barman	journalist

To give two important reference points, two additional elements were imposed onto the grid in spite of the fact that they were not nominated by Anthony. They were:

myself as I am at Univeristy
myself as I would ideally like to be

Imposing the 'self elements' in this way is important – especially in the area of Management Education. The self elements tend to elicit the important *core* constructs and there is the suggestion that the ideal self image is one of the best predictors of future behaviour. Other self constructs which could be used are: myself as I used to be; myself as others see me; and myself as I will be in the future. However, care must be taken not to overload the grid with too many self images.

The *second stage* was to elicit the *constructs* or the qualities and characteristics the jobs may have. Each job was written onto a file card and Anthony was presented with three of the file cards drawn at random. He was then asked to say which of the three jobs was the odd-man-out. Once he had made his choice he was asked to say *why* the job he had nominated was the odd-man-out. The reason he gave was used as one of his constructs and was entered down the side of his grid. The procedure was repeated with different triads of cards until no new constructs were forthcoming. At the end of the process, Anthony's list was:

business and commerce	stay in one place
uses brain	teaching something
has responsibility	solving problems
involves excitement	highly paid
concerns figures	involves meeting deadlines
have to think fast	challenging
purely physical	has authority
outside	has status

The *third stage* consisted of producing the grid shown in Figure 1 and presenting it to Anthony P. with instructions which produced a mental set to work along the rows rating each element on each construct using a seven-point scale.

	Historian	Businessman	Teacher – FE	Clerk	Postman	Climbing Instructor	Nurse	Accountant	Barrister	Naval Officer	Policeman	Fireman	JS Executive	Barman	Journalist	Self	Ideal Self
Concerned with business and commerce	1	7	1	5	1	1	1	7	5	1	5	1	7	1	6	1	5
Using brain	7	7	7	5	4	5	6	7	7	7	7	5	7	3	7	6	6
Responsibility	4	7	7	3	2	7	6	6	7	7	7	6	7	1	6	1	6
Excitement	2	4	5	2	1	6	4	4	3	6	6	5	7	1	6	1	7
Concerned with figures	3	7	1	6	1	1	1	7	1	1	1	1	7	1	2	1	1
Have to think fast	1	7	1	2	1	4	4	6	7	7	6	5	7	1	7	4	5
Purely physical	1	1	1	1	5	7	4	1	1	3	5	7	1	3	3	1	6
Outside	1	1	1	1	1	7	1	1	1	7	6	7	2	1	7	1	7
Stay in one place	1	5	1	1	6	7	1	1	2	7	4	3	7	1	6	7	6
Teaching something	7	1	7	1	1	7	1	1	1	2	1	1	1	1	1	1	5
Solving problems	6	7	2	1	1	1	3	6	5	5	6	2	7	1	4	5	4
High pay	3	6	3	2	2	2	3	6	7	5	3	7	7	1	4	1	6
Have to meet deadlines	1	7	2	2	2	2	3	6	7	7	7	4	7	2	7	6	3
Challenging	3	6	2	1	1	3	2	1	6	6	6	3	7	1	5	1	7
Lot of authority	4	5	3	1	1	3	1	3	6	7	7	1	7	1	2	1	5
High status	3	5	1	1	1	1	1	4	6	5	3	1	7	1	5	1	5

Key: Rating Scale from 7 – very true to 1 – very untrue

Figure 1. Anthony's Grid

The *fourth stage* involved the analysis of Anthony's data matrix using one of the programs from the GAP package. The appropriate program for the analysis of an individual grid is the INGRID (Slater, 1972) program which largely consists of a principal component analysis. In essence, the principal component analysis scans the data matrix looking for recurrent trends. Once his trend has been identified its size is calculated in terms of the percentage of variance which it explains and then, it is possible to give names to the trends and say how heavily each element loads on each of the trends. In Anthony's case there were two main trends. The first trend accounted for 47% of the variance and seemed to be concerned with being a 'big shot'. The second significant trend accounted for 20% of the variance and was concerned with working outdoors.

In itself, this is important information. It indicates that Anthony's thoughts about jobs were not very complex. Since we could predict his ratings with 67% accuracy by knowing their loadings on just *two* trends. Furthermore, when we actually look at the nature of the trends, 'big shot—small shot' and 'indoor—outdoor' we can see that they are fairly superficial qualities.

Added insights into the way that Anthony viewed his occupational choices can be gained by constructing a mental map in which loadings of each of the jobs on the first two components are used as map references to pin-point the position of the jobs (see Figure 2). Anthony's cognitive map makes his dilemma crystal clear. He tends to divide the jobs in his conceptual scheme into four groups; indoor-small shot jobs; indoor-big shot jobs; outdoor-small shot jobs; and outdoor-big shot jobs. Ideally, Anthony would like to be an outdoor-big shot but he feels that he is becoming an indoor-small shot which is how he would characterize barmen, clerks, historians, and nurses.

The discrepancy between the position of his real self and the position of his ideal self seems to have been the cause of the internal tensions which lead him to seek guidance. There is a further interesting point. Before the results of the Repertory Grid analysis were available Anthony decided to give up his history course in favour of a degree in Management Sciences. This move can be readily interpreted in the light of his cognitive map. His change can be seen as an attempt to reduce the discrepancy between his ideal self and his real self on the major component obtained from his Repertory Grid. Instead of being an indoor-small shot such as an historian, he has decided to become an indoor-big shot such as an accountant, business man, or jet-set executive. Perhaps his next move is to reduce the discrepancy on the smaller component. He may use a degree in Management Sciences to gain entry into one of the occupations which is near to the position of his ideal self such as journalism, the police force, or the Navy.

Clearly, there is a direct parallel between this type of vocational guidance and the indepth management development and counselling which sometimes occupy the time of management educators. The procedures which would be used would be much the same as those adopted in the case of Anthony P. The main difference is that the elements would be drawn from a different domain and include such things as jobs at different management levels or jobs in different management functions such as sales, production, accounting, and personnel.

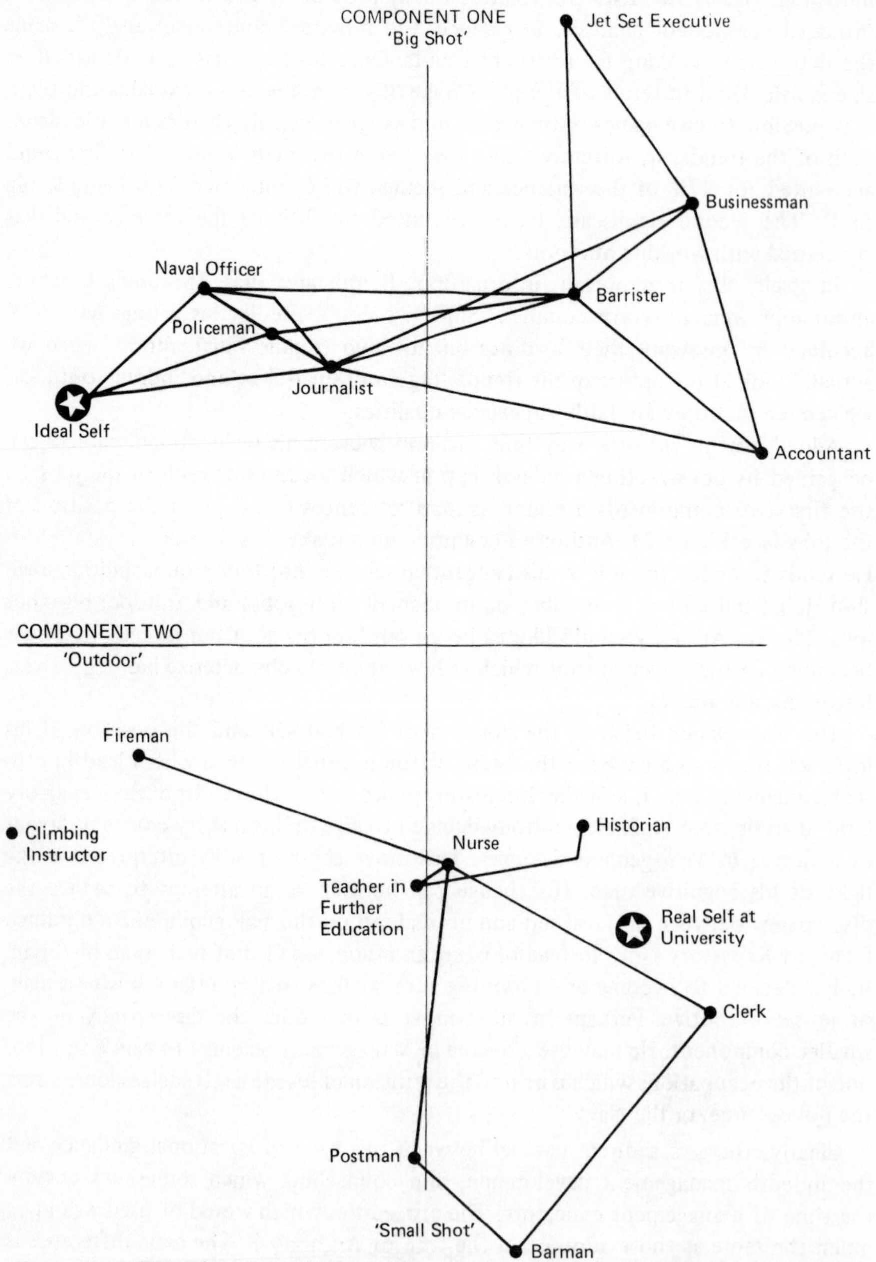

Figure 2. A Plot of Anthony's *Elements* using Loadings on the first two principal Components

APPLICATION TWO: MANAGEMENT JOB DESCRIPTIONS

The *second* application concerns the analysis of management jobs and the production of management job descriptions. Methodologically, it also demonstrates the use of an imposed set of constructs.

The study arose from an approach by the training officer of a large bakery chain. The bakery chain was following the very best of training practice and was starting its management training programme by first producing descriptions of managers' jobs. The Training Officer reported that some managers were having difficulties producing their own job descriptions and that most of the usual techniques seemed to be more suitable for manual jobs. Eventually, it was decided to use the Repertory Grid Technique to analyse the jobs of six different managers one of whom was the Factory Manager.

The *first stage* was to obtain a list of elements for the grid. In this case the elements were the tasks which the Factory Manager performed (in McCormick's terms these were the *worker activities*). Rather than ask a manager to fill in a questionnaire or maintain a log of his activities, it was decided to obtain a list of the managers activities by telephone. Every day for ten working days the Factory Manager received a noon telephone call and he was asked to list all the things he had done in connection with his job in the past 24 hours. At the end of ten days, the cumulative list was edited in order to avoid the duplication of identical tasks. The edited list was then returned to the Factory Manager for comment and it was accompanied by a specific request for him to add any other tasks which he might perform in the course of his duties at other times of the year. The list was again amended in the light of the Factory Manager's comments and the finalized list of tasks constituted the Factory Manager's list of elements.

In the *second stage,* instead of eliciting a list of constructs from the Factory Manager himself, it was decided to impose a list of 28 constructs which had been obtained from previous work with 74 managers in the communication industry. The objective of imposing a list of constructs in this way was to minimize the demands which were made on the Factory Manager's time.

In the *third stage*, the Factory Manager completed the grid of 28 constructs and 40 elements and rated each element on each construct using a seven-point scale. The resulting data matrix was again analysed using the INGRID program. An analysis of the variances contributed by each of the 40 tasks revealed that no single part of the Factory Manager's job stood out in terms of the demand it made of him. But, making checks on staff, taking disciplinary action, and making checks on machinery were, perhaps, a little more important than the rest. The principal component analysis suggested that the job is a rather complex one since the five significant components only accounted for 61% of the variance. More details of this principal component analysis are given in Figure 3.

The results from a parallel exercise with the Factory Manager's immediate superior gave some interesting comparisons. The General Manager's job seems to

		% of variance
Component 1	Monitoring Events	22
Component 2	Trouble Shooting	13
Component 3	Long Term Thinking	10
Component 4	Formal Relationships	9
Component 5	Paper Work	8
Total Variance attributable to 5 Components		61

Elements receiving high average Ratings

– making checks on staff	2.5
– taking disciplinary action	2.4
– making checks on machinery	2.0

Figure 3. Analysis of the Factory Manager's Grid

be rather simpler in that four principal components accounted for 65% of the variance. A comparison of Figures 3 and 4 will make the contrast between the two managerial jobs quite apparent.

The General Manager's job is, in Rosemary Stewart's (1967) terms one of an administrator-cum-emissary. The Factory Manager, on the other hand, is typical of Rosemary Stewart's troubleshooter category and he is almost architypal of Mintzberg's (1973) manager who is subject to much brevity, variety, and fragmentation of work. The comparison between the two job analyses has important,

		% of variance
Component 1	Organizing and Administration	31
Component 2	Informal Staff Relations	15
Component 3	Formal Staff Relations	11
Component 4	Giving Technical Advice	8
Total Variance attributable to 4 Components		65

Elements receiving high average Ratings

– liaising with Factory Manager	7.0
– attending company meetings	3.9
– attending progress meetings	3.3

Figure 4. Analysis of General Manager's Job

practical, implications for management succession and management education. Traditionally, General Managers are recruited from Factory Managers. Yet, this analysis suggests that the two jobs are fundamentally different and that success in the job as a General Manager will not necessarily follow from a success as a Factory Manager. At the very least, some form of management development will usually be required before a Factory Manager is fully equipped to succeed in the job of a General Manager.

APPLICATION THREE: TASK ANALYSIS

The third application of Repertory Grids also involves the analysis of jobs – or rather the analysis of one particular task in the job of a Training Adviser from one of the Industrial Training Boards. The third application also illustrates where the *elements* are held constant. One of the tasks of Training Advisers with this particular Board was to conduct a yearly Training Review Visit for each firm within his area of responsibility. The advisers were organized into teams and the way that two of these teams viewed the Training Review Visits was investigated.

The *first stage* was to elicit the elements and the elicitation took place as a part of one of their regular team meetings. The members of the teams were asked to

		% of variance
• FACTOR 1	INTERPERSONAL SKILLS e.g. ability to coach, sensitivity to others, listening, and reflecting	36
• FACTOR 2	REASONING AND ADMINISTERING(?) e.g. administration, assessing outcomes, listening, and reflecting	17
• FACTOR 3	TRAINING EXPERTISE e.g. knowledge of training techniques, selling skills, management training	14
• FACTOR 4	WRITING e.g. business knowledge, literacy, letter and report writing	11
• FACTOR 5	MAINTAINING CREDIBILITY e.g. business knowledge, long knowledge of firm, credibility (knowledge of industry), reasoning skills	9
	REMAINDER UNACCOUNTED FOR	14
		100

Figure 5. Component Analysis of Team A's Ratings

list, individually, the stages of a TRV as they saw them. Then, as a group exercise, the individual lists were pooled by writing the individual lists on a flip chart and discussing them. At the end of this stage, a list of ten mutually agreed phases of a TRV had been produced. In fact the same list of phases was used by both teams of Training Board Advisers.

The *second stage* was for each member of the team to elicit their own individual constructs using specially designed forms which identified triads of stages and then asked the Advisers to nominate the odd-man-out and give a reason for their choice.

In the *third stage* the Adviser completed his individual grid by rating each of the mutually agreed ten phases of the TRV on each of his own constructs. At the end of the third stage, eleven completed grids were available; six grids from Team A and five grids from Team B. All eleven grids had exactly the same list of elements – the phases of a TRV. But, each of the eleven grids contain the individual constructs from each adviser. In other words, the grids were aligned by element but *not* by construct. The most appropriate program from the Grid Analysis Package for analysing this data structure is the PREFAN program. The PREFAN program assembles all the grids and analyses them as one large grid. The output from the PREFAN program is very similar to the INGRID output. PREFAN was used to process the matrices from the two teams and some of the results can be seen in Figures 5 and 6.

		% of variance
• FACTOR 1	INTERPERSONAL SKILLS e.g. interpersonal sensitivity, empathy, personal enthusiasm	35
• FACTOR 2	REASONING e.g. analyzing, predicting, evaluating, judging, being objective	17
• FACTOR 3	WRITING e.g. making notes, persuasive letter writing, written presentation, presentation skills	14
• FACTOR 4	TRAINING EXPERTISE e.g. good subject knowledge, designing training	10
• FACTOR 5	CREDIBILITY AND POLITICAL SKILLS	7
	REMAINDER UNACCOUNTED FOR	17
		100

Figure 6. Component Analysis of Team B's Ratings

The similarity between the two sets of results is quite amazing. In both teams, the largest component can be labelled interpersonal skills and it accounts for 35% and 36% of the variance. In both teams, the second component accounted for 17% of the variance and it involved reasoning activities – although the composition of the second component was much clearer in the case of team B. The third and fourth components seemed to be juxtaposed for the two teams. There is a writing component which accounts for 11% and 14% of the variance. There is also a training expertise component which accounts for a surprisingly low 14% and 10% of the variance. Finally, there is a component which concerns establishing personal credibility with the owners and managers of the firms being reviewed. Clearly, this analysis has important practical implications for both the selection and training of Board Staff.

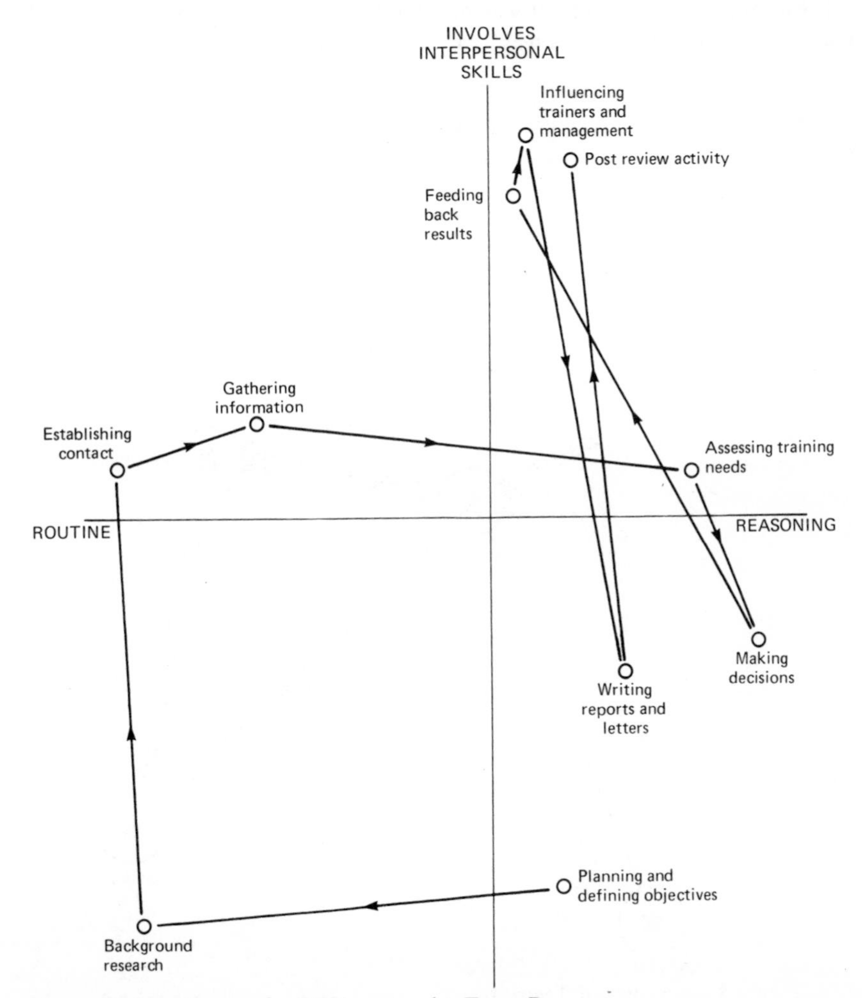

Figure 7. The Stages of a TRV as seen by Team B

Because the stages of the TRV usually have a clear temporal order, it is possible to adopt a technique advocated by Slater (1970) who attempted to chart the progress of therapy sessions in clinical psychology. The positions of each stage can be plotted on a two-dimensional map and, by joining the elements in the order in which they occur, it is possible to chart the progress of a training review visit over time. A map such as the one given in Figure 7 indicates that a Training Adviser will need to be able to adopt a flexible approach during the course of a Training Review Visit. In one stage he may need to be socially skilful in getting along with other people and in the next stage he needs to operate in a cool logical manner uninfluenced by personal pressures which may surround him.

One final aspect was made possible by the fact that the elements of the advisers' grids had been held constant. It was possible to compare the way that one adviser viewed the elements with the way that another adviser viewed the same elements

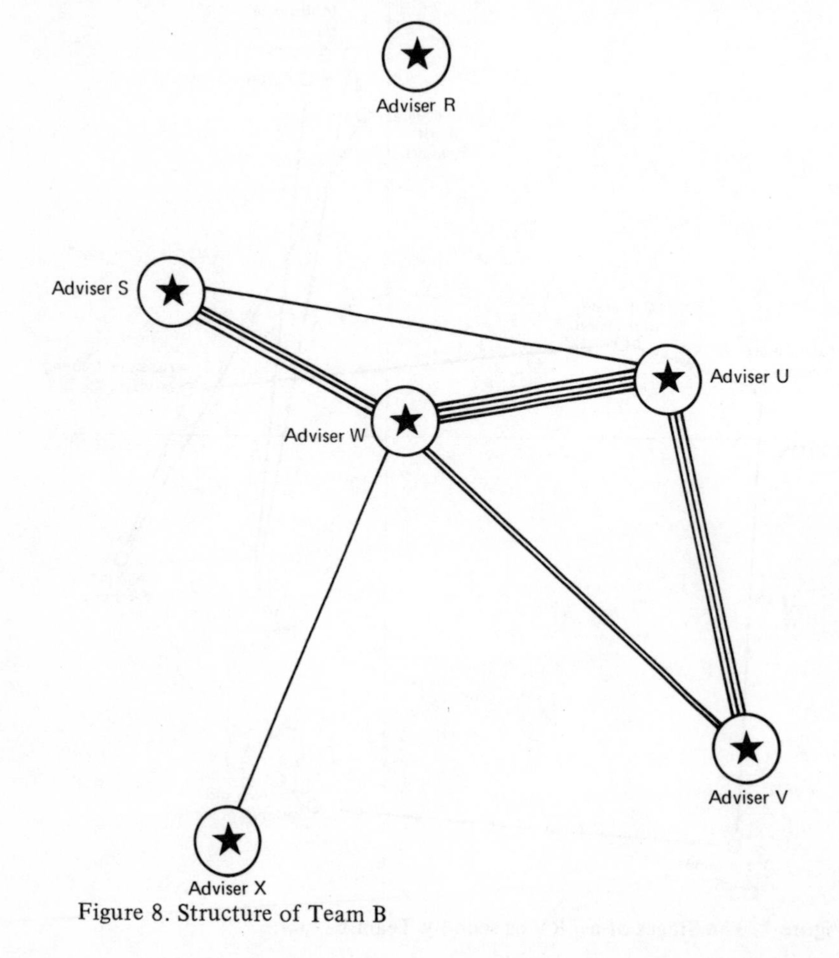

Figure 8. Structure of Team B

and to compute a co-efficient of convergence between every pair of advisers in a team. Using these co-efficients, a pictorial representation of the group's structure can be built up using a method which is analogous to Moreno's (1934) sociograms. For example, there was a co-efficient of 0.7 between advisers W and U. This indicates a close similarity in the way that they viewed the phases of a TRV and consequently advisers W and V appear close together and they are linked together by several bonds in Figure 8. A similar model could, of course, be produced for the other team. This diagram suggests that the other team has a looser structure and that they tended to show more differences in the way that they approach a Training Review Visit. Clearly, diagrams such as these can be very useful tools in the development and training of management teams.

APPLICATION FOUR: DEVELOPMENT OF MANAGEMENT APPRAISAL FORM

The last application focuses on a different aspect of Repertory Grid methodology. The centre of interest lies in the actual constructs which emerge rather than the results of a rigorous statistical analysis and it indicates how useful the classic elicitation techniques can be even when computer facilities are not available.

The setting was a large organization which had recently rationalized the structure of its lower and middle management. The existing management appraisal scheme was a casualty of this rationalization and it became necessary to devize a new appraisal form. After reviewing a number of approaches to the problem of management appraisal, it was felt that a series of behaviourally anchored rating scales (Smith and Kendall, 1963) was the most promising approach. However, this decision left two problems: (a) what dimensions should be scaled and (b) what behavioural anchors should be used? It was felt that Repertory Grid methodology could be adapted to obtain both the dimensions and the anchors. It was also felt that the most valid answers would be obtained from people who knew the job best; the middle and lower managers themselves.

To help the managers think about their jobs, ten general descriptions of the parts of their jobs were produced and the managers were asked to nominate actual parts of their own jobs which fitted these descriptions. Examples of these prompts were: something that I like doing; something that only a few of us have to do; something that is not very important; and something that makes me cross. In total, 74 different managers were questioned. For each one, triads from their list of parts of their jobs were selected and the manager was asked to nominate the part of his job in each triad which seemed to be the odd-man-out. He was then asked to give a reason for his nomination in terms of the personal qualities needed to do that task well. A typical reply would be, '. . . because that task needs to be done by a reliable person'.

In this application it was very important to obtain a deep and precise understanding of the exact meaning of each construct. So, a number of extra steps were added to the elicitation procedure. The first of these additional steps was to ask each manager for words or phrases which meant the same as the construct he had just given. For example, the manager may have replied that 'diligent' was similar in meaning to being a reliable person. Then, specific benchmarks were elicited for a person who was high, low, and medium on the construct. For example, the manager was asked to imagine someone who was extremely reliable and he was asked to say how that would show in the way that he did his work. Then, the manager was asked to imagine someone who was extremely unreliable and again he was asked to give a behavioural definition of extreme unreliability by saying how this unreliability would show in the way this imaginary manager did his work. Finally, a benchmark for someone with average reliability was obtained.

One point which seems to be overlooked in much of the literature on Repertory Grids is the possibility that there may be *two* constructs defining the odd-man-out in any given triad. Furthermore, this second construct may be less superficial and more fundamental. To contend with this possibility, attention was drawn to the initial triad and the manager was asked if there was any other way in which the task was the odd one out and if he gave a positive answer supplementary questions were again asked in order to obtain similies of the construct and then the high, low, and medium benchmarks for that construct. When this procedure had been exhausted for a given triad another random triad was drawn and the whole process was repeated until each manager gave no new constructs.

Exploring the meaning of construct in this way provides a very extensive and rich set of data. In actual fact, the process was repeated with all 74 managers and the combined results produced the 28 dimensions subsequently used in the job description of the Factory Manager. As far as the present application is concerned, each of the 28 dimensions was accompanied by a set of behaviourally anchored rating scales and subsequently each dimension with its benchmarks was scaled and used in a sample of management appraisals. Ultimately, when enough data for rigorous statistical analysis has been accumulated, it is hoped to reduce the number of dimensions involved in the appraisal scale by deducting those dimensions which contain redundant information.

These four applications indicate only some of the possibilities of using Repertory Grids in Management Education. Training Evaluation is one obvious application which has been successfully attempted by several researchers (Smith, 1978; Easterby-Smith and Ashton, 1975; Cooper and Oddie, 1975). Valerie Stewart (1975) has also indicated the use of grid methodology in identifying and developing management potential and in selection procedures. Finally, a number of applications outside the field of management education have been outlined by Slater (1976) and Smith and Stewart (1977).

PITFALLS IN THE USE OF REPERTORY GRIDS

In spite of the wide scope of its application, it is easy to abuse, intentionally or unintentionally, the Repertory Grid Method. Indeed, the pitfalls associated with Repertory Grids can be considered under three main headings.

Lack of Definition

Investigators and researchers intending to use Repertory Grids need to pay special attention to the definition of their objectives. Repertory Grids are very flexible tools and this allows the flexibility to travel on a wrong but parallel road towards an objective. The technique involves few constraints or built-in checks which force the user to think out the exact question he wants answering. A part of the problem is the apparent simplicity and ease of the first phase and once the list of elements has been produced the remainder of the process is almost mechanical. However, users should take great care at this initial stage to ensure that the *domain of elements is relevant to the objectives* and to ensure that the *people completing the grids will be able to understand the elements used* and that they have views on these elements.

In one market research example, a list of dog vaccines was obtained from the catalogues of drug companies and used as elements in a grid given to vets. Unfortunately, the vets concerned had no knowledge, no views, and no experience of more than half the elements on the list and the data needed considerable 'massage' before it could be brought to life and used.

Similarly, a grid with poorly defined objectives can fall down at the stage of eliciting constructs. A grid with people as elements can produce a hotch potch of constructs which refer to peoples' psychological qualities, their physical qualities, their roles, their backgrounds, and even their geographical locations. Usually, the user is most interested in the psychological qualities of people and if he has defined his objective with care he will be able to incorporate a set of instructions into the procedure for eliciting constructs which will enable the individual to focus on the most relevant domain. The *depth* to which investigators need to understand the constructs is another area which needs definition. Is it sufficient to elicit a one or two word construct, or is it necessary to evoke an extended elicitation procedure similar to the one described in the final application concerning the development of managerial rating scales?

If the objectives of a Repertory Grid are ill-defined a large and unwieldy grid often results and if a grid has a large number of elements and constructs completion is a major undertaking. A 20 × 20 grid requires 400 separate ratings. If each rating takes only 10 seconds, the respondent will take 67 minutes to complete the grid – in addition to the time needed for elicitation procedures. Clearly, with large and undefined grids, there is a great danger that rapport collapses and that the quality of response is poor.

Control and Experimental Design

A second group of pitfalls concerns the problem of how much control to exercise over the elements and constructs that are included in the grid. Inevitably, it also includes the problems of data analysis and experimental design.

The ideographic potential of Repertory Grids is a great asset in applications such as Vocational Guidance and Management Development. Unfortunately the freedom of the ideographic approach is a two-edged sword and it can turn out to be a liability to the unwary. For example, one Training Officer adopted Repertory Grids to evaluate one of his company's two-week courses in Human Relations. He allowed every participant complete freedom to adopt any element or construct which was meaningful to them as individuals. There were no constraints on the before and after grids that he obtained from either the control group or the training group. It may be that this large degree of freedom allowed him to obtain a very accurate picture of the thoughts of his respondents *but,* the results were useless as a form of evaluation. Because there was so much variation in the lists of elements and constructs there were no points of comparison between the control and training group, and the before and after grids. Consequently, the Training Officer's results were confined to remarks on the meta-structure of the grids such as complexity and tightness.

On the other hand, there is the clear danger of over control, where, in order to achieve comparable results which can be statistically crunched to the nth degree, everything becomes so specified that all individual meaning is excluded. Perhaps an acceptable compromise is to specify *either* the élements *or* the constructs. This strategy gives an adequate basis for comparison, yet it allows the individual freedom of expression. As a generalization it may be best to specify the elements since they are often easy to specify objectively. The freedom is then reserved for the constructs and usually, it is the constructs that are endowed with rich personal meanings. This strategy was adopted in the application concerning the Training Review Visits. A final variation on this theme is to elicit individual grids and then tack on a predetermined set of elements and constructs. Unfortunately, the effort involved in the analysis is often doubled and the resulting grids are often large and carry the danger of a poor quality of response.

Preparation and Technique

Finally, there are pitfalls concerned with the technique of the investigator and the thoroughness of his preparations. The deceptive simplicity of Repertory Grids can encourage a slap dash approach. In a scientific sense the situation is self correcting since poor technique tends to increase the error variance and produce 'conservative' results that are not significant. At least the false negatives do not find their way into the scientific literature. However, a large number of false negatives could well slow down the development of an area such as Management Education. There is no mysticism in Repertory Grids. It simply means that investigators must take the time to pilot their procedures and to train themselves properly.

As a rule of thumb, it seems to be necessary to administer six pilot grids before the procedures and instructions are acceptably clear and the investigator is sufficiently 'au fait' with the technique. Basic training is another problem. Certainly, most graduates can learn the basics of grid work during a two-day training course which involves four or five hours theoretical orientation followed by practical exercises where the skills of elicitation and administration are built up on a cumulative basis. It may be that a formal course is not necessary for Management Educators since they should have the skills and experience to build up their own training schedule. It may be that the key requirements are simply the time and the determination to do things properly.

REFERENCES

Cooper, C.L. and Oddie, (1975). Research questionnaire used in assessing training in social skills: a research note, *Journal of Management Studies,* February, 95–108.

Easterby-Smith, M. and Ashton, D. (1975). Using repertory grid technique to evaluate management training, *Personnel Review,* **4**, (4), 15–21.

Kelly, G.A. (1955). *The Psychology of Personal Constructs,* Norton.

Mintzberg, H. (1973). *The Nature of Managerial Work,* Harper Row, London.

Moreno, J.L. (1934). *Who shall survive?* Washington Mental and Nervous Disease Pub. Co.

Rump, E.E. (1974). Cluster Analysis compared with Principal Component Analysis, *British Journal of Social and Clinical Psychology,* **13**, 283–292.

Slater, P. (1970). Personal questionnaire data treated as forming a repertory grid, *British Journal of Social and Clinical Psychology,* **9**, 357–370.

Slater, P. (1972). *Notes on Ingrid 72,* St. George's Hospital, Clare House, Blackshaw Road, Tooting, London.

Slater, P. (1974). Cluster analysis vs. principal component analysis: a reply to E.E. Rump, *British Journal of Social and Clinical Psychology,* **13**, 427–430.

Slater, P. (1976). *Explorations of Intrapersonal Space,* John Wiley, London.

Smith, J.M. (1978). Using Repertory Grids to evaluate training, *Personnel Management,* February, 36, 38, 43.

Smith, P.C. and Kendall, L.M. (1963). Retranslation of expectations: an approach to the construction of unambiguous anchors for rating scales, *Journal of Applied Psychology,* **47**, 149–155.

Smith, J.M., Hartley, J., and Stewart, B.M.J. (1978). A case study of repertory grids used in vocational guidance, *Journal of Occupational Psychology,* **51**, 97–104.

Smith, J.M. and Stewart, B.M.J. (1977). Repertory Grids: a flexible tool for establishing the content and structure of a manager's thoughts, *Management Bibliographies and Reviews,* **3**, 209–229. MCB Press, Bradford.

Stewart, R. (1967). *Managers and their jobs: a study of the similarities and differences in the ways managers spend their time,* Macmillan, London.

Stewart, V. (1975). A technique for selection interviewing, *Industrial Training International,* **10**, (6), 179–181.

[illegible]

REFERENCES

[illegible] Journal of Management Studies [illegible]

[illegible] and Adams, [illegible]

Kelly, G. A. (1955) [illegible] of Personal Constructs, Norton.

[illegible] (1973) The Nature of Managerial Work, Harper and Row, [illegible]

[illegible] Washington: [illegible]

[illegible] Journal of Social and Clinical Psychology [illegible]

Slater, P. (1970) [illegible] Journal of [illegible] Psychology, [illegible]

Slater, P. [illegible]

Slater, [illegible] component analysis [illegible] Journal of Medical Psychology, [illegible]

Slater, P. [illegible] Wiley, London.

[illegible]

Smith, [illegible]

Smith, [illegible] and Stewart, [illegible]

Smith, [illegible] and Stewart, [illegible] Management [illegible] McGraw-Hill, [illegible]

Stewart, R. (196[illegible]) Managers and their Jobs, [illegible] London.

Stewart, V. [illegible] Industrial [illegible] 1[illegible]

Advances in Management Education
Edited by John Beck and Charles Cox

CHAPTER 13

Changing a Manager's Construction of Reality:

The Perspective of Personal Construct Theory on the Process of Management Education

John E. Beck

INTRODUCTION

Increasingly, management educators and trainers are turning to the use of Repertory Grids to evaluate the impact of their development programmes on trainees. It is recognized that grid data gathered before and after a course, might provide at least a partial answer to the continuing problems of programme evaluation. Smith (1980) in an earlier chapter in this book has outlined some of the ways in which grids have been used, and speculated on some of the further uses to which this technique might be applied. On the whole though, the increase in the use of grid methodology by management educators has taken place in something of a theoretical vacuum. In sharp contrast to the upsurge in interest in the use of grids, Personal Construct Theory (Kelly, 1955), from which grid methodoly has been derived receives relatively little attention from management educators. Yet the theory seems to provide a very useful perspective from which to view some of the current issues about the process of management education. Such issues as how to enable managers to develop skills in 'learning to learn', the use of 'safe' exercises or opening a manager to the emotional threat of failure in an Action Learning programme, the benefits of 'single loop' and 'double loop' learning, problems of transfer of learning, and the changing role of the management trainer.

This paper is presented in two parts. Part I will attempt to give a very brief overview of some of the core concepts in personal construct theory. In Part II these concepts will be used to examine how changes in the construct systems of participants in an experiential interpersonal skills training programme might be brought about, and the implications of taking this approach for management educators and for future research.

PART I

Personal Construct Theory (PCT)

It is beyond the scope of this paper to give anything other than a very brief overview of PCT. Those interested in gaining a more thorough grounding in the theory are recommended to read the excellent book by Bannister and Fransella (1971).

The model of man which Kelly proposes in PCT is that of 'man the scientist'. This means that man is trying to understand, to make sense of, and to be able to predict the world that he inhabits. He does this by identifying recurrent themes in his experience of the world, so that events with which he is confronted today are seen as similar to, but not exactly the same as, the events of yesterday. In saying that man 'identifies' recurrent themes in his experience, it is not assumed that man 'finds' or 'discovers' these themes in the real world. On the contrary it is assumed that man 'invents' or 'imposes' these themes on his experience in order to make sense of it. This does not mean to imply that man is out of touch with reality, enslaved by the delusions which he imposes on his experience. But it does accept that man cannot contact reality directly, and must build up or construct a model of that reality. The validity of the model can then be tested by how well it enables him to predict or anticipate future events, and this testing will indicate how useful the model is. This very firmly anchors the model which is built up to the future events which man is attempting to anticipate.

Each individual will of course develop his own idiosyncratic model of the world. Each of us not only has unique experiences of the world, but the understanding we evolve of those experiences will also be unique. This means that there are alternative models or constructions of reality to the ones which we customarily employ. There are the alternative models which other people use, and there are the alternative models which we as individuals can invent in order to understand our experience, and anticipate future events in a new way. There is no inherent rightness or wrongness of the models we invent, the only test of the models is the extent to which they help us predict future events. The better models will help us understand and give accurate anticipations of a wider range of events than the poorer models.

While there are differences between individuals in the way in which they see the world, there will also be some similarities. The very fact of sharing a similar culture and language means that the models of reality we build up will be open to influence by other people. One way of construing the role of the trainer is that of helping the trainee to explore and reflect upon his models of the world, test them out, and change them when they prove to be inadequate.

The Application of PCT to Management Education

The approach of examining how a manager organizes his experiences, and identifying the themes which he concentrates on is not unique to management educators interested in PCT. Earlier work by McGregor (1960) in indentifying the managerial 'assumptions' of Theory X and Theory Y, and by Blake and Mouton (1964) in proposing the 'concerns' which a manager might have for people and/or production are implicitly following a similar approach. They are both attempting to identify the models that a manager might use in getting things done through his subordinates, even if these theories suggest a somewhat restricted number of models available to the manager.

More recently proposals by Argyris and Schon (1974) of 'theories-in-use', and 'espoused theories', and the ideas proposed by Higgin (1975) of 'models of reality', and Radcliff (1977) of 'managerial paradigms' are all very similar to the approach being proposed in this paper. The unifying theme is that managers invent models of the reality of their organizational life which help them understand and anticipate what is going on. Further, that the process of management development involves enabling managers to test out, and when appropriate sometimes fundamentally modify these models or construct systems which guide their actions at work.

The Development of Construct Systems

The development of construct systems and the way in which constructs are changed are some of the key issues with which PCT is concerned. Kelly was, after all, a therapist concerned with helping his clients change and reconstrue the ways in which they see themselves and their world. Indeed the whole emphasis of the man-the-scientist model of man is the way in which a man's construct system develops as he gets to grips with a wider understanding of his world.

Kelly suggested that construct systems are developed by a process of elaboration, and that the elaboration of the system can occur in two different ways. One way is that an individual might confirm the validity of the constructs that he currently employs by using them to make sense of a novel situation. The novel situation is seen as very similar to other events which he has had to cope with in the past. This means that the constructs which are currently used remain essentially unaltered, apart from some minor changes in the detail of the construct to incorporate new aspects of the novel situation. Changes of this nature are essentially variations on old themes of his understanding, and this process is called increasing the *definition* of the construing system.

The second way in which a construct system might be elaborated occurs when an individual reaches out and attempts to get to grips with something which in the past he has poorly understood. The individual does not have a well-defined construct system to cope with those events. They are something of a mystery to him. His anticipations and predictions about these events tend to be at best sketchy, and at worst he might be totally bewildered by the uncertainty of what is happening. An example might be the culture shock experience by Peace Corps workers on their arrival in underdeveloped countries. In focusing his attention on these uncertain events the individual may invent new constructs, which he can impose on those events in order to gain some understanding of them. This means that new themes might become incorporated into the construct system, a process called the *extension* of the construct system. In extending the construct system the individual has increased the range of events of which he has some kind of understanding.

To give a hypothetical example of these two procedures at work let us imagine a person who tends to see most interpersonal relationships in terms of a central theme of 'power'. So that he sees most relationships as attempts by each person to control the activities of the other, by using authority, dominance, manipulation, or whatever. Imagine him now confronted by a couple who seem to be in love. He may see the potential for manipulation in that relationship, and decide that one good way of making himself more powerful is to get someone to fall in love with him. He has given his current model of the world greater definition. Or he may decide that something funny is going on in that relationship. Instead of controlling each other the lovers seem to want to give of themselves to each other, and what is more they seem to be enjoying it! In identifying that relationships can exist where people give rather than control, he has extended his model by incorporating a new theme.

In situations where the construct system becomes more defined, it seems that the individual can understand what is happening by using constructs which are already available to him. The validity and usefulness of these constructs is confirmed, and by applying them to the new situation they will be slightly modified. In situations where the learner attempts to extend his system he may find that his current constructs do not help him understand, and he needs to invent new constructs to help him find some meaning in the situation.

If the extension and definition processes are successful, that is, they help the individual develop validated constructs, then both of these processes are what we would broadly term 'learning'. However it seems that many management educators are much more concerned with the dramatic extensions of the system, than the less dramatic definition. Trainers are, after all, in the business of change, and the more dramatic the change the more confirmation of the efficacy of our role. Argyris and Schon (1974) provide an example of this thinking in the distinction of 'single loop' and 'double loop' learning. Single loop learning involves slight modification in the means of applying the current theory-in-use (Kellian definition) whereas double loop learning involves a comprehensive change in the theory-in-use (Kellian extension). While Argyris and Schon recognize that single loop development can be of some value, their theory is much more concerned with the facilitation of double loop learning. But why? Do we really want managers to abandon the models of reality which have helped them so far in their careers? Are we saying that much of what has been learnt so far is useless? I think not. Enabling a manager to see the significance and relevance of his current constructs, is just as valuable as seeing the shortcomings of his system and encouraging him to develop a new model. This is not a plea for complacency either on the part of managers or management educators, but a plea to recognize the value of both means of elaboration. A plea also to recognize that the crucial test of the validity of a model is whether it helps the individual anticipate events. It may be that the manager already has available constructs which do help him understand what is happening, *to his own satisfaction*. If this is so we may be attempting to do him a disservice, let alone be wasting our energy in trying to get him to change his already adequate model.

Construct Systems in Transition

Successful elaboration of the construct system involves both successful definition and extension of the system. In general, definition will occur when anticipations are confirmed, and extension when they are disconfirmed. Disconfirmation might lead to more comprehensive changes in the construing system, and one of the key concerns of PCT is the effect of awareness of change in our construct systems. In general Kelly described what we would call 'feelings' or 'emotions' as an awareness that our current ways of understanding the world are being challenged and changed. In particular he gave precise definitions to the emotions of 'anxiety', 'guilt', 'threat and fear', 'hostility', and 'aggressiveness'. These definitions are couched in ways which might be different from the general understanding of these terms, or indeed the way in which other theorists have chosen to define them. But they are consistent with the general approach taken in PCT and will be used in this context throughout the rest of this paper. The definitions offered here have been paraphrased in order to make them more understandable to people who are not acquainted with PCT.

'Anxiety' is seen as an awareness that we do not have an adequate means of understanding the events which confront us. 'Guilt' is an awareness that we have not been able to establish the role relationship with others which we normally would in this situation. 'Threat' and 'fear' are seen as an awareness of change in our 'core constructs', core constructs being the constructs which we use to understand and maintain our identity or self image. 'Hostility' is seen as a possible response to invalidation of anticipation that the individual has about other people. The individual becomes hostile when he denies or distorts the discomforting evidence to make it appear that the prediction has been validated. He is in essence cooking the behavioural books. 'Agressiveness' has nothing to do with interpersonal antagonism, but is used to mean an active testing out and exploration of the way in which we understand a situation.

To these ideas have to be added other definitions which Kelly coined, but which were not included in the definitions of emotional states given above. These are the ideas of 'constriction' and 'dilation' which refer to how a person deals with incompatibilities in his construct system, and of 'looseness' and 'tightness' which refer to the properties of some constructs within the construct system. 'Constriction' refers to the situation where an individual becomes aware of inconsistencies in his construing of events, and resolves the inconsistency of concentrating on some aspects of the situation and ignoring others. 'Dilation' on the other hand, occurs when the individual is aware of incompatibilities in his system, and seeks to resolve these by gaining data about the situation in the hope that he can reorganize his construct system in a more comprehensive way.

'Tight' and 'loose' constructs are very important concepts in PCT and refer to how exact and unvarying the predictions or anticipations of any construct are. A tight construct is one which leads to unvarying predictions of events, whereas a loose construct is one which leads to varying predictions. A tight construct is therefore very easily tested, but is not very robust when it is invalidated. A loose construct can only be tested in general ways and can accommodate invalidation fairly easily since it leads to varying predictions about events. Bannister (1963) has shown that one response to invalidation is the loosening of what was previously a fairly tight construct. The loosened construct still retains its identity, but is now more flexible in dealing with the events that it is attempting to anticipate.

The concepts of tight and loose construing are linked by the idea of the Creativity Cycle, a cycle of construction which leads to the development of new ideas and constructs. The cycle begins with loose construing, and ends after the person has invented, tested out, and tightened new constructs by validating them. The Creativity Cycle is therefore largely related to the extension of an individual's construct system, since it involves the creation of new constructs to understand the experience, and the testing out the validation of the new constructs by running them up against reality. There is perhaps an analogy between the Creativity Cycle and the unfreeze/change/refreeze model proposed originally by Lewin. The loosening of the system can be seen as the unfreezing and the tightening as the refreezing.

It is important to bear in mind that tight and loose construing are neither good nor bad in themselves; what should be recognized is that they are both of value in promoting the development of the individual's understanding. They should be seen as activities which complement one another, as they do in the Creativity Cycle. At times it is appropriate to loosen construing in order to gain a wider understanding of the situation, at other times to tighten construing in order to make concrete predictions about the world which can be tested out. The man-the-scientist model of man is therefore reaffirmed, since these activities can be seen as the hypothesis generating–hypothesis testing activities which scientists follow as they elaborate their theories.

One means of encouraging an individual to loosen his construing which was identified by Kelly, and which is even more central to the client or learner centred approaches of Rogers (1951) is the uncritical acceptance of the learner. Again Kelly (1955) offers a definition of acceptance within PCT terms, which is the willingness of the therapist to see the world through the client's eyes. In the training situation this would mean that the trainer accepts the way in which the participant construes himself and his world and is willing to explore this with the participant. A simple extension of this idea means that acceptance of the individual can be part and parcel of any relationship. In particular the mutual acceptance of participants on an interpersonal skills course can encourage the participants to loosen their construction processes. Gibb (1964) has suggested that acceptance is a central issue for participants during the early phases of group development. Fransella (1970) has shown that participants in a therapy group moved from loosened to tightened construing in concert during the course of the group. This offers some evidence that acceptance and the associated loosening of construing, followed by tightening and the testing of new constructs, does enable participants to elaborate their constructions of interpersonal relationships.

These then are some of the concepts which Kelly used to describe the awareness of change in construct systems, and some of the possible responses to that change. They are of particular importance to the PCT model which is being developed in this paper to explain the elaboration of the construct system of a participant on a human relations training programme. But there is much wider scope for the application of these ideas to other management training and development programmes. If one accepts that one view of management training and development is the process by which managers are enabled to elaborate their current construct systems to cope with new systems, roles, and responsibilities, then these ideas can be used to identify the problems which confront the trainee, and the strategy which he is adopting to elaborate his construct system.

PART II

The PCT Model of Learning from Experience in Human Relations Training Programmes

So far this paper has been concerned with giving a brief overview of some of the important concepts of PCT and, in passing made brief reference to some issues in management education. In this section these concepts will be used to develop a model of how a participant might learn from an experience-based human relations training programme. Experiential learning programmes have principally been developed to promote the acquisition of interpersonal skills and personal growth. The emphasis that experiential methods place on the participant gaining insight and personal meaningfulness have made these methods particularly relevant to interpersonal skills training. In contrast there has been relatively little use of methods which promote insight and meaningfulness in learning technical skills, although as Boydell (1976) points out there may well be scope to apply these methods to these areas.

What, then, are the features of experiential programmes which enable the participants to gain insights and make the learning personally meaningful to them? Perhaps the first feature is that the learning is not programmed, in the sense that the participants will not learn the same (nor necessarily similar) things, and how they learn them can be different. This does not mean that the learning has no objectives, but these objectives will be generalized foci of learning, rather than precise explicit behaviours. This apparent lack of precision in objectives and structure means that there is scope for the participant to project the constructs that he currently applies to interpersonal relationships into this ambiguous situation. These constructs not only act as means of understanding what others are doing, but also act as guidelines for his own behaviour in that situation. The focus of the learning is therefore what the participants make of the situation they are in.

The second feature is that in most experiential exercises the participants are asked to reflect on what has happened, what they did, how they felt, and so on. In doing this the participants are being invited to explore how they understood the situation, and how this affected their behaviour. They are being asked to get in touvh with the constructs, or theory-in-use which they used to make anticipations about that situation. These reflections are usually shared with the other participants in the exercise in an open forum. The sharing of reflections can create a number of interesting learning opportunities. Not only can each participant gain feedback from the others about the impact of his behaviour, but also whether the others were seeing the situation in the same way as himself. This is likely to have the effect of validating or invalidating the constructs he was using to make sense of that situation and his role in it. It also means that he can be confronted by very different interpretations of what was going on. If the individual explores the alternative constructs which other participants use to understand that situation, then he may find that there is something of value in the models of reality which other participants use.

The plenary sessions also give participants the opportunity to relate what happened in the exercise with what has happened in other situations. The generalization from the here-and-now of the immediate experience to the there-and-then situation at work allows them to share and confront the meaning which they have imposed on their working lives.

The freedom which the participants have to explore and test out the situation that they find themselves in, can also encourage them to experiment with what is going on. This can mean experimenting with different constructs or roles which are currently in their repertoire, to see how effective these styles are in this situation. Or it can mean exploring and experimenting with the alternative models employed by other participants. This will enable the experimenting participant to discover some of the implications of taking that model, and whether there seems to be anything of value to him in adopting or modifying it.

A number of learning models have been proposed to describe how participants learn from experiential methods. One of the best known models was proposed by Kolb, Rubin, and McIntyre (1974). They suggest that learning from experience is a cycle of four phases, starting with observation of events, giving rise to reflections about the events, leading to abstract conceptualization or the establishment of general principles, and finally leading to experimentation with behaviour, this leads to new events to be observed and the cycle is repeated. The understanding of experience, and the ways in which models of that experience are built up is fundamental to PCT. Kelly (1970), in similar vein to Kolb *et al*, suggested that experience was a cycle involving the following phases: anticipation, investment, encounter, confirmation or disconfirmation, and constructive revision leading to new anticipations.

To illustrate the model, it is possible to apply it to what typically happens during a short experiential exercise, for example a group decision-making exercise. The participant enters the exercise with some expectations or anticipations about how the group should set about its task, and about the role he might take in relation to others. In doing this he is using themes or constructs which he has found helpful in the past in working with groups. He invests himself in the task by acting out the assumptions and expectations that he has about groups and himself in groups. He is not a passive observer of what is going on, but is intimately concerned with making the thing work and getting something out of it. The encounter occurs between his anticipations of what is likely to happen in the group and what actually happens. This means that the way in which he broadly construed the activity is either confirmed or disconfirmed.

Let us take the situation where his expectations of what is likely to happen are confirmed. The group operates in a fairly similar fashion to other groups of which he is a member, and he felt fairly comfortable and effective with the role that he took. This does not mean that he has learned nothing new from that experience. For one thing he has learnt that he can have confidence in the constructs that he currently employs because they do help him anticipate what is going on. For another it is likely that the constructs he employs will have undergone some change as a result of that experience. These will be principally changes in the definition of those constructs, but nevertheless they may be significant changes in their effects on his behaviour. For example, he may have felt that if perhaps he had been a 'little more insistent' in the group he would have had greater influence, and decide that in future he will try to be a 'little more insistent' to see what happens. These may be variations on a theme which he currently uses, but nevertheless these variations are changes. These changes in the definition of a construct are the constructive revisions which occur when a construct is confirmed, and lead to new anticipations which he can apply to the situation and himself in similar circumstances.

Let us now take the situation where the participant's anticipations about that situation are largely disconfirmed. In some way he just cannot understand what is going on, he has a problem in squaring his expectations with the events that he observes. Depending on the nature of the problem or problems, and his sensitivity to them, he may experience the emotional states which Kelly suggested indicate an awareness that his construct system is being challenged and changed. He may experience anxiety if the group is behaving in ways that he has never experienced in a group before. He may experience guilt if he is unsuccessful in his attempts to establish with others a relationship or role which he has played successfully before. He may experience threat or fear, if he gets feedback from the other participants that he is not the kind of person he thought himself to be.

These then are some of the problems or dilemmas that he may experience as a result of the disconfirmation of his expectations. How he copes with those problems will determine the way in which his construct system is revised. He may adopt a hostile approach to the disconfirming data, and by reinterpreting the disconfirming data convert it into data which validates his expectations. He may discredit the source of the invalidating data, or he may seek out other participants who seem to support his view in a hostile pairing relationship. A hostile approach by forcing validation of current constructs leads to greater definition of those constructs rather than an extension of the system. A hostile approach to a problem seems to be non-growthful since it involves distortions of reality rather than an improved ability to cope with reality as it is. Argyris and Schon (1974) use the term 'self sealing processes' to describe the kind of learning which hostility produces. On the other hand it may be that the participant just cannot afford to be wrong, since if the central beliefs he has about himself are invalid he may feel that he has to begin a whole new process of reconstructing his life. A daunting prospect, and one which he must feel free to veto.

Another approach to the problem might be to constrict the diversity of events which the participant is attending to. If he concentrates on the familiar events, the events that he can understand, then he might be able to successfully ignore the disconfirming data. Events are rarely so chaotic that we cannot find something that we can make sense of. Again because the participant is reluctant to have his anticipations invalidated, then he is likely to define his current construct system rather than extend it.

On the other hand the participant might widen or dilate his perspective on the events in order to get more data about what happened. He may ask the genuine question 'What is going on?' so that he can explore the alternative constructions which other participants have placed on those events. He may be attempting a fairly major reprganization of his construct system in order to make it a better model of reality. This major reorganization of the system might well involve the extension of the system, and the invention of new themes to cope with reality. The invention of new constructs is a very ambitious undertaking, and not the only means of resolving these problems, (see Bannister and Fransella (1971) p. 158). The participant could redefine events within his current system, yet the invention of new themes might be the only way to gain a wider understanding of his world.

The process by which new constructs are invented is far from clear, and there seem to be no hard and fast rules which will guarantee the extension of an individual's construct system. In general terms the Creativity Cycle would seem to give some insights into the process, but even this does not explain how an individual gains the flash of insight which restructures his perceptions, and provides a new theme to explain the observed events. Much of what follows is therefore speculation about how the creation of new constructs might be facilitated and fostered within the group of participants on the experiential programme.

The Creativity Cycle starts with loosened construing, i.e. constructs which have varying predictions, and finishes with tight, validated constructs, i.e. constructs with unvarying predictions. There are a number of ways by which the construction process can be loosened, of particular importance within this context are the invalidation of current constructs, and the acceptance of participants for one another.

There are a number of possible sources of invalidation for course participants.

There is the self-generated invalidation where events just do not work out as we expected them. Then there is the invalidation from other participants who do not confirm our view of things, and perhaps more significantly have alternative models of reality which might explain events better than our own. If the participant has the reflective skills to be sensitive to this invalidation, and does not react in a hostile manner, then his construct system might well become loosened.

Acceptance has been identified by T-group theorists as a crucial issue, both for the development of the group and for the individual development of participants. If acceptance does lead to loosened construing then it is interesting to note the emphasis which Revans lays on the 'comradeship in adversity' and mutual acceptance of members of his learning sets, which might promote the loosening of the members' construction processes. Acceptance also has implications for the accepting participants, since in being prepared to explore the world through someone else's eyes, they may experience confrontation of their current constructs, particularly if the accepted person is seeing the world in a very different way.

The loosening of construction is the first phase of the Creativity Cycle, and indicates the readiness of the system to invent and incorporate new constructs. In social situations, such as an interpersonal skills laboratory, some of the sources of new constructs will be other participants and the trainer. If the participants are enabled to explore and experiment with each others' constructs or models of reality, then it may well be that they will find something of value in these alternative models. In 'trying on someone else's constructs for size' we are able not only to see what their model is like, but also to explore some of the implications of using that model for ourselves. This is not to suggest that second-hand models will be taken on wholesale and unaltered, but in exploring the implications of the model we may well modify it. These processes are of course dependent upon the participants being aware of their models, being prepared to share them, and feeling free enough to experiment with alternatives. All of which says something about the learning climate which is necessary for this kind of development. A climate which supports this learning would be low on defensiveness, high on trust, and placing a high value on experimentation.

This means of changing construct systems shows how other participants' constructs might be incorporated into the system, rather than the way in which new constructs might be invented. Of course new constructs can be invented in a creative way. This might be by individual acts of creativity where the participant relies principally on his own resources to restructure his experiences, as in the meditation and enlightenment-seeking activities of Eastern philosophies. Or it might be by collective acts of creativity in which participants invent new, shared themes to understand their experience.

The final phase of the Creativity Cycle is in the tightening of the newly invented or incorporated themes. The tightening of the construct involves testing out the construct to see the extent to which it does help the participant understand and predict events. In this way the construct is tested against reality to see whether it

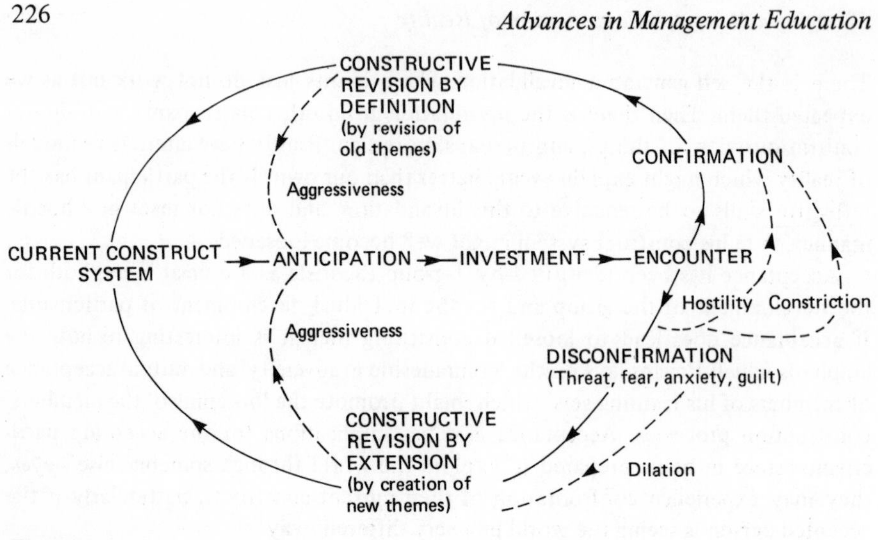

Figure 1

gains general validation and acts as a good guide to expectations, or whether it is a poor predictor and generally invalid. In the latter case the construct might well be loosened again, and the Creativity Cycle begins anew.

This active testing out of a construct is what Kelly described as aggressiveness, and can be seen as the participant setting up real-life experiments with his behaviour to test out new anticipations. The essence of aggressiveness is that the participant is actively seeking feedback about the success of his experiments, and is open to feedback about the failures. Quite obviously it is a much more valid experiment if it is tested in conditions which approximate most closely to his back-home situation. This might indicate that the accepting experimenting climate of the workshop which helped to loosen his construing and encourage creativity, might not be the most appropriate situation to test out the new themes, and points to a very real problem of transfer of learning; a point well illustrated by Harrison (1962) who has shown that participants on T-groups develop more 'personal' and 'social' constructs, but these may not generalize to people outside the group.

The process by which constructs are changed as a result of experience can be illustrated in Figure 1, in which the basic cycle of experience has been elaborated to incorporate the influence of the transition states. Those familiar with the work of Hampden-Turner (1966) will probably recognize a similarity between this model, and Hampden-Turner's existential model of learning in T-group situations. It is interesting that both Kelly and Hampden-Turner produced their models in the same year, 1966, but neither refers to the work of the other.

In summary, this section has attempted to illustrate the way in which a participant's understanding or construction of himself and his social relationships might be changed as a result of participation in an interpersonal skills workshop. The development of the construct system occurs by increasing the definition of the current constructs, or by the extension of the system by creating new constructs. The successful elaboration of the system will depend in part on the way in which the participant copes with the confirmation or disconfirmation of his current model and the emotions generated by the experience.

THE IMPLICATIONS FOR MANAGEMENT EDUCATORS AND FUTURE RESEARCH

One thing which has to be emphasized about Personal Construct Theory is that it is not just a theory of cognitive development, an accusation which is often made by its critics. Inextricably woven into the theory are central concepts of emotions and conations which make the theory a theory of the whole person. One of the objectives of this paper has been to suggest that an awareness that our construct systems are undergoing change (emotion) is part and parcel of our developing a better understanding of ourselves, and our relations to others. This is equally true in any training or development scheme, whether it is an action learning programme, promotion, job rotation, or in fact in any situation in which we are confronted by a different and perhaps perplexing world. To take this point further, perhaps one way in which we can aid the learner is to help him to become aware of these transitions as he experiences his everyday life. In this way the learner may be able to identify for himself the growth points of his own development. He may be able to question for himself what is making him feel anxious, threatened, or guilty; to identify whether he is adopting the best development strategy by becoming hostile, or withdrawing from the problem by constriction; to identify for himself how he might aggressively test out the validity of his model of the world to know whether it does help him understand and predict his new situation. Concern with issues of this nature are surely part of the process of learning how to learn.

A more comprehensive view of learning to learn is proposed by Thomas and Harri-Augstein (1977) in which learning to learn is seen as the learner developing skills in reflecting on the meaning which he is ascribing to events in his world. He is helped to do this by a 'learning conversation' with a tutor, who feeds back the learners cognitive reflections, offers personal support during the change process, and develops with the learner ways of evaluating his learning. Gradually the learning conversation goes on more inside the learners head than with the tutor as he becomes a 'self-organized learner'. There would seem to be tremendous scope for the development of learning conversation schemes, to enable managers to become self-organized learners and use their everyday experiences as learning opportunities. While recognizing that this might be a fairly costly scheme, it would seem to be particularly appropriate for managers embarking on major career developments, to smooth the transition into the new role.

An alternative approach has been to feed back to participants in an interpersonal skills workshop the results of a questionnaire which attempted to measure their emotional response to the events on the workshop. The questionnaire was originally designed as a research instrument to measure anxiety, hostility, threat, guilt, aggressiveness, constriction, dilation, and acceptance. The feedback was particularly effective for those participants who were identified as acting in a hostile manner towards disconfirming data. Feedback of data of this kind might provide the basis of a learning skills course, to enable managers to identify their usual responses to their experiences, and develop more effective learning strategies.

A point made earlier in this paper is that minor modifications in current models of the world can be just as valuable as fundamentally changing these models by incorporating new constructs. While Argyris and Schon (1974) pay lip service to the importance of single loop development, the objective of their training is to supplant current managerial models, Model I which emphasizes rationality, winning, non-expression of feelings, and controlling others, with Model II which emphasizes openness, owning feelings, and participative relationships. While it is appreciated that Argyris and Schon are attempting to change the culture of the organization by this management development programme, it must be pointed out that if a manager exists in a Model I culture, then his model is perfectly adequate in helping him understand that organization. This does not mean that he should not be aware of alternative models, but essentially the choice of which model he operates and which model he elaborates during training is his. In contrast it is Argyris and Schon who have identified the alternative Model II, and who have arranged the learning goals of their programme to enable the participants to explore the implications of Model II. Yet the participants are meant to learn something about employing a more participative style with their subordinates.

An alternative view of an effective executive is not that he is slavishly committed to one model of reality, but has a variety of models and also some working guidelines which indicate which model is appropriate in what kinds of situations. This would suggest that as trainers we have to identify processes and techniques which enable the participants on our programmes to identify and test out their current models of reality, to identify the situations in which the model is adequate as well as inadequate, and to concentrate as much on refining current models as we do on elaborating new models.

One further point about Argyris' approach is that, if we compare his ideas of the early 60's (Argyris, 1962) with those of the 70's (Argyris, 1976), there seems to be similarity in the factors which he suggests restrict or promote individual effectiveness within the organization. The ideas proposed in the 1976 paper seem to be modifications of the earlier model of interpersonal competence and organizational effectiveness. Within the terms of the later model this would seem to show single loop development of his ideas (a slight modification of the current theory-in-use). This demonstrates the worth of single loop development for no one can deny the tremendous value both theoretical and practical, that Argyris and Schon's model has had upon the management development world. Curiously though, the emphasis of their work, as with many writers on management education, is on double loop learning and the construction of new models rather than in the modifications of the old.

Finally to make some comments on Action Learning programmes, and in particularly the emphasis which Revans (1973) places on the importance of emotional threat in learning. He suggests that managers operate in threatening environments, where if one does make a mistake there is usually some negative consequence for being wrong. He goes on to suggest that the use of exercises in which there is no threat for getting things wrong only serves to teach managers how to behave in non-threatening situations and are therefore unrelated to the real world. In contrast Moore and Anderson (1969) suggest that the lack of personal threat in exercises encourage the participants to explore the situation, and experiment with their behaviour, and that these processes are crucial to learning.

Are these two opposed points of view irreconcilable? If we re-examine the Creativity Cycle then apparently they are not. The Creativity Cycle emphasizes the importance of loosened construing leading to the creation of new constructs, which can then aggressively be tested out in reality, leading to tight validated constructs. The processes of loosening and tightening are therefore complementary as a means of producing new validated constructs. It seems that the low threat/high acceptance which Moore and Anderson suggest are crucial will encourage loosened construing. Whereas the high threat/low acceptance conditions of implementing the Action Learning proposal will make the fellow tighten his construing so that he can test out and validate his model. These processes are therefore not mutually exclusive, but are appropriate at different times in the development of new models. The comments which Revans makes about the climate of high acceptance between fellows during the meetings of learning sets suggests that this is the situation in which participants' constructions are loosened. With interaction with other fellows new constructs can be created, and finally tested out as the fellow gets to grips with implementing his solution to the problem.

This paper has attempted to show some of the value of taking a PCT approach to the problems of management education and development. The utility of the theory is that it not only addresses itself to theoretical issues, but has practical implications for trainers and the programmes which they design. There are perhaps changes in the theory which would make it even more appropriate to management educators. In particular it seems that the clinical pedigree of the theory does tend to emphasize the pathological side of experience by concentrating on 'guilt', 'fear', 'threat', 'anxiety', etc. While the definitions of these states are not meaningless to management educators, there are more positive feelings which our trainees experience during their development programmes. 'Challenge', 'excitement', 'involvement' are but a few of the feelings which need some definition within PCT terms. Mildred McCoy (1977) has elaborated on Kelly's original definitions of emotions, but for our purposes we need to make this elaboration even wider. Because of issues like this it is not suggested that PCT has the answers to all of our problems, but it does pose some very good questions which are worthy of the attention of all involved in management education.

REFERENCES

Argyris, C. (1962). *Interpersonal Competence and Organisational Effectiveness,* Irwin Dorsey.

Argyris, C. (1976). Learning environment for increased effectiveness, in C.L. Cooper (ed.), *Theories of Group Processes,* John Wiley, London.

Argyris, C., and Schon, D. (1974). *Theory in Practice,* Jossey Bass.

Bannister, D. (1963). The genesis of schizophrenic thought disorder: a serial invalidation hypothesis, *Brit J. Psychiat,* **109**.

Bannister, D., and Fransella, F. (1971). *Inquiring Man. The Theory of Personal Constructs,* Penguin, London.

Blake, R., and Mouton, J.S. (1964). *The Managerial Grid,* Gulf.

Boydell, T. (1976). *Experiential Learning,* University of Manchester, Department of Adult Education.

Fransella, F. (1970). . . . And then there was one, in D. Bannister (ed.), *Perspectives in Personal Construct Theory,* Academic Press, London.

Gibb, J.R. (1964). Climate for trust formation, in L.P. Bradford, J.R. Gibb and K.D. Beene (eds), *T-group theory and laboratory method,* John Wiley, London.

Hampden-Turner, C.M. (1966). An existential 'Learning Theory' and the integration of T-group research, *Journal of Applied Behavioural Science,* **2**, (4).

Harrison, R. (1962). Impact of the laboratory on perceptions of others by the experimental group, in C. Argyris, *Interpersonal Competence and Organisational Effectiveness,* Irwin Dorsey.

Higgin, G. (1975). Scarcity, abundance and depletion. Inaugural lecture. Loughborough University of Technology.

Kelly, G.A. (1955). *The Psychology of Personal Constructs Vols. 1 and 2,* Norton.

Kelly, G.A. (1970). A brief introduction to Personal Construct Theory, in D. Bannister (ed.), *Perspectives in Personal Construct Theory,* Academic Press, London.

Kolb, D.A., Rubin, I.M., and McIntyre, J.M. (1974). *Organisational Psychology. An Experiential Approach,* Prentice-Hall, Englewood Cliffs, NJ.

McCoy, M.M. (1977). A reconstruction of emotion, in D. Bannister (ed.), *New Perspectives in Personal Construct Theory,* Academic Press, London.

McGregor, D.V. (1960). *The Human Side of Enterprise,* McGraw-Hill.

Moore, O.K. and Anderson, A.R. (1969). Some principles for the design of clarifying educational environments, in P.A. Goslin (ed.), *Handbook of Socialisation Theory and Research,* McNally.

Radcliff, P. (1977). Management and Education: Current Problems, Future Needs, and Possibilities. Unpublished M.Sc. thesis. University of Bradford.

Revans, R.W. (1973). The response of the manager to change, *Management Education and Development,* **4**.

Rogers, C.R. (1951). *Client Centred Therapy,* Houghton Mifflin.

Smith, M.J. (1980). Application and Use of Repertory Grids, in J.E. Beck and C.J. Cox (eds), *Advances in Management Education,* John Wiley, London.

Thomas, L.F., and Harri-Augstein, E.S. (1977). Learning to learn: the personal construction and exchange of meaning, in M.J.A. Howe (ed.), *Adult Learning. Psychological Research and Applications.* John Wiley, London.

Advances in Management Education
Edited by John Beck and Charles Cox

CHAPTER 14

Reflective Learning

Richard Boot and Philip Boxer

Reflective Learning is a method of facilitating learning from experience. So why not stick to the more commonly used term 'experiential learning'? There are a number of reasons for this and in this paper we hope that by describing what we mean by reflective learning those reasons will become clearer. A useful starting point might be to state one of our basic assumptions which is that experience alone is not learning and does not guarantee that learning will take place. It is no use providing people with 'experiences' either in the classroom or in the workplace in the hope that they will learn. Whether or not they learn will depend on what they 'do' with that experience. This fact is recognized in the old cliché that there is a difference between the man who has lived one year thirty times and the man who has lived thirty years once. It is also recognized in the idea of an experiential learning 'cycle' expressed by many practitioners in the field and explored in some detail by Kolb and others (Kolb and Fry, 1975). A closer look at this cycle will give one indication of why we choose to refer to the methods we are developing as reflective learning. Figure 1 represents our version of the learning cycle.

For us the major aspect of learning is *not* change in overt behaviour as a result of experience but the process of discovering new, personal meanings in that experience. Those meanings may lead to new forms of personal action and so be observable in terms of changed behaviour, but equally they may not. The stage in the cycle that influences the quality of learning from experience (i.e. the extent to which it leads to new meaning) is reflection – the process of thinking back on, reworking, or searching for meanings in experience.

For many management trainers or educators, their main intervention in the learning cycle is at the first stage. They provide 'an experience' in the form of a

The authors would like to acknowledge the support and assistance given during this project with Ellerman Lines Ltd of Don Young, Group Personnel Director and Mick Crews, Group Management Training and Development Manager; and of other consultants on the project, Fred Kohler and Tony Blake.

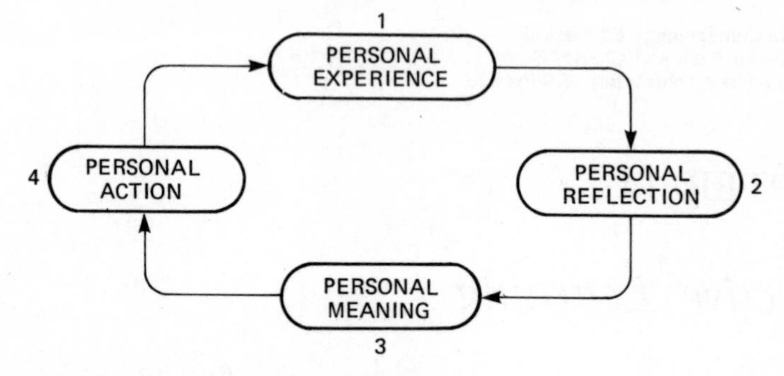

Figure 1. Learning from Experience

structured exercise, a business game or simulation or something similar. Indeed, as Boydell points out, for many this is what experiential learning is (Boydell, 1976). The methods we are developing, however, involve intervention at the second stage. Their purpose is to encourage and support personal reflection by the use of reflective techniques. We are making a conscious distinction here between the terms 'method' and 'technique'. The distinction is to us a very important one and worth elaborating.

We have frequently been struck by the fact that different trainers can use an identical technique and claim to be involved in the same process and yet seem to provide quite different experiences for the learner. In our use of the terms this is because the learner experiences more than the technique. He experiences the method, of which the technique is only one part. The other part of prime importance is the ideology of the trainer. Brown (1973, p. 179) defines an ideology as 'a system of beliefs about social issues, with strong effects in structuring thoughts, feelings, and behaviour'. This term has been preferred to alternatives like theory or philosophy because of its greater connotation of involvement of the trainers own value system. By making this distinction between technique and method it is possible to avoid some of the circularity that goes with the debate about whether technology is neutral or whether there is always an inherent set of values. In educational terms it is our contention that techniques may be neutral but methods can never be. The implications of this have been noted by others. For example Cooper and Levine (1978, p. 12) state:

> It is terribly important for trainers to be aware that their behaviour reflects, communicates and in many cases, models certain values which can influence immediate learning and subsequent behaviour of participants.

Postman and Weingartner (1971, p. 43) make the same point, perhaps more forcefully.

> There can be no significant innovation in education that does not have at its centre the attitudes of teachers and it is an illusion to think otherwise. The beliefs, feelings, and assumptions of teachers are the air of a learning environment; they determine the quality of life within it. When the air is polluted, the student is poisoned, unless of course, he holds his breath.

How then might this distinction between technique and method evidence itself in practice? To answer this we can refer to the different trainers mentioned earlier, all of whom would claim to be involved in the same activity – experiential learning. Their technique is to set up and run the NASA group decision-making exercise, widely used in management training (Pfeiffer and Jones, 1969). Their objectives in running the exercise, however, and the values implicit in those objectives are quite different. The first wants the participants to learn 'that'. In other words the exercise is used as a subtle variant of the information transmission method. It is intended to provide empirical evidence for the 'truths' about group decision-making that the participants are made aware of in accompanying lectures or recommended reading. They learn 'that' group decision-making takes longer in elapsed time as well as man-hours than individual decision-making, and 'that' groups produce more and better solutions to problems than do individuals. Problems arise for the trainer when, as sometimes happens, the outcomes of the exercise fail to support these 'truths'. He is faced with explaining how this particular group is the exception to the rule or why it was a bad exercise anyway, or worse still why the participants did it wrong.

The second trainer wants the participants to learn 'how'. His method is basically conditioning. His intention is to reinforce those behaviours which he regards as essential for effective teamwork and to extinguish those he regards as dysfunctional. He may get into trouble if questioned too closely on his definition of effectiveness.

The third uses the exercise as a vehicle to provide the opportunity for participants to explore and make sense of the way they relate to others and to collective tasks. As a trainer he cannot know in advance what they will learn in terms of facts and behaviours. His intention is to facilitate reflection and the discovery of personal meaning. He may encounter difficulties with those who are expecting to be 'taught' or 'trained'.

The point of these examples is that, whatever is learnt from the technique, the methods of the three trainers are teaching very different lessons about who is responsible for the learning that takes place, who determines what is good and bad behaviour, what is the nature of knowledge, and what is worth knowing. These lessons have their origin not in the technique but in the ideological standpoint from which it is applied. Figure 2 represents the relationship between technique and method diagrammatically. It also indicates our own ideological position and refers to a particular technique that has been developed to support the Reflective Learning Method.

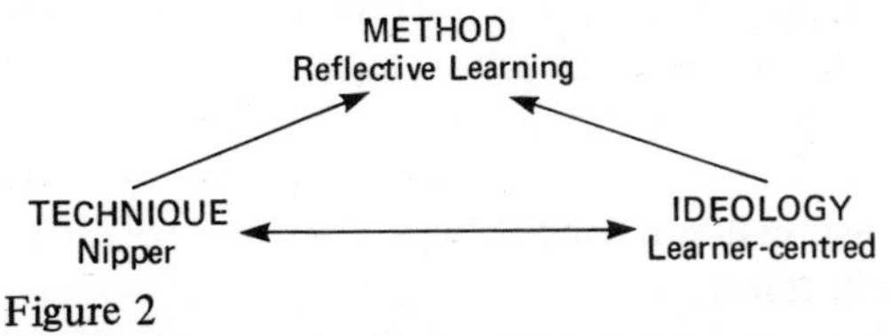

Figure 2

In the following sections we shall be looking more closely at the ideology of reflective learning, the technique, and the method in practice. We shall also be discussing the implications for subsequent research.

THE IDEOLOGY

We like to think that we are involved in the development of a truly learner-centred method of management development. But what is learner centredness? We believe this is something about which many trainers deceive themselves. For some it simply means 'not lecturing', for others it means 'activity based', for yet others it means 'individualized'. While all of these approaches may be part of learner centredness they are not synonymous with it. There are other ways of being trainer-centred than standing in front of a group with a piece of chalk in one's hand. The central issue seems to be one of control. Who determines what is to be learnt, why, and how? There are subtle ways in which the trainer can delegate this control or determination to the 'subject matter', or, and this is a particular concern of ours, to the technology. So the participant is given total freedom to learn the 'right' answers to questions regarded as important by the trainer. This may take the form of 'guess my list' discussion leading or it may take the form of 'individualized' programmed learning packages. On the latter Rowntree (1974, p. 97) has the following to say:

> Resource materials are sometimes so preselected, prestructured and virtually predigested (what Edgar Friedenberg calls the 'TV-dinner approach' to educational packaging) that the student is left no freedom to use the package in his own way and take from it just what he needs. We should be suspicious of monolithic packages that assume that all students have the same objectives and the same learning style.

But any attempts to define learner centredness in terms of the techniques employed is likely to be inadequate in that it implies that the choice as to what techniques are appropriate remains with the trainer. Learner centredness expresses itself in the relationship established between the trainer and the learner and in particular in the location of control in that relationship. It also expresses itself in the way the trainer defines, implicitly or explicitly, his own role in the learning process. Rogers (1969), who is probably the best known proponent of the learner-centred ideology insists that the role should be that of a 'facilitator' of learning. (A term which, it seems to us, does not sit easily on the British tongue but for which we have not yet found a suitable alternative). And he is quite clear about what that role involves. Amongst other things he suggests it involves establishing a suitable climate for enquiry, helping the learners clarify their own goals and purposes, making available the widest possible range of resources for learning from which the learner can choose those which are appropriate to his own purposes, and regarding himself as a flexible resource to be utilized by the learners. (Note that this last point could involve him in employing a whole range of different educational techniques, including lectures).

And what does this mean for the development of particular techniques? Here again we quote Rowntree (1974, p. 97):

> . . . they should impose minimum constraints on teachers and students who wish to choose from among them and combine them with other resources and experiences in personally meaningful ways. Better may be to hack out a path to your own destination than to ride the royal road to someone else's.

He expresses the principle that has guided our development of a range of computer aided techniques at the London Business School (with support initially from the National Development Programme in Computer Assisted Learning and currently from the Training Services Division of the Manpower Services Commission).

THE TECHNIQUE

The technique which we wish to describe is a flexible system known as NIPPER. It will probably be clear from what we have already said that we do not regard this as the only technique of relevance nor do we believe its use will inevitably result in reflective learning. But we do believe that when applied within a learner-centred approach it can be a very poweful catalyst in the reflective learning process.

NIPPER is based on the principles of Personal Construct Theory and the Repertory Grid Technique. Although different in some important respects from the conventional Repertory Grid it is still prone to the same kind of abuse and distortion that Fransella and Bannister (1977) caution against in the use of that technique. The intention in the design of the technique is to minimize the constraints it places upon facilitator or learner. In this connection it is important to emphasize that we have not developed a 'package' which the learner opens at one end, is guided through, and then is dropped out at the other. A better analogy would be a box of Lego bricks which the facilitator or learner can put together into any shape to suit hiw own purposes. NIPPER, then, consists of a series of modules each designed to support the Reflective process within individuals and groups. It places no constraint on the content or implicit structure of the 'subject matter' being reflected upon. Obviously our preference is that these be determined by the learners themselves on the basis of what they regard as significant in their own experience. The role of the computer is restricted to aiding the process of learning from that experience by feeding back to the learners patterns which appear to emerge in their reflections upon it. It does not in itself draw any conclusions from or attribute any meanings to those patterns. The intention is to provide the learners with the opportunity to do that for themselves.

To make it possible to demonstrate some of the forms in which these patterns might be fed back, we have chosen a hypothetical example. Our concern at this stage is simply to describe the mechanics of the technique and for this reason a fairly trivial but tangible subject matter has been chosen. It involves Richard reflecting upon a current problem of choosing a new car.

The starting point for the exercise is my thoughts and feelings on the subject. Here NIPPER requires that I distinguish my thoughts in terms of 'elements' and 'concepts'. The term 'elements', in this context, is used to refer to specific examples from the chosen subject area. They might be critical incidents at work, current options open to me, people I deal with, past decisions I have made or whatever. In this example they are the particular cars I am considering. 'Concepts', on the other hand can be used to express subjective, evaluative ideas or feelings which describe how I experience, react to, or respond to those elements. In this example they are not the hard analytical facts such as purchase price, miles per gallon, etc. that might allow me to define the range of cars to be considered. Rather they are expressions of the values implicit in my personal statement of preference for one car rather than another. I am required to state the elements I am considering and the concepts I am using to differentiate between them (see Figure 3).

```
How many elements do you wish to consider at this stage?
(You may add more later if you wish).
?6
Please type in your element names, one per line
(Element names should not be more than 20 characters long)
< DYANE
< GOLF
< CITROEN GS
< RENAULT 12
< RENAULT 14
< PEUGEOT 304
Do you wish to amend any of these element names?
?NO
How many concepts do you wish to use at this stage?
(You may add more later if you wish)
?9
Please type in your concept names, one per line.
(Concept names should not be more than 20 characters long)
< FUN
< CAMPING
< ME
< COMFORT
< STAID
< CHEAP TO RUN
< LASTING
< SOLID
< EASY TINKER
Do you wish to amend any of these concept names?
?NO
```

Figure 3

I am then encouraged to reflect upon the extent to which I feel each concept applies to each of the cars. I express this by representing each car by a letter and positioning the letters along a scale provided for each concept (see Figure 4).

Thus I think of the Dyane as a lot of 'Fun' and the Citroen GS as a little less but still quite high. The Renault 12 and the Peugeot in contrast I rate as rather low

WHEN RATING THE ELEMENTS AGAINST EACH CONCEPT
USE LETTERS TO REPRESENT THE ELEMENTS AS FOLLOWS:–

a – DYANE b – GOLF
c – CITROEN GS d – RENAULT 12
e – RENAULT 14 f – PERGEOT 304

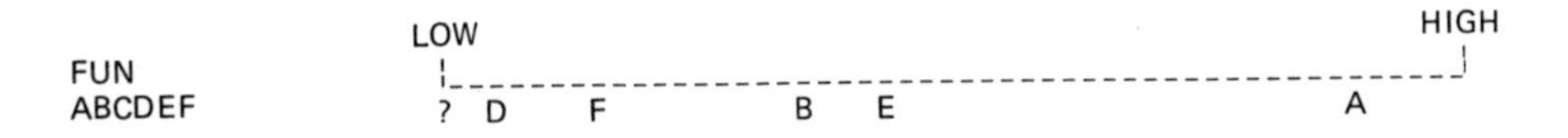

Figure 4

on fun and so on. Eventually then I will have entered into the computer a pattern of ratings for each of the concepts (see Figure 5).

a – DYANE b – GOLF
c – CITROEN GS d – RENAULT 12
e – RENAULT 14 f – PEUGEOT 304

```
               LOW                                                              HIGH
FUN            ¦--d----f---------b---e------------c---------a-----¦
CAMPING        ¦-------d------------b---f-------ec---------a-----¦
ME             ¦---d---------f---------be-------------a-----c-----¦
COMFORT        ¦-----------d-------ea-----f---b--------------c----¦
STAID          ¦---a-------ce------b--------------------fd-------¦
CHEAP TO RUN   ¦-------c-----b-------e---f----------d------------a-¦
LASTING        ¦----f-----d----------------------be--ac----------¦
SOLID          ¦a-----d---------e-------bc--------f---------------¦
EASY TINKER    ¦c-------------------ab-----e----f-----------d----¦
```

Figure 5

This stage, however, represents more than the mere 'inputting' of data. It is an important part of the reflection process. As I rate the cars I am inevitably forced to become more aware of, or at least clarify for myself, the real meaning to me of each of the concepts when applied to this kind of decision.

As was said earlier, once this information is entered, it is possible to ask NIPPER to feed back to me the various patterns that appear to be emerging in my reflections so far. It can do this in a number of different ways. For example it can represent the similarities in the ways I have used the various concepts in the form of a diagrammatic tree or 'dendrogram' (see Figure 6). This tree suggests to me that the concepts I have used to differentiate between the cars cluster together into three distinct families: one family consisting of 'fun', 'me', 'camping', and 'lasting'; the next of 'comfort' and 'solid'; and the third of 'staid', 'easy tinker', and 'cheap to run'. It rests with me to reflect upon these family clusters that NIPPER has identified and consider whether they are in any sense 'meaningful' for me. In the context

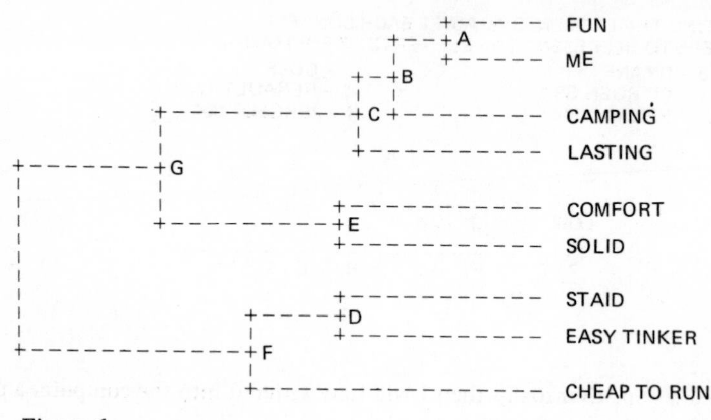

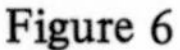
Figure 6

of this example 'meaningful' might imply that they represent some underlying concepts which are important influences upon my order of preference among the cars.

If, as in this case, it feels that they do, then NIPPER can help me explore what those underlying concepts might be. It does this by presenting the same information in a different way. It presents each of the links in the tree to me in turn (starting with the closest) and suggests that I consider what it is that underlies the two concepts that are being linked (see Figure 7). In this example the closest link is between 'fun' and 'me'.

(11) FUN AND ME => A [DIFFERENT]

Figure 7

For me the underlying concept is 'different'. The next closest link is between 'different' and 'camping' (see Figure 8).

(15) A [DIFFERENT] AND CAMPING => B [HOLIDAY CAR]

Figure 8

Here the underlying concept is 'holiday car'. As the process goes on I can build up a clearer picture of the concepts underlying the patterns represented in the tree diagram (see Figure 9). It can be seen that NIPPER labels each of these underlying concepts with a letter of the alphabet. Each of these letters represents one of the links in the tree diagram. By referring back to that diagram we can see that I have identified the concepts which underlie each of the 'family' clusters. Thus 'good bet' underlies cluster 'C'. 'Relaxing drive' underlies cluster 'E'. And 'sensible' underlies cluster 'F'. In addition I am able to make a meaningful link (G) between C and E

(11) FUN	AND ME	=> A[DIFFERENT]
(15) A [DIFFERENT]	AND CAMPING	=> B [HOLIDAY CAR]
(18) B [HOLIDAY CAR]	AND LASTING	=> C [GOOD BET]
(20) STAID	AND EASY TINKER	=> E [RELAXING DRIVE]
(29) D [ORDINARY]	AND CHEAP TO RUN	=> F [SENSIBLE]
(39) C [GOOD BET]	AND E [RELAXING DRIVE]	=> G [MY KIND OF CAR]

Figure 9

which represents 'my kind of car'. This in turn sets off further reflections upon the role of 'sensibleness' in my own decisions about car purchase. And so the process goes on.

If I wish, NIPPER can provide me with the opportunity to go through a similar process, focusing on the cars themselves (see Figure 10).

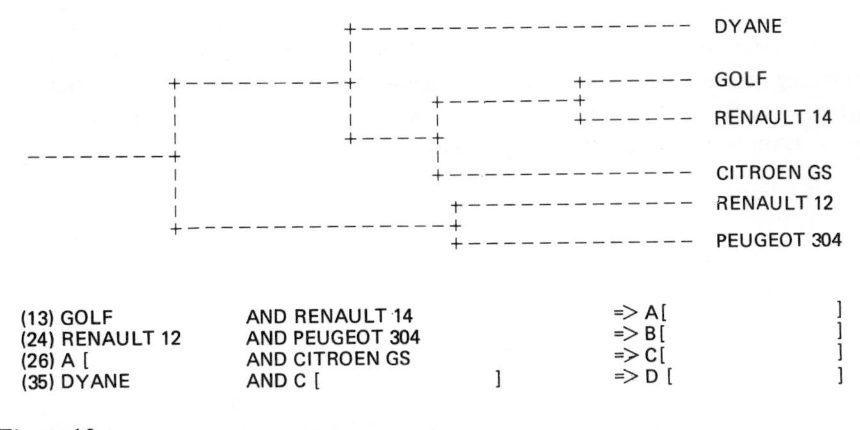

Figure 10

I may, however, be interested in more than identifying underlying patterns in the way I have considered the subject matter so far. I may for example wish to extend the range of concepts I am conscious of using when making choices of this kind. NIPPER can help by taking each car in turn and representing on a single line how different on average the cars are from it in terms of the concepts I am explicitly using so far (see Figure 11). It encourages me to reflect upon the differences expressed so far and consider whether they 'feel' right. Taking the Golf as an example, it would seem that the Renault 14 is much less different from it than all the other cars. Does that feel right? If not, why not? For me the answer is no, and the concept which differentiates further is 'flexibility'. I could continue to do this for each of the cars and so bring to the surface a number of new concepts which express the way I evaluate them, but which I have not considered explicitly so far. I could add these to my existing concepts and go through the same process as above, thus extending my understanding of the patterns implicit in my judgements about cars. NIPPER, then, is by its nature a dynamic process.

For the purposes of this example, however, I shall stay with the original con-

```
a – DYANE                    b – GOLF
c – CITROEN GS               d – RENAULT 12
e – RENAULT 14               f – PERGEOT 304

              LOW                                                              HIGH
DYANE         |a------------e---cb---------df--------------------------|
GOLF          |b-----e-----cf---a--d-----------------------------------|
CITROEN GS    |c------------be--a------f---------d---------------------|
RENAULT 12    |d------------f------eb-----a-----c----------------------|
RENAULT 14    |e-----b-----acf----d------------------------------------|
PEUGEOT 304   |f------------bde----------c--a--------------------------|
```

Figure 11

cepts, and ask for an indication of how the overall patterns in them seem to apply to the particular cars I am considering (see Figure 12). This suggests to me that I am thinking of the Citroen GS as not very 'sensible' but as a 'good bet' and a 'relaxing drive' – in fact as 'my kind of car'. The Renault 12 on the other hand I regard as very 'sensible' but definitely not 'my kind of car'.

1 DYANE
2 GOLF
3 RENAULT 14
4 CITROEN GS
5 RENAULT 12
6 PEUGEOT 304

	1	2	3	4	5	6			
1	++	–	=	+	––	–	FUN	GOOD BET	MY KIND OF CAR
2	++	–	–	++	––	–	ME		
3	++	–	+	+	––	–	CAMPING		
4	+	+	+	+	––	––	LASTING		
5	–	+	–	++	––	+	COMFORT	RELAXING DRIVE	
6	––	+	–	+	–	++	SOLID		
7	––	–	–	–	++	++	STAID		SENSIBLE
8	–	–	+	––	++	+	EASY TINKER		
9	++	–	–	––	+	–	CHEAP TO RUN		

Figure 12

There are a number of other aspects of NIPPER as a technique, including some which support pairs or groups of individuals in the exploration of shared experiences. But as our purpose in this section was simply to give some indication of the mechanics we shall not go into these. One thing, however, will probably have become clear. That is that its real virtue lies not in 'teaching' managers 'what they should know' but in helping them explore their own experience in order that they may better learn from it.

THE METHOD IN PRACTICE

This section describes a particular application of NIPPER within the context of a Workshop designed for Ellerman Lines Limited. The particular form of NIPPER which I used is fully described elsewhere (Boxer, 1979). Needless to say, the views expressed in this section are my own, and should not be taken as representing the views of others involved in designing the workshop. The workshop was designed over a period of eight months leading up to October 1978.

The proposal initially put to Ellermans had the following objectives:

- To generate a network of people who can and do manage their own development in the direction desired by Ellerman Management.
- To develop an internal consultant to be capable of maintaining and expanding that network within the Ellerman group of companies.

The essence of the Workshop was that it was concerned with developing 'learning to learn' competences in relation to the participant's own job. It was designed to involve five different sessions of varying lengths over a period of six months totalling 11 working days. Evaluation of their effectiveness was dealt with by giving Ellermans the following guarantee:

> At the conclusion of the Workshop each participant shall be able to manage his or her own personal development, shall be confident of that ability, and shall be willing to take full responsibility for that development. If it is determined that any individual is *not* so able, confident, and willing, then Boxer, Blake, and Kohler shall refund 75% of the Workshop fees related to that person's participation.

Between this first draft proposal and the final form of the Workshop, much development work was done. During the development process, three strands were discernable: firstly, there was the process of learning about Ellermans as a context to the Workshop. This process culminated in detailed briefings about the potential participants. Secondly, there was the process of 'contracting' with the organization. This did not just mean agreeing on a final form of words arising out of the initial proposal, but involved ensuring that the climate of expectations surrounding the Workshop would not only enable the participants to draw benefit from it, but also enable Mick Crews to manage the impact on Ellermans expected to result from the Workshop. Thirdly, there was the process of designing the form of the Workshop itself and deciding how the boundaries between the different sessions and Ellermans would be managed.

The Ellermans Context

Ellerman Lines Limited had been a very private Private Company. The Sunday Telegraph said about it on June 27th 1976:

> For 40 years the company ran on until by the time of the shipping slump in the late 1960's, the Ellerman Lines, largely through lack of direction and professional management, was in trouble. Real losses in one year were £4 million, rising to £6 million the next.

Under the Chairmanship of Dennis Martin-Jenkins, however, this began to change.

In 1973 the company was divisionalized into Shipping, Transport, Travel, Brewing, and Investment Services; and in 1970 Peter Laister was brought in as Group Managing Director from British Oxygen. Ellermans had traditionally been a paternalistic institution with closed boundaries operating with very low financial gearing in a stable environment. The implicit managerial assumptions had been that managing was a purely technical and routine operation. The introduction of new senior management from outside combined with reorganization of traditional activities had begun to change these implicit assumptions, but it was the primary purpose of the Group Personnel Function to accelerate this development towards a new managerial culture more appropriate for the 1980's.

The contents of the Personnel Function Mission for 1978/79 provides a useful summary of the strategy of which the Workshop would form a part:

> 'the mission is to develop a management culture which can be defined as moving towards the following characteristics:
>
> – more generalist
> – more visionary and enterprising
> – realistic
> – integrative
> – team working
> – achieving
> – adaptive and self-developing
>
> The mission will never be fully achieved, and the idea of movement "away from" and "towards" is an important one. Some of the essential initiatives for implementing the mission are: getting the top people right, developing a management "network", developing key management systems, developing Divisional and Group Boards and Management Development and Training'.

Mick Crews had already considered using a teaching approach aimed at supporting this mission through the use of self-directed use of teaching material. The need to which the Workshop was responding was therefore to support the mission similarly, but to do so with much less emphasis on pre-structured material.

Contracting with the Organization

By August 1978 our contacts at Ellermans felt that we could deliver something that would meet their need, though they were not precisely clear how we would do it. That was not surprising since the three of us did not finalize the form of the first Workshop until the end of September. Two parallel strategies were being pursued (implicitly) by us however. One strategy was concerned with the contract we would make with the actual participants who would be doing the work on the Workshops. The other involved working through the contacts at Ellermans to ensure that if the Workshop was effective, then it would be legitimate for the participants to ask for 'space', i.e. if the participants were to become self-developing, then it would inevitably lead to attempts to change some of the patterns of working within Ellermans. Effective contracting with the organization was therefore necessary to ensure that what energy was released could be usefully focused on the organization. The reverse side of this contracting was that its failure would lead either to a great deal of anxiety for the participants or to their departure from Ellermans.

The result was a memorandum which outlined the basis of the proposed Management Development Workshops, and sought approval to proceed. The argument was that a series of Workshops were necessary at this time because:

– The Group's development in part depended upon the availability of more highly skilled middle and senior managers.
– The current ability of the organization to facilitate management development was limited in both the line and in Personnel Departments.
– The current management development practices – i.e. the Management Review of Appraisal and Counselling – were not yet mature.
– Expectations of career and individual development has been raised by various statements and actions over the previous two years.

On September 12th the proposal to run a series of Management Development Workshops for Middle Management was approved. The first of these was to commence on November 7th with the first session. The plan was to commence a second Workshop at the end of January or early in February the next year. During September and October we were briefed on about 30 potential participants, and nominations were asked for from Divisions.

The Shape of the Workshop

The Workshop was to be designed to give the participant a space within which to manage his own development. The three of us, in designing the Workshop, had to contend with the fact that we were very different in our background and experience. In order to harness this difference we had to develop some vision of how the Workshop could be. The result was a series of sessions and an initial Contract Interview. The first session was to start about one week after the Interview, to last three days, and to be followed the next week by a further two-day session. In both these sessions the concern was to be coming into focus and clarifying the participant's contract with himself. About two months later the third session of two days was to be concerned with helping the participants to draw on each others' strengths and to extend what they were doing. The fourth and final three-day session one month later was then to enable the participants to own the process as a whole and thereby be able to manage it for themselves.

We did not try to, nor was it possible to tell the participants what we would be doing during the Workshop – that had to be his choice. The Contract Interview therefore involved enabling the participants to decide whether or not they wanted to work with us, and placing responsibility for evaluation firmly in their hands. In return for that, we decided to ask the participants to accept three conditions:

- Throughout the Workshop you will only act in ways which *you* choose.
- You will accept a duty to express yourself always in *your own* individual way.
- You will accept responsibility wholly for your actions *throughout* the period of the Workshop.

Our intention in imposing these conditions was to clearly break any connotations the participants might have of the Workshop with normal learning contracts – most contracts involve the participant in letting someone else choose what he is to do, how he is best to do it, and thereby handing *in loco parentis* powers to the teacher. The belief that we could be any different was based on the idea that we could work with them through the medium of our relationship with them, rather than through the particular things we chose to do with them. This meant of course being able to act resourcefully as each moment arose; but it also meant trying to adopt particular relationships with them in order to create a space within which they could choose to move. This concept of different focus within a relationship was to be present also in the form the Contract Interviews were to take and in the way we used physical space during the Workshop.

The first focus was associated with Fred Kohler and was 'Doing'. Its symbol was the individual expression – a display (as in exhibition) which would open possibilities of communication and which was constructed in as many different media and alternative forms as possible. The expression was of what the participant found true and significant; for session I it was based on the past and present; for session II on the present and future. 'Doing' was to be analogous with focusing a reflex camera – the participant needed to introduce coherence, clarity, and composition to his picture, even when the object of his focusing was moving. The second focus was associated with Tony Blake and was 'Being'. Its symbol was the Address Book containing extra leaves for the participant to record any golden rules he might wish to remember. 'Being' was to be a focus on the experiential method of learning, and the Address Book represented the mutual support which could be drawn from other participants. The third focus was associated with myself and was 'Knowing'. Its symbol was the Journal which we had specially printed for the participants. The Journal contained a summary of the sessions at the beginning, and then a pair of facing pages for each day over the period of the Workshops, except during the Workshops themselves when there were three pairs of pages each day for morning, afternoon, and evening. The left hand of each pair was ruled and intended for recording *what* was happening. The right hand page was left completely blank, and was intended for recording *how* the participant experienced what he experienced. The 'Knowing' focus was not therefore a 'facts' kind of knowing, but rather was the inner kind of knowing developed by the reflective method of teaching and essentially complementary to the experiential method.

In the descriptions of the sessions which follow, I can only describe them as I experienced them, since at no time did the consultants work together apart from interviewing. Early in October participants were selected for the Workshop, and a memorandum sent to them explaining that there would be a briefing, that they could decide whether or not they wanted to go on the Workshop, that there would be some kind of 'project' involved, and that this was 'the first money-back guarantee *ever* on this kind of management development'. The result was 14 nominees whom we met over a period of four days at the London Business School. The evening before meeting us they met Mick Crews, and were filled in informally on what the Workshops were about.

The Contract Interview

The three of us produced our own individual expressions for the Interview. During the initial period however we talked generally about the participants, talked about the kinds of 'projects' they might undertake, and tried to say what we would not be doing. When there were no more concerns that they wanted to deal with collectively, we handed out the contract, the Address Book, and the Journal, and briefly took them through their contents. We then broke into three rooms. In one room I introduced half of them to the reflective method of learning, while in a second room Fred Kohler interviewed them individually on the focus they might wish to pursue. In a third room the remainder of the group had an informal discussion with Tony Blake.

My aim was to introduce the participants to the implications of considering their experience both in terms of *what* they experienced and also *how* they experienced – the distinction underlying the left-and-right-hand pages of their Journal. I started by asking each participant to list a number of significant past experiences from which he felt he had learnt something. In doing this I had to help him not to deal with his experience in terms of stereotypes, but to get back to what actually happened; and also to choose experience which was not so extended in time and space that he felt unable to reflect without fragmenting it. When he had identified a number of different experiences, I then asked him to express *how* he felt them to be significant in terms of personal concepts of value. The difficult part here was to treat the feeling as a facet of himself rather than a property of the experience. This process of referencing the feeling within himself was the beginning of reflecting on personal meaning, and when expressed in the form of a pattern along a continuum, provided the basic data needed for the application of the reflective technique.

The patterns thus produced were a side product of a conversation between myself and the participants. The conversations felt very personal and reflective, although their content was always under the participant's control. What I was doing was managing the process, and thereby giving them a strong feeling for my mode of working. As a result of the interviews, eight individuals contracted for the first Workshop, three contracted for the second, two decided not to come on a Workshop at this time, and one never made it to see us.

Session I

The participants started filling in their Journals on day one, and planned what to put into their individual expressions. On the evening before the first session we assembled in the hotel and occupied three rooms. One room was a large assembly room which was to be Fred Kohler's base and in which the exhibition stands were placed. I also put a computer terminal in this room for using NIPPER. The two other rooms were drawing rooms en suite – I had table and chairs and flipchart paper, Tony had the bar and easy chairs. The three consultants had agreed to eat together on a separate table, but otherwise to operate autonomously. The next morning we found ourselves amongst eight participants, none of whom had any idea of how they were to start.

In the intervening period I had processed the data from the contract interviews. Not everyone had produced data, but for those who had, I had promised to return an analysis so that they could work through it if they wanted to. This I did, and out of the next three days, a pattern began to emerge. Working either from the interview data or from new patterns produced from conversation at the time, I would work reflectively through their 'dendrogram'. The criterion for whether or not they needed to produce new data was the 'experience difference analysis'. This enabled the participant to check whether differences made explicit in the data between his experiences corresponded to his intuitive feelings about their difference – and if not then what new concept patterns to add. On average it took about 20 minutes to produce a new analysis, which would then support about three hours reflective working. Expressing concept patterns consciously was in itself a learning process of varying difficulty. The 'dendrogram' then provided a technique for exploring the question: 'What underlying patterns are there in how you experience yourself in relation to this particular problem context?' At its easiest, the answer to this was an affirmation and extension of what they already knew intuitively. At its hardest, it involved a major struggle within the participant leading to self-confrontation, possibly for the first time.

It is impossible to convey hours of personal interaction in any useful way. The conversation however felt like a struggle with the participant's external rational being. The eventual locating of their internal being in the conversation not only led to new questions to take up with Tony Blake, but also to new ways of structuring activity which they took up with Fred Kohler. Figure 13 shows a 'dendrogram' produced at this stage.

Session II

Session II occupied two days at the end of the following week at the same hotel. In between the two sessions participants had been home and spent one or two days in the office, and had had a chance to digest some of the issues raised by session I. I had spent time with everyone at this stage, but not everyone had 'worked through'

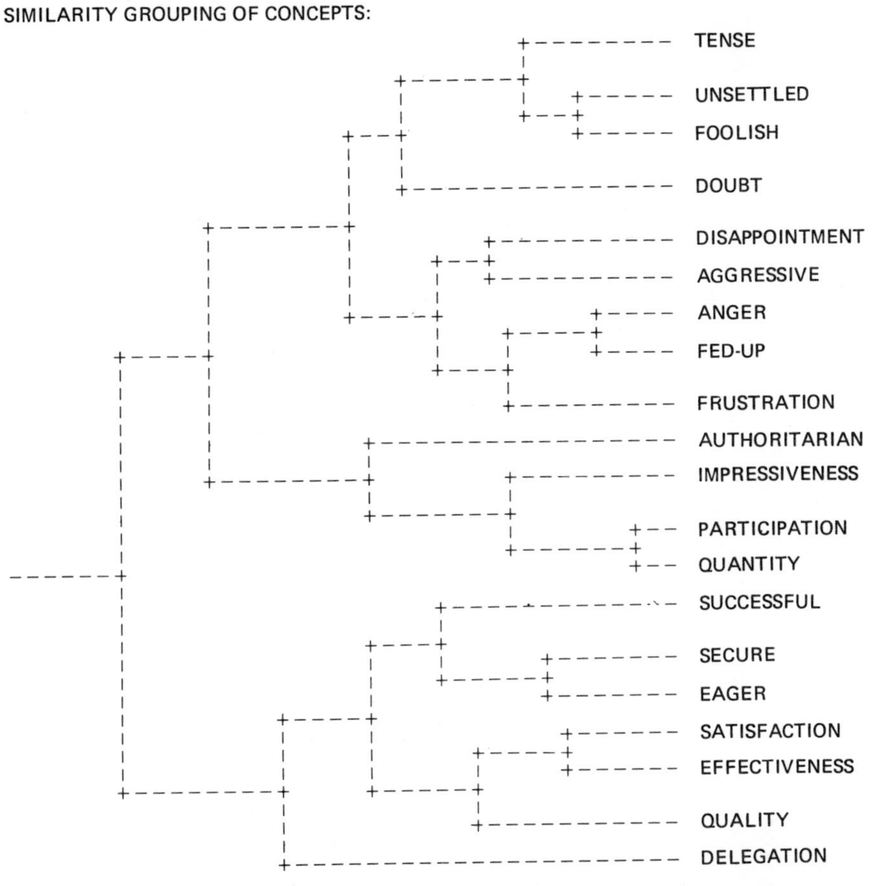

Figure 13. A Session I Dendrogram

reflectively. As the Workshop progressed therefore, there was an increasing dispersion in the stages the participants had reached, as defined by the original design. This had as much to do with their internal readiness as with the particular work context in which they had to operate.

After having established the reflective mode of working, the participant found himself faced with a new perspective on himself which needed working through. The corollary to the patterns in his experience of himself was stereotype responses to certain kinds of problem in his environment, and also in his way of dealing with others. The second of these two was left until session III when it was likely to be more of an issue. I worked on the first in session II partly by seeking to recreate the participant's work environment using paper and pencil, and partly by repeating the reflective process with a future orientation rather than a past one. Figure 14 shows a pattern analysis applied to the same data as in Figure 13. For reasons of confidentiality, the option names have been omitted, but from the figure it can be seen

PATTERN ANALYSIS OF OPTION PREFERENCES:

	1	2	3	4	5	6	7	8	9	10	11	12	13	14	15	16	
1	+	−	++	++	++	+	+	−	+	+	+	−−	−−	−	−	−−	TENSE
2	−−	−−	++	++	−	−	−	+	+	++	+	−−	−	−	+	−	UNSETTLED
3	−−	−	++	++	−	−	++	+	+	++	+	−−	−	−	−−	−	FOOLISH
4	−	−	+++	−	++	+	++	++	−	−	−	−	−	−−	+	+	DOUBT
5	++	−	++	++	−	+	++	+	−	−	−	−−	−	−	−−	−−	DISAPPOINTMENT
6	+	+	+	++	++	+	+	+	−−	−	−−	−−	−	−−	+	−−	AGGRESSIVE
7	+	+	++	++	++	−	++	+	−	−	−	−−	−	−−	−−	−−	ANGER
8	+	+	++	++	++	−	+	−	+	+	−	−−	−	−−	−−	−	FED-UP
9	+	−	++	++	+	+	+	+	+	+	+	−−	−−	−−	−−	−	FRUSTRATION
10	++	+	−−	+	++	−−	−	+	+	++	+	−	−−	−−	+	−	AUTHORITARIAN
11	++	++	−	−−	+	−	−	−	+	−	−−	++	++	+	+	−−	IMPRESSIVENESS
12	++	++	−	+	+	+	+	−	+	−	+	++	−−	−−−	−	−−	PARTICIPATION
13	++	+	+	++	+	+	+	−	−	−	+	+	−−	−−−	−	−−	QUANTITY
14	+	−	−	++	++	−	−−	−	−	−−	−	++	+	+	+	+	SUCCESSFUL
15	+	++	−−	−	−−	−	−	−	−	−−	+	++	++	++	+	+	SECURE
16	++	++	−−	−−	−	−	−	−	−	−	−	++	++	++	+	+	EAGER
17	+	−	−	−−	+	−	−−	−	−−	−−	−	++	++	+	++	+	SATISFACTION
18	−	+	+	−−	++	−	−	−	−−	−−	−	++	++	++	+	−	EFFECTIVENESS
19	−−	−	+	−−	−	−	+	+	−−	−	−	++	+	+	++	++	QUALITY
20	++	+++	−−	−	−	−−	−−	+	+	+	+	−	+	+	−	−	DELEGATION

Figure 14. A Pattern Analysis showing Groupings of Options (Corresponding to Columns) and their Associated Value Connotations

that they fall into groups which have characteristic connotations in terms of the individual's concepts. Working with the individual at this stage therefore involved exploring how he could create movement for himself along these dimensions and to what extent he was restricting himself through stereotyping rather than because of any particular restrictions in his environment.

The individual expressions of participants had acquired a great deal more focus between session I and II. By the end of session II the initial euphoric mood of the participants had begun to turn into cautious optimism. The three of us working in the Workshop space had enabled each participant to leave with a personal focus which he could pursue. Shortly afterwards we heard that they had organized a get-together to begin to give each other support. Mick Crews was invited to this, and amongst other things, the participants decided where they would like to meet next.

Session III

For session III I decided not to take the computer terminal. This turned out to be a mistake as one of the participants decided that he would like to work through a reflective analysis. I was able to do the first stage of identifying patterns, and explaining what we were working towards. Without the programs for doing pattern analysis however, it was not worth trying to do the next stage. This session ran for two days in January 1979 and at this stage my mode of working was with participants in groups of two or more. The object of the reflective method was to develop participants' awareness of the internal meanings present in interpersonal activity so that they could deal with that as well as task activity. This involved enabling them to express these different aspects of themselves and further to confront stereotyping – both of themselves and of others.

Session IV

The last session for this group took place over three days, at the end of February. One participant had waited until now to work reflectively, so NIPPER was of particular use to him and one other during this session. In addition to working with these two, my mode of working was with the group as a whole. One important activity was to help participants to find some way of seeing the Workshop as a whole. We ended up with seven of the eight working through a particular Division's problems with a view to developing a new strategic plan for it with two members of that Division present. The group was able to manage its own process so that it could use each individual effectively as a resource, while at the same time surprising itself at its ability to work on a work task. The emphasis throughout this session was on payoff for Ellermans.

Postscript

By the end of the Workshop, the participants talked freely amongst themselves and to me about experiencing 'breakthrough'. This breakthrough was particularly associated with working reflectively. What seemed to be happening was that the reflective method had enabled them to 'know' in a conscious sense what and how they were experiencing both within and outside the Workshop. This 'knowledge' was enabling them to manage their own learning in qualitatively different ways. NIPPER as an analytical technique was an essential part of this process, not because it was doing something which could not otherwise be done, but rather because it enabled the individual's reflection to sustain a very high degree of focus on the quality of his own experience. The reflective method therefore complemented the work of Tony Blake and Fred Kohler.

One of the issues raised by the high internal orientation of the Workshop was the kinds of payoff which would appear legitimate for Ellermans. There was no doubt amongst the participants of the fact that there would be payoff, though there were no particularly obvious 'projects' going on. In one or two cases, a very high degree of anxiety was experienced, as participants experienced the confrontation between their internal needs and what they were presently doing outside. The other side of this was that the Workshop had very rigid timing, and did not fit the readiness of all those who contracted. All of these things meant that Mick Crews had quite a large 'change manager' role to play within Ellermans in between the sessions, and there was pressure for more work within the sessions on projects and payoff earlier on.

The other issue was around the staff/student ratio – three to eight was extremely high. On the second Workshop there were ten participants, and whereas for the first Workshop I had worked one-to-one, on the second one I worked predominantly with a group throughout, although the group had permeable boundaries. Fred and Tony however continued to work in one-to-one. In the long run I felt that the norm would have to be one-to-many, but still with the flexibility to work one-to-one. As experience with the Workshops within Ellermans grew, the organizational necessity for the money-back guarantee diminished. It had a danger of becoming the famed Catch-22 for the participant, but even so, my views on the feasibility of evaluation still lead me to want to keep it in some form. The form of the Workshop is still being developed, however, and at the time of writing I am only half-way through the second Workshop.

IMPLICATIONS FOR RESEARCH

By way of pulling together some of the themes running through what we have said so far, we would like to draw attention to what we believe are some of the implications of the reflective method for research. These can be loosely categorized into implications for the research process and implications for the content of research.

With regard to the research process perhaps what stands out most clearly is that the traditional academic split between teaching and research loses a lot of its meaning. That split is largely dependent upon a view of knowledge as concrete and existing outside of persons. This view of knowledge leads to a fairly logical division of labour between quarrying knowledge (researching) and selling it (teaching). We believe that in the field of human experience, at least, knowledge or more correctly knowing, is a process of discovering personal meaning. This implies regarding the research 'subject' as just that, i.e. not as research 'object'. The person becomes his own researcher. The role of the facilitator is to aid him in his research activity.

This leads on to implications for the process of educational research in particular. For a start it implies a move away from overt behavioural definitions of learning and their concomitant before/after externally evaluative research methods. What becomes important is the learner's own construction of the learning process. In NIPPER we have a potential vehicle for helping learners explore that process. But will it not influence the results of the research? Of course it will. But we believe that this is true of all research in the social sciences. Research is intervention. We would like to make sure that that intervention is facilitative and not alienating.

What of the content of research? Here there are a number of things in the field of management education and development which we would like to see explored more fully. Not surprisingly, high on our list would be the differing training ideologies and their impact on learners and the learning process. Here again NIPPER might serve as a useful vehicle. Perhaps equally predictably we would like to see research leading to a fuller understanding of the impact of technology on learning. In particular we would like it to lead to the development of less alienating and less overdetermining computer software and hardware.

We have seen from the Ellerman's case study that the reflective method has implications for the design of whole learning 'events' and this is another area we believe deserves further attention and experimentation.

Finally we would like to see research leading to a greater understanding of the personal, organizational, and institutional pressures that often lead to the rejection, by learners, trainers, and training managers alike, of truly person-centred methods of learning. Clearly for all involved they represent a higher degree of risk-taking than conventional methods. But is this the only reason for rejection? Are there some definite 'contraindications'? If so what are they? Or could it be that we are totally misguided in our belief in their value? Reflection tells us we are not.

REFERENCES

Boxer, P.J. (1979). 'Reflective analysis: user documentation', *International Journal of Man Machine Studies,* in press.

Boydell, T. (1976). *Experiential Learning,* Manchester Monographs 5, Department of Adult Education, University of Manchester.

Brown, L.B. (1973). *Ideology,* Penguin, Harmondsworth.

Cooper, C.L. and Levine, N. (1978). 'Implicit values in experiential learning groups: their functional and dysfunctional consequences', in C.L. Cooper and C. Alderfer (eds), *Advances in Experiential Social Processes,* pp. 1–27, John Wiley, London.

Fransella, F. and Bannister, D. (1977). *A Manual for Repertory Grid Technique,* Academic Press, London.

Kolb, D.A. and Fry, R. (1975). 'Towards an applied theory of experiential learning', in C.L. Cooper (ed.), *Theories of Group Processes,* pp. 33–57, John Wiley, London.

Pfeiffer, J.M. and Jones, J.E. (1969). *Structured Experiences for Human Relations Training Vol. 1,* University Associates, Iowa.

Postman, N. and Weingartner, C. (1971). *Teaching as a Subversive Activity,* Penguin, Harmondsworth.

Rogers, C.R. (1969). *Freedom to Learn,* Merrill, Columbus.

Rowntree, D. (1974). *Educational Technology in Curriculum Development,* Harper and Row, London.

Advances in Management Education
Edited by John Beck and Charles Cox

CHAPTER 15.

Ten Years of Transactional Analysis:

An Account and Evaluation of the Development and Applications of Transactional Analysis

Mary Cox and Charles Cox

INTRODUCTION

The aim of this paper is to give some account of the state and status of Transactional Analysis (TA) at the present time, with special reference to the usefulness of the theories and their applications in organizational settings. The evaluative comments in this paper are partly based on research data, and partly on some years of practical experience of teaching and applying TA. They are intended to offer tentative appraisal, and more importantly, to provoke further speculation on the problems, and especially the limitations, of techniques of evaluation of TA and behavioural models in general.

The general questions to be answered here are:

1. What is TA?
2. What has been achieved so far?
3. Who uses TA and how?
4. How can both achievements and potential be evaluated? What does evaluation show so far?
5. What potential has TA as a development tool?
6. What are some typical criticisms and perceived limitations of TA?
7. Can anyone use it – *should* anyone use it?

A basic knowledge of TA is assumed in the reader. For guidance, either 'Born to Win' by Muriel James and Dorothy Jongeward (1971) or 'I'm O.K./you're O.K.' by Thomas Harris (1973) are recommended as basic introductory reading.

1. WHAT IS TRANSACTIONAL ANALYSIS?

Transactional Analysis is a model of human behaviour based on interrelated concepts and theories, developed originally by Dr Eric Berne more than twenty years ago and subsequently extended by others, notably Claude Steiner, Robert and Mary Goulding, and Jacqui Lee Schiff.

TA has four main parts: *'Structural Analysis'* – the analysis of the individual personality in terms of *'ego-states'*; *'Transactional Analysis'* – the analysis of the patterns of interactions between individuals; *'Game Analysis'* – the analysis of the hidden levels of interactions; *'Script Analysis'* – the analysis of the personal historical causes of behaviour patterns. In addition there are significant conceptual additions, for example, *'Stroking'*, *'Time Structuring'*, *'Symbiosis'*, *'Passivity'*, and *'Discounting'*.

The origins of TA are in psychotherapy, and until the last ten years the main use of TA has been in a variety of clinical settings. It has provided a diagnostic tool and a model for generating options for change and growth, for individuals who themselves have not been satisfied with their own level of functioning. Over the last decade it has been recognized, and experimented with, as a tool for change and development with groups of people and organizations.

The clinical use of TA is a special field and outside the scope of this paper, but some limited comment may, at times, be appropriate since the clinical uses have paved the way for other applications, and in so doing, have left their marks. Not the least of these is a suspicion of TA as potentially dangerous and possibly unethical when used outside of a therapeutic setting.

Over twenty years Berne's original ideas and theories have been extended, and in some cases changed, and new concepts developed. One outstanding feature of TA is its generative quality. It excites the kind of conceptual challenge that leads to elaboration and growth, both in terms of the concepts themselves, and of the variety of ways in which they might be applied. One major area for such creative transposition is that of management and organization development.

> Every organization faces not only the task-orientated problems of getting the job done, but also those problems that have to do with people dealing with people. As a consequence, a rising consciousness grows . . . concerning 'people problems'. Training departments, management development departments, and people in organization development have all turned to the behavioural sciences for answers. It was not until recently that the behavioural sciences had something practical and usable to offer.
>
> . . . Transactional Analysis is an intelligent, thinking approach to understanding the motivations and sources of human behaviour. Almost anyone can learn and apply its basic principles. Not only does it offer a basic method of understanding communications between people, but it also offers a blueprint for change.
>
> It is a most appropriate interpersonal relationships tool for organizations because it is a non-threatening, practical, interesting, and often fun approach to learning about people. In addition, Transactional Analysis helps us understand how the scripts of an organization can be analysed and changed. Such an analysis is a fresh approach to organization development.
>
> (Jongeward, 1973)

So, in 1979, 18 years on from the first major publication of TA theory by Eric Berne (1961) what is Transactional Analysis? It is still an important psychotherapeutic tool, more so in the United States than here. It is a model of human behaviour that offers insights into and diagnosis of human interaction. It is a theoretical framework embodying definite fundamental assumptions about human life that offers choices for change. It is a language that can provide common understanding for conflict resolution, and problem-solving.

Based on a growing body of knowledge and experimentation, the areas of application are as diverse as alcoholism and literature, or management development and counselling the dying.

2. WHAT HAS BEEN ACHIEVED SO FAR?

Without doubt, the best account of how TA is being used and developed is to be found in the 'Transactional Analysis Journal' (TAJ), the official quarterly publication of the International Transactional Analysis Association (ITAA). Further mention of this professional body will be made later. The TAJ provides a forum for theory development, conceptual exploration, reporting on-going work, and research, and for exchanging ideas, comment, and critiques. The regular publication of a well supported, stimulating journal of high professional standards is in itself an achievement.

There is now a vast amount of TA literature, including major works e.g. Berne (1961), (1963), and (1964), Steiner (1974), Schiff (1975), and Jongeward (1973); through well-edited handbooks bringing together theory, research, and technique (Barnes, 1977), and a mass of paperbacks, pamphlets, and articles presenting TA for Teachers, TA for Women, TA for Managers, and even TA for children. One single significant feature of all this material is that the contributors are still for the most part Americans, and there remains much scope for European writers since there are sufficiently strong cultural variations to warrant 'translation' of some of the terminology and concepts.

A different, and perhaps more significant, indication of the achievement of growth and firm establishment of TA, are the national and international organizations. The first of these in both historical terms, and in importance, is the International Transactional Analysis Association, in California, which had its foundations in the San Fransisco Social Psychiatry Seminars led by Eric Berne. The ITAA which has a membership which includes subscribers from all over the world, is still the major professional body providing standards for both practice and training and accreditation. In Britain, since 1975, there has been the Institute of Transactional Analysis (ITA) which began with a handful of interested and part-qualified TA practitioners, and now has a membership of approaching 200 persons from all over the British Isles with a core of experienced, accredited TA practitioners and trainers. The ITA publishes its own quarterly Bulletin (*Transactions: British Transactional Analysis Bulletin)*, and mounts a three-day conference each year. More recently, interested individuals and groups throughout Europe, in an effort to pull together resources, and organize professional facilities, have formed the European Association of Transactional Analysis (EATA) which has as part of its aims and objectives (as does ITA) to set professionally recognized standards for training and practice, and to work alongside ITAA but autonomously, in order to meet the special needs of European practitioners. The growth and development of these three major organizations represent a significant level of interest, commitment, and hard work in the service of Transactional Analysis.

In addition there are thriving groups of Transactional Analysts across the world, as far apart as South America, Canada, Japan, India, and Australia. These organizations and individuals have in common their commitment to TA and their striving to work to and to maintain high standards of professional conduct, whilst trying for the balance between rigour and experimentation. This is not an easy task in the early stages of a new discipline.

In the United Kingdom, there are at the time of writing six accredited TA trainers offering full training programmes in London, Birmingham, and Scotland, as well as any number of special workshops, groups, and seminars, and there are over twenty on-going treatment groups led by either accredited or supervised therapists. Over the last three years the interest in TA both as a therapy and as a training and development tool has maintained a steady level, as evidenced by the number of enquiries received by the ITA.

3. WHO IS USING TA AND HOW?

The following comments apply only to the United Kingdom, unless otherwise stated. A good account of the use of TA in organizational and management development in the United States will be found in Jongeward *et al.* (1973), and details are given of specific companies, contracts, and programmes. At the time of writing we have no specific knowledge of the application of TA other than clinical with regard to the Continent though through personal contact it would seem that there, too, TA is being used increasingly in organizations.

The use and applications of TA falls mainly into three categories – clinical, organizational, and special fields, though there are overlaps, especially between clinical and special fields.

In the UK the primary clinical practitioners of TA are persons who are either fully accredited with ITAA or in training for accreditation and are presently under qualified supervision. There are initial requirements for clinical training so that clinical practitioners are usually already trained in one of the helping professions, e.g. doctor, social worker, psychologist. There are TA groups and workshops available led by persons who may have only read some TA books or who may have had a great deal of TA training but have chosen not to work for accreditation. More will be said about the ethical problems posed by this situation in a later section. At the present time, along with other forms of counselling and para-medical treatment, TA is not subject to laid-down codes of practice other than those demanded by the law in general.

At least as significant in terms of amount and growth (spread) is the use of TA as a tool for personal development, especially related to particular kinds of work (special fields). The client or learner will very likely come from any one of a number of helping professions, e.g. social work, medical profession, marriage guidance, teaching, hospital service, prison service, and local government. Sometimes the main aim is the development of greater personal skills on the job, sometimes the objective is better team work and staff/customer or client relations in general.

The third main users of TA are industrial and commercial organizations who, through both their internal training departments and through external consultants, incorporate Transactional Analysis into their training and staff development programmes. A special sub-section here are the consultants and trainers themselves who may use TA for better personal understanding of their work whilst never using it explicitly with their clients, or who may teach TA and coach participants in the applications of TA in the work situation, either as the main framework for organizational development or as a part of broader based training programme.

In an attempt to find out more about the way TA is being used we wrote, with a questionnaire, to the 160 largest manufacturing companies in the UK (taken from the Times Top 1000). 71 companies responded (44%), of these 47 do not use TA. As far as we know then, only 24 of the largest companies are using, or have used TA. We do not, of course, know anything about the vast number of smaller companies or the non-respondents. Out of these 24 companies, 13 use TA as simply part of wider training programmes, 2 run special TA programmes and 7 do both; of the remaining 2 companies, one occasionally sends staff on external courses and one has ceased to use TA.

We asked for information about the way in which TA was being used. Typical responses were as follows:

'As an awareness tool – for behaviour'
'For Sales Training'
'For improving sales/customer relations'
'Interpersonal skills training'
'Team building'

All levels of management from 'Top level' to first line supervisors were mentioned.

We were also interested in the evaluation of TA training. Of the 22 companies currently using TA on internal programmes, 11 had attempted some form of evaluation. In most cases this was fairly informal – of the course evaluation questionnaire type. Only two companies had attempted a more rigorous evaluation. Typical comments on the outcomes of evaluation were:

'Gave greater understanding of own and others behaviour'
'Participants like it – see more benefit than any other part of course'
'Over half the participants express keen interest in TA'

Among more negative comments were:

'More use in home and social life'
'Negative reaction to terminology and methodology'.

The companies not using TA gave a wide range of reasons, many of them, perhaps, predictable. Again we quote a sample below:

'We do not do interpersonal skills/behavioural training'
'Dislike the jargon'
'We use other techniques which we see as more effective'
'Gimmicky, latest fad'
'No expertise in the company'
'No felt need'
'Culturally unacceptable'

This data seems to confirm our general view derived from experience that there is a significant minority of management trainers enthusiastically using TA with apparently beneficial results. Many others will have assessed TA and decided for one reason or another that it is not for them, with another significant group reacting with suspicion and hostility. It is also worth adding that many of the respondents not actually using TA had, nevertheless, attended courses and recorded that they had transferred much of the approach and philosophy to their own work.

One other aspect we checked in our questionnaire concerned the qualifications of the trainer responsible. In only five cases was an officially accredited TA trainer involved. In all instances this was an external trainer. Often his main role was to train in-company staff, who actually ran the programmes for managers. So here, as with clinical users, the trainer may or may not be himself fully-trained or qualified to use TA in the sense of having professional accreditation. What does seem certain is that a large number of teachers and trainers have discovered TA through books or courses, have been excited by it through seeing its potential, and have added it to their 'tool-kit'. Whatever the ethical issues raised by this, it nevertheless seems an appropriate usage and development of TA.

4. HOW CAN WE EVALUATE WHAT HAS BEEN DONE SO FAR?

An examination of the (limited) range of reports of the attempted validation of TA and its applications suggests that they tend to fall into two broad categories. We have called these *experimental* research and *empirical* research. There is a third approach which tends to overlap these two, which is concerned with *testing the conceptual power* of the theory.

Experimental Research

What is meant here by experimental research is the classical type of study, which in its purest form involves the testing of a hypothesis, by the manipulation of an *independent* variable in order to measure changes in one or more *dependent* variables. Great care is taken to ensure the 'objectivity' of the measurements, and results are subjected to careful statistical analysis. The key question here is to what extent is this an appropriate method for evaluating changes in human behaviour, that are frequently more internal (attitudes, feelings, values) than external (new or different amounts of specific behaviours).

The crux of the matter seems to lie in the fact that for an experiment to be acceptably rigorous there must be some measurable results. This has often led to research being designed around particular given measures and what those may indicate, rather than grappling with the problem of finding suitable measures for complex human behaviour.

Researchers, to be sure, do manage to devise counting and measuring techniques which relate to complex global behaviour. For example, Pinsker and Russel (1978) tested subjects for fingertip skin response to positive verbal stroking. Their account is careful and precise, as presumably was the experiment itself. The results showed 'a significant increase in fingertip skin temperature in experimental subjects, whereas the control group showed no significant changes in skin temperature.'

Two questions come to mind after reading the account, especially the Discussion. Why is it not enough simply to allow the subject to report what response he/she has to the given stroke? Secondly, and more importantly, the concept of stroking in TA is related to psychological well-being. Does the fact that the skin temperature increases (measurable positive response) mean that the subject/client *must* be responding to the stroke and therefore his/her psychological state changed in some way, even if he/she does not register the response consciously in some reportable way, such as 'feeling'? The Discussion includes the following remark:

> Being able to verify whether or not the therapist's positive verbal strokes are *actually being accepted* (our italics) by the client might be very useful in establishing rapport, particularly for beginning therapists. Many people have difficulty in asking for help and a stroking interviewer might make this approach easier.

Apart from the possible effect on the client of being attached to an electrical device during the first interview, there still remains doubt about the fundamental correctness of the interpretation of any measured skin response. If the client does not have the conscious awareness of being positively stroked, then is he being stroked? Is it either appropriate or helpful to say, in effect, 'Look here, I'm positively stroking you even though you don't seem to be aware of it.' This one example raises many questions about the relevance of the research, about the usefulness, and more fundamental questions about the interpretation of the experimental results and the implications of the interpretation.

One of the difficulties facing those wanting to evaluate any psychological theory is that of finding that when they have reduced the problem to manageable (measurable) terms, they may be left with a sound experiment that does not go even part way to answering the original important exciting question about some global aspect of human functioning. This is not meant to imply that experimental research has no value, but simply, that there are dangers. In order to establish what value, if any, experimental research does have, it is necessary to examine the research which has been published.

On sifting through the TAJ what emerges is that TA and special applications of TA go through a fairly common, stage by stage, process of innovative conceptualization, theoretical elaboration, practical application, abstraction, and speculative generalization, and then research. By 1977 and 1978 there start to appear research articles of the standard and worth typically found in any professional journal. The following is a small sample.

Spencer (1977) studied 'The effectiveness of an Introductory Course in Transactional Analysis' – data was collected via a follow-up questionnaire after a 12 week study course. Results were of the 'most/many felt they had gained from the course' kind. Bloom (1978) studied 'Attitude Changes During a Four-Week TA Workshop' – data collected from a projective psychological test. Results were the recorded changes between pre- and post-testing and showed significant changes.

Aronson (1977) in 'What does a Woman Want?' (in relation to career and personal needs) collected data from contracts made by participants during training workshops. Results obtained by categorizing responses and interpreting findings gave the general conclusion that women are 'getting ready to choose autonomy over desirability – but wish they did not have to make the choice.' Lindquist (1977) makes an interesting contribution which uses other people's research (fact finding) to break myths contained in women's scripts, especially in relation to conflict over whether to work outside the home or not. This last example is interesting because whilst not of itself a piece of research it would not have been possible without someone doing some thorough research beforehand.

Two further reports are of interest. Brennan and McClenaghan (1978) and Kramer (1978) were both experimenting with the development of better instruments for use in research in TA. Brennan and McClenaghan developed 'The Transactional Analysis Behaviour Questionnaire'. They report 'The evidence of psychometric reliability encourages the claim that basic TA concepts are 'real', that they are not purely hypothetical, and that they can be measured by standard psychometric procedures'. Kramer's article reports the development of 'An instrument for Measuring Life Positions'. The findings show that 'The test meets rigorous psychometric standards of test reliability and validity'. Kramer suggests that 'Instruments that measure TA (life) positions may prove to be valuable clinical tools. Preliminary information about a client can be gathered . . . (and) progress can be monitored on a regular basis, and discussed with the client'.

Finally, Sowder and Brown (1977) reported an experiment to test the validity of Berne's concepts of PAC, Transactions, and Time-structuring. The experimental design is one of those rare ones that after stating the general propositions to be investigated, formulates the appropriate null hypotheses. Data was collected from recorded observations and was treated statistically. The statistical data is summarized and shows no support for the null hypotheses but offers contrary significant findings.

By way of comment on the above it can be said that soundly constructed research, such as most of this is, is undoubtedly a valuable method of evaluation, provided the material being researched is not fragmented or diminished in the service of the research technique itself such that the product is demonstrably reliable data, but which, in practical terms, is meaningless. What is needed, not only in relation to researching TA and its applications, but for the whole of the behavioural sciences, is more thoughtful and creative consideration of the problem of how to measure without distorting or destroying that which is measured. In addition, more work along the lines of Kramer, and Brennan and McClenaghan, is needed to develop specific instruments for TA research.

Empirical Research

What is meant specifically here by empirical research is the more pragmatic approach of 'do it and see what happens' but with a little more structure, for example, 'set goals, plan action, operate, check results'. This is, in fact, how competent, effective practitioners work, whether they be therapists, managers, trainers, or for that matter, cooks. In addition they are willing to 'mix and fix' a little as they go along, i.e. they operate a continuous action and feedback cycle and have faith in their own capacity to adapt to the situation or the demands of the problem as they work with it. Over a period of time such people build up experience of what is effective behaviour; they acquire 'know-how'. They also develop something else – wisdom, a quality often either overrated and put beyond the reach of ordinary mortals or undervalued and dismissed as non-rational and non-scientific.

The TAJ is a major source of reports of the various techniques and methods used to diagnose and to solve problems, and to 'cure' malfunctioning. Three such accounts are quoted for illustration.

Wright (1975) in a brief article gives a clear straight report of how one manager put TA concepts to good use in his work to improve supervisory relationships with 'perceived' good results (but not ones that were measurable in any scientific way). '. . . to the manager (TA) was simply God sent because *it was working.* Inspection personnel were starting to limit their feedback to only the specifications of the product and, in turn, production personnel no longer had a need to defend themselves from attack'. Wright concludes:

> The manager in this company was able to reach his people through TA concepts, and all concerned have benefited by his original efforts. As James and Jongeward so beautifully put it, 'Effective managers are often those who are able to touch and recognize others appropriately.' TA has helped this manager to do just that.

Frank (1975) gives an account of how not only basic TA concepts can be used for solving organizational problems, but how the methodology of TA can provide a powerful structure for such problem-solving, e.g. contract building, use of appropriate levels of confrontation, avoidance of 'games'. One of the basic TA concepts that Frank uses to clarify and strengthen his work as a consultant is 'Ego state contamination'. Identifying contaminated thinking, and diagnozing the precise contamination, is fruitful activity in that it provides the key to what kind of confrontation will be most effective in getting a positive client response. Frank gives a helpful table of typical Parent and Child contaminations which manifest themselves when managers are confronted with Adult questions and actions.

Babcock (1975) gives yet another account of the practical kind. Babcock teaches TA to staff in 'a large, complex, city public health system.' She writes,

> Transactional analysis has proven to be a tool these workers can use for relating to their clients and for dealing with their system. The topics they find most useful include ego states, learning to use contracts, and counting themselves as OK important people (an attitude which the system tends to de-emphasize).
>
> In this article a statement of the problem in a typical large public system is followed by examination of the passive responses they (the staff) had learned to use in discounting themselves. The final section of the article lists alternative active responses, all of which they have used with success.

What do reports such as these show concerning the effectiveness of TA? There is inevitable bias. People mostly only report their successes. Even so, the amount of reported success is sufficient to be significant in itself. TA training and practice has been received with excitement and enthusiasm, participants have reported constructive change and feelings of being 'enabled' by the insights gained. Consultants and managers have reported using TA concepts and techniques successfully for problem-solving at both interpersonal and organizational levels, in a wide variety of settings, ranging from industry to public service, from educational establishments to prisons.

Testing the Conceptual Power of TA

One of the attractions of TA lies in its conceptual power. One manifestation of this is the ability to re-interpret in terms of Transactional Analysis a remarkably wide range of other psychological theories. As the context of this paper is management education we will, here, confine ourselves to a consideration of some theories relevant to management, in an attempt to demonstrate briefly how TA can show connections between and give greater insight into such theories.

McGregor's (1960) 'fundamental assumptions' theory can be readily 'translated' into TA concepts. The basic difference between the *X* and *Y* assumptions may be effectively described in terms of 'Life Positions', and the consequent supervisory style of each set of assumptions may be analysed in terms of typical transactions and stroking patterns. Theory *X* assumptions relate to 'I'm OK/You're not OK' in the ways shown in Figure 1. Theory *Y* assumptions relate to 'I'm OK/You're OK'

I'M OK/YOU'RE NOT OK *THEORY X POSITION*		*I'M OK/YOU'RE OK* *THEORY Y POSITION*	
Relationship:	Symbiotic	*Relationship:*	All ego states available
Position Characteristic:	Control Lack of Trust Autonomy and Authenticity unacceptable.	*Position Characteristic:*	Co-operation shared responsibility
I'M NOT OK/YOU'RE NOT OK		*I'M NOT OK/YOU'RE OK*	
Relationship:	Ritualistic or Non-existent	*Relationship:*	Symbiotic
Position Characteristic:	Alienation caused by either hostility or anxiety or both.	*Position Characteristic:*	Accommodation, autonomous and authentic behaviours not permitted.

Figure 1. McGregor's Assumptions Theory related to 'Life Positions'

and the supervisory style will be based on mutual respect for Authenticity, Sponteneity, and Intimacy. All levels of transacting are acceptable and games are avoided. Associated stroking patterns are shown in Figure 2. The authors have found the most constructive way of modelling Theory *X*/Theory *Y* is by using Jacqui Schiff's (1975) *Passivity* and *Discounting* material and the concept of *Symbiosis* (Cox and Cox 1977).

I'M OK/YOU'RE NOT OK *(THEORY X)*	*I'M OK/YOU'RE OK* *(THEORY Y)*
Boss: Works for 'thank you' strokes (appreciation strokes) Discounts strokes, feels frustrated, feels justified in giving negative strokes. Little or not sponteneity	*Boss and Subordinates:* give and receive contitional and unconditional strokes from all ego states. Sponteneity manifest and mutually appreciated.
I'M NOT OK/YOU'RE NOT OK *(ALIENATION)*	*I'M NOT OK/YOU'RE OK* *(THEORY X)*
Little or not stroking Ritualistic relating	*Subordinate:* Works for praise (Conditional stroking) or plays games to get kicks. Gives 'thank you' strokes (Conditional stroking) Little or no sponteneity

Figure 2. Characteristic Stroking Behaviour related to McGregor's Assumptions Theory and 'Life Positions'

A major advantage of being able to use TA in conjunction with McGregor's theory is that a much finer analysis can be made of the different behaviours deriving from the two sets of assumptions. In addition the analysis can be made so that the limited transactions deriving from Theory *X* quickly expose in a recognizable way the hidden assumptions. The symbiotic model makes very clear the discounting of the subordinate. A second advantage is that participants are much less likely to see Theory *X* and Theory *Y* as a 'Behavioural Spectrum'. The Life Positions model highlights the fact that the two approaches are *fundamentally different.*

Randall (1973) has made a similar comparison and integration of TA and Blake and Mouton's (1964) Managerial Grid in which he describes each of the key grid positions in TA terms. Again one effective advantage of doing this is that the specific behaviours of each style can be readily identified.

Two further major theoretical models which have had considerable impact on managerial thinking are Maslow's (1954) hierarchy of needs and Herzberg's Hygiene/Motivator theory (Herzberg *et al.* .1959). Both these models fit well with McGregor's Assumption theory, and both relate well to the basic assumptions and values of TA. Herzberg's work supports the view of the individual as responding well to recognition (stroking) of personal ability, achievement, responsibility. In TA terms, *autonomy* is valued.

Maslow's view of the individual as striving for self-actualization is similarly comparable. An interesting aspect of Maslow, and one which has often been highlighted as a weakness in his theory, is that although the prediction is that an individual will work upwards through the hierarchy, which is developmentally progressional, the fact is that individuals appear to be working on meeting needs at, say, the Esteem level, at the expense of 'lower level' needs, e.g. Affection needs. Over the last few years most trainers teaching Maslow have been obliged to concur that the theory does not quite fit observable behaviour, and that people do seem to move up and down the hierarchy rather than progressing neatly up through it. This usually has to be explained by referring to 'individual differences'.

Script Analysis, in particular the effect of stroke patterns on early life decisions, is a powerful model for further explaining the 'individual differences' and in a way that keeps Maslow's basic theory intact. For example, a person who has been raised with mainly conditional stroking, will quite likely have decided that the way to get needs met is through recognition for performance (esteem needs), and because there was an imbalance in terms of insufficient unconditional stroking they have decided (accepted a 'Don't get too close' injunction) that affection needs cannot, in fact, be met, so will by-pass that level on the hierarchy.

5. WHAT ARE THE POTENTIAL USES FOR TA AS A TRAINING AND DEVELOPMENT TOOL?

The main way in which TA is currently used in the UK is by teaching the language and concepts to groups of participants either as a special training event, or as part of a broader staff development programme. The groups may be from mixed backgrounds and levels or they may be work teams or they may be homogenous, e.g. all supervisors. A company may decide to 'expose' only senior and middle managers to a short series of workshops, or may commit themselves to a long term programme involving all levels, including shop floor and offering follow-up 'advanced' training.

When used in this way, TA is contributing to the development of *personal* and *interpersonal skills.* The aims, at the personal level, are likely to include greater self-awareness, listening skills, effective self-expression, increased adaptability in responding to others (i.e. increasing options for responding); at the interpersonal level, aims are likely to include greater skill and sensitivity in giving and receiving feedback, help-giving, and help-receiving skills (e.g. joint problem-solving, appraisal interviewing, counselling), greater awareness of stereotyping and projection, increased willingness to risk open sharing to develop mutual trust.

The areas in which increased interpersonal effectiveness are likely to have pay-off are numerous and include line management, sales/customer contact, communications, and relations between interviewer/candidate, shop floor/supervisor, trainer/participant, consultant/client, and manager/union official. Many participants report using company-given TA training in their private lives and have greatly appreciated this incidental pay-off.

TA has also been used to specifically develop *group skills* (and, related to personal development, leadership skills, and assertion skills). A one-off programme may be developed for a specific team, or the team building may arise naturally as part of an on-going TA development programme. The understanding of games, time-structuring, and the Schiff (1975) passivity material is particularly useful here. TA is also an effective framework for analysing 'group process'.

In *organization development,* a key focus is the structuring of the organization and the way this structure affects the levels of personal, interpersonal, and group skills. TA offers a way of examining the organizational climate in terms of the organization's script, and the extent to which autonomy is both permitted and valued. For example, organizations with a strong line management structure may manifest symbiotic chaining resulting in increasing alienation (passivity) the nearer one gets to the shop floor level (Cox and Cox, 1977). The script analysis can throw light on other significant organizational features, such as the predominating stroke patterns, the attitudes to power and authority (using Life Positions), the dominant values of the organization (e.g. creativity, service to the community, efficiency) and the typical transactional patterns, including games.

In some ways, organization development is like individual therapy. TA offers the consultant not only a tool-kit of concepts and techniques, but also a methodological framework for structuring his organizational intervention. The consultant (or for that matter, trainer or manager) need not use TA explicitly with the client. Indeed, it is important in the early stages for the consultant to use the client's language to avoid 'mystification' – a typical way in which the 'professional' either sets up or colludes with the client in establishing a relationship based on 'I'm OK/You (the client) are not OK'. If it becomes appropriate to use TA explicitly as part of the OD plan then all those involved in the process need to have some basic instruction in order to avoid both confusion and 'one-upmanship'. We would stress here that it is possible and feasible to use TA as both the main diagnostic tool and the framework for the planned intervention without ever using TA language. This holds true for the trainer teaching group and interpersonal skills and for the manager (or any individual) in the work situation. TA can be used effectively as a 'one-sided' tool.

6. WHAT ARE SOME TYPICAL CRITICISMS AND PERCEIVED LIMITATIONS OF TA?

As mentioned already, TA literature is biased towards reporting success. Nevertheless, negative feedback is available through the direct personal comments of participants. We have summarized below some typical views and reactions taken both from our own experience and from discussion with other trainers, managers, and TA practitioners.

(i) The Language is too American, too 'Slangy': There is too Much Special Jargon

Reaction ranges from outrage and complete rejection of TA to dislike of the labels but acceptance of the ideas. The issue here is not whether the language is OK or not OK but the fact that it is such that it can and does create a real barrier to understanding and accepting the concepts for some people.

(ii) The Model is too Simple to Adequately Describe and Explain Human Behaviour

This reaction is most common when the teaching is limited to very basic concepts, especially when only first order (and basic functional) structural analysis is taught. There is also rejection of 'reducing' people to simple diagrams and complex attitudes to simple models such as the OK Corral.

(iii) 'It's all Just Common Sense'

This reaction is the obverse of number (ii) – and may be summarized as 'Surely everyone knows all this, why are you making it more complex with all these diagrams and special words.'

(iv) 'You Can't Analyse Human Behaviour'

This usually represents a rejection of any psychological theory but TA is especially objected to because it attempts to be so specific.

(v) Objection to 'Proliferation'

This reaction is based on the feeling (and fact) that there are already any number of theories of human behaviour. How does TA add anything to these or in what way is it better?

(vi) TA is Dangerous

TA is seen, in common with some other psychological theories and techniques, as being potentially damaging. First, on the basis that 'a little learning is a dangerous thing' there is a fear that people might find themselves being analysed and judged (and possibly treated) wrongly and unfairly. Inadequate understanding of the concepts might lead to misuse.

Second, there is a fear that sudden insight, or sudden revelation might lead to an individual being seriously disturbed both emotionally and psychologically. A more general form of this fear of 'nervous breakdown' is expressed by 'Don't you think it's better not to dig too deep? It only creates problems and makes people unhappy.'

Third, there is also a fear that if 'others' learn TA effectively, 'They' might be able to manipulate or exploit 'us'. Also 'You are teaching us to manipulate people. Don't you think that is wrong?'

Fourth, there seems to be some resistance on the grounds that consciously choosing new behaviour is to be 'not genuine', and that to stop and analyse own and others' behaviour is unnatural and will spoil a relationship.

(vii) 'The Model is Wrong' (and Anyway you Can't Prove what You're Saying is Right!)

For some people both the models themselves and the language of TA which is the conceptual basis of the models are simply rejected as wrong or invalid. A major objection of this kind stems from the way in which TA can dramatically expose ulterior motivation and unconscious behaviour. The issue is one of working with *interpretation* of observable behaviour together with making value judgements based on interpretation.

(viii) Does TA have a Lasting Effect?

A number of participants including many who are enthusiastic about TA express concern that they will not be able to remember so much new material and special language for more than a few months after the workshop, especially if they do not have contact with anyone else familiar with TA.

These are only some of the perceived limitations of TA. We feel certain that there are others which we have not expressed adequately here. The issue for discussion here is not whether the criticisms of TA are valid or justified or whether they can be dismissed through reasoned argument and presenting contrary data but the *fact that such criticisms do exist.* It is a real limitation of TA that its effect on some people is negative, and often dramatically so. It is our experience that rarely are participants left indifferent. The issue seems to us a relatively simple one – either you like TA and find it useful or you do not. We return to the nub of our comments in the section on empirical evaluation. It would seem that the appropriate way to present, use, and evaluate TA is the rather old-fashioned approach of 'Suck it and see!' on the basis that you can always spit it out if you do not like it, and since there is no evidence to date of TA being toxic, no harm will have been done. Or will it?

7. CAN ANYONE USE TA – SHOULD ANYONE USE IT?

TA in itself is indeed non-toxic. It is simply a conceptual model, a theoretical framework. However, embodied in the conceptualization both implicitly and explicitly are value structures and practical techniques. These are open, like nuclear power, to misuse. It is not so much TA that demands careful scrutiny but the practitioner using it.

One of the attractive and powerful features of TA is that it is quickly and relatively easily understood, at the basic level. This means that anyone who has read a book or attended one basic course has the basic tool-kit. There is increasing evidence from talking with people and from our own discussion with specialist groups that TA is being taught and practised by people who have very limited training in the subject and none at all in the practice of techniques particular to TA. On the other hand there is similarly gathered evidence that most of these people are professionally trained in a related discipline, such as social work, teaching, training and development, or para-medicine. There seems to us no reason to suppose that such people will not use TA as an additional tool with the same professional integrity and care that they already bring to the practice of their particular specialism. In any case, we see no acceptable way of preventing this kind of use of TA. A positive move to set professional standards and safeguard both the public and TA practitioners themselves is the development of the professional organizations.

In Britain, professional training for accreditation is available and the Institute of Transactional Analysis has as one of its main objects to encourage such formal training as a way of ensuring high professional standards. The requirements for acceptance into training are particular and specific, and the training programme includes a specified number of hours of attendance at teaching and training workshops, together with a specified length of time under qualified supervision. Qualification is by written examination and a viva with a panel of experienced accredited practitioners. It is not usually possible to get accreditation in less than one year and typically takes between two and three years.

The ethical issues raised in connection with the use of TA either in teaching or practice, are the same basically as those raised in any situation where the safety and well-being of any human being is concerned. It is our belief that, in general, ethical considerations should, and for the most part will be, taken into account more or less explicitly *in the initial contract for which the teacher or practitioner and the participant/client are both jointly responsible.* If difficulties are experienced that cannot be resolved by the two parties concerned then the Ethics Committee of the Institute of Transactional Analysis is available for consultation.

CONCLUSION

In this paper we have given a definition of TA and some examples of its use and areas of application. We have quoted research and reports which give account of some results and effects of the use of TA in various settings. We have added to this our own summary of typical criticisms and perceived limitations of TA. In addition we have attempted to show that TA can be related to existing theory and practice in management education, (and we have given some example approaches for applying TA in organizations). Finally, we have touched on some ethical considerations and outlined how professional training both in TA and related disciplines should serve to ensure that TA is used with care and consideration.

Our closing comment is a grateful acknowledgement of all the help and enlightenment we have been given by our colleagues and peers, who have shared their experience with us; by a number of experienced TA practitioners who have shared their expertise with us; most of all we would like to thank the hundreds of participants who, in working with us, listening to us, and sharing their reactions with us, have given us knowledge and insight, and helped us to develop our own wisdom.

REFERENCES

Aronson H.L. (1977). What does a woman want? *Transactional Analysis Journal,* **7** (2), 141–144.

Babcock D. (1975). Teaching caregivers to win, *Transactional Analysis Journal,* **5** (4), 392–395.

Barnes G. (1977). *Transactional Analysis after Eric Berne,* Harper and Row, New York.

Berne E. (1961). *Transactional Analysis in Psychotherapy,* Grove Press, New York.

Berne E. (1963). *The Structure and Dynamics of Organisations and Groups,* Grove Press, New York.

Berne E. (1964). *Games People Play,* Grove Press, New York.

Bloom W. (1978). Attitude changes during a four-week TA workshop, *Transactional Analysis Journal,* **8** (2), 169–172.

Blake R.R. and Mouton (1964). *The Managerial Grid,* Gulf, Houston.

Brennan T. and McClenaghan J. (1978). The transactional behaviour questionnaire, *Transactional Analysis Journal,* **8** (1), 52–55.

Cox M. and Cox C. (1977). Alienation in the workplace: a transactional analysis approach, in R.N. Ottaway (ed.), *Humanising the Workplace,* Croom Helm, London.

Frank J.S. (1975). How to 'cure' organisations, *Transactional Analysis Journal,* **5** (4), 354–358.

Harris T. (1973). *I'm O.K. – You're O.K.* Pan, London.

Herzberg F., Mausner B., and Snyderman B.B. (1959). *The Motivation to Work,* John, Wiley, New York.

James M. and Jongeward D. (1971). *Born to Win,* Addison-Wesley, Reading, Mass.

Jongeward D. *et al.* (1973). *Everybody wins: Transactional Analysis and Your Organisation,* Addison-Wesley, Reading, Mass.

Kramer F. (1978). Transactional analysis life position survey: an instrument for measuring life positions, *Transactional Analysis Journal,* **8** (2), 166–168.

Lindquist R. (1977). Scripts people give working women, *Transactional Analysis Journal,* **7** (2), 139–140.

Maslow A.H. (1954). *Motivation and Personality,* Harper and Row, New York.

McGregor D. (1960). *The Human Side of Enterprise,* McGraw-Hill, New York.

Pinsker E.J. and Russell P. (1978). The effect of positive verbal strokes on finger-tip skin temperature, *Transactional Analysis Journal,* **8** (4), 306–309.

Randall L. (1973). The transactional manager: an analysis of two contemporary management theories, in D. Jongeward *et al., Everybody Wins: Transactional Analysis and Your Organisation,* Addison-Wesley, Reading, Mass.

Schiff J.G. *et al.* (1975). *Cathexis Reader, Transactional Analysis Treatment of Psychosis,* Harper and Row, New York.

Sowder W.F. and Brown R.A. (1977). Experimentation in transactional analysis, *Transactional Analysis Journal,* **7** (3), 279–285.

Spencer G. (1977). The effectiveness of an introductory course in transactional analysis, *Transactional Analysis Journal,* **7** (4), 346–349.

Steiner C. (1974). *Scripts People Live,* Bantam, New York.

Wright A.L. (1975). TA in the electronics industry, *Transactional Analysis Journal,* **5** (4), 377–378.

Advances in Management Education
Edited by John Beck and Charles Cox

CHAPTER 16

Management Educators and Their Clients

Charles Magerison, and Ralph Lewis

INTRODUCTION

'Those that can, do, those that can't, teach'

This well-known aphorism sums up the negative aspects of what many practical people feel about those who occupy educational roles. It, in a sense, can be seen as an inverted form of snobbery, an attempt to get even with those who supposedly have conventional wisdom on their side. However, the extent to which those who educate can put into practice that which they teach is often questioned, especially in management education.

Stories about the mis-management of management schools abound. One hears of the 'time-and-motion' experts arriving late, the in-fighting of the behavioural scientists and their lack of concern for colleagues, the failure of management educators to specify objectives, or finance lecturers who do not budget effectively. These stories are told with great relish. Whether they are true is another matter; the stories have entered the folk lore of modern business life. The reasons for these attitudes are of interest as they affect the relationship between the management educator and his client. It is this relationship that will be examined in this paper.

The question that this paper will be addressing is whether these perceptions of the role of educators are founded on a factual base or upon prejudice? The political and status issues that, of course, affect relations between groups will be left aside for the moment. The issue is whether these two groups approach the problems and opportunities that the world offers in a similar or in a different way? If there are differences is there anything that can be done to help communication?

The research is founded upon a study of the work preferences of teachers of management in a large business school and of their clients, both practising managers and MBA students. The result of these studies is that the criticisms that are levelled at management educators would in one sense appear to be valid. They do think in different ways from their students. This, we believe, is because of individual differences, rather than being detached from the industrial world. Equally, the evidence suggests that criticisms that are often levelled at students would also appear to be valid, such as their concern for example, with instant and easy solutions. To understand these differences and the basis on which the research is founded, it is necessary to look at the model of work preferences that was used in the research (Margerison, Lewis and Hibbert, 1978).

WORK PREFERENCES AND APPROACHES TO LEARNING

We have been considerably influenced by Carl Jung's typology of personal constructs (Jung 1923). Jung is well-known for his philosophical views, and for his psycho-analytical work. However this work on psychological types has not been fully explored. Indeed it has been dismissed by a number of writers as of little use. Our work would suggest that these views are misplaced and that the explanatory value of Jung's framework is very strong and moreover fortified by scientifically derived data.

For example, Eysenck (1976) has been very scathing about complexity of the theory. Even Storr (1973) queries Jung's schema when he is discussing different ways of working and learning. The issues raised then are fairly controversial. However, on the other side there is a great deal of substantive research to show that the theory has at the very least some restricted and practical outcomes. These have been a result of a number of studies for example, Kilmann and Mitroff (1977), Brawer and Spiegelman (1964), and Bradway (1964).

The foundation of Jung's typological theory is based upon four major propositions. These are:

(a) people have different ways in which they relate with other people in the world
(b) people have different ways of gathering and generating information
(c) people have different ways of using information and making decisions
(d) people have different emphasis on the priority they assign to gathering information or using information

As the Jungian typology is the centre of discussion of the relationship between academics and their clients, we need to examine in more depth the key factors that Jung mentioned. These are outlined below:

Relationships – Extraversion or Introversion (E or I)

This is how Jung differentiated the way in which various people establish relationships with others and the world. The terms have become well-known and part of everyday language. To him they had special significance and special meaning.

Clearly each person has some orientation to being extraverted in some situations and introverted in others. The important point however, is that given a choice or opportunity most of us have a preference to orientate our lives and behaviour towards a more introverted or extraverted approach. This is the key point that Jung brings out in his work. It is a point which we will examine in the relationship between management educators and their clients. Is there any difference between the teacher and the student? If so, what are the implications for education and for the relationship between them?

According to Jung a key characteristic of extraverts is that they are orientated to 'external objective conditions.' We also think of the extravert as a person who easily makes good social relationships. However, such a person can also be easily bored and seeks change and novelty.

The introverted person in contrast is more able to keep his own company and prefer a quieter social life. As Jung wrote 'the introvert interposes a subjective view between the perceptions of the object and his own action.' The introverted person therefore has his own personal view of how he sees the world. This is not easily changed. Many introverts find that it is difficult to sustain a high degree of social activity for a long time and are extremely sensitive to interpersonal relationships. They therefore very often prefer to work more on their own or with people who they know well rather than go out and about making many contacts with strangers.

Gathering Information – Sensing or Intuition (S or N)

Here Jung distinguishes between a *sensing* approach and an *intuitive* approach. The *sensing* person will prefer to gather information in a practical way. He will like to measure, weigh, and generally identify information in a specific way. He likes to touch, smell, see, and work with tangible issues. Essentially he will be happier dealing with matters of fact. He likes to work with objects that can be verified through his senses.

In contrast the *intuitive* person generates information largely through his insight. While he will start with a real situation which is measurable he quickly likes to move to create ideas based upon his original insight. He will play with possibilities and consider what might be. His emphasis is continually on looking at new things and new ways. He is a considerable innovator and will often go beyond the facts. He will therefore be open to criticism but often makes considerable leaps by his intuitive grasp of reality. It may take some time for people to catch up and prove or disprove the insight. It is however a very different way of generating information. People are often suspicious about other people's intuitions but no one should totally rely on the tangible and verifiable reality of the practical world.

Again there is no right or wrong approach to acquiring information. All of us use both intuition and sensing. However, as Jung emphasised, given a choice we tend to move towards one or the other in the way in which we construct our day to day behaviour. Obviously this is important in an education setting. Does the teacher work mainly on a creative plan where he is asking the students to develop ideas and consider possibilities, or is he working on purely practical down to earth tangible plans where everything must be measured and assessed and proved before the next step is taken?

Using Information – Thinking and Feeling (T or F)

There are also major differences in the way people can reach decisions. Jung noted this and distinguished between *thinking* types and *feeling* types when it came to decision making.

The person who prefers the *thinking* approach will make decisions mainly upon the facts available in terms of what is in his judgement the most valuable way of resolving the issue. Such a person will emphasize logic and analysis and detachment in coming to a decision.

In contrast a person who stresses a *feeling* approach will take decisions primarily on his or her personal beliefs. The term feelings really means personal values. A person who has strong values will take information and relate it to his beliefs whether they be religious, political, or humanitarian. The important thing is that such a person does not have to weigh the evidence based upon direct calculation but judges more by his inner feeling of what is right or wrong.

Gathering Information or Using It – Judging and Perceiving (J or P)

Finally Jung emphasizes that most people have a preference either for gathering information or for using information. Those who prefer to gather information he says will have a preference for *perceiving* and understanding. They will always wish to listen, read, observe, and obtain a substantial amount of information before making decisions.

In contrast those people who prefer using information will like to try and resolve issues rather than have them drag on while people generate a lot of information. Such people Jung referred to as being *judgmental.* They like a more orderly approach to life where things can be decided upon and clarity brought to bear upon the situation. This judgmental approach is probably seen as decisiveness and a desire for producing order.

Again there is no right or wrong between these two. It is a question of which is most appropriate. The emphasis is a function of preference in one's orientation to working and living. It is these key factors of preference and a way of operating that we looked at in assessing the relationship of management educators and their clients.

WHAT SORT OF CLIENTS DO WE HAVE?

To test out some of the above ideas, we worked with three groups. These were respectively: educators, management students (MBAs), and practising managers. They were asked to complete the Myers–Briggs Type Indicator This is a questionnaire designed to operationalize the Jungian constructs that have been outlined. Full details are given in the Myers–Briggs Handbook (1962).

The main independent studies on the Indicator however, have been carried out by Stricker and Ross (1964a, 1966). They note that in terms of 'continuous scores', the Indicator seems to have about the same reliability as better known personality inventories. Overall, their conclusions are that there is some evidence for restricted facets of the typology and that the MBTI certainly measures variables which are related both to measurements made on other personality questionnaires and to behaviour.

In essence it assesses the extent to which people have particular preferences on the scales which we have shown below:

(E)	Extravert	Introvert	(I)
(S)	Sensing	Intuition	(N)
(T)	Thinking	Feeling	(F)
(J)	Judging	Perceiving	(P)

It is possible therefore to discover the range of a person's preferences on each of these scales and also to identify a particular area of preference within which they feel most easy when working.

The sample of those responding to the questionnaire are shown below:

Management Educators	31
Management Students (MBAs)	140
Managers	343

The management educators are all members of the faculty of a large business school. They were invited to respond to the questionnaire as part of an internal research project conducted by one of the authors. This was therefore a voluntary exercise.

The management students were all students of an MBA programme at the same University business school. They were asked to fill this in at the beginning of their course year. Although it was a voluntary exercise everyone filled it in as, at that part of the course, they felt they should help. However a voluntary exercise conducted at the end of the year showed that 97 per cent of the students again filled in the instrument. Therefore we would see the results as acceptable, particularly as there was little change between time one and time two measurements (Chilmeran, 1978).

The managers came from a wide variety of industries and filled in the questionnaire as part of the management programmes they were on. Some of these were conducted at the University business school and some within their own companies.

ANALYSIS OF THE DATA AND FINDINGS

The results of the study are given below. Table 1 gives continuous scores of the academics, managers, and MBAs on the MBTI scales. It should be noted that a '100' is the mid-point between extraversion and introversion and correspondingly so on the other scales. Thus, any scores greater than '100' reflect that preference for

Table 1. Continuous Scores of Academics, Managers, and MBAs on MBTI Scales

	ACADEMICS (n = 31)		MANAGERS (n = 343)		MBAs (n = 140)	
EI	100	(I)	102	(I)	107	(I)
SN	127	(N)	87	(S)	102	(N)
TF	90	(T)	90	(T)	88	(T)
JP	94	(J)	85	(J)	92	(J)

introversion and scores below '100' reflect a preference for extraversion. The greater the deviation from '100' the stronger the preference for either introversion or extraversion. Figure 1 shows the results in a diagrammatic form.

In Table 2, we have shown the differences between the three populations on a percentage basis. This illustrates the major overall differences in preferred operating ways particularly between the management educators and their clients.

Extraversion – Introversion

Breadth v. Depth

As can be seen there is virtually no difference between academics and managers. Both contain roughly equal proportions of extraverts and introverts. There is however, a significant difference ($\alpha < 5\%$) between MBAs and academics. What are the implications of this? Introverts like quiet for concentration, preferring to work on one thing at a time, and work happily alone. Their main emphasis is on thinking

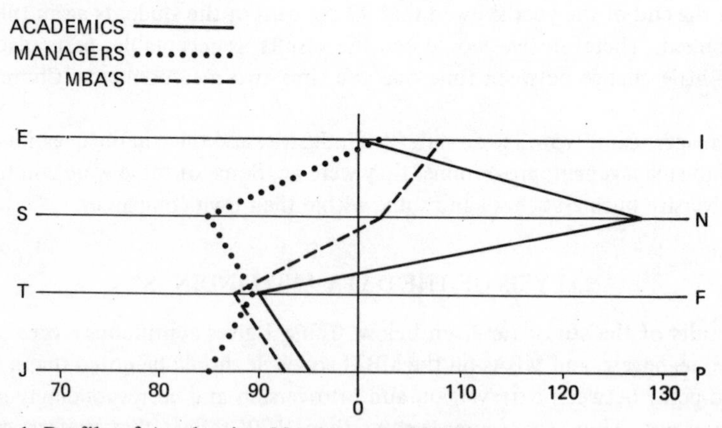

Figure 1. Profile of Academics, Managers, and MBAs

Table 2. Distribution of the Three Groups Showing Differences in Gathering and Using Information

		Using Information			
		Thinking		Feeling	
Gathering Information	Sensing	Academics Managers MBAs	3.5% 50% 40%	Academics Managers MBAs	3.5% 18% 7%
	Intuition	Academics Managers MBAs	67% 22% 36%	Academics Managers MBAs	26% 10% 16%

through ideas and projects before they act. It is perhaps hardly surprising that the MBA students tend to be more introverted that either academic or managers. They are a self-selected group whose main interest is in studying and gaining new knowledge. One of the results of this which has been documented by Chilmeran (1978) is that the MBAs as a group tended to feel in their relationship with the academic teaching staff that they were being asked to do too much at a too superficial level. Many comments on their programme were couched in terms such as, 'We need more time to look at things in depth.'

Sensing – Intuition

Practicality v. Imagination – What's new that we can use?

This is probably the most interesting and significant of the MBTI scales. It is certainly a very powerful predictor of the differences between academics and managers with, as can be seen, MBAs being a medium between the two. The differences between managers and academics were significant at the 1 per cent level. If we look at Table 2, of 31 academics tested, 29 preferred the *intuitive* approach. That is, over 93%. On the other hand, 68% of the managers preferred a *sensing* approach with only 32% preferring the *intuitive* approach. Before going on to discuss the implications of these differences, it should be noted that even this 32% of intuitives within the managerial population is high if one compares it with evidence from America on normal populations. One reason for this we would suggest, is the high proportion of managers attending the business school who have had further education, and almost by implication tend to be orientated towards theoretical aspects.

Intuitives enjoy solving new problems and working in an unstructured way. They dislike routine, are impatient with details, are very often ready to jump to conclusions based upon insufficient evidence. Most important of all, however, is the fact that they tend to work from implicit internal models, whereas the sensing type works with an external reality. This differentiation is not new. For example, it has been examined using a different basis by McKenney and Keen (1974). The sensing type, in contrast, dislikes new situations, likes established routines, prefers simple explanations, and dislikes ambiguity in a great number of aspects.

There are therefore, two very different types in terms of their approach to work which are being examined. On initial reading it seems incredible that these types actually communicate at all. The manager, and here we are talking about the overall profile, is orientated, in terms of the Jungian concept, to a much more practical and down to earth type of reality than the academic. The academic's reality is for him, ideas, not the production of tangible goods. In a very real sense therefore, the differences which are postulated by conventional wisdom and mentioned at the beginning of this paper, exist. As can be seen from Figure 1, academics are much more theoretically and idealistically inclined than managers. They have a preference for more complexity than managers and also again because of the sensing/intuitive differences, a more positive attitude towards change than managers.

Because of these different work preferences the approaches of both groups towards problem-solving will be different. We can expect the academic to be concerned with problem definition. That is, he will be problem centred, curious, and seek to explore the complex world. The manager in general, will be more concerned with solutions. That is, he will take a problem and find practical answers.

What will happen then when the two groups come together? The management educator will be talking in terms of the problem or process. He will be asking the manager to define his terms, to sort out his assumptions, to define his objectives. On the other hand, the manager will be saying to himself and to the academic, 'Why do I need to go through this rigmarole; just give me the answer to solve the problems I have? Do not talk to me about these fancy theories of yours.' If they can communicate however, then there is likely to be mutual benefit for each side. Each possesses skills and expertise in a particular part of the problem-solving cycle that the other does not have.

The manager often needs management educators to compliment his style – to enable him to define the problem and define his objectives. In this way much time and effort can be saved by avoiding the trial and error process of trying out one solution after another. Similarly, the management educator will be encouraged to keep his feet firmly on the ground and will not be liable to drift off into the rarified atmosphere of ideas that have little relevance to industrial modern life. In other words, we are talking about a partnership. In such an arrangement, each side appreciates and works with the other but does not attempt to force the other to work in the way contrary to their preference.

One of the interesting results of the data is that the MBAs on the Sensing – Intuitive scale come mid-way between managers and academics. This is really to be expected as essentially the group that we were dealing with, average age 31, had a great deal of experience in business and industry but were very much a fringe group compared to the majority of managers in that their concern was also with an academic degree.

Thinking – Feeling

Let us sit down and work this thing out rationally

This is the sort of comment that all respondents in our sample could be expected to make. They all seem to emphasize a thinking approach. As can be seen from the data there is virtually no difference between the three groups on the Thinking – Feeling scale. In other words all three groups considered themselves rational and logical in the way they approach decision-making and problem-solving. Thinking types tend to be relatively unemotional and disinterested in people's feelings. They prefer analysis rather then deciding on the basis of values and beliefs. In terms of the Jungian functions one would therefore expect them to be better at dealing with technical problems rather than dealing with people. In many ways this may reflect part of the problem with management today. With the exception of a small minority of people in all these groups the majority preferred working with technical things, ideas, rather than dealing with people. One of the conclusions of Jung's theory is that the opposing function to the one you prefer is very often under utilized, simply because you prefer not to use it. You therefore end up lacking skills in that area. This may well reflect the need and desire of many managers to develop their skills in dealing with people.

Judging – Perceiving

Let's get into the action and stop talking

This sort of reaction is one that we would predict the managers in our sample to have on this scale. It basically distinguishes between those who prefer to make decisions and those who prefer to understand the background rather than make a decision. As would be expected academics (and MBAs) were much more interested in understanding situations and problems, rather than taking immediate action. The management educators' clients therefore may well see him as someone who is 'soft' in comparison to themselves. They would suspect the academic of not being tough enough to make decisions and implementing them, but rather sitting on the fence. In contrast the academic will often criticize the manager for rushing into a decision before sufficient research has been done. Now this also says something about the attitudes both parties have to risk-taking. The important point is that individual differences can explain the behaviour, and moreover there is a tendency for each group to choose occupations that allow for different work patterns on decision-making.

LEARNING

In the area of learning, managers and educators are also different. This has already been discussed in a previous article (Lewis and Margerison, 1979). The MBTI has been related to the Kolb Learning Style Inventory. If we take the NT group of

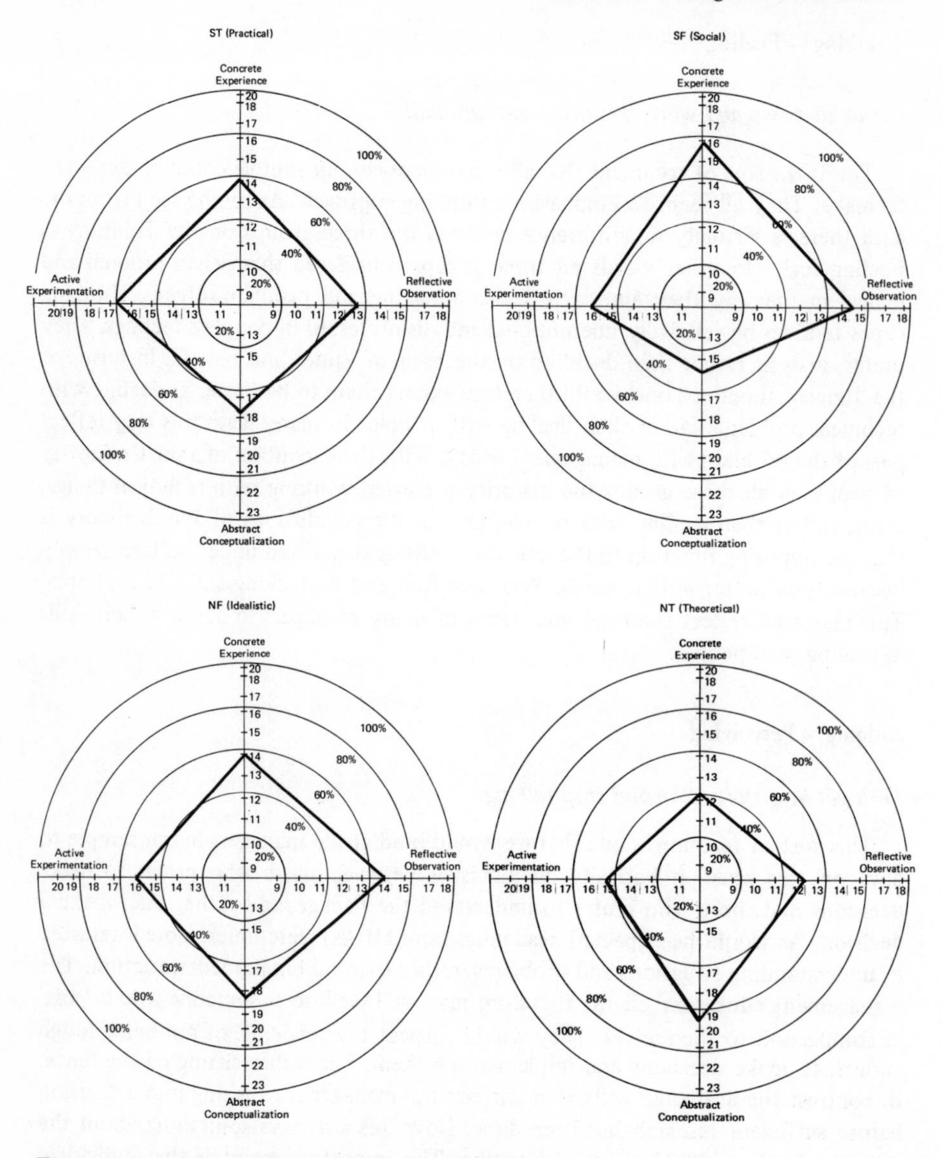

Figure 2. Learning Profiles of Main Jungian Types

which academics are basically composed and the ST group of which managers are basically composed and plot their learning styles, two different learning styles become apparent (see Figure 2).

It can be seen that in terms of the Learning Style Inventory, academics learn by thinking and discussing ideas on abstract levels. Managers on the other hand need to learn by actually doing things by trial and error. Processes that educators set up for learning reflect their own learning styles, i.e. they are basically orientated towards lectures, absorbtion of theoretical models, and 'rich' in information provision such as learned papers. It is not surprising therefore that the clients of management educators are liable to say to them, 'This process is not satisfactory for us; give us something practical to do.' For effective learning by a manager to take place, the educator needs to build in experiential learning and provide participation for the manager to test out his learning if effective reinforcement is to take place.

Of course, this is not an area which has any easy solution. It has already been shown that the educator has skills that are different to the manager's skills. Does the educator pass on his skills to the manager, knowing that the manager would prefer not to work in that way, or does he do what has often been suggested by the practitioners of action learning, and that is adopt the manager's preferred style wholeheartedly?

ORGANIZATIONAL STRUCTURES

One of the most interesting aspects of the differences that we have been discussing is the implication that it has for the type of organization that the manager and the academic prefer to work in. The main reason for this is that each needs a different environment in which to work in the way they prefer. It is suggested that the manager (STs) prefers a disciplined bureaucratic organization with a well-defined hierarchy and clear policies and rules. He prefers a fixed structure because this enables him to get on with what he enjoys doing – practical, everyday matters at hand. Discussions with people about feelings and intuition would not allow him to do this.

On the other hand management educators (NTs) prefer structures which are de-centralized, which have no clear lines of authority, and no tight rules. This is because the management educator in general, has to have autonomy in order for him to utilize his intuitive work preferences. When we look at the different types of organizational structure we can see that the management educator works in a way which is typically concerned with team/project groups (on courses for example) and will experiment with matrix management systems. These are areas which industrial organizations are now beginning to explore and put into practise. There is much therefore, that management educators could discuss and share with their clients as regards to problems and benefits of these types of organization.

CONCLUSIONS

In this paper we have examined some of the issues that have arisen from testing the conventional common sense distinction between management educators and managers. This has been shown to be correct and to raise a number of issues. What it further does, is to show that educators and their clients are not necessarily in competition but in fact are complementing each other and that the partnership if developed with mutual respect on each side, could be extremely valuable, not just in industry but also for management schools.

However, much management teaching is done using theoretical models and cases rather than real-life practical examples. Managers are likely to see such discussions about change based on models, as threatening, simply because it is an area where they do not have expertise. The normal reaction then of a manager is to dismiss the educator as one who is impractical. Let us hope therefore that by developing an understanding of the way managers think and work, the educator can avoid these differences. Then we can hear comments such as 'teaching and managing are just the different sides of the same coin – we had better learn from and teach each other'.

REFERENCES

Bradway K. (1964). Jung's Psychological Types, *Journal of Analytical Psychology*, **9**, (2), 29–35.

Brawer F.B. and Spiegelman, J.M. (1964). Rorschach and Jung: a study of introversion – extraversion, *Journal of Analytical Psychology*, **9**, (2).

Chilmeran A. (1978). *The Influences of the MBA Programme upon its Participants*, Unpublished Paper.

Eysenck H.J. and Wilson G. (1976). *Know Your Own Personality*, Penguin.

Jung C.G. (1923). *Psychological Types*, Kegan Paul, London.

Kilmann R.H., Lyles M.A., and Mitroff I.I. (1977). Designing an effective problem-solving organization with the MAPS design technology, *Journal of Management*, **2**, (2), 1–10.

Lewis R.G. and Margerison C.J. (1979). Working and learning – identifying your preferred way of doing things, *Personnel Review*, 8, (2).

McKenney J.L. and Keen P.G.W. (1974). How managers minds work, *Harvard Business Review*, 52, (3), 79–90.

Margerison C.J., Lewis R.G., and Hibbert C. (1978). Training implications of work preferences, *Journal of European Industrial Training*, **2**, (3), 2–4.

Myers I.B. (1962). *The Myers–Briggs Type Indicator*, Educational Testing Service, Princeton.

Storr A. (1973). *Jung*, Fontana.

Stricker L.J. and Ross J. (1964a). An assessment of some structural properties of the Jungian personality typology, *Journal of Abnormal Psychology*, **68**, 62–71.

Stricker L.J. and Ross J. (1964b). Some correlates of a Jungian personality inventory, *Psychol Rep.*, **14**, 623–643.

Stricker L.J. and Ross J. (1966). Intercorrelations and reliability of the Myers–Briggs type of indicator scales, *Psychol Rep.*, **12**, 287–293.

Advances in Management Education
Edited by John Beck and Charles Cox

CHAPTER 17

Evaluation of Management Training: A Focus on Change

Chris Brewster

This paper reports upon some tentative and limited steps that have been taken to evaluate management training by changing the focus of evaluation from the process of training to its effects in and on the organization. The approach here is conceptual in the main and there are more than enough issues to grapple with in this area. The spectre of methodological difficulties waits in the wings; the view of evaluation presented here may help to overcome some of those problems.

Evaluation received a good deal of attention in the Sixties and early Seventies. Since then, however, although the necessity for evaluation is accepted in theory it is perhaps most generous to say that it is often carried out in an unstructured and unsystematic manner. The last few years have seen few major advances on the early theory and few attempts to make theory and practice more consistent. Yet there are increasing pressures upon us to 'prove' that training and development activities are worthwhile: the time when such activities were seen as a 'Good Thing' and unchallenged 'appears to be well on its way to passing from a reality to a memory' (Kane, 1976).

The research I report upon is currently being undertaken by the Industrial Relations Unit of the Air Transport and Travel Industry Training Board (ATT/ITB). As part of that work over 300 managers have been interviewed in the last three years prior to attending courses in man-management. Courses have been organized for companies ranging in size from those with under 200 employees to those with over 5,000 and training for complete management teams has been, or is being, undertaken in a dozen organizations. Evaluation studies are, so far, being conducted in three organizations.

Before following through the reasoning that led to the adoption of the approach we are now using it may be helpful to clarify the definitions of 'manager', 'training', and 'evaluation'. Managers are defined in the terms of the organizations that we are working with, except that those with the title, but no staff, are excluded. 'Superintendents', 'Supervisors', and 'Duty Officers' who control staff and have no, or little, involvement in performing the task supervized are included. Personnel specialists are excluded. Training is defined as any systematic learning and/or teaching activity which is aimed at improving management within the organization.

There have been many definitions of evaluation (see for example Mahler, 1953; Martin, 1957; Meigniez *et al.*, 1963) and there is little to be gained by adding to this list. Matt Whitelaw in his excellent review of 'The Evaluation of Management Training' (Whitelaw, 1972) finds two definitions of particular use and they will be adopted here. The 'Glossary of Training Terms' defines evaluation as the 'assessment of the total value of a training system, training course or programme in social as well as financial terms' (Department of Employment, 1967). Hamblin defines the term in the broad sense as 'any attempt to obtain information (feedback) on the effects of a training programme, and to assess the value of training in the light of that information' (Hamblin, 1970). This seems to be a useful definition and the word evaluation will be used in this sense to include 'social as well as financial terms'. I shall be concentrating, however, on more systematic attempts to carry out the process.

This paper suggests a small, but I hope useful, change in the way evaluation is seen. To understand the reason for this change it is necessary to:

1. Review some of the conceptual problems involved in conducting evaluation;
2. Examine the levels at which evaluation has been proposed;
3. Consider the choice of objectives to which these levels relate;
4. Relate evaluation to change.

It will then be possible to indicate the way that the evaluation process may be assisted by changing the focus to what will be called below context evaluation and re-evaluation.

PROBLEMS

The evaluation of management training is important, but it is fraught with difficulties. As a Central Training Council report put it:

> The effectiveness of management training at managerial levels is difficult to assess and often impossible to measure. But unless the attempt is made, useful lessons may go unlearnt, the planning of future programmes may suffer and valuable resources in terms of managerial time and effort may be wasted.
>
> (CTC, 1969)

It is worth reviewing some of the difficulties, briefly, before examining the proposals that have been made to overcome them and considering the new proposal advanced here.

The Limitations of Training

The impact of management training will vary from one situation to another and the evaluator must be clear about the limitations of training. Training cannot 'solve' many management issues – it will not prevent problems or conflicts arising, it will not ensure that factors such as trade union policy or fuel price rises do not impede management's attempts to handle the problems, and nor can it ensure that even the best-trained manager will not make mistakes.

The impact of the training will also be affected by the situation that exists in the organization prior to, during, and after the training; and by the motivation of the managers involved. Where motivitation is high the training will have more impact. To some extent this can be created during the training, but other factors can have an effect: the managers will not learn, and the training will have failed, if they are not motivated to do so. (Gagne and Bolles, 1969).

The Nature of the Managerial Task

It is widely recognized that evaluating management training involves greater difficulty than the evaluation of training for physical tasks covering a limited number of correct procedures. As Rosemary Stewart has put it:

> 'Managerial work is varied and complex,' and yet 'We know too little about the nature of managerial jobs to be able to select and train managers satisfactorily, or to evaluate their jobs. Most of all we are ignorant about the difference between jobs.' (Stewart, 1976).

The management task is often concerned with unusual 'one-off' problems involving a wide range of possible options, and frequently involves decisions that are a matter of interpretation and judgement in an area where there are no 'right' or 'wrong' ways of operating. In the man-management field especially the manager may be trying quite simply to cope with and juggle a problem to which there is no solution. This implies obvious problems for someone trying to assess the success or otherwise of training for management.

Assessing Causal Relationships

Given the complexity of the management task and the extensive range of factors outside managerial control which affect performance, it is extremely difficult to assess causal relationships. There are many factors rooted in the background of each individual, such as skill, knowledge, and personality traits, which will be affected to greater or lesser extents by training. There are also a large number of factors at work outside the individual's control which may enhance or hinder the application of acquired knowledge or skills. These factors include the organizational climate, production systems, senior management, subordinates, and customers. Although these factors, in theory, may enhance or hinder the positive effects of training, in practice it would seem that it is the negative organizational influences that prevail (Sykes, 1962).

Unexpected Results

The problems created by the difficulty of assessing causal relationships are typified by the fact that training can have results that were neither planned for nor expected. Cowell (1972) argued that few evaluators are concerned with this problem although the fact that training can have unanticipated effects has been noted for some time (Fleishman *et al.* .1955). His own researches gathering information from trainees and their bosses about general management courses show little cause for concern: few were able to identify unforeseen effects. The problem may be more acute in the man-management area. To examine similar issues for a man-management course would necessitate asking subordinates too. As many managers know to their cost, it is not always easy to predict the way employees will react to management initiatives. This may well be an area where the more the training is successful in effecting change in the way the management team behaves, the greater will be the danger of unanticipated results.

The Limitations of the Behavioural Sciences

The behavioural, as opposed to, for example, the physical sciences, have a number of limitations and these apply, almost by definition, to the evaluation of management training. There have been attempts to move towards the precision of other sciences. Odiorne (1964), for example, suggests that the value of training must be assessed in strictly economic terms and decisions to invest time and money on training should be taken accordingly. This point of view has been opposed by Whitelaw:

> in the present state of development of quantification in the behavioural sciences the evaluation of management training will be a combination of quantitive techniques and subjective assessments,
>
> (Whitelaw, 1972).

and by Mahler (1953) who argued that attaching cost accounting concepts to training is not possible, especially in the context of a managerial job, and that evaluators should be satisfied with something less.

All the social sciences can – at least in theory – contribute to the field of evaluation:

> It is clear that the evaluation of training is not *a priori* a strictly defined part of the social and pyschological sciences, but a synthetic attempt to use various branches of these sciences in order to locate, define, and measure various kinds of changes, and, if possible, explain them.
>
> (Meigniez *et al.*, 1963)

Evaluations of training programmes are subject to the criticisms that apply to many research studies carried out by behavioural scientists e.g. subjective involvement by the researcher. Efforts have been made to design tests or questionnaires or to improve the statistical analyses of data but it is clear that such techniques can never overcome all the problems created by the social field in which such enquiries are being made.

Evaluation of Management Training as Heresy

It has been argued that it is seen by some as almost a heresy to wish to evaluate management training. Such training is an integral part of an overall approach by the management of an organization. On this view:

> investment in management education is the observable outcome of a belief in a certain style of management and, as such, 'cannot' and 'should not' be evaluated.
>
> (Hogarth, 1978)

Resourcing

Resourcing is of course a practical problem, but it has a conceptual angle, too, related to the view of evaluation as heresy and to its political nature. Decisions have to be taken about who undertakes the evaluation (trainer, accountant, external resource) and for whom. It is significant that most of the pressure for evaluation has to date come from trainers themselves. There has been increasing debate in recent years about measuring the resources used (or wasted) in training. Unfortunately the attempt to undertake a cost–benefit analysis of training has proven, so far, to be unsuccessful. (Thomas *et al.* .1969; Talbot and Ellis, 1969; Jones, 1971; Woodward, 1975).

The Political Nature of Evaluation

Problems raised by management style and by resourcing point to the 'political' nature of evaluation. Evaluation in any area can be seen as menacing to certain interest groups (Weiss, 1970; Banner, 1974; Angrist, 1975) and management training is no exception. It threatens, potentially at least, the trainer, the trainee, and those who are responsible for committing resources to the training.

Choice of Criteria

The political element is seen at its clearest in the decision as to whether or not to evaluate the training. It is also manifest in the choice of criteria. It is necessary:

> to examine the range of objectives perceived by those sponsoring the training (top management), those nominating or selecting course members, the trainees themselves, and the trainers. The range of objectives will be partly overlapping

> and partly conflicting. The degree of consensus is the main constraint preventing the definition of criteria for the evaluation of the programme. This consensus should not be assumed, it has to be clarified and probably negotiated before it can result in any operational criteria.
>
> (Thurley *et al.,* 1975).

Each person involved in any management or supervisory training will have their own objectives for the training and hence their own criteria. The evaluator will either have to choose those aspects of the objectives that can be found to be common, or the declared and written objectives, or to choose one set of objectives from amongst the many. Evaluation cannot proceed without this choice being made.

This particular problem is compounded by the increasing reliance being placed upon the trainee's own objectives and responsibility for learning. Almost by definition, there can be a process of rejecting, amending or supplementing original objectives in the course of any self-development activity. (Burgoyne, 1973).

Nature of Criteria

The nature of the criteria used for evaluation will help to resolve some of these difficulties, but it will give rise to others. Most management training courses are conducted in order to achieve a number of primary and secondary objectives. For evaluation purposes these objectives must be translated into criteria which the evaluator can use as a measure. 'Did the course (or how far did the course) achieve this objective?' If real progress was made in that direction the assessment is positive. If no real change, or a move away from that objective, then the assessment is negative.

The essential problem for the evaluator is whether to take broad or narrow objectives. The broad objectives may be more 'real', more akin to the purpose the training is aiming to achieve, but they are largely non-measurable. Data can be obtained if the criteria are narrowed down, but the evaluator is then measuring something that is less than the overall purpose of the training and having to make assumptions about transferability.

Failure of Previous Attempts

There have been few reported attempts to evaluate management training. (This is perhaps not surprising given the problems outlined above). The record of those that have been undertaken is not always encouraging. Some, such as the attempts to reduce the whole exercise to financial terms, have failed because their concept of evaluation has been too narrow. Others have been too ambitious and have been unable to reach useful conclusions. (Hesseling, 1966).

These problems have all created difficulties for evaluators in the past and will do so in the future. Their importance, and in some degree the extent to which they can be surmounted, will depend upon the level at which evaluation is being attempted.

LEVELS OF EVALUATION

There have been many different classifications of the process of evaluation. Mahler (1953), for example, distinguished three approaches: common-sense, systematic, and experimental and there have been a number of attempts to classify learning objectives, and hence evaluation, into subject areas: cognitive, affective, psychomotor (Bloom *et al.,* 1956), social skills (Bales, 1961; Rackham *et al.,* 1974; Morrison and O'Hearne, 1977), and perceptual (Moore, 1967).

The most widely used classification has been put forward on the basis of the point in the training cycle at which judgement is made. Figure 1 gives a selection of the classifications that have been made on this basis. Some definitions may be necessary, although, as indicated there, different authors have used different words to refer to the same level.

Context: What training should be done? This type of evaluation collects data on the situation and training needs of managers to determine what training should be done and for whom.

Input: How should training be conducted? This looks at available data on who is to be trained and about what, on resources, methods, and media to determine what will be included in the training and how, when, and by whom it will be done.

Process: How well is the training being done? Evaluation conducted during the training is called process evaluation. It uses data on the effects that the training is having, and any assessment that can be made as to the causes of those, to measure, and perhaps to modify, the programme as it is being conducted.

These levels of evaluation take place before or during the training. Other levels have been termed generically 'outcomes' evaluation.

Reaction level: What did trainees think of it? This overlaps the process level. It can occur during training or immediately after the training and assesses the trainees' views of the training.

Learning/Immediate level: What has the trainee learnt? This form of evaluation can take place at the end of the training or some time later. It deals with such issues as the acquisition of new skills or knowledge as a result of the training.

Behaviour/Intermediate level: What changes have occurred in the way the trainee carries out his or her job? At this level the evaluation is concerned with the effects of the training back at the workplace. It assesses whether the manager is managing better.

KIRKPATRICK (1) 1967	*HAMBLIN (2)* 1968	*BOYDELL (3)* 1970	*WARR ET AL. (4)* 1970	*STUFFLEBEAM (5) ET AL.* 1971	*THURLEY ET AL. (6)* 1975
			Context	Context	Organisational Context
					Objectives
			Input	Input	
					Process
Reaction	Reactions		Reactions	Process	Reaction
Learning	Learning	Knowledge Understanding Application	Immediate	Product	
					Content
Behaviour	Job Behaviour	Transfer	Intermediate		
		Medium Term			
Results	Functioning	Long Term	Ultimate		

Sources:

1. D. L. Kirkpatrick, 'Evaluation of Training' in *Training and Development Handbook,* R. L. Craig and L. R. Bittel (eds), McGraw-Hill, New York 1967; and 'Evaluating a Training Program for Supervisors and Foremen', *Personnel Adminstrator,* Vol. 14, No. 5, 1969, pp. 29-38.
2. A. C. Hamblin, 'Training in Evaluation: A Discussion of Some Problems' in *Organizational Necessities and Individual Needs,* R. J. Hacon (ed.), Blackwell, Oxford 1968.
3. T. H. Boydell, 'What's It All About', *Industrial Training International,* Vol. 8, No. 7, July 1973 and *Validation,* (mimeo) Sheffield Polytechnic, 1970.
4. P. B. Warr, M. W. Bird, and N. Rackham, *Evaluation of Management Training,* Gower Press, London 1970.
5. D. L. Stufflebeam, W. J. Foley, W. J. Gephart, E. G. Guba, R. I. Hammond, H. O. Merriman, and M. M. Provus *Educational Evaluation and Decision Making,* F. E. Peacock, Ithaca, I11. 1971.
6. K. E. Thurley, D. Graves, and M. Hult, 'An Evaluation Strategy for Management Development', ***Research Bulletin*** ATT/ITB, Vol. 6, No. 2, Dec. 1975.

Figure 1. Some Developments in the Classification of Levels of Evaluation

Results/ Ultimate level: Is the organization functioning better? This level of evaluation examines the contribution that the changes wrought in the manager make to the overall operation of the organization in which he works. In his latest book, Hamblin breaks this level down into two: 'organization' and 'ultimate value' (Hamblin, 1974). This is a distinction that I have tried to build upon.

There are indications in Figure 1 of two main trends in the approach to evaluation. Firstly, there has been an increasing emphasis upon the value, almost the necessity, of context evaluation: a trend to relate the training more closely to the environment and training needs of the managers involved. The second change is an apparent concentration upon the training process itself, a concern with developing the training, understanding learning theory, and getting instant feedback on the training that has been undertaken. This could be seen as a trend towards the trainer and the training environment and away from the environment that the manager will have to cope with at the end of the training. In other words, evaluation of the training as a process rather than evaluation of its results.

I will argue that the first trend holds great potential for improving management training and could be used more widely. I will also suggest that the benefits from the second trend have been considerable but have been at the expense of an important element of evaluation.

Our approach developed from an assessment of the advances made in recent years by researchers into the evaluation of management training. These advances have been considerable, particularly at the reaction and immediate levels, but have served to highlight some of the limitations of concentrating on evaluation at these levels. A brief report of this assessment will lead into an examination of the objectives of management training and the details of our approach.

Evaluation at the Reaction Level

Evaluation at the reaction level is often of the 'what do you think of it so far?' kind. Systematizing this type of evaluation means creating a format for obtaining standard answers. Fairly sophisticated methods have been developed, (House, 1965; Kirkpatrick, 1967) but we have found the very simple method suggested by Warr, Bird, and Rackham (1970) to be useful. Figure 2 gives an example of the form we use. We have found that provided the trainees are informed that the exercise is to enable evaluation of the training, not themselves, the worries that led Kirkpatrick to insist on anonymity are unnecessary. Reaction evaluation can, of course, also be carried out on the overall management programme (Hogarth, 1978).

Whilst we have found this form of evaluation of immense use it has, in common with all reaction evaluation, severe limitations. The managers may be enjoying the course, for example, but in fact not be learning anything. The form in Figure 2 is

SESSION ASSESSMENT

NAME: ....

SESSION: .... COURSE: ....

Please give your reaction to the session by putting a tick in the appropriate space in each of the scales below.

ENJOYMENT of session

Did not enjoy it very much | | | | | | | | Enjoyed it very much

Amount of NEW INFORMATION picked up during session

Taught me little I didn't already know | | | | | | | | Taught me a lot

RELEVANCE of session to own job

Not very relevant to my job | | | | | | | | Very relevant to my job

DURATION of session

Not long enough | | | | | | | | Too long

About right

Figure 2

predicated on the reasonable assumption that if the trainees are expressing enjoyment, a belief that they have picked up new information of relevance to their job and have not been bored, then learning is more likely to occur. There is, however, no necessary correlation.

The reaction level evaluation also contains limitations concerning the 'halo' effect surrounding certain speakers, topics or methods of training and concerning the scales that it uses. For its purpose it is a valuable training tool, but it is clearly inadequate at other levels of evaluation.

Evaluation at the Immediate or Learning Level

Evaluation at the immediate outcome level is perhaps the most common in management training. Methods used have included questionnaires, rating scales, and trainer rating. Questionnaires have usually been used to check knowledge learning and the many techniques (such as essay questions, true/false, multiple choice) are well-known. Rating scales, such as those developed by Thurstone and Likert (Tiffin and McCormick, 1966), and others (Castle, 1952; Fleishman *et al.,* 1955) and the more elaborate semantic differential scales (Staats and Staats, 1958; Warr *et al.,* 1970), all aim to test the trainees' knowledge of aspects of the training on one or more of various scales. Rating by the trainer can be carried out in a great many ways and is often undertaken by the trainer during the courses as he conducts successive exercises designed to reinforce earlier learning. More systematic methods have been developed to analyse behaviours into categories. (Bales, 1961: Castle, 1972; Heyns and Zander, 1953; and Rackham, 1971). Each of these methods has its uses. For example, questionnaires are more effective in assessing knowledge acquisition, rating scales for assessing changes in beliefs (Fishbein and Ajzen, 1976).

The limitation of the immediate level of evaluation is that it is unable to measure the extent to which any changes in knowledge or skills are being or can be transferred back to the workplace.

Evaluation at the Intermediate or Job Behaviour Level

Identifying behaviour on the job is difficult. A number of methods have been tried and are reviewed in Rosemary Stewart's recent book (Stewart, 1976) and, as evaluation methods, by Hamblin (1974). They include continuous direct observation, random sampling, standard interval sampling, interviews and questionnaires, self-recording, role-set assessment, and the use of appraisal interviews. Less direct methods ranging from sophisticated critical incident techniques to output measures or customer complaints have been tried in the non-managerial areas but because of the nature of the managerial role will be more problematic when applied to management training.

Intermediate level evaluation is much closer to ensuring that training managers has been a valuable activity for the organization, but clearly it is possible for a manager to change his behaviour either in the direction intended by the course or in some other direction and in either case to have no effect, a possitive effect or a deleterious effect on the organization as a whole. This is the issue confronted by ultimate or long-term level evaluation.

Long-term or Results Level Evaluation

There have been very few studies of the impact of management training on organizations. Indeed it has been argued that the necessary 'information gathering would involve expenditure of a great deal of time and money. Thus, for short term training, it is unlikely to be worthwhile' (Williams, 1969). This lack of study of the impact of training on the organization is particularly unfortunate. As Hamblin has put it:

> . . . a trainee may react correctly but fail to learn; or he may learn, but fail to apply his learning on the job; or he may change his job behaviour, but this may have no effect on the functioning of the firm. Thus, ideally we should evaluate at every level. If we ignore the more distant levels, we will only discover the more superficial changes. If we ignore the immediate levels (i.e. reactions and immediate outcome levels) we are in danger of being unable to explain any changes that we discover because we have not followed through every link in the chain.
>
> (Hamblin, 1970).

OBJECTIVES

The level of evaluation that the evaluator concentrates upon will be determined to some extent by the nature of the objectives that have been set for the training. It is recognized that most, if not all, management training will have both 'principal' and 'modifying' criteria (Isaac and Michael, 1971) but it is usually possible to discern a distinction between educational or learning objectives and organizational objectives.

The authors of one of the earliest and most influential texts in this area, (McGehee and Thayer, 1961) defined this in terms of objectives related to changes in job performance and objectives related to changes in organizational performance. Furthermore, 'traditional training objectives have been identified as the needs of the individual or group of individuals' (Odiorne, 1970). The emphasis on individuals, coupled with that on measurement (Mager, 1975) has tended to ensure that most objectives that have been set have been *learning* objectives. This has caused evaluation of the objectives to be restricted to the learning, or at best job behaviour change, level.

Odiorne (1970) has argued that training should be about 'solving organization problems or introducing change *by means* of affecting individual behaviour', and that 'hesitancy in defining training objectives as organization objectives has led to numerous diversions and waste in training'. In man-management training the relevance of this approach can be discerned readily. The ability of the manager to handle this topic is dependent upon the organizational climate, the procedures and unions he has to deal with, and the actions of others in the management hierarchy as well as his own knowledge and skill. There is evidence to indicate that the effects of training can be overwhelmed if there has been no supporting change in the organization (Sykes, 1962).

Management training therefore should be placing its emphasis 'not only upon behavioural change in the individual but also upon change of the individual within his organizational context, and changes in the organizational context or organic system of which the individual is one interacting part' (Friedlander, 1967). The objectives of such training should be directed towards change in the organization rather than at elements of managerial performance. This change may not be accomplished solely by the training. Other, mutually supporting, strategies will be involved and the objectives should be stated broadly enough to encompass them.

The Mant report (Mant, 1969) found that

> 'Where companies felt they had in fact coped successfully . . . they had done so overwhelmingly as a result of improved organization structures, clearer objectives . . . rather than as a result of training.'

There is no reason why the training should not have as an objective some changes, greater or smaller, to the organization. The report also stated that

> 'where training has been perceived as successful it has been closely linked to the job, usually by some form of problem-oriented project work.'

EVALUATION AND CHANGE

Training that is aimed directly at change within the organization provides an opportunity for a different kind of evaluation. Most discussion of evaluation to date, even the more recent and rigorous studies such as those by Burgoyne and Stuart (1977) have concentrated upon evaluation of learning objectives. The reasons are clear: it has been found difficult to establish the link between the training and any change in the organization. This is particularly so where the manager being trained is sent on external courses.

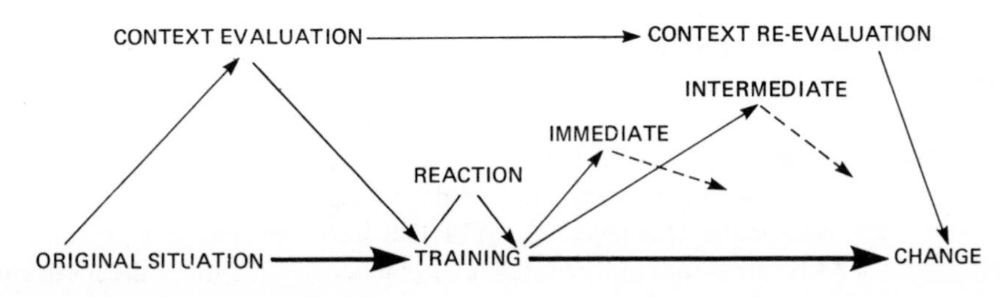

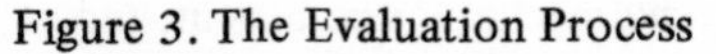
Figure 3. The Evaluation Process

Where the training has as an objective some greater or lesser change in the organization the position is different. Here we can assess the change. Figure 3 indicates this additional option, which we have called Context Re-evaluation. The bottom line indicates training as a process to create change in the organization. Context evaluation is undertaken to assess the original situation so that the training is relevant. The other levels of evaluation take place at varying distances from the training itself and have a greater or lesser assumed relationship to change in the organization. What is new here is context re-evaluation.

This is an attempt at evaluation at Hamblin's 'Organization' level (Hamblin, 1974). We have called it context re-evaluation in order to emphasize the approach that we have adopted. Hamblin argues that there are no techniques at these levels which are specifically relevant to the evaluation and control of training, although he suggests that some (self-diary studies, activity sampling, work study, open-ended interviews, and patterns of work-flow) have potential. Our approach, which uses the interview mechanism in part, may indicate another technique.

Context re-evaluation is evaluation of the changes that are made in the organization as a result of training. It falls short of ultimate or results level evaluation in that we are not able, at this stage at least, to measure the success of such changes in improving financial or other indices of company performance. It does, however, move us one stage nearer that level of evaluation.

Evaluation of management training at this level involves a number of prerequisites:

1. *Context Evaluation* – we must know what the situation was prior to the training.
2. *Training of the Management Team* – training that is company based, involves those with managerial authority, is aimed at change directly and which examines policy issues.
3. *Follow-up and Supporting Action* – to make the changes that the course has identified as necessary.
4. *Context Re-evaluation*

Context Evaluation

Although, as shown in Figure 1, there has been an increasing emphasis upon context evaluation it is still true that it is honoured more in the breach than the observance. Methods range from 'as an experienced tutor I have an intuitive grasp of the situation managers are in' through to some highly sophisticated techniques. Many of these latter concentrate upon the manager, almost in isolation. But managers do not act in isolation: they act in the context of their organization, of an economic system, a market, trade union involvement, and a management team.

Our man-management training at the ATT/ITB starts, invariably, with context evaluation. This is carried out in three stages. Firstly, we gather data on the company generally. (We already have details of the industry and market it operates in, and of company size, profitability, ownership, and recent history). By meetings with senior executives and Personnel department staff information is obtained on various aspects of the company, particularly on man-management – hierarchical organization; rules, policies, and procedures; the formal communication system; union position and industrial relations history; budgets and budgetary authority, manning levels, and salary administration.

The second stage consists of interviews with the managers. These last for 60–90 minutes each and are conducted by means of an administered, structured questionnaire. Managers are asked about:

1. The job – reporting relationships
   employees supervized
   main work activities, key results, constraints
   budgets.
2. Involvement with employees and employee representatives.
3. Communication to employees and employee representatives.
4. Grievance and disciplinary issues.
5. Negotiations.
6. Experiences of conflict.
7. Involvement with Personnel department.
8. Communications with other managers.
9. Company policy.
10. Background and experience.
11. Previous man management training.
12. Perceived training needs.

The questions attempt to concentrate on facts (e.g. 'what issues have you dealt with?') rather than opinions ('what is going wrong?'). By means of these two stages we cover the Organization Analysis, Operations Analysis, and Man Analysis facets identified by McGehee and Thayer (1961).

The third stage is to combine the information and documentation of the first, with the computer analysis and the interviewers' understanding gained from the second stage, to write a report and check back with the company.

The context evaluation provides two vital benefits. Firstly, the training can be structured in a direct and immediate way to reflect the needs of the managers involved. Secondly, it provides a base line from which evaluation at other levels can be undertaken. If we do not know where we started from no amount of work will enable us to show whether we have advanced.

Training the Management Team

Company-based training is likely to be, in practice, a prerequisite for evaluation at the organizational change level. This is an unhappy conclusion for the great mass of general, publicly-available courses. It may be that the absence of attempts to evaluate at this or the results level reflects the dominance of such courses and the great difficulty of applying context evaluation or making change to an environment outside the control of the trainer or trainee. Eccles (1973) has shown how the educational institutions are attempting to overcome this problem by operating *within* the trainees' working environment.

Company-based training, which can of course be conducted externally or internally and will often involve the use of external training resources, provides several advantages. Tailoring training to needs is easier, transfer of learning more likely, the achievement of consistent management action more possible and, crucially here, it provides an opportunity to examine and perhaps to change the organization that the managers work in.

Where the trainees do have managerial authority, i.e. either they (or someone involved with running the course) can carry out decisions that are made, then the training can be aimed directly at organizational change; it can be pro-active. Berger (1977) found that transfer of learning for management required that the manager 'must have the autonomy to change the way in which he performs his job,' and, indeed, that 'the more autonomy a person has in his job and the less rigid the structure of the job content, the more he will transfer learning from the course.'

Two points may be made about this finding: firstly it emphasizes once again that the manager does not operate in a vacuum and that the training for him should reflect the context in which he works; secondly, it is possible, as part of the training programme, to vary and/or increase the 'autonomy to change' that the manager has. This does not imply that a seminar leads directly to changes in the organization. It does imply, though, an understanding on the part of senior executives in the organization that training is about change, it involves the creation of a climate in which change is seen as being the outcome and as something positive rather than threatening and it calls for a willingness to examine all the issues that the management team wishes to cover. If, to take a simple example, problems exist in communications and management consistency a programme that examines the problem, looks at managers' suggestions and perhaps establishes monthly management meetings may be more effective than a month of 'communications skills' training.

Methods for undertaking such training are legion but need not be very complex (Brewster and Connock, 1978). The process is based upon the concept that there is a limit to the extent to which training should try to change the manager. The change may be needed in the context in which the manager works. Mager and Pipe said:

> Rather than change what he can do, change something about the world in which he does it so that doing it will be more attractive, or less repulsive, or less difficult.
>
> (Mager and Pipe, 1970)

We would only dissent from this in that we see changes in duties, responsibilities, authority, communications patterns, procedures, and policies as concomitants of, rather than an alternative to, training.

Follow-up

Changes that are discussed during the training need to be followed up after it. Some typical changes that have been suggested in the man-management area we work in include changes to the composition and role of monthly management meetings; a re-examination and rewriting, or re-negotiation of, rules and procedures; increases in middle management authority for disciplinary action, and changes to reporting relationships.

Where the training is company-based, involves managers with sufficient authority, and has these kinds of organizational changes as its objective then it becomes possible to end the course with a series of individual action plans, proposed changes within the organization, and issues that are still unresolved and a mechanism for handling them.

We have then, at appropriate points within our training, an opportunity to carry out job behaviour evaluation – by checking back on the outcomes of the individual action plans – and to assess the extent to which there have been changes within the organization or steps taken to bring it about. These two areas overlap to some extent and our evaluation mechanism attempts, therefore, to cover both.

Context Re-evaluation

Context re-evaluation is an almost self-explanatory term. It is long-term evaluation. Its purpose is to establish whether structural or organizational changes have occurred, how far they have been in line with the management team's wishes, and how beneficial they have been.

The process that we have used involves, substantially, a repeat of the context evaluation plus a series of additional investigations. By repeating the context evaluation we have a simple and direct measure of the extent of change that has taken place during and since the management training programme. The additional investigations are carried out as part of the repeat interviews with the managers between 12 and 18 months after the training. The additional data is derived from a note of all the issues raised and decisions taken during the training and from a form of critical incident technique concentrating upon situations that have arisen since the completion of the training and of subsequent organizational change (Flanagan, 1954; Kay, 1959). By this means, examining incidents, problems and issues that have been dealt with since the course, and by comparing the results of this questionnaire with the original training needs identification survey as assessment can be made of some of the effects of the training.

CONCLUDING POINTS

Three simple points can be made in conclusion. Firstly, this approach does not help us to evaluate the training *per se.* As has been indicated, training is a change mechanism. In my experience the organization is concerned to evaluate the change and have confidence that the training has contributed to that change. This evaluation measure is more relevant to those requirements than assessments of extent of learning for example. Context Re-evaluation examines the change, and can tell us something about the extent to which the training programme contributed to that change if it is used with the other levels of evaluation rather than as a replacement for them. Given that, a sensible assessment can be made of the extent to which the training has been a catalyst.

Secondly, this approach enables some, though by no means all, of the problems of evaluation to be faced. It clearly recognizes the limitations of training and the complexity of the managerial task and can deal with unexpected results. It is still bound, of course, by all the limitations of the behavioural sciences and deals with the problem of causal relationships by, in effect, sidestepping them and choosing criteria that make the causal relationships less important. Perhaps one of its major benefits is that it can operate with the objectives of the trainees as they are identified at the beginning of the training and as they are amended and supplemented during the course of it; objectives that are generally expressed in organizational rather than training terms.

Thirdly, and related to this second point, this approach needs to be developed. It needs further refinement in the man-management area; it would be interesting to see if it could be applied to other aspects of management training. Context re-evaluation does raise a large question against the value of general management training courses run for trainees from a range of organizations. There is, in theory at least, no reason why this approach should not be adopted for courses which aim much less directly at change and it would be interesting to compare the results.

It is an approach that is simple and practical and which makes sense to managers being trained and to the senior executives in their organizations. And it is an approach that, combined with the other, more learning-based evaluative techniques, provides a much wider possibility of being able to make a clear assessment of the value of management training.

REFERENCES

Angrist, S.S. (1975). Evaluation research: possibilities and limitations, *Journal of Applied Behavioural Science*, **11**, 75–91.

Bales, R.F. (1961). *Interaction Process Analysis :a Method for the Study of Small Groups*, Addison-Wesley, Cambridge, Mass.

Banner, D.K. (1974). 'The politics of evaluation research, *Omega*, **2**, 763–774.

Berger, M. (1977). Training and the organisational context, *Journal of European Training*, **1**, (2), 7–12.

Bloom, B., Engelhart, M.D., Furst, E.J., Hill, W.H., and Krathwohl, D.R. (1956). *Taxonomy of Educational Objectives*, David McKay, New York.

Brewster, C.J. and Connock, S.L. (1978). Feeding company policy into IR training, *Personnel Management*, **10**, (8), 28–35.

Brewster, C.J. and Connock, S.L. (1979). An integrated apporach to IR training, *Industrial and Commercial Training*, **XI**, (2), 69–71.

Burgoyne, J.G. and Stuart, R. (1977). Learning theory/outcomes of MD programmes (4 articles), *Personnel Review,* **5**, (4), 19–29, **6**, (1), 5–6, **6**, (2), 5–14, and **6**, (3), 39–47.
Burgoyne, J.G. (1973). A new approach to evaluating management development programmes: some exploratory research, *Personnel Review,* **2**, (4), 40–44.
Castle, P.F.C. (1952). The evaluation of human relations training for supervisors, *Occupational Psychology,* **XXVI**, (4), 191–205.
Central Training Council. (1969). *Training and Development of Managers :Further Proposals,* Management Training and Development Committee, CTC, HMSO, London.
Cowell, D. (1972). Evaluating the effectiveness of management courses, *Journal of European Training,* **1**, Spring, 55.
Department of Employment. (1971). *Glossary of Training Terms,* HMSO, London.
Eccles, T. (1973). Developing management skills and improving organisational performance, *Personnel Review,* **2**, (4), 46–52.
Flanagan, J.C. (1954). The critical incident technique, *Psychological Bulletin,* No. 51, 327–358.
Fishbein, M. and Ajzen, I. (1976). *Belief, Attitude, Intention, and Behaviour :An Introduction to Theory and Research,* Addison-Wesley, New York.
Fleishman, E.A., Harris, E.F., and Burtt, H.E. (1955). *Leadership and Supervision in Industry – an evaluation of a supervisory training programme,* Ohio State University Bureau of Educational Research Monograph No. 33.
Friendlander, F.I. (1967). The impact of organizational training laboratories upon the effectiveness and interaction of ongoing work groups, *Personnel Psychology,* **XX**, 289–307.
Gagne, M., and Bolles, D.M. (1969). A review of factors in learning efficiency in Holding, D.H. (ed.), *Experimental Psychology in Industry,* Harmondsworth.
Hamblin, A.C. (1970). 'Evaluation of Training', *Industrial Training International,* **5**, (11), 33–36.
Hamblin, A.C. (1974). *Evaluation and Control of Training,* McGraw-Hill, London.
Hesseling, P. (1966). *Strategy of Evaluation Research in the Field of Supervisory Management Training,* Van Gorcum, Assen.
Heyns, R.N. and Zander, A.F. (1953). Observations of group behaviour in Festinger, L. and Katz, E. (eds), *Research Methods in the Behavioural Sciences,* Holt, Rinehart, and Winston, New York.
Hogarth, R.M. (1978). Assessing management education. A summary of the CEDEP project, *Journal of European Training,* **2**, 2.
House, R.J. (1965). Managerial reactions to two methods of management training, *Personnel Psychology,* **XVIII**, (3), 311–319.
Isaac, S. and Michael, W.B. (1971). *Handbook in Research and Evaluation,* Robert Knapp, San Diego.
Jones, J.A.G. (1971). Towards a cost–benefit approach to evaluating management training, paper to IPM National Conference.
Kane, J.S. (1976). The evaluation of organisational training programmes, *Journal of European Training,* **6**, 289–338.
Kay, B.R. (1959). Key factors – effective foreman behaviour, *Personnel,* No. 36.
Kirkpatrick, D.L. (1967). Evaluation of training in Craig, R.L. and Bittel, L.R. (eds), *Training and Development Handbook,* McGraw-Hill, New York.
Mager, R.F. (1975). *Preparing Instructional Objectives,* Fearon Publishers, Belmont.
Mager, R.F. and Pipe, P. (1970). *Analyzing Performance Problems,* Fearon Publishers, Belmont.

Mahler, W.R. (1953). Evaluation of management development programmes, *Personnel,* **XXX**, (2), 116–122.
Mant, A. (1969). *The Experienced Manager – A Major Resource,* BIM, London.
Martin, A. (1957). The assessment of training, *Personnel Management,* 88–93.
McGehee, W. and Thayer, P.W. (1961). *Training in Business and Industry,* John Wiley, New York.
Meigniez, R., Gauchet, F., Stalker, G.M., and Thurley, K.E. (1963). *Evaluation of Supervisor and Management Training,* OECD, Paris.
Moore, M.R. (1967). *A Proposed Taxonomy of the Preceptual Domain and Some Suggested Applications,* Educational Testing Service.
Morrison, J.H. and O'Hearne, J.J. (1977). *Practical Transactional Analysis in Management,* Addison-Wesley, Cambridge, Mass.
Odiorne, G.S. (1964). The need for an economic approach to training, *Journal of the American Society of Training Directors,* **XVIII**, (3), 3–12.
Odiorne, G.S. (1970). *Training by Objectives : An Economic Approach to Management Training,* MacMillan, New York.
Rackham, N. (1971). *Development and Evaluation of Supervisory Training,* Research Report 71/1, Air Transport and Travel Industry Training Board.
Rackham, N., Honey, P., and Colbert, M. (1974). *Developing Interactive Skills,* Wellens Publishing, London.
Staats, A. and Staats, C. (1958). Attitudes established by classical conditioning, *Journal of Abnormal and Social Psychology,* **LVII**, 37–40.
Stewart, R. (1976). *Contrasts in Management,* McGraw-Hill, London.
Sykes, A.J. (1962). The effects of a supervisory training course in changing supervisors' perceptions and expectations of the role of management, *Human Relations,* **XV**, 227–243.
Talbot, J.R., and Ellis, C.D. (1969). *Analysis and Costing of Company Training,* Gower Press, London.
Thomas, B., Moxham, J., and Jones, J.A.G. (1969). A cost–benefit analysis of industrial training, *British Journal of Industrial Relations,* **7**, (2), 231–264.
Thurley, K.E., Graves, D., and Hult, M. (1975). An evaluation strategy for management development, *Training Research Bulletin,* **6**, (2), Air Transport and Travel Industry Training Board.
Tiffin, J. and McCormick, E.J. (1966). *Industrial Psychology,* George Allen and Unwin, London.
Warr, P., Bird, B., and Rackham, N. (1970). *Evaluation of Management Training,* Gower Press, London.
Weiss, C.H. (1970). The politicisation of evaluation research, *Journal of Social Issues,* **26**, 57–68.
Whitelaw, M. (1972). *The Evaluation of Management Training – a Review,* Institute of Personnel Management, London.
Woodward, N. (1975). The economic evaluation of supervisor training, *Journal of European Training,* **4**, (3), 134–147.

Advances in Management Education
Edited by John Beck and Charles Cox

CHAPTER 18

Transfer of Learning – There Are Two Separate Problems

David Casey

PART I TWO PROBLEMS IN ONE

First - the Problem We Created for Ourselves

Who has ever heard a manager use the expression 'Transfer of learning'? Trainers, on the other hand, worry a lot about it. And so we should worry because we have invented a significant part of the problem ourselves. We did this by putting learning in a separate place from work, so that there is now a space between the two. Having invented that space we devote a lot of time trying to solve the problem of transferring learning across the space. I shall call this problem the transfer of learning from course-to-work. It is certainly felt to be a major problem and much research has been devoted to it. Vandenput's (1973) work in Belgium, has identified factors inhibiting course-to-work learning transfer whilst Baumgartel and Jeanpierre's (1972) research in India has identified conditions for maximum likelihood of learning transfer across the course-to-work gap.

This problem of transfer of learning from course-to-work does not exist in vocational skills training. A typist can learn her skills on a training course and transfer those skills easily to any office typewriter. The skills required by the craft apprentice can be developed in the training shop and can easily be transferred to any workshop. This is because the skills are separable, recognizable, teachable, and usable, independently of the environment. A newly qualified secretary will of course be very nervous about her first job but although the social impact of a new job on a young person may be tremendous, there is a great deal of confidence in the fact that sooner or later a boss will call her in for dictation and she will be using her shorthand skills, developed on a training course, with very little problem of transferring the skills she has learned to her new place of work.

We seem to have used roughly the same learning model for management education, possibly because management is clearly vocational and clearly needs skills. The thinking presumably went like this – there are recognizable, discrete skills of management and therefore these must be teachable by a process similar to that used in vocational skills training. Provided we select the right skills, they should be transferable to most management situations just as other vocational skills are transferable to most work situations.

But managers were not able to transfer new skills from the courses we invented to their managerial places of work. In my view this is because the learning model is inappropriate. The model which works for other vocational skills training will not work for management skills training. In the UK we became aware in the 60's and 70's that it was not working to our satisfaction as trainers, nor to the satisfaction of senior and thinking men in industry (see the Owen Report 1971). However, we should never forget that it was approved and was valued by *those managers who attended our courses.* Now many of them are in senior positions. They remember our courses with pleasure quite simply because we put a lot of ingenuity into them – they were cleverly designed, interesting experiences. So the problem of transferring the learning from course-to-work was created by us in designing all these fascinating courses which were enjoyed for their own sake with hardly a thought given to how managers were to use what they had 'learned'. We were using the wrong model, but now the wrong model is bedded down in solid and widespread approval by middle and senior managers. And we did it. It is our own fault.

The well-known problem can be drawn quite simply, using an arrowhead to represent transfer of learning and using numbers to indicate separate work experiences (see Figure 1).

Second Problem – Much Deeper

Now I would like to describe the deeper problem, the one we should have been addressing all the time instead of inventing the course-to-work transfer problem. All this time there already lay, deep in the activity of management itself, a learning problem of such dimensions that most people could not see it and many people still cannot see it today. Our cavorting about with the course-to-work transfer problem

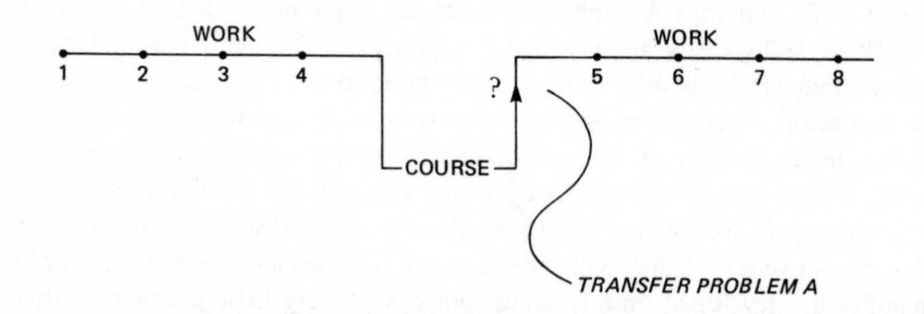

TRANSFER PROBLEM A This transfer is concerned with translating CONCEPTS into ACTION. Concepts, models and ideas stack up during a course largely because teachers are afraid their sessions might be a flop. We are all scared of flops – so we arrive armed with plenty of concepts. Unfortunately this keeps the course intellectually stimulated and exhilarated – making the transfer problem at the end of the course even *more* difficult. Concepts breed more concepts – not action.

Figure 1. The Well-known Transfer Problem A: Course-to-work

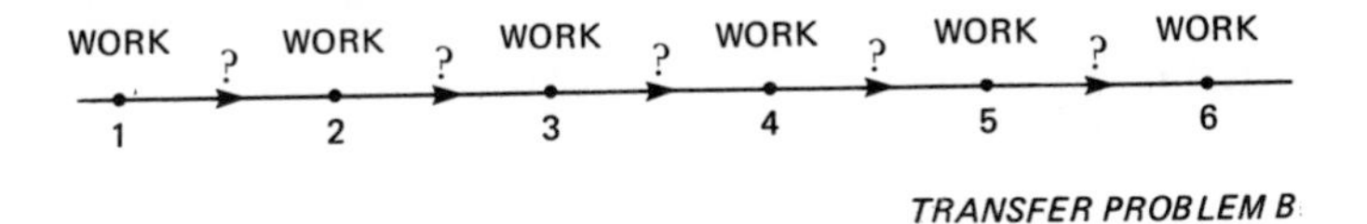

TRANSFER PROBLEM B This is the transfer of learning from experience-to-experience, and is really at the heart of management development. Human beings learn this way all the time – management education can do no more than speed it up and perhaps make the process more comprehensive and effective. Management cannot be learned without concepts of course, but the *concepts are derived from work* experience and applied to subsequent work experiences, rather than discovered on a course, as in model A. Although it is a very natural learning process it requires the ability to do two things at once – work and learn – which is more complicated than Problem A, where so-called 'learning' is separated from work in a very deliberate way.

Numbers are used in diagrams throughout this chapter to indicate consecutive work experiences. Any particular work experience may be a day, a week or a month. The regular spacing between numbers is for simplicity and convenience only.

Figure 2. The More Difficult Transfer Problem B: Experience-to-experience

has given us an illusion that we have been making progress. The unpalatable truth of the matter is that even if we had a magic wand and with one wave could spring a 100% solution to the course-to-work transfer problem we should then have to face the deeper issue of experience-to-experience transfer of learning, the *nature* of which is different. It can be illustrated – using the same symbols as before (see Figure 2).

Why Problem A and Problem B are Different in Nature

Figures 1 and 2, and the brief descriptions of the two transfer problems A and B, do not fully explain why the problems are different in nature. Let us go a little deeper. Problem A is concerned with transfer from cognitive activity to whole-person activity, whilst problem B is concerned with transfer from whole-person activity to whole-person activity, *via* a cognitive interpolation.

The enormous difficulties of attempting to transfer learning from a course to real management work is graphically illustrated by Figure 3, which assumes human activity to consist of emotional, cognitive, physical, and moral activities, each of which may operate independently or in combination with the others. It does not matter if you disagree with my arbitrary division of human activity into the four categories – that is not the point. The point is the *multiplication factor* from an *artificially simplified* single activity, to the reality of a jumble of interrelated, contemporaneous activities in real life.

The corresponding drawing for model B, transfer from experience-to-experience, is shown in Figure 4. Here the cognitive activity comes forward into sharper focus than the others, exercizing a co-ordinating role on the other activities, both in retrospect and in anticipation. The *transfer mechanism is cognitive* – it is the intellectual process which comes in between whole-person management actions, by means of which some sort of crude sense is made of the bewildering world of action. If a person can't do this, that person will not grow as a manager, for he will not learn as a manager.

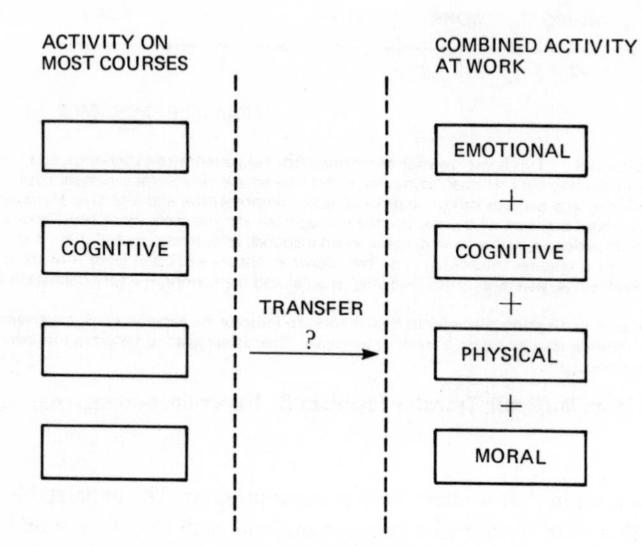

Figure 3. Transfer of Learning Problem A: course-to-work

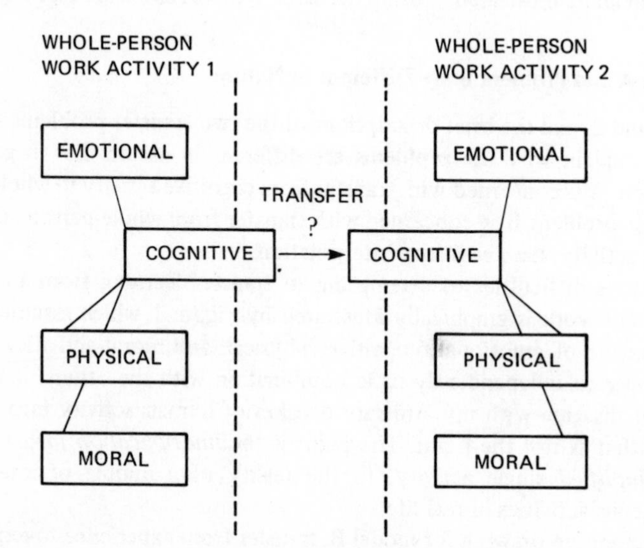

Figure 4. Transfer of Learning Problem B: Experience-to-experience

To solve the problem of transfer from experience-to-experience each whole-person experience must be interpreted by an intelligent looking back. In this looking back a manager will use models, theories, frameworks, and principles (whether his own or someone else's). Using the same models he must then look forward to make intellectual sense of his next whole-person activity, in the light of what he saw when he looked back. I am not suggesting that it will ever be possible to decide what to do purely intellectually and carry it through – management is much too human and dynamic for that. However, the learning we must surely be aiming at is *intelligence-led* in contrast to learning driven by instinct ('Don't ask me why – just do it!') or by emotion ('Next time I'll get even with her') or by habit ('We *always* meet on Tuesdays'). This is not to say that instinct, emotion, and habit can be eliminated in some crazy attempt to strip down managers to cold calculating computers. Quite the opposite – emotional, moral, and physical activities are the very essence of management and so must always be the vehicle for learning about management. But this can only happen if these human activities are recognized cognitively by the manager for what they are; only a manager who has become aware of himself and his own capacities and values is really able to handle the confusing interplay between himself and events around him, which is what the task of managing calls for.

If management were less of a whole-person activity and more of an intellectual activity, courses would work because the transfer would be from one cognitive activity to another. But management is very definitely a whole-person activity – a manager in action is often physically, emotionally, and intellectually at full stretch. Transfer of learning from one whole-person experience to the next whole-person experience can only be achieved by a learning model which accepts the trauma of real management action for what it is – a bewildering and punishing assault from all sides on a person's mental, emotional, physical, and even moral capacities all at the same time. Perhaps this is why the young, intellectual whizzkids of the 60's – mostly in the City – blew themselves out pretty quickly. The 70's have seen experience and judgement being valued once again – certainly it is experience and judgement which the bulk of middle managers need. For them, management development is an incremental process; there are no step-function changes, and no shortcuts. For them, management development is learning from one whole-person experience to the next. And it is our job to help them along this steady gradient, just a little faster than they would travel without our help.

I have now tried to explain why the old problem of course-to-work transfer, and the deeper problem of experience-to-experience transfer are different in nature. It is a very short step from here to a far-reaching conclusion. My conclusion is that courses are quite irrelevant to *management* education, *even though 90% of management eduction is based on them.* Holding on with all our strength to that particular truth, let us move on to see what can be done about transfer from experience-to-experience.

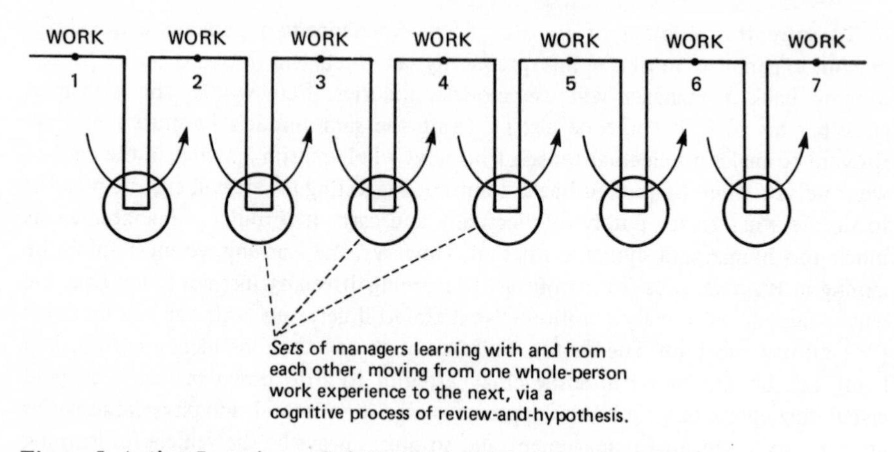
WORK
WORK
WORK
WORK
WORK
WORK
WORK
1
2
3
4
5
6
7
Sets of managers learning with and from each other, moving from one whole-person work experience to the next, via a cognitive process of review-and-hypothesis.

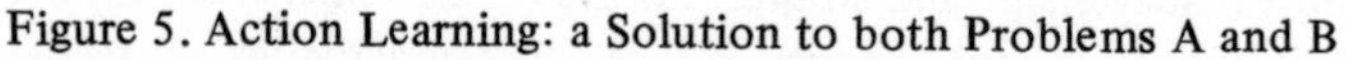
Figure 5. Action Learning: a Solution to both Problems A and B

The Attraction of Action Learning

There was one person who saw both transfer problems. We were making heavy weather of management education in the UK when in the mid-70's Reg Revans, now himself almost in his mid-70's, came out of exile and said quite simply 'Courses won't work. We must give management education back to the managers and let them learn with and from each other during real work'. There is in this statement the solution to BOTH problems – if only we had the wit to see it and the courage to do it. The trainers said they understood '. . . Revans has said what we were all feeling in our hearts'. Problem A would disappear because if there is no course there is no course-to-work transfer of learning problem. Problem B – the deep problem of transfer of learning from experience-to-experience – can also be solved by managers learning with and from each other during real work. Revans' model for management education can be drawn as in Figure 5, using the same symbols as before with arrowheads for transfer of learning.

Action learning became the most talked of and widespread topic of interest in management education. A wave of excitement passed through the management training world. The concept was so simple and easy to understand. Admittedly the role of the trainer did seem a bit tricky (see Garratt, 1977, and Casey, 1976), but within the capacity of any experienced trainer, it was simply an extension of his teaching role in which he could deploy some new skills.

But what has actually happened in the UK in the last five years?

Failure of Action Learning Programmes

What went wrong? I believe it has a lot to do with the word 'Programme'. Action learning as an *idea* was not found to be usable, people clamoured for something they could get hold of, managers had been so brainwashed by our ingenuity in putting on stimulating courses that they expected a structured thing. At the same time trainers, bemused by years of course-ingenuity, wanted to get started and 'get a programme off the ground'. The questions that those of us working in action learning were most frequently asked by trainers were these:

- How do we sell action learning programmes?
- How do we launch action learning?
- How do we convince top management that an action learning programme is right for them?
- How do we design a programme?

All these questions assume there is a *thing,* a programme to design and sell. Here we were again, taking the best single idea of the last decade and subtly changing it into a course with all the re-entry and transfer of learning problems all over again! Perhaps the trainers did not understand after all.

We now have people stomping the country hawking around incomplete action learning sets, desperately looking for set members to complete their numbers. This is no way to use Revans' important idea. As Robert Pirsig (1974) says, 'the fanatic is only a fanatic because deep down he has real doubt'.

At the worst extreme, an action learning programme which has been cobbled together for the sake of 'doing action learning' can suffer from all the disadvantages of any training package, *including* the familiar transfer of learning problem at the end of the programme. The worst extreme would be represented by Figure 6.

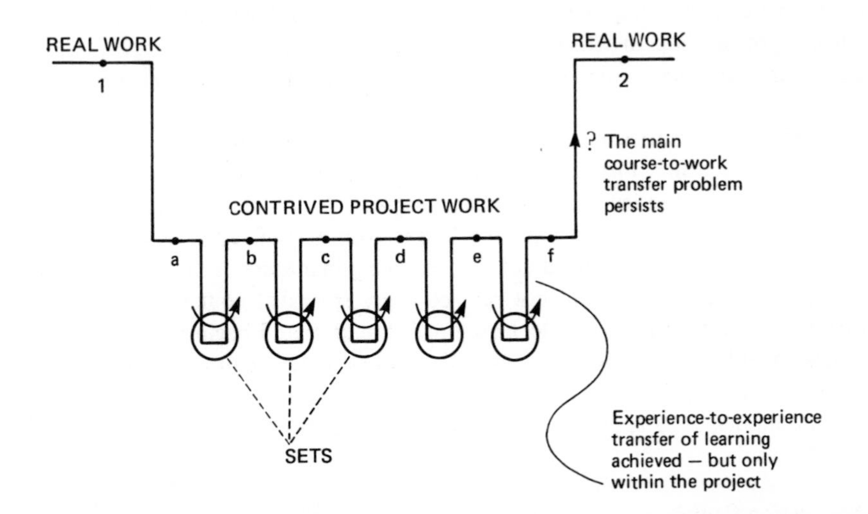

Figure 6. The Extreme Case: a Contrived Action Learning Programme with many of the Faults of any Training Package

In this first part of my paper I have tried to expose two separate problems of learning transfer in management education and have introduced Revans' concept of action learning, a concept which is just as vulnerable to misuse and abuse as any other. In Part II I would like to tell a story, the story of one company's struggles, over a long period of time, to do something about ideas of this nature which lay around in the organization for nearly two years before the strength was found to use them. The story is not complete – in a sense it is never ending – and the ideas are still developing. The ideas were entirely strange to them and it took all this time for managers to unveil for themselves the deceits of traditional management education (which we management educators have perpetrated for so long) and get on with the real job of management education, which is transfer of learning from one work experience to the next.

PART II ONE COMPANY'S STRUGGLES WITH THE TWO TRANSFER PROBLEMS DESCRIBED IN PART I

Ideas without a Name

A chemical company in which I am working as a consultant has taken the brilliantly simple idea that managers learn better with and from each other and has used the idea without once saying 'action learning' let alone 'action learning programme'. This company has made an interesting and brave attempt to pull itself up by its own management development bootstraps for a few years, with a fair degree of success: training is happening; appraisals are happening; individuals are developing. But still there seemed to be something missing – some central forum – a place where management could be talked about. Management ideas needed an eighteenth century coffee shop in which they could be aired, exposed, challenged, and reinforced. In short the company felt the need for a tradition – and set out to create one.

I had clear memories of a pivotal course we ran in Reed International (Casey and Berger, 1973) which turned out to be the seedbed for ideas about management style, teamwork, and leadership in that company. Now the idea began to take root in my client company, of a basic, backbone course – of say two weeks – which would represent the starting point for all young managers in their exploration of management ideas. It would not replace other specialist courses for individuals, where specific techniques could be learned, but it would begin to form a base of management ideas, from which we hoped a tradition and a culture would spring.

Many managers had doubts – a forum for debate was all very well they said, but how would managers apply the concepts and ideas back at work?

Application Groups

Then the idea slowly began to emerge of *Application Groups.* If application groups could be organized after the course to focus on the application to real work problems of whatever skills had been learned, managers would be able to help each other jump the gap from course-to-work. And if the application groups could continue meeting regularly for a comparatively long time – perhaps up to a year – managers would be able to help each other take succeeding hurdles in their stride as they battled over the more gruelling track of transferring their learning from experience-to-experience, at work. We thought once a month was a minimum requirement for meetings. If the level of trust was high and the small application groups were sufficiently bonded, commitment to meet would be high. What would they do?

At this stage we were not sure. We felt each person should feel responsible for his own destiny and yet the application group as a group would clearly be responsible for something. To make matters more difficult the person's boss would have to be engaged in some very meaningful way → *application on the job* would be a meaningless phrase without the boss's full involvement.

Individual Contracts

Suppose we asked each participant to negotiate a contract with his boss which defined exactly what he would achieve in his application group? This would link his boss into the whole process of his development. It would also give him a goal, expressed either as a business goal or a development goal. At this stage in the debate an interesting shift had occurred in company thinking. No longer was the two-week course the main thing – several perceptive senior people were beginning to see the application groups as potentially more valuable. In their minds, what had started as the follow-on to a course was now being viewed as the real development activity, to which the opening course would be no more than the curtain-raiser.

The idea of an individual contract between each participant and his boss took some time to gestate. Eventually it became explicit in a document reproduced verbatim in Appendix I. But that came later. Before we could create such a clear-cut document there were anxieties ahead. Some of those showing anxiety were the personnel and training people in the company.

A New Role for Personnel and Training Specialists

It will be seen from the contract document in Appendix I that a special role eventually emerged for the four company personnel and training people. Their job would be to help the learning along. We avoided referring to them as trainers, because we did not wish their role to become tutorial; they were encouraged to focus on *processes.* The idea behind this is that if management learning is to be transferable from one experience to the next, not only must the experience be a whole-person experience – the person must also be able to see the *underlying form* (Pirsig, 1974) or the underlying *processes* (Casey, 1978) taking place. The recognition of these underlying processes is the cognitive bridge required for learning transfer (see Part I). It is only these underlying processes which are sufficiently general to be transferable from one unique experience to the next.

The personnel/training staff were to increase awareness of processes taking place in two places: in the application groups themselves, and in each personal task (see Appendix I). In the application groups the processes would be interpersonal – task processes and maintenance processes – as in any working group. In each personal task the processes would be what I have called elsewhere *managerial processes* (Casey, 1978). So the personnel/training facilitators would have to keep their wits about them and it became clear to us that the four personnel/training specialists would themselves need training if they were to perform this difficult facilitating role well. At first this seemed like a major obstacle to further progress – nor was it the only obstacle in our path.

Three Difficulties

Three main problems began to bug us about this time:

1. Most managers still expected a course. This is our fault, but they still expected it!
2. How were we to get started? Some sort of legitimization was needed. It seemed somehow awkward to get groups of managers to start sharing difficulties of application of management skills in the proposed application groups. Isn't this what managers did every day at meetings? Why some special 'application groups' in addition? Wasn't it taking learning away from work, yet again? The ideas were fragile and hard to keep in focus. I was grateful to Lenin for the one thing I remember him writing: 'It is necessary to know at every moment, how to find the particular link in the chain which must be grasped with all one's strength in order to keep the whole chain in place and prepare to move on resolutely to the next link' (Carr, 1950). The link I felt I had to hold on to was the central belief that these managers could learn from each other and from their work – they did not need any management experts. But they still had to get started.
3. The four personnel and training people needed training for this new role. How were they to get it?

All three problems were accepted by the company as opportunities and challenges. Acknowledging managers' expectations for a course, we decided to put on a course for one week but not two. This satisfied expectations for a course and also enabled us to get started by legitimizing the whole process. Running a course may sound like a denial of the arguments put forward so far in these notes. There were, however, other valid reasons for a residential week in this organization, apart from satisfying expectations for a course. The other reasons are concerned with the nature of my intervention as an OD consultant to the total organization and the need to get the managing director and senior managers involved in management development. But these OD considerations are beyond the scope of this article, concerned as it is with transfer of learning – in this case transfer of learning of the course participants.

Recognizing that the personnel and training people needed training we designed a parallel training programme for them during the first week's course. We were now moving towards an overall strategy which attempted to cope with all three problems.

An Overall Strategy Emerges

Criteria for selection were established and 20 junior managers were invited to take part, first time round. The one-week residential course was to be followed by six one-day meetings of the application groups, one a month for six months. There was no special ending event, our belief being that if application to work had been achieved, there would be nothing to have an event about. The whole six months can now be drawn as in Figure 7, using the same symbols as before, with arrowheads for transfer of learning. Notice that transfer of learning arrowheads are absent in the first work experience sequence from 16 to 19 and no transfer is claimed immediately after the course. However, in the sequence 21 to 26 the transfer is achieved via the application groups. This builds into a habit for each manager and in subsequent work experience sequences, from 27 onwards, transfer takes place without the help of application groups. The long-term achievement, therefore, is to enable each manager to maximize the learning opportunities of his future managerial life.

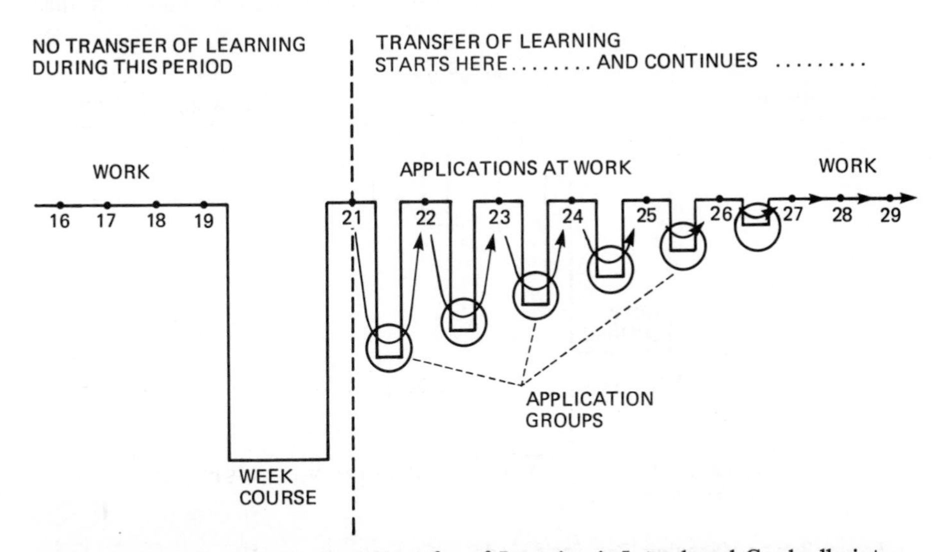

Figure 7. Overall Strategy: how Transfer of Learning is Introduced Gradually into Daily Work

During the life of the application group (sequence 21 to 26) a gradient is assumed to occur. At first the application groups will feel akin to the course, since the groupings are unique to the course and did not exist in the organization before the course. In the early stage application groups will feel an affinity to the course culture and at a psychological distance from work. As the monthly meetings progress, the content of application group discussions will be the work of each individual, taken in turn, and this will gradually close the gap between the application group discussions and the day-to-day work of each member, so that by the time sequences 26 and 27 are reached the gap will have vanished. This could not happen if members were working on projects separate from their daily work. The diagram in Figure 8 was in essence created by the managing director who was the only one shrewd enough to see that sequences 27 onwards were the only ones that mattered in the long-run and it was he who insisted on calling the sequences from 27 onwards 'Phase III', where the rest of us had been thinking of two phases only – course plus application groups. The managing director's model of the whole activity is shown in Figure 8.

The Opening Course is no longer What it Seems

In all of this excitement about application groups we had lost sight of the opening course! The overt aims of the opening course were to develop some management skills, but senior management came to realize that the really important underlying aims were first to *form the small application groups* and second to provide a learning arena for the personnel and training people to learn their new role as facilitators. In other words, the one-week course were nothing more than

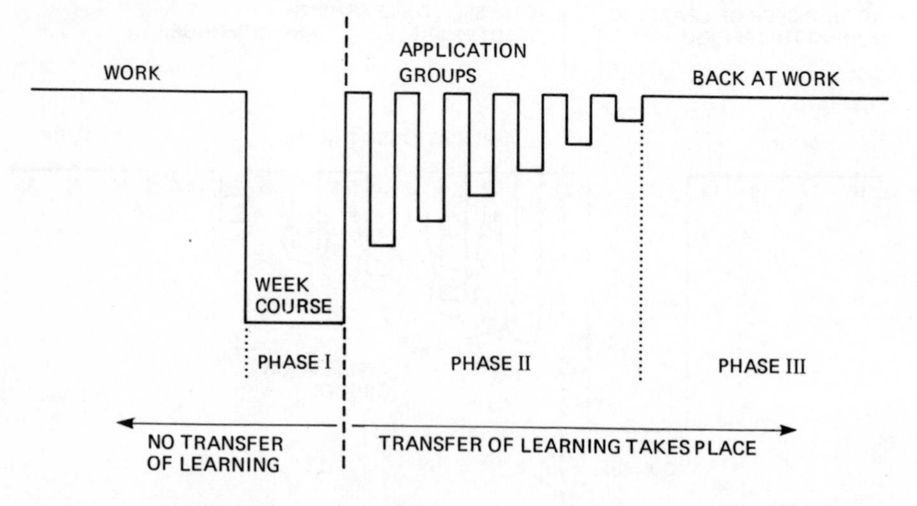

Figure 8. The Managing Director's Model – Including Phase III

preparation for the application groups (and incidentally it would satisfy managers' expectations).

The one-week course was to be taught by line managers from the company. They would teach management skills to the 20 junior managers split into four groups of five. The groups would come to function as teams during the course. Once they had worked together for this week, with some process consultation provided by the personnel and training people, they would later become the application groups where the real learning would take place – on-the-job – managers learning with and from each other. The idea of this course had overcome our second difficulty of getting started with application groups and had somehow legitimized the application groups as different from everyday meetings.

We prepared for the opening week knowing that it had to feel good to the participants in terms of skill development but deeply aware that the real purpose, and the real test, was whether this week could achieve two things:

1. Formation of application groups
2. Training the four personnel and training specialists for their special role as facilitators in the application groups.

The design of the week therefore gave over the major part of every day to practical work in the groups of five. Practical skill-development exercises were devized and run by company line managers who were the teachers during this week. During the formal teaching and practical exercises the personnel and training people sat in, beginning to operate in their new role as facilitators – a role which was to become crucial in the following six months.

In describing this week as a vehicle for forming application groups and training group facilitators, I am aware of seeming to throw away the value of any skill development resulting from the exercises. This is quite deliberate and emphasizes my belief that skill development for managers is not useful if carried out separately from the job, because management is such a whole-person activity. However, there were enormous benefits of an OD nature derived from this week, e.g. the total involvement of the Managing Director and his senior colleagues in designing the week, preparing talks and exercises, and managing the week's work. Again, I make only passing reference to the OD dimension in this article, because the article is concerned with transfer of learning and for this purpose the focus is on the participants.

Because I do not believe that learning developed in a one-week management course is transferable to work, I have not described the content of the week in any detail. For this purpose the week was not useful (to be *useful,* learning must be transferable to work). However, I would like to describe briefly how we tried, during this opening week, to equip the training and personnel staff with transferable skills for *their* new facilitating roles in the application groups.

Training the Facilitators

From early experience of action learning (Casey and Pearce, 1977) I felt that the three internal personnel and training people who were available together with a selected line manager, did possess the personal characteristics and motivation required for the role of facilitator in each small group. They would work in the opening week with one group during practical skill-development exercises and they would stay with the same group for its further six-month period as an application group. They would play the role of catalyst/process consultant/set adviser/facilitator, using what skills they had plus any additional skills and insights which could be added during the first week by means of a parallel training programme specially designed for them. I was asked to undertake the parallel training programme.

The community consisted of four elements:

Participants
Company Line Managers as Trainers
Personnel/Training People as Facilitators
Myself as Consultant

During the first week, line managers would train the participants, and this process would be catalysed by the personnel/training specialists. I was to train the personnel/training people, acting as 'consultant-to-the-consultants'. This second-order shadow consultancy role (Schroder, 1974) is, incidentally, a very satisfying role and is consistent with my philosophy as a consultant of doing only that which cannot be done from within the client system.

Before the whole adventure started I ran a couple of seminars for the four facilitators and they did some reading. During the first week (see Figure 9), it seemed sensible to use the same learning model for the facilitators' parallel training programme as we were using for the participants themselves. We would then be modelling the message to some extent and reinforcement was likely. During the day, while line managers were teaching participants, and facilitators were catalysing this process, I circulated round the four learning groups, observing the facilitators in action.

Every evening, while the participants were having dicussions with top management, the four facilitators met as a group, to exchange experiences and learn with and from each other – this time I acted as facilitator to them. Since the learning design for the facilitators themselves was a replica of the learning design for the managers' groups, there were two levels at which the facilitators learned: (i) by getting help from their peers on their direct task of facilitating; and (ii) by experiencing a learning group at first hand as a member.

At the end of the first week the facilitators felt ready to act in this capacity once a month for the second phase – in the same groups which had now become application groups. In this period I would visit the company once to enable them to

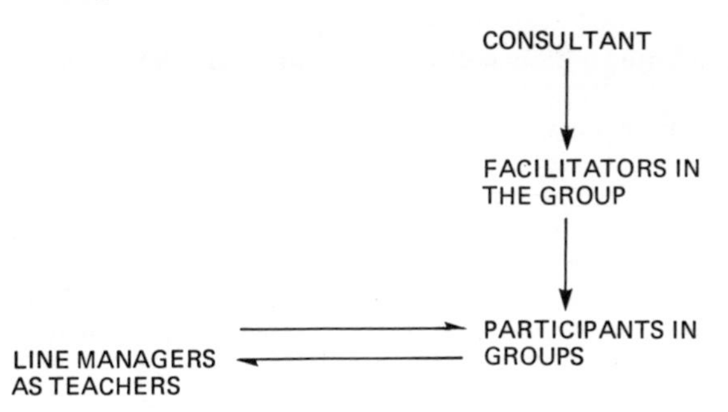

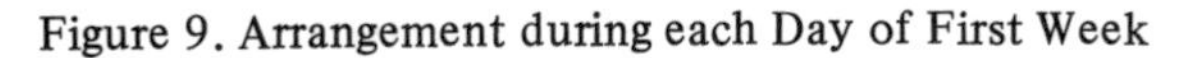

Figure 9. Arrangement during each Day of First Week

review experiences together, although there was nothing to stop them doing this among themselves without my being there, if they found the need to touch base together.

Experiences and Conclusions to Date

It is impossible to draw firm conclusions from an activity still going on. Experiences to date are encouraging and on-going changes are being made by the company to cope with emerging problems. The successes can be listed as:

- In two years the company has moved from doing almost nothing about management development, to enthusiastically mounting a regular internal development activity of some significance. The second and third activities are scheduled. It would seem that the creation of a tradition is well under way.
- The activity is designed and run internally. The managing director feels it is his programme and he is seen by the company at large to have ownership of it. Heads of functions (Finance, Marketing, R & D, etc.) feel responsible for presenting each day of the opening course, leading their own teams of specialists in doing this.
- Company personnel/training staff are working in a new and challenging role as facilitators of application groups in the second phase. This has enhanced their own development as educators, the relations between each other, and their relationships with their colleagues.
- The benefits of the opening week have not been limited to what the company expected (management skills) nor what I expected (formation of application groups and facilitator training). This quotation is from a line manager after the opening week:

  'Commercial managers from the course have been much more willing to consult with or involve other departments, now understanding how they are affected, the benefits to be gained, and how best to go about it.

Two plant managers on the course responded very well to manufacturing services' request for a reduction in stocks of parts, etc. They now more readily accept that the plant difficulties involved are outweighed by benefits to the Company.

Course members now move more confidently in other areas of the Company using other course members as contacts. I do this myself.

The three course members from my own department have all benefited a great deal. Bill and Andy in particular now see their jobs and scope of influence and effect in a very different way. I have noticed them practising their group skills in routine meetings.'

– The line manager who acted as a facilitator, wrote after the first few meetings of his application group in phase II:

'The group very quickly re-found the skills developed during phase I. It was very interesting again to observe the relationship between the two impetuous group members and how the others reacted. All showed a great deal of interest in the other group members' projects and became even more enthusiastic once they had identified as individuals how they could play a constructive role. This they found much easier for some projects than for others.

All five recognized the learning potential for them from the projects. The group had some difficulty in controlling the rate of progress. At the start it did appear that they intended to complete all projects at one meeting. Once they had recognized this problem and discussed it they did settle down to a comfortable and realistic pace.

The true value of phase II has now been realized. It has not been easy over the last three months to think about phase I, to use and develop the knowledge and skills gained. Without phase II much of the benefits gained would have been lost.'

However, all is not plain-sailing and problems have arisen. Since the second activity with new participants is going to start before the first ends, overlapping by several months, there is every opportunity to adjust, as experience is gained. (The learning transfer model applies to those running the activity, just as it does to participants.) Two of the more important lessons learned are these:

– Bosses of participants were not involved enough. This resulted in some participants being pulled in different directions in phase II, their bosses expecting normal work, whilst their application group expected devotion to the personal task. The deep involvement of bosses in phase I seems necessary to prevent this dichotomy arising in phase II.

– The facilitators' lack of experience is showing through in places. Inexperienced facilitators can allow application groups to look outside the group to the 'then-and-there' for solutions to group failures – such as sluggish work – when a more experienced facilitator would insist on focusing on the 'here-and-now' dynamics of the group itself as the only sure way of solving the group's internal problems. To help in the solution of this kind of facilitator problem the four facilitators have come to realize how vital it is to meet regularly as a group of facilitators and share concerns. Whether this 'set of facilitators' needs the on-going services of a 'facilitator-to-the-facilitators' remains to be seen.

RESEARCH NEEDED

The opportunities for pragmatic, usable research in this field are boundless. Many of us are blundering forward without the support of the research findings we urgently need. The three topics which follow, are suggestions only, picked out to give the flavour of the kind of issues which need to be researched:

1. *What makes a good facilitator?* From my limited experience I am beginning to think that a really competent small group trainer will make *any* set or application group a really useful learning experience for the members. Less experienced small group workers may need *either* excellent personal tasks in the group – very carefully chosen – *or* a high level of commitment from the task clients, whether they are the bosses of the participants or not. It would be valuable to know if this is the case.
2. *Is the assumption contained in Part II of this article valid* – that application groups dealing with personal tasks which are closely bound up with participants' jobs, will experience a gradient of feeling; a gradual moving *away from* the community of whatever opening event took place, *towards* the ambiance of their jobs? The assumption continues that learning transfer will then take place from one job experience to the next job experience. This needs to be checked out by research. It is important, because if it is true, any project which is not part of a person's normal job is not a useful task for this kind of management education experience, however cleverly contrived.
3. *How frequently should application groups meet?* Are there any criteria an application group can use to decide on the periodicity of its meetings?

These, and other questions like them, are being asked by more and more people in management education. Between us, our experiences are growing to quite a formidable level, and yet I know of very little attempt to collect together the evidence and to research such questions, so that we can begin to feel some more solid ground under our feet.

REFERENCES

Baumgartel, H. and Jeanpierre, F. (1972). Applying knowledge in the back home setting, *Journal of Applied Behavioural Science,* **8**, (2).

Carr, E.H. (1950). *The Bolshevik Revolution,* Penguin.

Casey, D. (1976). The emerging role of set adviser in action learning programmes, *Journal of European Training,* **5**, (3).

Casey, D. (1978). Project training for managers – the underlying paradox, *Journal of European International Training,* **2**, (5).

Casey, D. and Berger, M. (1973). Leadership training can have factory payoff, *Journal of European Training,* **2**, (2).

Casey, D. and Pearce, D. (1977). *More than Management Development – Action Learning at GEC,* Gower Press.

Garratt, B. (1977). Don't call me teacher, Chapter 11 of *More than Management Development – Action Learning at GEC,* Gower Press.

Owen, T.B. (1971). *Business School Programmes – the Requirements of British Manufacturing Industry,* BIM.

Pirsig, R.M. (1974). *Zen and the Art of Motor Cycle Maintenance,* Bodley Head.

Schroder, M. (1974). The shadow consultant, *Journal of Applied Behavioural Science,* **10**, (4).

Vandenput, M.A.E. (1973). The transfer of training, *Journal of European Training,* **2**, (3).

APPENDIX I INTERNAL COMPANY COMMUNICATION QUOTED VERBATIM

Basic Management Course – the Phase II Contract

Phase II is quite complicated, although simple in design. Each *Application Group* consists of 5 course participants plus a facilitator. Each participant has a *Personal Task.* It is his own task, for which he is totally responsible – the group help him, but do not take over his responsibility. In the final analysis he does his *Personal Task* in whatever way he decides – even if this means going against the recommendations of the Group.

His Personal Task is set up by negotiation between his boss and himself in the fortnight after phase I, before the first group meeting in phase II. It may be a concentrated attempt to develop one or more of the skills highlighted in the phase I week; it may be a project; it may be a defined part of his job; or indeed his whole job. Whatever his *Personal Task* is, he must agree it with his boss and *it must be committed to paper* for clarity and understanding. In a sense it is a contract – the participant agrees to achieve certain goals (business goals or development goals) in six months and his boss agrees to help and support him, knowing that the *Application Group* will also be making every effort to help and support him as well, without taking away his responsibility.

So in each *Application Group* there are five *Personal Tasks.* There is also a *Group Task.* The *Group Task* is different. It is to help each individual member perform his *Personal Task.* The group does not carry corporate responsibility for any individual's *Personal Task;* it does carry corporate responsibility for helping him.

Finally, there is the *Facilitator.* His job is to facilitate maximum individual *Learning,* and also maximum help from the group to each participant. The facilitator will try to ensure that each individual learns all he can from his *Personal Task,* consolidating the learning from phase I, working in some defined relationship with his boss – the exact relationship will depend on the *Personal Task.* He will learn something about how groups work. He will learn something about himself and how others see him. His tutors in all this will be his boss, company experts, and his peers, aided and abetted by the personnel specialist in his group. The potential to learn is there; each participant must himself take advantage of that potential.

The end product will be a manager more skilful in whatever defined area of management skill his boss and he contracted to improve during phase II of the Basic Management Course.

Advances in Management Education
Edited by John Beck and Charles Cox

CHAPTER 19

Promoting Useful Management Learning: Problems of Translation and Transfer

Don Binsted, Roger Stuart, and George Long

SECTION I

LEARNING AND ACTING

Much emphasis is apparent in recent years of the need to educate, train or develop managers, (Leggatt, 1972) (Department of Industry, 1977). Such development may aim to improve performance in some current work role or prepare the person for some different and generally more demanding role. The emphasis on 'learning to carry out a role' may seem to focus learning to an undesirable degree in the eyes of a liberal educator. Nevertheless, this is the business most of us find ourselves in. Thus management development is concerned with both learning and acting (managing) and not with learning alone. This section explores some ideas about the relationship between the two, and is the first of a trilogy. Section 2 explores some strategies and tactics for designing suitable learning events. Section 3 explores some specific designs which link learning and acting.

TRANSFER AND TRANSLATION

The notion that acting and learning are two different things is supportable by dictionary definition at the least. The notion that acting and learning may be connected, is also widely accepted, but in the management development field, this becomes an imperative. The question for the management trainer or teacher is 'how is this connection accomplished?' First let us introduce two concepts which link action and learning.

1. *Transfer.* The concept of transfer of learning into the job situation is well-established, and is often described as a problem, e.g. 'how to ensure that learning on the course is transferred into the job', (Bylham and Robinson, 1977; Stiefel, 1974; Huczynski, 1974, 1978). 'Transfer' is thus to do with 'how learning is used to modify action in the context of the manager's role'.

2. *Translation.* The concept of translation of desired action into learning is much less recognized although the problem which is involved is all too apparent. This problem may appear in the form, e.g. 'how to decide what has to be learned to improve performance', or 'what learning is relevant to a manager's role', (Huczynski, 1978). Translation is thus to do with 'how action (hoped for) dictates what learning is appropriate'.

Thus it can be suggested that transfer and translation as defined above are *reciprocal connections between learning and action* (see Figure 1).

It is suggested further that both are necessary for achieving successful development of managers, (e.g. improved performance). Failure of *either* will result in the learning and the acting becoming separated. If for example there is poor perception of what has to be learned to improve performance, (poor translation), then however effective the learning process, transfer of learning to improve that area of performance will be poor.

TYPES OF LEARNERS

The model developed so far of reciprocal transfer and translation makes no reference to the most important element of the situation, e.g. the *learner.* Indeed this appears to be a neglected element in some of the work in this area. Thus Huczynski (1977) focuses on the important aspect of the organizational climate, and the development of application skills (1978). Stiefel (1974) cites factors such as similarity between seminar learning and the job environment, organizational barriers, time and congruence between learning intensity, and required behavioural intensity.

Variations between individual learners is also an important factor to be considered. A number of ways have been proposed for differentiating between various types of learners, or learner characteristics, for example the Kolb learning style indicator, (Kolb, 1971). This measures certain dimensions, (concrete experience,

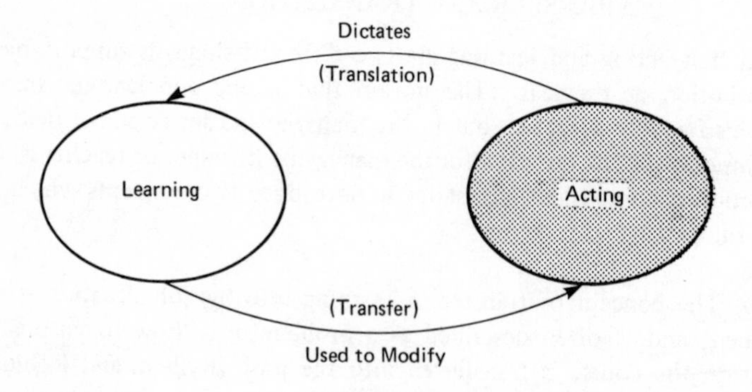

Figure 1

reflecting observation, abstract conceptualization or active experimentation) which differentiate between four dominant styles of learner, viz. convergers, divergers, assimilators, and accommodators, (Kolb, 1977).

The Self-Developing Manager

We would like to postulate a particular learner who seems to exist at least in some people's minds as some sort of ideal person. Since we attempt to describe an ideal, the extreme end of some dimensions, inevitably there will be some element of caricature; but this should not divert attention from the seriousness of the intention to describe a model of an ideal. This learner is the *Self-Developing Manager.* He is the person who always learns from his experience, swiftly and *correctly*. He never makes the same mistake twice. In a few weeks he seems to learn what others take years to learn, or never do at all. For him acting and learning seem to be not only simultaneous but synonymous, as in Figure 2. His method of solving problems is

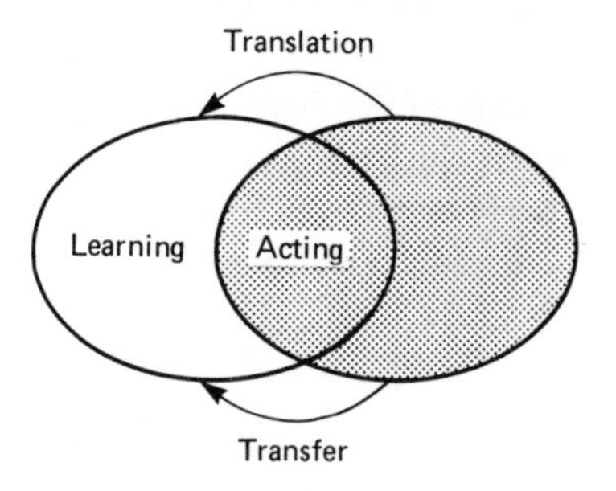

Figure 2

represented by Kolb's cycle of learning, (Kolb, 1971, 1977), (see Figure 3). His learning is balanced, continuing, pushing forward into new concepts, experiences, etc. He discoveres things, which lesser mortals would pass over. He is experimental by inclination, learns from his mistakes which are never disasters, but stepping stones to more learning. He senses what he does not know and is able to interrogate

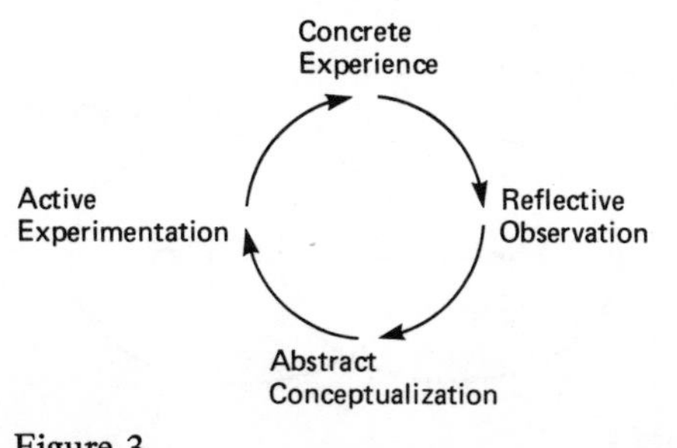

Figure 3

bodies of knowledge efficiently, whether these be in books, reports or his colleagues' heads. He is capable of deep reflection and has an ability to accurately conceptualize feedback and observation of his experience. He learns independently and is strongly motivated to improve performance and learn what is required to achieve that. He is self-aware, knows what effect he has on others, can read and interpret human interactions, of which he is a part. He will be aware of his own attitudes and values and the effect these have on his behaviour, and will achieve *affective* learning from almost any situation. Practice of a skill will improve it to a high standard compared with his colleagues. Above all he has an insatiable appetite to learn and grow psychologically and has a seemingly inexhaustible supply of energy to achieve it. Problems fascinate him, almost anything interests him. Because his action and learning are closely integrated, see Figure 2, his translation and transfer connections are strong and for him non-problematical. Such a person would require little formal management development.

Although there may be some element of caricature in the foregoing we can recall at least one person who fits such a model and many more who have many of the characteristics described.

Moving away from our paragon of the Self-Developing Manager (SDM) there are two other models of managers which are identifiable in terms of their learning preferences. These can most easily be recognized when they move temporarily from their work environment into a temporary learning environment such as a management course, workshop, or conference (see Figure 4).

The Expatriate

One type is identified by Benne, as the *expatriate* who comes to the learning event, and becomes fully and enthusiastically identified with it (Benne, 1976). *He learns a great deal,* the event opens up new ideas and horizons for his thinking, and he develops an ongoing interest which will perhaps stimulate learning in the future. However he fails to apply his new found learning in action in his role as manager. He does not see how the learning can be applied to his job, *but this does not particularly worry him;* he has learned a lot, and enjoyed the course. Based on the model in Figure 1 the *transfer connection* does not take place, as shown in Figure 5.

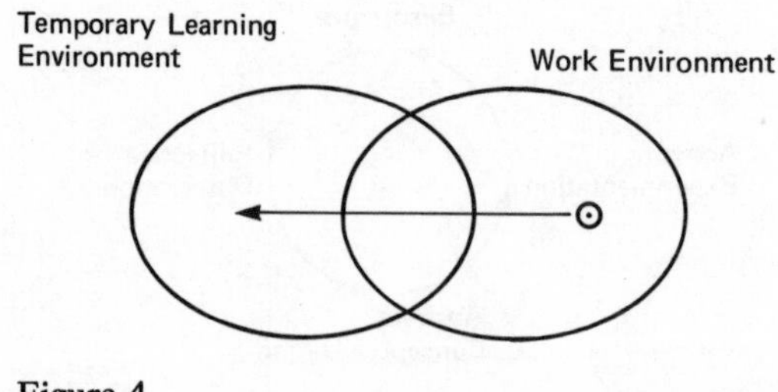

Figure 4

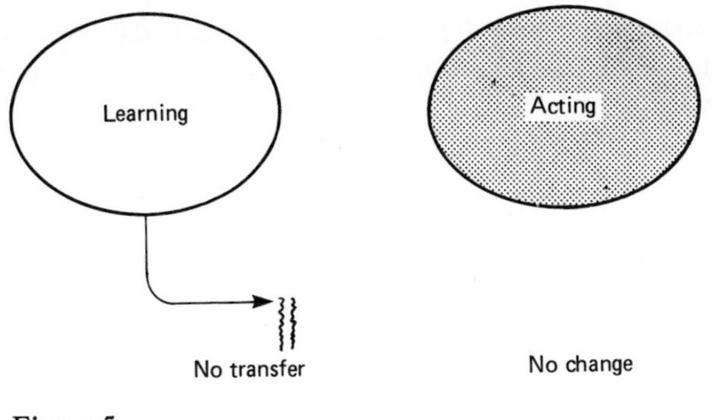

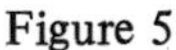

Figure 5

The Tourist

The other type is identified by Benne as the *Tourist* (Benne, 1976). He comes to the learning event determined not to become involved in the learning. He will seek to keep his distance from the other participants, the staff, and the contents. He is likely to emphasize how special are his back-home circumstances and vast his experience of the practical things of his role. He is likely to describe the learning event as academic, too theoretical, impractical, not relevant to his situation. He cannot see anything in the learning event which looks like his action situation. In his case this *does* matter to him, and will effectively cut him off from learning. In his case the *translation connection* does not seem to be present. Again based on the model in Figure 1 we could show the Tourist manager reaction as in Figure 6.

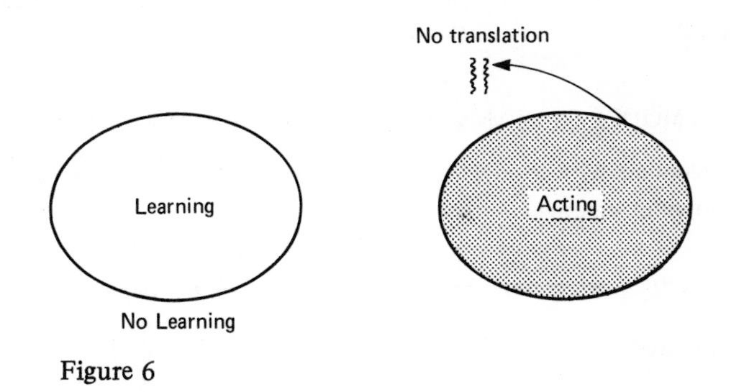

Figure 6

In both the case of the Tourist and the Expatriate in a learning event, the effect is the same; *learning and action are disconnected. Both* the connections, translation, and transfer are missing; but the start or cause of the breakdown is different. In the case of the Expatriate the learning occurs but is not *transferred,* whereas for the Tourist the learning is prevented by any *translation* link. He just does not see how what he does in role (action) is reflected or identifiable in the learning event.

The 'self-developing manager' previously described, if attending a learning event, will not react in either the tourist or the expatriate pattern. He will quickly see the relevance of what is happening in the learning event, i.e. he will identify his action situation in the learning event and thus can be said to have made a strong translation connection. Similarly when learning has taken place, having already been convinced of its relevance, transfer back into action will be highly likely. This embraces what Benne (1976) calls a 'Learner' reaction. In a learning event our Self-Developing Manager will have *both* strong transfer and translation connections as shown in Figure 7.

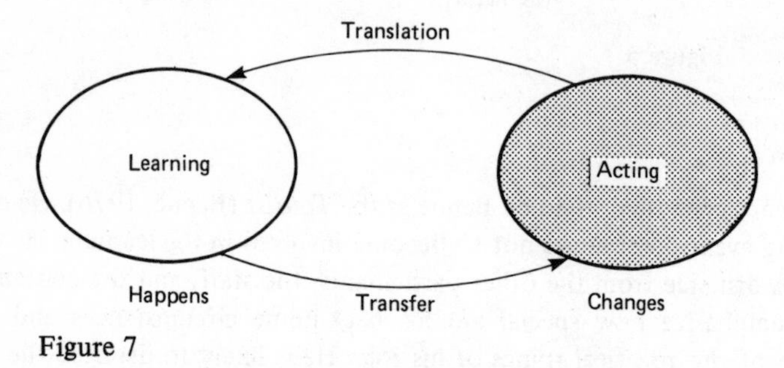

Figure 7

To make a point which is perhaps self-evident our model of a Self-Developing Manager (SDM) also makes him an ideal student or workshop participant. Again individuals may spring to the reader's mind. Thus the Expatriate and the Tourist in a learning event can be seen as *opposite reactions* and both are unsatisfactory for different reasons.

A MODEL OF MANAGEMENT LEARNER REACTIONS

The first element of a model of management learner reactions can then be a dimension shown in Figure 8.

Expartiate ←——————→ Tourist

Figure 8

The reactions of our Self-Developing Manager in a learning event include both the reaction of the Expatriate (full identification with the learning event) and the Tourist (full identification with the work situation). But *additionally* the reactions are satisfactory in the sense that learning and action are strongly connected. Thus the next element is a management learner model need to show the SDM reaction as a *synergystic addition of the reactions of both the Expatriate and the Tourist;* see Figure 9.

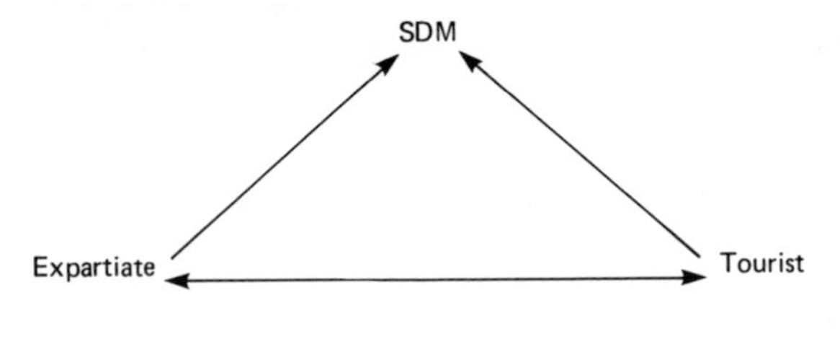

Figure 9

This releases us from the dilemma of an Expatriate–Tourist dichotomy which we would argue is dysfunctional. The model can be completed by recognizing a learner whose reactions are *mixed,* (some Expatriate and some Tourist) but who does *not* connect learning with action. Additionally there is one who does not react in *either* way, who does not appear to react at all, who may be described as '*Turned-off*'. These can be incorporated in a two dimensional model which contains the

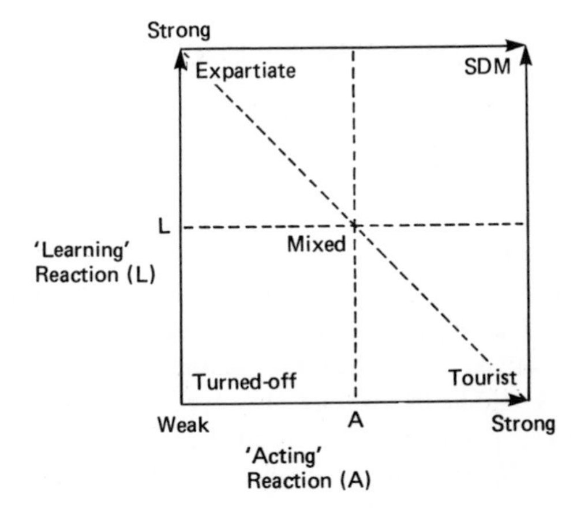

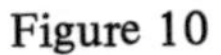
Figure 10

learner reactions already developed, as shown in Figure 10. The two *dimensions* can then be described as:

(a) Strength of a 'Learning' reaction. A strong reaction being associated with a high level of involvement and learning in the *learning* situation.
(b) Strength of an 'Action' reaction. A strong reaction being associated with a high level of involvement and learning in the *action* situation.

Thus the five categories of management learner can be summarised as in Table 1.

It must be noted that the dimensions of the management learner model in Figure 10 are 'reactions' of a learner in a learning situation. It is tempting to speculate that people have fixed orientations which correspond to these reactions but

Table 1

Strength of Learning Reaction (L)	Strength of Acting Reaction (A)	Category of Learner
Strong	Weak	Expatriate
Weak	Strong	Tourist
Weak	Weak	Turned-off
Moderate	Moderate	Mixed
Strong	Strong	Self-Developing Managing

such a model would be simplistic, suggesting that people's reactions would be fixed under all circumstances, and predictable, regardless of the design or type of learning event in which they found themselves.

DESIGN IMPLICATIONS

The model suggests that a management trainer or teacher running a learning event is likely to find some distribution of learners who react in the various ways described, the majority of whom (if the distribution is even) will *not* transfer learning readily to the work situation, for one reason or another. The more hopeful assumption is that although learners may join the course, workshop, etc. with a particular orientation, this and their reactions are likely to *depend on and change with* the design of the learning event, and also on the time engaged in it. If the goal of any management activity is to encourage learning which is transferable to the job, then a *meta-goal* could be to generate SDM type reactions from each learner to the extent to which this is possible, so that strong transfer and translation connections are made and learning is carried through to acting in the job role.

By considering the learner reactions model (Figure 10) and the learning and acting model in Figure 1 we can now make some propositions about how to accomplish this.

Proposition 1. For effective learning which is transferable to the manager's work role, the learner needs to make strong translation *and* transfer connections between learning and action, *for himself.* The trainer/teacher cannot do this for him. One aspect of this is the issue of ownership of learning goals or topics to be covered, in say, a workshop. High ownership would suggest a strong *translation* connection.

Proposition 2. For people exhibiting a strong learner reaction and a low action reaction *(Expatriate)* a *transfer* connection needs to be made (since it is this which is the primary cause of the unsatisfactory nature of his learning; see Figure 5). That is to say the learning which has occurred needs to transfer into action.

Table 2

Predominant *reaction* or orientation	*View* of learning environment		*Connection* which requires primary attention
	Learning event	Work situation	
Expatriate	Satisfactory	Unsatisfactory	Transfer
Tourist	Unsatisfactory	Satisfactory	Translation
SDM	Satisfactory	Satisfactory	Neither
Mixed	Partially satisfactory	Partially satisfactory	Indeterminate but some of each
Turned off	Unsatisfactory	Unsatisfactory	Both

Proposition 3. For people exhibiting a strong action reaction and a low learning reaction (Tourist) a *translation* connection needs to be made (since it is this which is the primary cause of low learning, see Figure 6). That is to say the action needs to be *translated* into the learning event so that learning activities are perceived as real, relevant, etc.

COMMENT

In both propositions 2 and 3, opposite strategies are suggested to initiate a change which will eventually lead to *both* connections being made as in proposition 1. Both strategies can be achieved by *high reality* learning events, (Binsted and Stuart, 1979), i.e. one in which the learner perceives a close relationship between the activities in the learning event and his work activities. For people exhibiting both a strong learner *and* strong action reaction, (SDM) *neither* strategies are called for.

Other differences which are of interest to the trainer or teacher are the ways in which people with predominantly fixed reactions or orientations are likely to view different learning environments. These can be summarized as in Table 2.

CONCLUSIONS

These models thus give clues to what might be effective strategies to facilitate learning which results in some change of behaviour within the job role. The overarching strategy suggested is to design management development activities which encourage learners to move towards exhibiting SDM reactions and conversely to discourage the other types of reactions. Thus design strategies will seek to facilitate translation or transfer connections or both. Which strategy is most needed can be ascertained by looking for potential and actual learner reactions. Suggestions about how to do this follow in Section II.

SECTION II

In this section we would like to consider the range of strategies and tactics which are, or could be, open to the designer of managerial learning events who is particularly concerned to overcome the problems of translation and transfer. Having identified the options open to the designer, we will present some of our ideas as to what underlies the various strategies and tactics – 'what makes them tick?'.

THE CONCEPT OF 'DISTANCE'

In Section I we discussed how a manager's learning and his acting may become separated, the translation and transfer connections being weak or missing altogether, and tourist and expatriate reactions observed. It is as if the experiences a manager accrues in, for example, a learning event belong to a different 'world' to that he experiences through acting in his work situation. The worlds of learning and acting are remote or *distanced* from one another. As represented in Figure 11, translation and transfer problems can be seen as the problems of connecting, linking two distant worlds. The greater the distance between the two worlds, the more problematic becomes their linking together. Strategies and tactics for facilitating translation and transfer problems can be seen, then, as ways of *reducing the distance between the experience of learning and the experience of acting.*

As we will go on to discuss later in this paper, the concept of distance is a complex one. Before we proceed any further in the disucssion, it is, however, important to distinguish between actual, objective distance and subjective, *'psychological distance'.* Hence, a learning event may *actually* be located in a hotel which is 200 miles from the place of work. This distancing *may* be seen and acted on as such, producing tourist and expatriate reactions. Thus, for the Expatriate being 200 miles from work might be a case of 'out of sight, out of mind!'. The SDM reaction, in contrast, is one in which the cue of, for example, physical distance does *not* produce a psychological distancing. Despite physical separation, the manager is able to transport himself, mentally, backwards and forwards from the learning experience to his work situation. In its ultimate form, the SDM reaction is one of being psychologically in 'both places at once'. Though physically distanced, for the SDM, the two worlds are *pyschologically close,* if not one in the same.

STRATEGIES AND TACTICS FOR REDUCING DISTANCE

In attempting to strengthen translation and transfer connections, the designer of managerial learning events utilizes the various strategies and tactics which will reduce the perceived psychological distance between learning and acting.

To reduce the tourist reaction and *facilitate the translation process it is necessary to 'take the job nearer to the learning'.* This strategy will be achieved by the manager being better able to see his work experience and problems reflected in the goals and

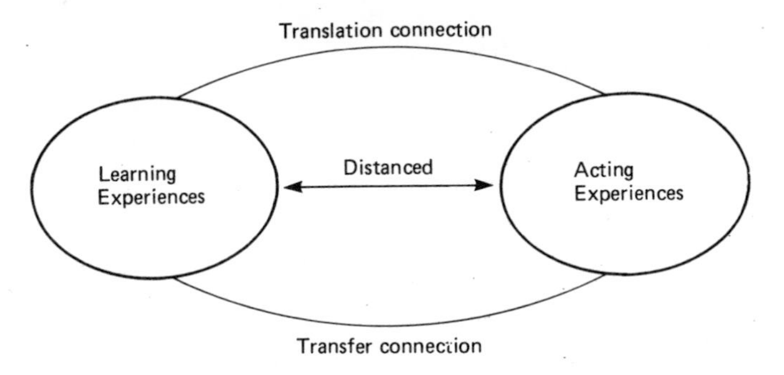

Figure 11

the activities of the learning event. The learning event will be perceived as relevant, that is, related to his real world of work.

To reduce the expatriate reaction and *facilitate transfer of learning, it is necessary to 'take the learning nearer to the job'.* In this strategy, the learner is enabled to identify his learning experience as being of direct use in the work situation.

What, then, are the development activities which appear to make significant and specific attempts – whether explicitly or implicitly – to reduce distancing between learning and acting? Rather than detail specific examples of such activities, we prefer to present a crude, but nevertheless we believe a useful, categorization of the range of strategies and tactics open to the designer of management learning events. This categorization is presented in Table 3. Five basic strategies are identified along with specific examples of some of their allied tactics. As will be seen from the Table, some activities strengthen translation connections, some transfer connections, and some both.

Many of the strategies and tactics referred to in Table 3 have been alluded to, and in some cases focused upon in other papers in this book. Our subsequent Section III will deal with some of the less commonly utilized tactics within this framework.

THE PROCESS OF DISTANCE REDUCTION?

So far in our discussion of transfer and translation problems, we have talked largely at the level of manifest characteristics, (Burgoyne and Stuart, 1977). Thus, we have described typical, observable learner reactions, and suggested a range of strategies and tactics which appear useful in terms of reducing both tourist and expatriate reactions and promoting SDM reactions. In suggesting the notion of psychological distance, we started to probe beneath the surface of these activities and to look at their underlying processes. Thus we saw the SDM reaction as one in which – despite apparent cues to the contrary (e.g. physical separation) – the manager was able to interrelate his learning and acting experiences. We would now

Table 3

Strategy	*Tactics*	*Connections most likely to be strengthened*	*Comment*
(i) *Integration* Learning Acting	e.g. Coaching; On job problem-solving; Job change; Special Assignments.	Translation and Transfer	Acting and learning indistinguishable, are one and the same activity
(ii) *Taking Learning to the Job*	e.g. Projects; Action Learning; Action Planning sessions; Creating a pull (e.g. superiors ownership, expectation of application); Learner centred de-briefings.	Transfer	Application of learning a part of the learning event, or planned before and during the event.
(iii) *Taking the Job to the Learning*	e.g. Clinics; Action Learning; Mini learning events; Problem definition sessions; Critical incidents.	Translation	Work problems identified before the learning events and/or brought into the event as vehicles for learning.
(iv) *Create a range of activities within the learning event*	e.g. Optional sessions; Modules; Choices; Resource 'Laboratories'; Learning Communities.	Translation	Allows learner to select activities most near to his work problems
(v) *Create Job based development activities*	e.g. Change/application opportunities; Licenced experimentation.	Transfer	Job is freed up, changed, enlarged, to facilitate experimentation and application

like to pursue this discussion further, and to put forward an abstraction which seems to move us towards a greater understanding of the transfer and translation processes. In particular we would like to flesh out what may be implied in the notion of psychological distance.

Cognitive psychologists (e.g. Horrocks and Jackson, 1972) have postulated that as we accrue experience in our lives, so these experiences are taken in, processed and built up into 'schema' or private 'maps of the world' as we have experienced it. These maps in their turn underlie how we interpret, attach meaning to, and subsequently act in new situations. These new experiences then themselves produce further data which is taken in and integrated, adding to ('assimilation') or modifying ('accommodation') our schema. This experiential learning process – learning through experience – is represented in Figure 12.

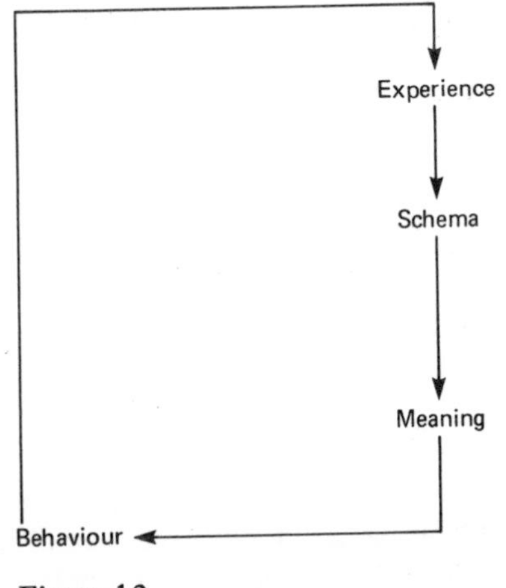

Figure 12

The maps which an individual builds up of his world are to varying degrees integrated with one another, some people achieving a greater degree of integration or 'wholeness' than others. To pursue the geographical analogy, some people's maps may be integrated at the level of continents, whilst others might be integrated at the level of individual countries. The extent of the implications that an individual can see for an event occurring in a state or county within one country will depend on the level or degree of this integration.

To bring us back to the worlds of learning and acting, it is our contention that the experiences accrued within these worlds can be interpreted on schema specific to these worlds (as represented in Figure 3) or on schema which integrate and transcend the two worlds (Figure 4).

Figure 13, we would suggest, represents the processes underlying the tourist and expatriate reactions. Here the maps of the learning and action situations are separate and distinct. Thus, the tourist reaction is one in which the manager is unable to

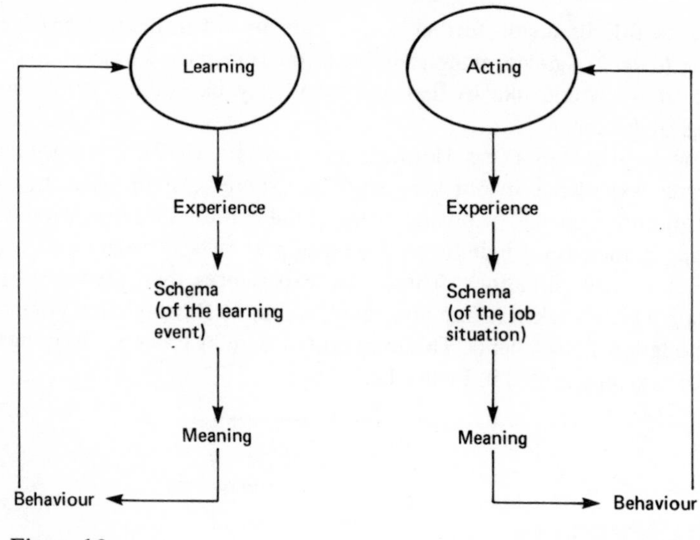

Figure 13

perceive the learning event from the (separate) schema of his work experience. That is, the translation connection is not achieved. Conversely, the expatriate reaction is one in which the learner fails to perceive/attach meaning to the work situation from the (separate) schema of his learning experience. That is, the transfer connection is not made. Figure 14 depicts the cognitive processes underlying the SDM reaction.

The schema derived from learning and acting have been integrated, and the learning and job experiences will be given meaning from the same schema base. Psychologically, the SDM's maps are not separate and distanced – consequently neither the translation nor transfer connections are problematic.

This abstraction, and the suggested processes underlying the erosion of psychological distance, has a number of implications for the strategies depicted in Table 3. For example, 'learner-centred de-briefings' – which may follow a behavioural simulation – may be seen as attempts to link the learner's experiences to his schema of the work situation. However, since each learner's life experience is likely to have been individual and unique, so too, then, will his maps be unique. Thus strategies such as de-briefing will only work to the extent that the *learner's rather than the trainer's, schema are invoked.* Ultimately the transfer connection is personal and individual, and cannot be done for him. Similarly will depend the success of coaching sessions.

To take another example, (and it is for the reader to invoke his own unique experiences and test them out on this framework) action learning projects (Mansell, 1975) will succeed to the extent to which the activities engaged in do not generate, and in turn are processed on, schema particular to the learning event but are processed by the schema which the manager has derived from his work experience. The extent of the translation and transfer problems will depend on the extent to which

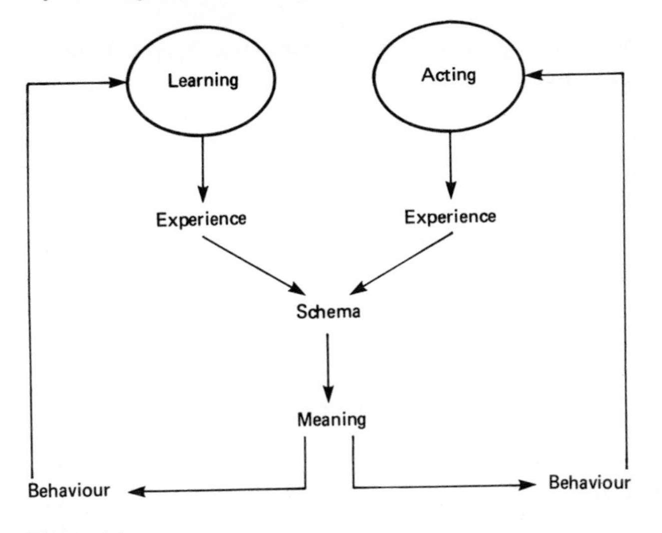

Figure 14

this is accomplished. On this basis, tactics such as putting the learner in a consultant rather than a managerial role, as an outsider rather than an insider, in an unfamiliar organization, though offering potential for a rapid and rich acquisition and building of schema, must be considered against the situations represented in Figures 13 and 14.

SDM REACTIONS, COGNITIVE MAPS, AND MANAGERIAL EFFECTIVENESS

It is consistent with our abstraction to suggest that the ease with which translation and transfer connections are made will depend ultimately on the richness of the maps that an individual has built up from his experience. This is not to suggest that other factors are not of importance. Thus, for example, the development and possession of transfer skills which facilitate the learner's interventions in the work situation are of obvious significance, (Huczynski, 1978). So too is building up the confidence of the learner so as to encourage him to actually attempt to apply his learning (Byham and Robinson, 1977). The identification of organizational factors hindering the enactment of learning in practice has been a further significant input into this area (Vandenput, 1973). Nevertheless, we would contend that of fundamental importance, a *sine qua non* in terms of facilitating useful learning, is for the learning and work experiences to be connected at the schema level. Further, that the development of these connections will depend upon the richness of the individual's schema.

The centrality of an individual's schema in understanding managerial activities is supported by Burgoyne's research, (Burgoyne, 1977). Researching the relationship between the self-development process, the possession of a rich cognitive map of managerial skills, and managerial success and effectiveness, Burgoyne found that '... the results give general support to the hypothesis that managers with *richer* cognitive maps of managerial skills and qualities are *more* effective and successful ...' He saw his results as offering '... weak support for the conclusion that a rich cognitive map of managerial skills and qualities is a part of the self-development process which *causes* managerial effectiveness and success ...' Thus the SDM reaction *may* be seen as one which not only makes light of the establishment of translation and transfer connections between learning and acting, but, even more pertinently, could be a mode of behaving which is predictive of perceived effectiveness in the job of managing.

IMPLICATIONS FOR RESEARCH

Much of the content of this section has been derived from our abstractions, observations, and experiences of practice, supported by the pertinent but scant theory in the literature. We would be the first to admit, and indeed advocate, the need for further research in this area. In particular, there is a *need for research which 'gets inside the learner/manager's head'*. Much of the previous research on translation and transfer has been devoted to exploring the objective context in which the learner/manager operates.

There is a need, then, to explore people's subjective, perceived world; to understand the basis on which they act or react; to identify what they take into and take away from their experiences. A side effect, but nevertheless an important consequence of such studies would undoubtedly be a *recognition of the uniqueness* of the learner/manager, for his schema are as individual as his life experiences and how he perceives them. A further implication would be to shift attention away from 'T' (the tutor, trainer, coach, etc.) towards 'L' (the learner/manager). At the end of the day, the resolution of translation and transfer problems rests with the learner/manager. Though integration of his schema can be facilitated, it *cannot be done for him.*

Finally, we feel that more research is needed to consolidate the suggested links between SDM reactions and processes, learning, and acting. As was stated at the start of Section I, the legitimization of researching into, and the practising of management development activities, comes ultimately from the acquisition of useable learning leading to improved proficiency in the managerial work role.

SECTION III

The first part of this paper argues that successful management education links and ultimately integrates the worlds of learning and action by ensuring that both translation and transfer connections are effected. In this context it is interesting that, in the literature at least, the problem of translation has been somewhat neglected. This is especially unfortunate since translation is the logically prior process and determines how the participant engages with a management learning event. The process of connection or engagement with its attendant problems will be a function of the mix of participant's learner reactions, the Tourist experiencing problems of translation, the Expatriate those of transfer, whilst the self-developing manager has reached the happy state of being able to connect and integrate by himself.

The second part of the paper discusses the strategies the management educator can use to reduce the psychological distance between a participant's schema or 'cognitive-map' of learning and action. The discussion is advanced by the categorization of a number of management teaching methods indicating the strategies that they can be used to promote.

In this part of the paper we would like to further the consideration of these ideas by examining their implications for the choice of teaching methods when designing management learning events.

A CHALLENGE FOR MANAGEMENT EDUCATION

One of the challenges then for the management educator is to make a judicious choice amongst the teaching methods he has in his repertoire, to ensure that individually or in combination they facilitate translation and/or transfer, and that this facilitation is not achieved to the general detriment of either of the learner reactions identified. Meeting this challenge, teaching methods require a certain robustness, contributing to the solution of two separate if related problems, whilst achieving their goals and maintaining their appeal to an audience which is most likely to be heterogenous in respect of the learner reactions it displays.

To meet this challenge the management educator must be able to identify the learner reactions of participants prior to observing their consequences. As mentioned earlier, reflecting on past courses, conferences or other learning events, we can often identify participants whose behaviour, in one or more sessions conforms to the broad descriptions, almost stereotypes, that have been outlined. Fortunately, a number of sources other than observation can also be used to estimate the extent and nature of an audience's heterogeneity. Evidence for the range of orientations can be gleaned from pre-event questionnaires. Such questionnaires, by identifying the balance of participants, are a useful aid when determining the particular mix of teaching methods which can be effectively used. Looking at questionnaire responses often shows the Tourist airing his concerns that the course will be full of jargon, which as if to compound the felony will be elaborated into 'airy-fairy theory' which may be the stuff of academic ivory towers but has scant value in the real world he lives in. Expatriate responses have a markedly different flavour and often revolve around the expectation that the course, workshop or whatever, will provide an opportunity for the real exploration of important issues, completely untethered from the chains of day-to-day routines and drudgery. Whilst these reactions, in their extreme forms, reveal an equally ill-balanced approach, the self-developing manager in his replies shuns neither theory nor practice but rather looks forward to an event which can justify itself by the short or long term impact it has on his job.

A further, retrospective, source of evidence comes from post event, reaction-type evaluations (Warr, Bird and Rackham, 1970). On re-examining some of our own post workshop data, we have found a tendency to be seduced by the enthusiasms of the Expatriate who saw the week, already in the past tense, as thoroughly interesting and refreshing. The worrying quality of these replies is the way in which the week is seen as an isolated self-contained event which is somehow insulated from the past and the future. We have also warmed to the response of the Tourist who reports that he has managed to collect a few useful ideas and techniques, ideas and techniques that are analogous to the souvenirs which sit on our mantelpieces after our holidays. Interestingly and less immediately satisfying, are the somewhat more circumspect and conditional responses of the self-developing manager who reserves his judgement until ideas and insights can be put into practice and stand the test of the 'cold light of day'.

Although not fully reported, these examples illustrate some of the re-interpretations which can be made of pre-course questionnaires and evaluation data, when examined from the viewpoint of learner reactions. Being able to identify these reactions before, during, and after the event is an important step in our ability to estimate the contribution particular teaching methods can make to learning event design.

PROBLEMS OF DISCUSSING TEACHING METHODS

Like all attempts to discuss teaching methods this one faces some endemic problems. The first is what can be called the STEIN fallacy. Whilst in some essential way it may be true that 'a rose is a rose is a rose', this becomes a dangerous half truth when applied to a discussion of teaching methods. The labels given to the various management teaching methods are general enough, the lecture, seminar, management game, role play, etc. These labels establish a currency in which the definition of the methods is treated as non-problematic. Even so we have all, for example, sat through lectures which demonstrate and use a wide variety of characteristics and media; indeed we have all probably given lectures or talks which if placed side by side would be so distinct, that the injustice of giving them the same label would be clear.

Although the labels given to various teaching methods are taken for granted, the veneer of certitude, with which the relative advantages of one method over another are compared, is readily punctured. In some small-scale research Crawford (1976) using management teaching methods as the elements of a repertory grid found an enormous variety of rather individualistic constructs that were for the most part only explicable in terms of respondents practice and experience. This diversity strongly suggests that the label we give to a management teaching method be it the lecture or action learning, is insufficient to convey the detail or the spirit of the event, and that this spirit is itself a function of the particular teacher and his audience.

A further problem arises from the fact that teaching methods are most frequently discussed in isolation. It is too easy to forget that in practice methods are used in contexts which involve long albeit broken sequences. Participants in management learning events have prior histories of experiences with various teaching methods and bring expectations and preferences which form part of the contract they establish with the teacher or trainer and which will facilitate or inhibit the successful use of the method on any particular occasion (Stuart, 1978). These expectations can themselves offer an indication of the participant's learner reaction. The Tourist often has an impoverished model of teaching methods. Most of the things he has learnt in the past, opposed to 'picking up from experience', come from school or college experience based on a staple diet of lectures given by subject experts with a degree of clarity and delivered at a pace just above that of dictation. The Expatriate by contrast revels in a wide experience of teaching methods although he tends to reject anyting which is not participative or experiential. Their preferences for methods and their stance on other educational issues shows the Tourist leaning towards Theory X and the Expatriate Theory Y (see Stiefel, 1975). Rather than labour the point it just seems easy to forget that the suitability of a teaching method will depend on the climate that is established and on the legitimacies of the situation as discussed in a rather different context by Steele (1976).

A problem allied to that of discussing teaching methods in isolation is to discuss them like patent medicines, a description of how to use the method is supplied with a list of its indications (advantages) though rarely with its contra-indications (disadvantages). The method is presented by its enthusiastic users as a panacea for all management education problems. The unwary teacher or trainer, following these testimonials often uses the method with disappointing results.

The management teaching methods in our repertoires form the building blocks of course design. Sometimes through time and other pressures we resort to a particular well-used case study, a good steady management game, our favourite role play. Often successful, the main dangers of this method of design lie in its susceptibility to unanticipated changes and the extent to which it prevents an accurate diagnosis of current participants' needs.

CRITERIA FOR ASSESSING TEACHING METHODS

Bearing in mind the general difficulties outlined in the previous section, what we need to do is to establish a series of criteria with which to judge a teaching method's ability to deal with the problems of translation and transfer and the heterogeneity of learner reactions it is likely to encounter.

To foster translation a method should have preceived relevance, gain commitment, be compatible with the goal of promoting participant's responsibility for their own learning, and be sensitive in its use of language.

The first criteria for successful translation is that the method should help participants use or see the relevance of their own action schema. The diagnosis of their everyday activity as managers is a crucial aid to the identification of what needs to be learnt. This diagnosis can be prompted by a reassessment of current satisfactions, with a view to further improvement, of dissatisfactions, with a view to remedy, or routines and procedures, with a view to removing the blinkers of current practice in an attempt to isolate or identify alternative courses of action. Through its goals, content or processes the method needs to harness the energies of the participants gaining their commitment to learn and take an active part in the event.

Even if it is initially teacher centered, like a lecture, the method, as was contended earlier in this paper, should be consistent with the aim of helping participants to take responsibility for their own learning. Not only by making the connection in a particular event, but also by developing the meta skills, to make connection unaided and through the integration of action and learning schema developing away from their current orientation toward that of the self-developing manager.

Particularly important is the method's use of language. There are many reasons for the use of technical language, not the least of which is its ability to express the nuances and subtleties of action which everyday language fails to convey. However, the more derogatory description of technical language, 'jargon', indicates a serious problem that course participants encounter. In the same way that real tourists seem unwilling to learn the language of the country they are visiting, Tourists on management programmes often see the use of non-familiar language as the first sign of the need for a siesta. Jargon turns people off precisely because it uses ideas which although they may have counterparts in the participants own schema are unrecognizable, alien, and foreign. Translation is difficult enough to accomplish with a shared language, almost impossible without one. Unless language is used in a sensitive fashion participants and trainers will spend their time talking at each other rather than to each other.

The problem of transfer has been widely recognized and the literature referred to earlier contains a discussion of the features of teaching methods and programmes which promote it. Rather than duplicate those discussions, we would like to focus on three of the characteristics that equip a teaching method to deal with the problem; they are its ability to take into account the organizational context in which learning is to be applied, the role reality of the method, and the extent to which learning and action are consciously and constantly related.

To ensure transfer, participants must have the capacity to carry learning forward into action; seen in this light transfer is a form of organizational intervention. In the same way that Blake and Mouton (1976) have identified external consultants using ideas and theory as an intervention strategy we need to acknowledge that our participants if they have learnt and changed their schema will face the problems of intervention when they try to apply their newly acquired insights. Teaching methods must recognize these difficulties and ensure that insights are not only judged according to their academic elegance but also in terms of their likely effects if implemented in the participants' organizations. The extent to which a method promotes speculation without attempting any 'grounding' is a measure of the extent to which it divorces its responsibility to directly tackle the problems of transfer.

If transfer is seen as a function of the participant's immediate, rather than his long term, activity it can be suggested that teaching methods should promote a degree of 'role-reality'. He should be encouraged to react as himself in his current job role, not as a student, nor as the hypothetical managing director of a hypothetical enterprise. Departing from this role reality may well cause frustrations when new ideas have been vetoed or snarled in the cogs of bureaucracy. The manager gets scant comfort from the rueful reflection that his good idea worked on the workshop.

As Huczynski (1978) points out leaving action planning to one session at the end of an event is a recipe for problems, although special sessions of one sort or another throughout the event is a partial solution. Ultimately the challenge is that every method used should eventually turn to the consideration of practical implications.

RETHINKING TEACHING METHODS

The second part of this paper indicates that some of the more recently developed management teaching methods, coaching, action learning, on-the-job problem solving, etc. have the potential to solve both problems. Whether this potential is realized will depend on the extent to which, in its execution, the method meets the criteria outlined above. As well as providing a framework for the assessment of new teaching methods, these criteria can also be used to reassess more widely used techniques, indicating their strengths and weaknesses, perhaps suggesting ways in which they can be modified. Rather than deal briefly with a wide range of methods, in the rest of this paper we would like to focus on two particular examples which have been used, with some success, to tackle the problem of translation. These methods are the incident process case study and the mini learning event.

INCIDENT PROCESS CASE STUDY

This is one of the family of methods that are known collectively as the case study. Within this family there are a wide variety of methods using a range of media, written, audio, and visual. There are also a number of process differences which become apparent when looking at the way the case study is used. Sometimes the teacher controls the proceedings, being located in the centre of a horseshoe of participants who are working as individuals. On other occasions syndicate groups make a series of presentations with the tutor making a few introductory and closing remarks.

Through the writings of Towl (1969), and others, the best documented tradition is that of the Harvard Business School. Even within that tradition there seems to be considerable variety. The academic descriptions have a very different flavour from the reports of one participant. Illustrating the private and individual nature of teaching Cohen (1979) describes the behaviour during a case presentation of his teacher McKay who brought

> 'a big fish to class. He had wrapped it into a newspaper and the newspaper into two layers of foil. He carefully pulled it out . . . and laid it on the newspaper for everybody to see. The fish had a reddish head and a yellow almost golden belly. "Here's what happens" McKay said pointing to the dead fish "to those who open their mouths at the wrong time".'

More seriously, through the Harvard tradition, the promotion of the International Teachers Programme, and its widespread adoption in Management Schools, the case study has established itself as an important part of the management education scene. Describing its advantages writers have made a number of claims which suggest its suitability with different learner reactions. It might attract the Tourist, if as Zoll (1969) claims, it offers the possibility 'of promoting effective understanding and analysis or real complex problems.' This attraction is somewhat reduced since the 'real' problems are only on the rarest of occasions the 'real' problems encountered by the participants. One of the case study's appeals to the Expatriate is its safety, since as Hayward (1974) argues, 'the essential purpose of a case is to enable students to take part in a real decision-making process without the costs (other than to personal esteem) of making mistakes.'

As a method the case study has been developing in a number of ways. Case writing courses have disseminated to teachers the skills of sensing critical management issues and preparing them for class discussion, especially in areas where there is a dearth of material. In attempting to deal with real complex problems cases have tended to become long and rather tortuous testing the patience of teachers and participants alike. So at the same time that the scope of case studies has been increasing a number of modifications have been suggested. Ehrenberg (1977) has attempted to reduce large cases, making them less wordy and simplifying the presentation of data. Other authors for example Dietzer and Shillif (1977) and Champion and Bridges (1969) have abandoned the long format and drawn up series of small mini cases based on management incidents.

These developments are essentially teacher centred. The teacher or trainer is seen as uniquely qualified in his ability to generate case materials. Zoll (1969) specifically warns us of 'one tendency learners have, when asked to report on their own cases early in a course, is to describe bizarre or very unusual situations.' This is a view we would disagree with. It is a dangerous assertion in so far as it inhibits the attempt to draw cases out of participants when as Foy (1978), we believe rightly, observes that 'in past experience of management education, every course member is a walking case if only he and his fellow members can be asked to look at the case.' This leads us to ask the question, can participants write useful cases? The greatest strength of the incident process case study, as developed by Pigors and Pigors (1961) is that it allows us to answer that question in the affirmative.

Predating Kolb, Rubin, and McIntyre (1971) by almost 200 years Paine (1776) argues that 'if we neglect to gather up experience as we go, we expend the knowledge of every day on the circumstances that produce it.' This quotation identifies one of the meta-skills we are attempting to develop in participants, a continuing sensitivity to events and the ability to learn from them. The incident process case study promotes and mobilizes this skill by first recognizing the knowledge that each participant on a course has as a result of his job experience. By formalizing some of that experience the incident process case 'captures' it so it can be shared with and examined by others.

The case is constructed by asking participants to go through four steps. Firstly, to think of a situation they have been involved in recently that contained an interesting incident, an important episode, something which perhaps heralded a change in a relationship, perhaps a surprising but illuminating statement or action that suddenly cleared up a nagging doubt about someone or something. A hallmark of the incident should be that it required the participant to respond, do something, or say something which affected the eventual outcome.

As a second step, bearing the incident in mind the participant is asked to write a few sentences which outline the background against which the incident took place. Where was it? What type of meeting was it? Was it the first time the parties had come together? What sort of atmosphere was there? The third step is to write a few sentences which describe the parties to the incident. What are their jobs? How old are they? Do they have any known quirks? What sort of mood are they in? Answering these and similar questions the participants are reminded to include themselves as parties to the incident. The fourth and last stage asks the participant to focus down on that part of the encounter or incident which made it notable, then to write a sentence or two which leads up to someone in the incident expecting them to respond. This may be what someone said. Did they pose a question? Did they make a challenging statement? Did they leave or close-up in some way? Did they surprise you by an unexpected request?

By going through these four steps, most participants can construct a small, usually half page study which contains a number of interesting issues. Two examples are given below:

Example 1: From a Postgraduate Student

At the company's Dumfries factory I was in the regular production planning meeting representing the marketing department. I was with the production scheduler who was about 50 years old and had worked his way up from the factory floor, and the assistant materials flow manager who was about 30. I was a 25 year-old marketing assistant.

Our current promotion required the production of certain items. The assistant materials flow manager kept on saying no. I was persistent and the exchanges got quite heated although not unfriendly. Eventually the assistant materials flow manager said he was under specific instructions not to produce the goods and left the room.

About five minutes later an argument approached the room, the assistant materials flow manager was accompanied by the manager who was again about 50 and was known to hate marketing. He stood over me and said 'Just who the bloody hell do you think you are coming up here with your damned ridiculous requests?'

Example 2: From a Training Board Adviser

I was making a regular visit to the director of a small company which had 12 staff in three branches. In keeping with previous visits the atmosphere was relaxed although I suspect she saw me as an intruding civil servant. We talked about training, merchandizing, and display. There was a natural pause in the conversation, she looked up, and said, 'While you are here perhaps you could tell us how soon a new branch ought to start paying for itself.'

These two examples are obviously rather different; the teacher or trainer can to some extent control the topics of the incidents by the initial instructions being focused on particular kinds of problems. Each of these examples took about ten minutes to write after a ten minute briefing.

When the cases have been written participants take it in turn to verbally present them. Then, depending on the size of the group there is a period for each member to ask one or two questions. These questions allow a degree of clarification and probing which help develop diagnostic skills. After the question time each member of the group has to present his solution: what he would have done in the circumstances that were outlined. The group then has the opportunity to compare their suggestions with what actually happened. This cycle of question, solution, and comparison can be repeated for each of the cases.

As a teaching method the incident process case study seems to have many appeals: its reality, the fact that the author is present, the opportunity to hear and discuss exactly what did happen. It seems to meet many of the criteria mentioned earlier: it has personal relevance, does seem to hold participants interests, gives them practice of some of the meta-skills required to move towards an SDM orientation, and is certainly in the appropriate language. In a way more formal case studies do not; this technique seems to generate an excitement and interest which is revealed in the pace and activity of the session. Because the trainer has not had the opportunity to prepare beforehand, he is clearly in the same boat as the other participants; he can only offer a reasoned view about what he would do in that situation. The similarity between the participants and the trainer's role allows the barriers between them to weaken and for the responsibility for learning to be shared.

THE MINI LEARNING EVENT

The mini learning event is another technique which allows participants to take their job to the learning. To call mini learning events a technique is something of a misnomer since it can have many forms, rather it is a process which enables participants to experiment and practice ideas with a view to solving the problems they encounter in their work activity. This process has been developed primarily for use in our workshops with management teachers and trainers. It consists of four stages: diagnosis, design, implementation, and review.

The workshop is split into groups of 4–6. Then with tutorial aid, if required, participants are asked to individually think of a problem they have in their work as a teacher or trainer. This could be a small recurring problem or a large infrequent one. The first part of the task is designed to help people to identify the problems they want to work on. The initial identification is followed by a further analysis to try to distil out the essence of the problem, to get to the heart of it, to strip away the extraneous.

The diagnosis completed, the participant has to design a learning event to help him explore the problem he has identified. A constraint upon this design is that it should last no longer than half an hour, this requires a further stage of refinement, miniaturization. The problem having been distilled out must be reduced in size until it can be meaningfully tackled within the constraint of the time allowed.

The design having been completed the participant implements his activity with the other members of his group. During this implementation the participant has to ensure that his participants will also learn something useful. They are not in any sense guinea pigs with one participant doing something to them, neither are they expected to role play; rather they are to be themselves and it is from that standpoint that in the post-event review they feed back to the designer their opinions as to what was achieved, how it was achieved, and how it could be improved. This review is of course two-way and allows the designer to check his assumptions, ideas, and design strategy, as well as giving him feedback on his achievements and interactive skills.

The mini learning event gives participants wide freedom in the types of event they design. In the past some people have used the opportunity to experiment with unfamiliar techniques, typically drawn from the experiential area. Other participants have in the past been more interested in processes and have designed events around issues like selling ideas to a potentially disinterested group, for example making a case for management development.

The only real constraint on the nature of the event is the imagination of the participants; past experience has suggested that amongst management teachers and trainers there is a rich vein of creativity. A number of fascinating designs have been enacted and judging from evaluation data it is a well-received process. In terms of organization there is a need for about two hours individual preparation time usually followed by between three and four cycles of half-hour events followed by a one and a half hour de-brief. The number of cycles required is usally less than the number of participants as people often either identify similar problems or want to try working on team designs.

The method again firmly hands responsibility over to the learner. He has the opportunity to spend time thinking about his work problems, reacting to them, and practising their solution. This process requires the connection of translation and through tutorial interventions specific problems which the Tourist may encounter can be picked up and dealt with. The Tourist has a chance to work on real problems in an exercise that is not a simulation, nor a role play, but a real event with peers as the audience.

Perhaps its major advantages as a method are in its ability to create a supportive climate in which experimentation is encouraged and in which mistakes can be discussed and rectified rather than punished.

CONCLUSION

In concluding this section of the paper we would like to add a reflection. Many of the teaching methods we use are implemented without consideration of the problems we have identified, being teacher centred and somewhat didactic at first sight they seem ill-equipped to contribute to the integration of action and learning schema. What then are the modifications that need to be made to them before they can help participants gain the meta-skills which distinguish the Self-Developing Manager from the Tourist and the Expatriate?

REFERENCES

Benne, Kenneth D., and Demorest, Charlotte K., (1976). Building the conference community, in Warner Burke and Richard Beckhard (eds), *Conference Planning* (2nd Edn), University Associates.

Binstead, D., and Stuart, R., (1979). *Designing 'Reality' into Management Learning Events 1. Towards Some Working Models,* The Centre for the Development of Management Teachers and Trainers, University of Lancaster. Forthcoming in Personnel Review.

Blake, R.R., and Mouton, J.S., (1976). Consultation, Addison-Wesley.

Burgoyne, J.G., (1977). 'Self development, managerial success and effectiveness: some empirical evidence', *Management Education and Development,* **8**, 16–20.

Burgoyne, J.G., and Stuart, R., (1977). 'Implicit learning theories as determinants of the effect of management development programmes', *Personnel Review,* **6**, (2), 5–14.

Byham, W.C., and Robinson, J., (1977). Building supervisor confidence – a key to transfer of training, *Personnel Journal,* May, **56**, (5).

Champion, J.M. and Bridges, F.J., (1969). *Critical Incidents in Management.*

Cohen, P., (1979). *The Gospel According to Harvard Business School,* Penguin.

Crawford, C.W., (1976). Some teacher perceptions of business teaching methods, unpublished MA Dissertation, University of Lancaster.

Dietzer, B.A., and Shillif, K.A., (1977). *Contemporary Management Incidents GRID INC.*

Department of Industry, (1977). *Industry Education and Management.*

Ehrenberg, A.S.C., (1977). Case Reduction, Proceedings of the Marketing Education Group Conference 1977.

Foy, N., (1978). The Missing Links: British Management Education in the 80's, Oxford Centre for Management Studies.

Hayward, C., (1974). Case study developments in the UK, *Industrial and Commercial Training,* 480–2.

Horrocks, J.E., and Jackson, D.W., (1972). *'Self and Role. A Theory of Self-Process and Role Behaviour',* Houghton-Mifflin Co., New York.

Huczynski, A., (1977). Organisational climates and the transfer of learning, *BACIE Journal,* June.

Huczynski, A., (1978). Approaches to the problems of learning transfer, *Journal of European Industrial Training,* **2**, (1).

Kolb, D., Rubin, I.M., and McIntyre, J.M., (1971). Learning Style Inventory, *Organizational Psychology An Experimental Approach.*

Kolb, D., and Plovnick, M., (1977). The experiential learning theory of career development, in John Van Maanen, (ed.), *Organisational Careers. Some New Perspectives,* John Wiley.

Leggatt, T.W., (1972). *The Training of British Managers: A Study of Needs and Demand,* NEDO, HMSO.

Mansell, C., (1975). 'Action learning at G.E.C.', *Management Today, UK,* May, 62.

Paine, T., (1776). American Crises, (quoted by Pigors and Pigors).

Pigors, P., and Pigors, F., (1961). Case Method in Human Relations: The Incident Process, McGraw-Hill.

Steele, F., (1976). Is organizational development work possible in the UK culture, *Journal of European Training,* **5**, (3), 105–110.

Stiefel, R. Th., (1974). Learning transfer strategies in management training, *European Training,* **3**, (1).

Stiefel, R. Th., (1975). Towards a more humanistic approach in management education, *MEAD,* **6**, (3), 156–65.

Stuart, R., (1978). Contracting to learn, *MEAD,* **9**, (2), 75–84.

Towl, A.R., (1969). To Study Administration by Cases, Harvard.

Vandenput, M.A.E., (1973). 'The transfer of learning: some organisational variables', *Journal of European Training,* **2**, (3), 251–262.

Warr, P.B., Bird, M., and Rackham, N., (1970). Evaluation and Control of Training, Gower.

Zoll, A., (1969). Dynamic Management Education, Addison-Wesley.

Advances in Management Education
Edited by John Beck and Charles Cox

CHAPTER 20

Reflections

J.E. Beck, C.J. Cox, and P. Radcliff

In this final chapter we are setting out some thoughts and ideas which have occurred to us during the preparation of this book. Some of these arise from the content of the papers and from events at the conference at which they were first presented. As Michael Reynolds points out in Chapter 3 the process is often as important as the content. This was true of the conference and it is a point we will discuss in a later section. It is in no way claimed that these are the only, or even the main, conclusions which can be drawn from the preceding chapters. They are simply points which have occurred to, and intrigued us.

MODELS AND CONCEPTUAL FRAMEWORKS

To us, one of the major themes of this collection of papers is the search for *conceptual frameworks.* This is at two levels. Some contributors are concerned with theories to conceptualize the learning process – trainers' models, as it were. At this level one striking feature is the popularity of Kolb's experiential learning model. This, or very close variations, is used in very many of the papers in this book. The other level is models for managers to use in structuring and ordering their own experience. Many papers are implicitly concerned with both levels, John Morris in Chapter 8, for example. One interesting point arising from this paper concerns managers' liking for 'simple' models – metaphors and mandalas. Possibly the high popularity of Transactional Analysis with many managers (as pointed out by Cox and Cox in Chapter 15) is due to its combination of relative conceptual simplicity with wide and precise applicability.

The choice of a number of papers concerning Personal Construct Theory and Repertory Grid techniques, possibly represents only a personal bias of the editors. Our belief, however, is that this is a theory which can have applications at both trainer and manager levels, providing insight into the process by which managers develop their conception of the world (as outlined by Beck in Chapter 13) but can also be used as a framework to help managers develop their own concepts. One approach to this is discussed by Boot and Boxer in Chapter 14. One encouraging aspect of their approach is that it is consistent with one of the other main themes of this book – an increasing emphasis on self-development and personal autonomy.

SELF-DEVELOPMENT AND PERSONAL AUTONOMY

Again there may be an element of self-fulfilling prophecy in identifying this theme. It is an area we considered important from the start, and specifically invited the paper from Boydell and Pedler (Chapter 11). However the need to take personal responsibility for one's own learning and the problems (as well as advantages) this creates is an important element in many other papers. Of particular interest is Reynold's comment (Chapter 3) concerning those 'unplanned events' which can be such a fruitful source of learning. If we could only learn how to 'plan' them and to ensure useful learning when they do occur, we could greatly increase our skill as trainers.

We suspect that the answer to this problem lies in one of the models put forward by John Morris (Chapter 8) when he talks of *'Design, Trust, and Negotiation'.* Very often the trainers' trust in the participants is low, leading him to set up a tightly designed programme with all possible eventualities covered. This is colluded with by the participant who has insufficient trust in either himself or the trainer, and so also demands high supportive design. Thus by definition 'unplanned' events cannot occur. What is needed is more negotiation – particularly role negotiation – between trainers and participants leading to higher trust and clear *contracts* concerning objectives and methods. Some of the ideas in Chapter 19 by Binsted *et al.* are also relevant here. If participants are either 'tourists' or 'ex-patriots', involvement and trust will tend to be low. Again learning from unplanned events will be less probable. This will be further affected by the 'content' of the training. It has been noted, for example, that one the main strenghths of Action Learning is that the tasks are *'real'* and require high emotional commitment, in a way that, for instance, management games and stimulations can rarely generate. Thus it could be that for the individual to take responsibility for his own learning and to learn from all the events in a programme (planned and unplanned), trust must be high, and this may be more easily achieved with 'real-life' tasks, where there is less tendency (or reason) to be suspicious of possible manipulation by the trainer. Another approach lies in the work reported by Keslake and Radcliff (Chapter 4) in using 'outward bound' type exercises for management training. Getting the group safely down a rock face is also a 'real-life' task.

THE ALTERNATIVE TO FORMAL EDUCATIONAL SYSTEMS

Much has been written in recent years about the failure of the formal education system to cope with rapidly changing society. 'Formal education has not prepared citizens for living, experiencing, and learning in, or coping with the dynamics of, and turbulence of contemporary society'. Kahn and Bruce-Briggs (1973) refer to 'educated incapacity'; Freire (1972) to a 'banking approach' to education, whereby man is educated as a spectator to, rather than a recreator of, his own reality; whilst Fromm (1966) goes so far as to refer to 'necrophily man' – a state where man is trying to reduce a complex reality to a series of mechanical and inorganic relationships. Processes of education must be found to integrate learning with reality and the fostering of skills in learning and conceptualizing from experience. Burgoyne and Cunningham place their emphasis on identifying the skills of the facilitator. John Morris in his chapter points to the use of Joint Development Activities to focus on effective mangement learning from exploring business opportunities rather than business problems. The papers here in this book outline a number of choices and emphasize methods of making the learning process fully effective, rather than a concern for socialization of mangers into a particular set of roles and values in a passive, static reality.

TRAINER IDEOLOGIES

In recent times the ideology which seems to have had most influence on the way in which trainers have viewed learning, personal development, and their role in relation to trainees has been the humanistic approach principally advocated by Carl Rogers. The espoused values of this ideology reflect the influence of the post-war sensitivity training movement on trainer attitudes. This influence can be seen clearly in the themes which unite a number of chapters in this book which emphasize self-direction, the learner finding personal meaning in the learning, and the integration of thought, feelings, and action into a whole-person approach to learning.

There seem to be a number of papers, however, where this ideology is tempered with what is perhaps a more hard-headed approach to learning. An approach which recognizes the value of humanistic principles in promoting human growth and development, but which also recognizes that in painfully few organizations, including very often the training organizations which espouse humanistic values, do humanistic principles apply. The problems posed by these papers is how to enable management trainees to get to grips with the reality of their sponsoring organizations as it is, warts and all. The process of enabling a trainee to develop a greater understanding of his organizational life may or may not be helped by confronting him with a very different, supportive culture in the training situation. The suggestion is that what are needed are programmes which enable mangers to adapt to their organizations as they are, yet still be able to identify opportunities for self-development within the particular culture of their organization. This theme is considered explicitly in the papers by McGivering and Beck and is implicit in the approach by Cox and Cox, Keslake and Radcliff, and Binsted, Stuart, and Long.

THE ROLE OF RESEARCH IN MANAGEMENT EDUCATION

The role of the researcher is to help mangement educators prepare effectively for the future possibilities of management education. Much needs to be done to establish effective relationships between the researcher and the developer of mangers. The requirement is for research relationships which foster the development and application of the research findings by the practitioner in management education. By integrating research and action, social scientists can contribute to the solution of social problems before they reach crisis proportions. The critical factors are dissemination and utilization, both of which lay very much at the heart of the conference and this ensuing book.

Research can also play a direct part in the process of educating managers. Gruber and Niles (1973) draw attention to the fact that the cycle of research is often very similar to that of managerial activity. Consequently research projects offer an underutilized educational opportunity for managers – there would appear to be much to be gained by greater use of the research component in management education.

TWO CULTURES

We have already mentioned that the conference on which this book is based was an attempt to get interaction between academics and management training practitioners. This objective was not achieved, partly because of the design of the programme, but partly also because of a difference in value and culture between these two groups. Indeed one fear which we have is that the conference may have served to validate the negative stereotype which the parties held about each other, rather than formed the basis for communication and joint development between the parties. At its worst the stereotype which academics seem to hold about practitioners is that they are behind the times, interested in 'nuts and bolts' matters rather than the broader philosophical issues in management education. Similarly practitioners in their worst moments seem to see academics as 'airy-fairy', fashion and fad conscious, interested in nothing but ideas and building models rather than in doing things, and having little relevant to say about practical problems. There can be no doubt that there was hostility between the parties at the conference with all of the usual dynamics of intergroup conflict that this creates. Small groups of practitioners and coteries of academics spent longer interacting within their groups than in talking to one another, and when interaction did occur it tended to be of a negative nature.

There are of course inherent contradictions in the attitudes which the parties took to each other which tend to make this conflict self-fulfilling. If academics emphasize the importance of reflection and learning from experience, how come they seem to be unprepared to learn anything from the practitioners' reflections on their experiences? If practitioners see research as too "academic" and divorced from reality, how come they do not try to shape the nature of research by sharing their problems?

It would be naive to assume that solely by exhortation we could get the academics and practitioners to work closer together. However, we must realize the need to work in tandem, if management education is to have an impact on a management which is increasingly sceptical about our efforts. The most realistic solution would seem to rely on individual initiatives by academics and practitioners to ensure that good ideas are tested out in practice, and that research concentrates its efforts towards solving real-life problems.

REFERENCES

Freire P. (1972). *Pedagogy of the Oppressed,* Penguin, London.

Fromm E. (1966). *The Heart of Man,* Routledge and Kegan Paul.

Gruber W.H. and Niles J.S. (1973). Research and experience in management, *Business Horizons,* August, 15–24.

Kahn H. and Bruce–Briggs B. (1973). *Things to Come,* Macmillan International, London.

INDEX

Abstract conceptualization 56–58, 113, 280
Acceptance 220, 225, 228
Acquisition 57
Action 323, 327, 329
Action learning 5, 98, 107, 115, 123–140, 141–144, 161, 229, 308–310, 352
    Background 123–126
    Design issues 123–140
    Groups 129–133
    Managing the environment 135
    Projects 126–127, 134
    Roles 128, 137
    Set advisor 142–150, 158–162
    Sets 129–133, 142–150, 155–159, 161
    Structural arrangements 133
Action planning 47, 87, 93
Action research 106, 109
Active experimentation 56–58, 113, 280
Activity
    Cognitive 305–307, 311
    Emotional 305–307
    Moral 307
    Physical 305–307
    Whole person 305–307
Aggressiveness 219, 226, 228
Anxiety 219, 226, 228, 243, 250
Application groups 310–315, 317, 319
Appraisal 70, 209–210
Argyris, C. 217, 218, 228
Assessment of teaching methods 341–343
Authority 31
    Based on knowledge 32
Autonomy 352
    Laboratory 166

Beer, S. 106, 107
Behavioural change 86, 92, 94
Being
    External 246
    Internal 246–249
Berne, E. 253–254
Blake, R. 105, 116, 264

Career development 14, 70–77
Career history 59, 64
Case studies 343–346
Coaching 69
Cognitive map 197, 201, 335–338
Concepts 236–240, 245, 246
Conceptual frameworks 351
Concrete experience 56–58, 113, 280
Conditioning 233
Conflict 12–13
Constriction 219, 224, 227
Constructs 198, 199, 203, 206, 209
    Core 199, 219
Construct system 217
    Constriction 219, 224, 227
    Definition 217, 223
    Development 217
    Dilation 219, 224, 227
    Elaboration 217–221, 224–226
    Extension 218, 224
    In transition 219

Construing 215–230
  Loose 220–221, 225, 229
  Tight 220–221, 225, 229
Consultancy skills development 23, 35
Context evaluation 296
Context of management education 1
Context re-evaluation 299
Contracting 242–245, 311, 341, 352
Control 76
Control systems 88
Counselling 150, 151
Creativity 3
Creativity cycle 220, 224, 229
Crisis 180, 181
Culture 104
Cybernetics 106

Democracy 2, 22, 26, 27, 31
Design 109–112, 330
Development
  By self 165, 166, 170, 191
  Of self 165, 170–173, 191
Developmental
  Models 172–174, 182–185, 188–190
  Stages 57
Dilation 219, 224, 277
Discontinuity 3, 103
Distance 332–333
  reduction 332–337
Double-loop learning 218, 228

Education
  Formal 352
  As socialization 29
Elements 197, 198, 203, 205, 235
Encounter groups 142, 143, 145, 150, 154, 155, 159
Evaluation 85
Evaluation of training 6, 283–300
  And change 295
  Levels 289–294
  Of management training 283–300
    criteria 288
    as heresy 287
    the political nature of 287
    problems 284–289
Existence 174–179
Expatriate 326, 328–330, 335, 339, 341, 352
Experiential groups 150, 153
Experiential learning 55, 172
Extraversion 272, 275, 276

Facilitating 141, 142, 145, 153, 161
Facilitator 142, 145, 150–153, 234, 251
  Training 314–317, 319
Fear 219, 226, 228
Feedback 49, 227
Feeling 274, 275, 279
Focus 243–245, 249, 250

Game analysis 254
Grid Analysis Package (GAP) 198, 201, 203, 206
Growth 174–179
Guilt 219, 226, 228

Harrison, R. 104
Herzberg, F. 264
Hostility 219, 226, 228

Ideology 232–235, 251, 353
Incremental development 174, 175, 179–182, 193, 307
Industrial democracy 2
Integrated learner 57
Integration 57, 63
Introversion 272, 275, 276
Intuition 273, 275, 277

Jargon 342
Job description 203
Joint development activities 97–120
Judging 274, 275, 279
Jung, C. 272

Kelly, G.A. 197, 215–230
Key development events 172–174, 190, 193
Kolb, D.A. 25, 55–64, 113–114, 222, 231, 279, 325, 345, 351

Leader 150, 152–158
Leadership 48, 51
Learner centred 234–235
Learner types 324–328
Learning 49–51, 279
  Abilities 55–69
  Catalyst 148, 149
  Community 37, 166
  Cycle 222, 231
  Environments 56, 59, 61

Learning (*contd*)
Experiential 55, 231, 233, 244, 281
Goals 46, 50
Intelligence led 307
To learn 147, 150, 167, 191, 227, 240
Managers 55
Self directed 165–168
Strategies 331, 332–333
Style 56–57, 62, 113
Style inventory 57–58, 280
Systems 7
Liberating culture 31
Life position 262

Management
Analysis 73
Education cultures 354
Educator 275, 278, 279–281
Student 275
Manager 251, 275, 277–278
Managerial
Grid 105
Role 4
Managers' expectations 312–314
Mandala 115, 116
Maslow, A.H. 264
McGregor, D. 28, 262
Meta-goals 330
Metaphor 115–118
Method 231–233
Mini-learning event 347–348
Model 100, 101, 115–118, 351
Morris, J. 98, 100, 101
Myers Briggs Type Indicator 274, 279

Negotiation 109–112
Network 240
NIPPER 235–240, 246, 249–251

Objective detachment 33
Objectives of training 294
Off-the-job 69
Organizational
Adaptability 3
Climate 15
Culture 91, 104, 188–190, 353
Development 28, 35, 265
Structure 281
Outward Bound 41, 52

Participation 21, 26, 27, 31, 34, 86, 281
In education 28, 34
In work 27
PEGASUS 198
Perceiving 274, 275, 279
Personal
Action 231
Construct Theory (PCT) 6, 197, 215–230, 235
application to management education 216, 218, 227–230
application to human relations training 221–227
Meaning 231, 233, 245
Person orientation 104
Perturbation 181–182, 185–187, 193
Power 152
Orientation 104
Principal components 201, 203, 205
Problem-solving 75, 78
Process 21, 29, 32
Awareness of 21, 311–312
Consultancy 24, 148, 149
As material for study 32
Psychodynamics 146
Psychological types 272–274

Quality of managerial life 11

Randomness 115
'Real-life' tasks 352
Re-entry 92–93
Reflection 231, 233, 245, 247–251
Reflective learning 231–251
Reflective observation 56–58, 113, 280
Refreezing 50
Relatedness 174–179
Repertory grid 6, 197–213, 235–236
Control 211
Objectives 211
Pitfalls 210
Preparation 212
Repetition 115
Research 354
Content 250–251
Empirical 261
Experimental 258
Process 250–251
Responsibility 66–68

Revans, R. 5, 107–108, 115, 124, 125, 133, 229
Reward systems 89
Rogers, C. 34
Role 4, 12
 Analysis 87–95
 Conflict 94–95
 Expectations 87–94
 Focal 91
 Formal 88
 Latent 91
 Relations 5
 Set 12
Role analysis model 87–95
Role orientation 104

Schema 335–338
Schon, D. 217, 218, 228
Script Analysis 254
Self-actualizing 170, 178
Self awareness 307
Self-confidence 65–66
Self-development 4, 165–193, 242, 325–326, 332, 333, 337–338, 342, 352
 Strategies 168, 170, 187
Self efficacy 66–71
Sensing 273, 275, 277
Set – *see* Action learning
Single-loop learning 218, 228
Socialization 26, 27, 29
 Through process 29
Social responsibility 1
Specialization 57
Stereotypes 354
Step-jump development 174, 175, 179–182, 193
Strategy 313
Stress 9–19, 49
 Audits 17
 Coping with 17
 Managerial 9–19
Stroking 259
Structural analysis 254
Support group 190
Systematic training 166, 167, 190
Systems theory 76, 109

Task analysis 205
Task orientation 104
Technique 231–235
T-groups 142, 145, 150, 154, 160
Theoretical models 5
Theory *X* 262
Theory *Y* 262
Therapy 150, 151, 160
Thinking 274, 275, 279
Threat 219, 226, 228
Tourist 327, 328–330, 335, 339, 341, 352
Trainer centred 234
Trainer ideologies 353
Training
 Limitations 94
 Needs 80–83
 Needs analysis 74
 Needs identification 73–78
 Objectives 294
 Role 311–313, 315
 Systematic 166, 167, 190
Training advisor 205–209
Transactional analysis 6, 253–269
 Applications 264–266
 Conceptual power of 262
 Criticisms 266–268
 Empirical research 261–262
 Evaluation 258–262
 Experimental research 258–261
 Management development 254, 257, 261
 Organizational development 265
 Professional associations 255
 Psychotherapy 254
Transfer course-to-work 303–308, 311
Transfer experience-to-experience 303–308, 310–311, 313
Transfer of learning 86, 303–319, 323, 326, 330, 339, 343
Transfer of training 7
Translation of learning 323, 326, 330, 339, 343
Trust 109–112, 352
Turbulence 3

Unfreezing 50
Unplanned events 352

Values 86–87, 90, 274
Viable system 106, 109
Vicious circle 68–69
Virtuous circle 68–69
Vocational guidance 198–202